The Greek Exodus from Egypt

THE GREEK EXODUS FROM EGYPT
DIASPORA POLITICS AND EMIGRATION, 1937–1962

Angelos Dalachanis

berghahn
NEW YORK · OXFORD
www.berghahnbooks.com

First published in 2017 by
Berghahn Books
www.berghahnbooks.com

© 2017, 2020 Angelos Dalachanis
First paperback edition published in 2020

All rights reserved. Except for the quotation of short passages for the purposes of criticism and review, no part of this book may be reproduced in any form or by any means, electronic or mechanical, including photocopying, recording, or any information storage and retrieval system now known or to be invented, without written permission of the publisher.

Library of Congress Cataloging-in-Publication Data

Names: Dalachanis, Angelos, author.
Title: The Greek exodus from Egypt : diaspora politics and emigration, 1937–1962 / Angelos Dalachanis.
Description: New York : Berghahn Books, 2017. | Includes bibliographical references and index.
Identifiers: LCCN 2016053294 (print) | LCCN 2016055556 (ebook) | ISBN 9781785334474 (hardback : alkaline paper) | ISBN 9781785334481 (ebook)
Subjects: LCSH: Greeks—Egypt—History—20th century. | Greeks—Migrations—History—20th century. | Egypt—Emigration and immigration—History—20th century. | Egypt—Ethnic relations—History—20th century. | Nationalism—Egypt—History—20th century. | Egypt—Politics and government—1919–1952. | Egypt—Politics and government—1952–1970.
Classification: LCC DT72.G7 D36 2017 (print) | LCC DT72.G7 (ebook) | DDC 304.8089/8906209045—dc23
LC record available at https://lccn.loc.gov/2016053294

British Library Cataloguing in Publication Data

A catalogue record for this book is available from the British Library

ISBN 978-1-78533-447-4 hardback
ISBN 978-1-78920-835-1 paperback
ISBN 978-1-78533-448-1 ebook

This book has been produced within the framework of the Unit of Excellence LabexMed – Social Sciences and Humanities at the heart of multidisplinary research for the Mediterranean (reference no. 10-LABX-0090). It has benefited from a French state grant administered by the Agence Nationale de la Recherche for the project Investissements d'Avenir A*MIDEX (reference no. ANR-11-IDEX-0001-02)

In memory of my grandmother Popi

Contents

List of Tables	viii
Abbreviations	x
Acknowledgements	xii
Introduction	1

Part I The Politics of Remaining in Egypt (1937–60)

Chapter 1. End of an Era (1937–52)	11
Chapter 2. Egypt at the Forefront (1952–60)	47

Part II Change and Adjustment (1937–60)

Chapter 3. The Labor Market	77
Chapter 4. Education	120

Part III Leaving Egypt before 1960

Chapter 5. Mobility, Migration, and Repatriation	151
Chapter 6. Decongestion	180

Part IV The Exodus

Chapter 7. A Fulfilled Prophecy?	201
Conclusion	239
Bibliography	248
Index	268

List of Tables

Table 1.	Population of Egypt, 1907–60	3
Table 2.	Occupations of Greek citizens in Egypt, 1950	81
Table 3.	Geographic distribution of Greek citizens in Egypt, 1897–1947	83
Table 4.	Citizenship of people of Greek origin in Egypt, 1927	94
Table 5.	Greek businesses and professionals in the Alexandria district, 1936 and 1958	108
Table 6.	Greek schools in Egypt per consular district and per level of education, 1955	130
Table 7.	Distribution of pupils of Greek citizenship per nationality of school, 1948–49	132
Table 8.	Distribution of Egyptiot pupils per school type, 1954–55	135
Table 9.	Visitors with Greek citizenship from Egypt to Greece and the purpose of visit, 1931–40	153
Table 10.	Repatriation and migration of Greek citizens from and to Egypt, 1931–40	154
Table 11.	Exit visas issued by the Greek consulate general in Alexandria, 1951–53	167
Table 12.	Exit visas issued by the Greek consulate general in Cairo, 1951–53	168
Table 13.	Migration of destitute Greeks from Egypt under the auspices of the WCC/ICEM, 1952–61	192

Table 14. Dispersion of the Greeks who left Egypt, 1945–January 1963 — 193

Table 15. Market value of nationalized foreign capital under the July 1961 laws (in LE) — 209

Table 16. Market value of the capital belonging to Greek citizens nationalized in the aftermath of the July 1961 laws in Alexandria and Cairo (in LE) — 209

Table 17. Number of declared definitive departures of Greeks from Alexandria, per month, 1960–64 — 220

Table 18. Number of declared definitive departures of Greeks from Cairo, per month, 1960–64 — 220

Table 19. Number of departees from Alexandria and Cairo consular districts and destination, 1960–64 — 221

Table 20. Percentage of departees from Alexandria and Cairo consular district and destination, 1960–64 — 222

Abbreviations

AGCCA	Archive of the Greek Chamber of Commerce of Alexandria
AGKA	Archive of the Greek *Koinotita* of Alexandria
AGKC	Archive of the Greek *Koinotita* of Cairo
AGKS	Archive of the Greek *Koinotita* of Suez
AICEM	Archives of the Intergovernmental Committee for European Migration
AP	Antifascist Vanguard (Antifasistiki Protoporia)
AYE	Archive of the Greek Ministry of Foreign Affairs
CADN	Nantes Diplomatic Archives Centre
CS	Central service
EAM	Greek National Liberation Front (Ethniko Apeleftherotiko Metopo)
EAS	National Liberation Association (Ethnikos Apeleftherotikos Syndesmos)
EDA	United Democratic Left
EEC	European Economic Community
ELIA	Hellenic Literary and Historical Archive
EOKA	National Organization of Cypriot Fighters
FLN	National Liberation Front, Algeria
FMFA	French Ministry of Foreign Affairs

FO	Foreign Office records, National Archives of the UK
GCCA	Greek Chamber of Commerce of Alexandria
GCCC	Greek Chamber of Commerce of Cairo
GKA	Greek *Koinotita* of Alexandria
GKC	Greek *Koinotita* of Cairo
GMFA	Greek Ministry of Foreign Affairs
GPD	Greek parliamentary debates
ICEM	Intergovernmental Committee for European Migration
KKA	Konstantinos Karamanlis Archive
KKE	Communist Party of Greece
KYP	Central Intelligence Service, Greece
LE	Egyptian pound
MAE	Archives of the French Ministry of Foreign Affairs
NATO	North Atlantic Treaty Organization
SCC	Suez Canal Company
UAR	United Arab Republic
UK	United Kingdom
UN	United Nations
US	United States
USSR	Union of Soviet Socialist Republics
WCC	World Council of Churches

Acknowledgements

This book is deeply indebted to Anthony Molho, an inspiring teacher who considerably shaped my historical thinking, as well as to George Dertilis, Christos Hadziiossif, Alexander Kitroeff, Costas Gaganakis and Eleni Condylis, who were among my role models in my student days. Several colleagues who read the manuscript at different stages provided excellent feedback: Irini Chryssoheri, Sakis Gekas, Anthony Gorman, Kostis Gkotsinas, Mathieu Grenet, Jonathan Gribetz, Nikos Hadziioakeim, Heinz-Gerhard Haupt, Vicky Kantzou, Kostis Karpozilos, Alexander Kazamias, Manolis Papoutsakis, Alexis Rappas, Nikos Skoplakis, Robert Tignor, Theocharis Tsampouras, Katerina Trimi and Lina Venturas.

During this project, I had the chance to closely collaborate with scholars working in neighboring research areas, a fact that enlarged my perspective. I will always feel fortunate for my unexpected meeting with Vassilis Colonas and my collaboration with Mercedes Volait but also with Claudine Piaton and Nicolas Michel in the project "Isthmus". Brigitte Marin, Ghislaine Alleaume and the LabexMed team in Aix-en-Provence, along with the core team of the ERC project Open Jerusalem, namely Vincent Lemire, Leyla Dakhli, Yann Potin, Stephane Ancel, Falestin Naili, Maria Chiara Rioli, Yasemin Avci and Abdul-Hameed Al-Kayyali, nourished my thoughts and were invariably supportive.

The research for and writing of this work greatly benefited from the financial assistance of the Greek State Scholarships Foundation and the European University Institute in Florence. The French Institute for Oriental Archeology in Cairo and the French School at Athens greatly facilitated my work. I currently have the privilege to conduct research at the French School and to work closely with its director of modern and contemporary studies program, Tassos Anastassiadis. The LabexMed program of Aix-Marseille University provided generous financial assistance, while the Stanley J. Seeger '52 Center for Hellenic Studies at Princeton University provided the ideal environment to work on the manuscript and I am grateful to Dimitri Gondicas for this.

I am deeply grateful to all the Greeks from Egypt whom I met during my years of research. They made themselves available to provide assistance and discussed with me different aspects of their life in Egypt. I would especially mention Panayiotis Karmatzos, as our discussions have been a source of inspiration. I owe particular debts of gratitude to the late Sofianos Chryssostomidis, Euthymios Souloyiannis and Alekos Vlachos, but also to Michalis Fokas, Nikos Mastrandreas and Ioannis Misrekis. I am also grateful to Stefanos Tamvakis and Mary Kavoura for their help in Alexandria, the Koinotita, the Greek General Consulate and the Greek Chamber of Commerce of the city. The assistance of Christos Kavalis, president of the Cairo Koinotita, and Villy Politou, who was then responsible for the Koinotita's archives, was valuable on many occasions. My stay in Egypt would undoubtedly not have been so fruitful without the generous support of two dear friends: the late Melita Kosti in Alexandria and Jakob Lindfors in Cairo.

I am indebted to the staff of the Hellenic Literary and Historical Archive (ELIA-MIET), especially Mathilde Pyrli and Dimitris Bacharas. Many thanks also due to Vaso Lafiatoglou of the International Organization for Migration in Athens and Konstantinos Papantonopoulos, whose experience in migration matters was invaluable. I would also like to thank the personnel of the historical archives of the Greek Ministry of Foreign Affairs who have always been helpful during the many hours I worked there. I would also like to thank the staff of the historical archives of the French Ministry of Foreign Affairs in Paris and Nantes. Working at the British National Archives in London and at the historical archives of the World Council of Churches, the International Committee of the Red Cross and the International Organization for Migration, all located in Geneva, was an extraordinary research experience.

This is also the occasion to thank colleagues, friends and relatives who, in one way or another, contributed to this book: Francisco (Patxi) Appellaniz, Thierry Bonzon, Maud Chirio, Elena Chiti, Maria Dermitzaki, Charlotte Deweerdt, Annabelle Gallin, Nita Georgouli, Memi Katsoni, Anne Kazazian, Niki Koniordos, Alexander Lukas Krüger, Omar Nagati, Kostas Nitaris, Sayed 'Oshmawy, Apostolos Palierakis, Stavros Papakyritsis, Lily Papaspyropoulou, Sofia Papastamkou, Alkimos Papathanassiou, Evi Paradeisi, Antonella Romano, Katerina Stathi, Anna Laura Turiano, Elli Vintzileou and, last but not least, Damian Mac Con Uladh for his valuable help in the editing of the text.

My partner, Eugenia, now knows almost everything about the Greeks in Egypt. She read everything I wrote and heard (multiple times) everything about this project. Her patience and her incisive comments were invaluable. My parents, Irini and Giorgos, supported me continuously and in countless ways. My beloved grandmother, Popi, passed away a few months before these lines were written. This book is dedicated to her memory.

Introduction

"I am not a Greek of Egypt!" This is how I've answered the most frequent question put to me by Greeks since I started the research for this book. I knew about the Greek presence in Egypt from my schooling and gradually assimilated the collective conventional wisdom of post-1960s Greek society regarding it, which can be summarized thus: the Greeks of Egypt (also called the Egyptiot Greeks or Egyptiots) lived in Alexandria; they were rich and knew many foreign languages and, therefore, were cosmopolitans; they left Egypt because Gamal Abdel Nasser threw them out. Another assumption, common not only in Greece but also elsewhere, is that the Greek presence in Egypt had existed uninterrupted since the arrival of Alexander the Great and the foundation of the city of Alexandria in 331 BC. In a similar way, the mass departure of Egyptiot Greeks is somewhat framed within the context of the biblical exodus. According also to a commonly encountered scenario, the definitive departure of the Egyptiots was provoked by the Arab-Israeli conflict and decolonization. Therefore, similarities are sought with the definitive departure of Jews or the expulsion of British and French citizens in the aftermath of the Suez Crisis.

As I delved into the issue and heard more and more stories about the Greek presence in Egypt, many of these perceptions increasingly appeared partial or erroneous. In fact, it was my first visit to Egypt in 2008 that drastically changed my view and made me conscious of what my research was about. There, I met some of the few remaining Egyptiots. All of them were in agreement that the Greeks had not been expelled, otherwise they would not be there talking to me. An old Alexandrian, Alekos Vlachos, who had been caretaker of the city's most important Greek school since the early 1950s, reacted strongly when I asked him some questions that betrayed the latent power of the stereotypes: "But, what do you think? That they were all rich big shots here? Most of them were poor people!" As my research progressed, I visited Ismailia, where I met Ioannis Misrekis, a former Egyptian Suez Canal Authority employee and then president of the city's still active Greek association. He talked to me about the lack of solidarity among Greeks in the 1950s and 1960s, the position of the Greeks of the Suez Canal area who were caught between the Egyptians and the French and British, the prevailing feeling of uncertainty among them at the time regarding their future in Egypt, and the briefings that "some Alexandrians" had organized in his city in order to "push" them into leaving for Australia, but not Greece.

A historical study, this book follows the path of the Greek community from the late 1930s to its exodus in the early 1960s, which peaked in 1962. This path was not linear; nor was exodus the only outcome. At the beginning of the period under study, in 1937, the Capitulations, which provided special rights and tax and judicial privileges to foreigners, were abolished. Over the following years Greeks, along with other foreigners, experienced the rapid transformation of Egypt in political, social, economic, and cultural terms. The Egyptiot bourgeoisie controlled the Greek population's most influential and representative institutions, the Greek Koinotita of Alexandria (henceforth GKA) and the city's Greek Chamber of Commerce (GCCA). Many of the members of the GCCA administrative board also served on the GKA administrative committee and maintained close contacts with Greece's political elite and diplomatic authorities in Egypt. They constituted, in fact if not in name, the leadership of the Egyptiot Greek population.

The Egyptiot leadership collaborated closely with the Greek state in developing various political, economic, and cultural strategies, not only to ensure the long-term presence of Greeks in Egypt but also to promote their departure. Their often contradictory and ambiguous strategies were strongly opposed by the social and political forces of the Egyptiot Left, which was controlled by the Communists but also comprised Socialists and several progressive people. The Egyptiot Left had its own proposals regarding the long-term sustainability of the Egyptiot population. In hindsight, the various strategies of the Greek state and the Egyptiot leadership that aimed to keep the Greeks in Egypt appear to have been both insufficient and ill-conceived or were simply not adopted by all Egyptiots. It is a fact, though, that when the exodus commenced in earnest in 1960, the Greek presence had already decreased by almost one-third (see table 1) compared to what it was in the late 1930s. In the 1960s most of the Greeks residing in Egypt left the country that they almost unanimously called their "second country."

This study discusses the residence and departure of Egyptiots, either as repatriates to Greece or as migrants to other destinations. My interpretation principally rests on research in the community archives of the GKA and GCCA, the diplomatic archives of Greece, France, and the United Kingdom, and the records of Geneva-based international organizations such as

Table 1. Population of Egypt, 1907–60

	1907	1917	1927	1937	1947	1960
Egyptians*	11,189,978	12,512,106	13,952,264	15,734,170	18,966,767	25,984,101
European nationals						
Greeks	62,973	56,731	76,264	68,559	57,427	47,673
Italians	34,926	40,198	52,462	47,706	27,958	14,089
British/Maltese	20,356	24,354	34,169	31,523	28,246	
French	14,591	21,270	24,332	18,821	9,717	25,175
Others	–	–	–	–	16,664	
Other communities						
Jews	38,635	58,581	63,550	62,953	65,639	8,561
Armenians	7,747	12,854	17,145	16,886	–	–
Syrians, Palestinians, and other Arab nationalities	33,947	31,725	39,605	38,692	–	56,375

Sources: *Annuaire statistique, 1910* (Cairo: Imprimerie nationale, 1910); *The Census of Egypt Taken in 1917*, vol. 2 (Cairo: Government Press, 1921); *Annuaire statistique, 1927–1928* (Cairo: Imprimerie nationale, 1929); *Annuaire statistique, 1937–1938* (Cairo: Imprimerie nationale, 1939); *Annuaire statistique, 1947–1948* (Cairo: Imprimerie nationale, 1951); *Al-Qiraa al 'ama li soukan: jadawil 'ama* [General population census of Egypt: General tables] (Cairo, 1960); Floresca Karanasou, "Egyptianisation: The 1947 Company Law and the Foreign Communities in Egypt" (Ph.D. dissertation, Oxford University, 1992), 11.

* The numbers refer to the sedentary population.

the Intergovernmental Committee for European Migration (ICEM)—the precursor to the International Organization for Migration. These three different kinds of sources provide three respective views, which are often entangled. The elites of the Egyptiot community and Greek state produced most of this archival material, which consequently reflects their views.

As regards terminology, when referring to the Greeks in Egypt the study uses the term "Egyptiot Greeks," or simply "Egyptiot," regardless of the citizenship individuals may have held. The term is derived from the translation of the Arabic word *mutamassirun*, literally the "Egyptianized," into Greek and describes Greek people in Egypt. The *mutamassirun* were Egyptianized because "they recognize[d] both an affinity and conformity with the Egyptian way of life and yet, at the same time, a certain detachment from it."[1] To avoid more transliterations and to simplify matters, the text employs the term "community" used in the British Foreign Office records to collectively describe the Greeks in Egypt. All the Greek archival records consulted for this study described the movement of Egyptiots toward Greece as repatriation (*epanapatrismos*). This does not imply that the movement was forced; rather, the term is used to differentiate this movement from the emigration of Egyptiots to third countries. Lastly, the study does not use the term "exodus" in its biblical sense, which would necessitate a persecutor and a promised land, neither of which existed in the context under study. The term is used to describe the mass departure in the early 1960s.

Those Greeks who left Egypt during the period under scrutiny or their ancestors had arrived in the country from the nineteenth to mid-twentieth centuries. Initially, this movement essentially concerned big merchants and traders who were part of the Greek merchant diaspora around the Mediterranean and Black Sea. In Egypt they established nodes of their extensive commercial networks, encouraged by Muhammad Ali, the leader of Egypt from 1805 to 1848, who favored their settlement. Subsequently, migrants arrived and became engaged in a wide range of economic activities. Migration to Egypt even took the form of a mass labor movement, as was the case of thousands of Dodecanese islanders who came to work on the construction of the Suez Canal. The newly arrived Greeks not only settled in Cairo and Alexandria but also inhabited the old town of Suez and the newly founded cities across the Suez Canal area, Port Said and Ismailia, and penetrated the interior, namely the cities of the Nile delta such as Mansoura, Tanta, and Zagazig, and also Upper Egypt.

The Egyptiot population was a mosaic in terms of its origins: they came from many different regions of the Balkan Peninsula, Asia Minor, and the islands of the Aegean and the Ionian Seas. The push factors for this movement should be sought in the specific economic and social conditions prevailing in each of these areas. Migrants from the Peloponnese, for instance, were part of the successive waves of emigration at the end of the nineteenth century caused by overpopulation and unemployment in the mountainous parts of the region. Anti-Semitism pushed many Greek Jews from Epirus and the Ionian Islands to Egypt. After a decrease in numbers between 1907 and 1917, which was mainly due to the economic crisis in Egypt and the mobilization of Greeks during the Balkan Wars and World War I, the Greek population reached its peak in 1927, that is, after the influx of refugees in the aftermath of the defeat of the Greek Army in Asia Minor in 1922.

The migration of Greek people to Egypt was not an isolated phenomenon. Migrants from different areas and of different origin arrived in Egypt during more or less the same period. Italians, Maltese, and other non-Egyptian communities, namely Jews, Syrians, and Armenians, whose presence was largely linked to the Ottoman *millets*,[2] were also part of the so-called *mutamassirun,* or Egyptianized. They were socioeconomically diverse, middle to lower class in the majority, which distinguished them from the nationals of colonial powers, essentially the British, who were mainly military personnel, administrators, and businesspersons, and the mostly bourgeois Belgians and French when these were of metropolitan origin. A foreign economic elite, comprising members of almost all the above-mentioned groups, dominated economic activity in Egypt and exerted considerable control over its political system. This was mainly due to the British presence, which began in 1882, and the extremely favorable conditions for foreigners created by the Capitulations regime.

Even though Egyptiots were not in their majority citizens of a colonial power (see table 4), most of them benefited directly or indirectly from the semicolonial conditions created by the Capitulations and British protection. At the turn of the twentieth century, the Greeks constituted the largest foreign ethnic or national community in Egypt. Their principal unifying elements were language, the idea of common cultural origin, and, to a lesser extent, the Orthodox Christian religion. At the same time, they constituted a multifaceted entity in terms of local origin, citizenship, geographic settlement across Egypt, political beliefs, professional activities, social stratification, and economic status. While this book deals with the Egyptiot population as an entity, its limits were not tightly defined but fluid and constantly changing. Whether someone was considered a member of the community depended not only on all or some of the above criteria being met, but on who set the definition and how.

Throughout the period under scrutiny, the Greeks in Egypt found themselves entangled in different worlds that shaped the specificity of their presence. First, Egypt was a meeting point of two different kinds of Greeks living abroad. On the one hand was the diaspora that presupposes migration from a common national center, Greece, as was the case for many Egyptiots. On the other hand, there was the broader notion of *homogenia,* whose members never lived in Greece but migrated to Egypt from Asia Minor and other regions of the Ottoman Empire.[3] Second, the Greek population constituted an imaginary meeting point of two states: Egypt and Greece. Their name, "Egyptiot Greeks," ideally attributes their position between two geographically close countries and their hybrid identity, a characteristic of all diasporas. The Egyptiots also found themselves at the transition point from empire—Ottoman and British—to the Egyptian nation-state. This transition triggered Egyptian nationalism, which would generate it further, and concerned many aspects of political, social, economic, and cultural life. Finally, after World War II, the Egyptiot Greeks were at a flashpoint between imperialism and the communist "threat" in the Middle East, a determining factor for the Cold War alliances in the region, which became more complex after the creation of the State of Israel in 1948. These new alliances affected, to a great extent, the policies of both the Egyptian and Greek states and were also reflected in the political, social, and cultural realities of the Egyptiot population.

The book's historical narrative is structured around chronological and thematic axes in order to avoid the teleology inherent in the term "exodus." The division of the book into parts and chapters takes two distinct factors into account. First, the Egyptiot departure is examined as a product of the interaction between individual initiative and structural characteristics and change (such as the abolition of the Capitulations, conditions in the labor market, education, Egyptian legislation, and so on), which had short-, medium-, and long-term effects on the movement of Egyptiots. The examination of the individual initiatives is not restricted to the Egyptiot departees but also concerns people representing state, community, or international organizations. The book also takes into account that a historical study of migration requires the examination of practically all aspects of human activity: political, diplomatic, social, economic, and cultural. These two separate but also interrelated factors are reflected in the parts and chapters of the book.

Part 1 explores the political historical context beginning with the abolition of the capitulatory privileges—a major structural change—through to the eve of the exodus. It focuses on the policies that aimed to ensure the long-term presence of Greeks in Egypt despite the end of the economic advantages from which the community had benefited. The two chapters in this part discuss the policy of the Greek state toward its nationals abroad and the different strategies proposed by the Egyptiot leadership and the Left opposition to deal with the multiple transformations taking place at the local and international level. Chapter 1 focuses on the period from the abolition of the Capitulations in 1937 to the end of the transitional period in 1949 and the Free Officers coup in 1952. Chapter 2 deals with the period under the new military regime until Nasser's visit to Athens in June 1960.

Part 2 analyzes the efficiencies and deficiencies of the Egyptiot population in labor and education as well as the existing (or non-existing) efforts to adjust to the changing Egyptian context. Chapter 3 examines socioeconomic changes, through an analysis of the labor market, and chapter 4 focuses on the community's education system, its cultural and professional adjustment until the exodus. Part 3 deals with individual initiatives to leave Egypt. Chapters 5 and 6 address the different forms of mobility and emigration until 1960.

Part 4 is dedicated to the exodus that was triggered in late 1960. Chapter 7 addresses the immediate reaction of the Egyptiots to the socialist legislation enacted in the late 1950s and early 1960s. Taking a different and autonomous chronological focus than the previous six chapters, it argues that the exodus as a crisis situation was the expression and partly the culmination of a complicated process that had been developing over the previous decades. In other words, I devote the first six chapters to the period preceding the exodus to suggest that even before the exodus started, Egypt, for many Greeks, had already been "lost."

NOTES

1. Anthony Gorman, *Historians, State and Politics in Twentieth Century Egypt: Contesting the Nation* (London: Routledge, 2003), 174–75.
2. In the Ottoman Empire the term *millet* described confessional communities, which were allowed to administer themselves under their own set of rules. The main *millets* were the Greek Orthodox, namely the *millet-i-Rûm*, the Armenian and the Jewish.
3. Lina Venturas, "'Deterritorialising' the Nation: The Greek State and 'Ecumenical Hellenism,'" in *Greek Diaspora and Migration since 1700: Society, Politics and Culture*, ed. Dimitris Tziovas (Farnham: Ashgate, 2009), 125.

Part I

The Politics of Remaining in Egypt (1937-60)

Chapter One

End of an Era (1937–52)

In spring 1952, the post of Greek ambassador in Cairo became vacant. That August, Michail Melas was appointed head of the embassy in Egypt and would serve until April 1956. His delayed appointment was mainly due to the fact that none of his superiors sought the position. In his autobiography, Melas explains that the tough times had already started for the Greeks in Egypt and that the community dignitaries, who had strong links with the Athenian political elite, often blamed the ambassadors—who were from Greece and appointed by the Greek government, as were the consuls—for their own difficulties.[1] The picture Melas paints of the community dignitaries, who practically constituted the Egyptiot leadership, was that they were almost entirely oriented toward Athens, just a few months before the Egyptian military coup d'état and fifteen years after the abolition of the Capitulations. After years of "full unaccountability" and "important opportunities for easy enrichment," during which the Greeks constituted "a state within a state,"[2] the Egyptiot leadership needed to find a new path for itself and the community after the changes brought about by the winding down of the Capitulations. In the post-Capitulations environment, the community had the opportunity to emancipate itself and to create and reinforce its political, economic, social, and cultural ties with Egypt.

However, from 1939–40 to the summer of 1952, local and international developments roiled the community. During World War II, British troops were deployed in Egypt, where London tried to control the political situation. The exiled Greek government, along with the members of the main Greek resistance organization, the National Liberation Front (EAM), also established itself there. This peculiar coexistence of the Greek government, resistance groups, and the community shaped, to a certain extent, the different poles of postwar community political life. In the immediate postwar period, the international context changed radically after the creation of the Israeli state, the gradual decline of the colonial empires, and the simultaneous emergence of the two superpowers, the Soviet Union and the United States of America. In Egypt, a long period of political instability, which intensified after the war, ended in the Free Officers coup d'état on 23 July 1952. This chapter examines the positions of the different elements of Egyptiot community life and the Greek state from 1937 to 1952 as its members dealt with the issue of the long-term presence of Greeks in Egypt. It also looks at the relationship between the community leadership, Greek state, and Egyptiot Left, on the one hand, and the question of the community as a coherent and homogeneous entity and its relationship with a changing Egyptian context, on the other.

THE CAPITULATIONS AND THEIR ABOLITION

Following the Egyptian Revolution of 1919 against British occupation, the country became independent three years later in 1922 but only in name. The British continued to control foreign policy and the defense of Egypt. Their hegemony was confirmed in the first three conditions of the declaration of the British government with which they acknowledged Egypt's independence on 22 February 1922. With one of these conditions the British undertook the obligation to protect foreign interests and minorities in Egypt.[3] Thus, it is not surprising that the extension and consolidation of the country's national sovereignty became the main demand of Egyptian political life in the following decades. British power was somewhat diminished with the signing of the Anglo-Egyptian Treaty of 26 August 1936. Under this twenty-year treaty, Britain agreed to reduce its armed forces in Egypt to 10,400 men (10,000 soldiers and officers and 400 pilots) and to station them once it had constructed a new military base along the Suez Canal. The protection of the canal and, therefore, imperial communications was the main, but not the only, purpose of the British military presence in Egypt. London maintained the right to intervene militarily in the country in the event of an external threat. In exchange, it undertook to provide equipment and material to the Egyptian Army—whose hierarchy was opened up to the middle and lower strata—and train new officers. Among those who joined the military academy at that time was Gamal Abdel Nasser, a son of a postal clerk. Britain also supported Egypt's membership in the League of Nations, which permitted the latter to create embassies and enter the world diplomatic map. According to Article 12 of the Anglo-Egyptian Treaty, the protection of foreign interests would gradually pass to Egyptian authorities, for

Article 13 foresaw the abolition of the Capitulations, as they were a sticking point with all of the Egyptian political parties at the time.

The Capitulations were bilateral agreements between the Ottoman Empire and individual states regulating the rights and privileges of foreigners within the empire. In 1536, France became the first country to sign such an agreement with Constantinople, and other countries followed its example in securing extraterritorial legal rights for their citizens. Greece, as a relatively newborn state, having gained independence in 1830, endorsed the Capitulations in 1856. Apart from Greece, sixteen different states—Austria, Belgium, Brazil, Denmark, France, Prussia (and later Germany), Italy, Netherlands, Portugal, Spain, Sweden, the United Kingdom, and the United States—negotiated capitulatory privileges for their citizens at different times. However, contrary to the situation prevailing in the rest of the empire, in Egypt the Capitulations offered privileges that greatly exceeded those foreseen by the spirit and the letter of the agreements. As the British consul general—and Egypt's de facto governor—Lord Cromer stated, "The European who is privileged in Turkey, is ultra-privileged in Egypt."[4]

The Capitulations exempted Egypt's foreigners from almost all taxes.[5] For the Ottomans, the initial idea was to exempt Western Europeans from a number of commercial taxes in order to boost economic activity and trade; however, in Egypt these privileges developed into almost complete tax immunity. The Egyptian government was not allowed to impose taxes on the citizens of capitulatory states without the consent of those states. Using his influence, the British consul general managed to impose some minor taxes on the citizens of other capitulatory states in order to protect British interests. The capitulatory states in general, though, never consented to the imposition of income tax on their citizens but only minor taxes, as, for instance, a small residency tax or, in the 1930s, an automobile tax. Along with tax immunity, the Capitulations also guaranteed the freedom of movement and commerce. Thus, up to the 1930s, Egypt was open to anyone who wished to settle there and acquire—in a relatively simple procedure—a residence permit.[6] Moreover, they granted immunity from legal and judicial control. The Egyptian state had no right to promulgate laws referring to foreign citizens, over whom the Egyptian courts had no jurisdiction. In those cases where foreign litigants were of the same nationality, only consular courts were empowered to deal with them. Where the litigants were of different nationality, they were subject to the jurisdiction of the Mixed Courts, created in 1875. Appointed by the Egyptian government but always with the consent of the capitulatory states, judges of different nationalities served in these courts, which constituted a hybrid institution with its own regulations, an amalgam of the Napoleonic code, Islamic sharia, and Egyptian customary law.

Given the extensive privileges the Capitulations granted to foreigners, their abolition became a priority issue for the Egyptian nationalist movement. The Ottoman Empire had unilaterally suspended them upon the outbreak of World War I, a move the capitulatory countries officially recognized in 1923 in the Lausanne Treaty. In Egypt, on the other hand, the Capitulations remained in force during the 1920s and much of the 1930s. The Montreux Convention of 8 May 1937 finally abolished them, following almost a month of negotiations in the Swiss city of the same name.

The convention, proposed by the Egyptian government, was signed by twelve capitulatory states—Belgium, France, Denmark, Greece, Italy, Netherlands, Norway, Portugal, Spain, Sweden, the United Kingdom, and the United States. Austria, Germany, and the Soviet Union were not invited to Montreux, since they had already lost their privileges following World War I and the Russian October Revolution. The 1936 Anglo-Egyptian Treaty, though, allowed the remaining capitulatory states little room to maneuver. Ahead of the conference, it was a common expectation among foreign diplomats in Cairo that, if the capitulatory states rejected the Egyptian proposals, Egypt would proceed to abolish the Capitulations unilaterally. The perception was that Egypt's call to Montreux was less an invitation to negotiate than the announcement of a prearranged decision.

Egypt's main aim in Montreux was the abolition of the privileged status of foreigners and the affirmation of its sovereignty over them. This included introducing equality before the law for foreigners and Egyptians by placing all the country's residents under the jurisdiction of the Egyptian national courts, after winding down the Mixed Courts following a transitional period. Consequently, what was at stake at the conference was the length of the transitional period for the full implementation of the convention. The issue was essentially the manner in which such a radical change should be effected and the time frame within which foreign interests could adjust themselves to the new conditions.

The first article of the convention declared that "the High Contracting Parties ... agree ... to the complete abolition in all respects of Capitulations in Egypt" in October 1937. Eventually a twelve-year transitional period was agreed on. This was the original Egyptian proposal, to which the British had already agreed. The Italians also backed it. The French, on the other hand, had sought an eighteen-year transitional period, and the Greeks, even though they earnestly favored the French proposal, decided that there was no point in supporting it, as it would only displease the Egyptians.

The Egyptian government promised not to enact discriminatory laws against foreigners during the twelve-year transitional period, at the very end of which, on 14 October 1949, the Mixed Courts would cease to exist.

During the transitory period, the consular courts, which dealt with cases involving litigants of the same nationality, would also continue to operate. Following the conference, Nikolaos Politis, the head of the Greek delegation, highlighted the importance of the transitory period for the fate of the foreign populations in Egypt: "According to whether it is wisely or unwisely applied, the next twelve years will become a true period of transition, preparing the normal evolution of the present toward the future."[7]

To reassure the foreign delegations at Montreux, the Egyptian side added an annex to the convention stating that before the end of the transitory period, the Egyptian government planned to conclude treaties of establishment and friendship with the ex-capitulatory powers, which would reiterate the guarantees of nondiscrimination against foreigners provided for in the transitory period. The idea of new future treaties was unanimously accepted by the foreign delegations, who saw in them an opportunity to renew the privileged status of their citizens under the pretext of equality and reciprocity that a treaty of establishment required. David Ewan Wallace, the chief British negotiator, was left in no doubt that the planned treaties were simply old wine in a new bottle. "In reality the Capitulations constituted a kind of treaty of establishment," he acknowledged.[8]

Since participants had agreed on the outcome of many of the conference items beforehand, only two matters remained for the Greek delegation to consider: the unrestricted continuation of the professional activities of Egyptiots and the safeguarding of the national legal character of Egyptiot institutions. Chapter 3 examines the first issue. The second matter, the viability of Greek institutions, was more crucial than for any other foreign group residing in Egypt because these organizations constituted the main institutional mechanism for the perpetuation of the Greek presence in Egypt.[9] Even though people of Greek nationality—and sometimes also of Greek origin—could avail themselves of the services of each *koinotita* (*koinotites* in plural), their members mostly consisted of people who could afford the extremely high subscription and annual fees, namely the Egyptiot bourgeoisie. This was principally the case in Alexandria, whose Koinotita, the first to be established in Egypt in 1843, was considered *prima inter pares* among the other *koinotites*. In 1937, thirty-seven different such institutions were active in Egypt, constituting the administrative structure around which much of Greek political, social, economic, and cultural activities revolved.[10] The safeguarding of their national character was important because they dealt with not only the educational, religious, and welfare activities of the *koinotites* but also their property.

The discussion around the status of the *koinotites* was not new. Georgios Mavris, a doctor based in the Egyptian city of Zagazig, publicly raised it in a memorandum sent to the Greek government in 1911. He claimed that if the Capitulations were abolished, there would be no guarantee as to the national character of the *koinotites*.[11] On his way to Montreux, on 27 February 1937, Nikolaos Politis sent a memorandum to the Egyptian government concerning the issue. Egyptian parliamentarians, though, were not sympathetic to Greek demands for the administrative autonomy of the *koinotites* because this would imply the "extension of the Capitulations system."[12] For the Greek and other delegations at Montreux, though, the preservation of the national character of community institutions was a top priority. Eventually, under pressure from the British, the Egyptian government conceded, incorporating its decision in a separate letter from the Egyptian Prime Minister, Nahhas Pasha, to the British, Italian, French, and Greek delegations. Nahhas's assurances that Egypt would maintain the national character of these institutions for the transitional period provoked strong reactions from Egyptian MPs, who believed they were likely to provide a back door for Western intervention.[13] The issue of the status of the Greek *koinotites* in Egypt was finally settled in an almost definitive way at the end of the transitory period, on 10 February 1949. A Greek-Egyptian agreement dictated that in the event that a *koinotita* was dissolved, its property would pass to the GKA, the Koinotita in Cairo, or the Koinotita in Mansoura, depending on which was closest geographically. The last of these three bodies to remain would be entitled to claim the property of the other two, and in the event that all the *koinotites* were dissolved, their property would pass to the Greek state, which would be then obliged to offer it to charities set up for Egyptiots. Thus, the Greek state became—and still is—the ultimate owner of *koinotites* property.

The pronounced interest of the Egyptiots in the Montreux conference was lucidly expressed on the front pages of the Greek-language press in Egypt. Skepticism and anxiety regarding the future, along with rather superficial enthusiasm for Egypt's achievements, were common in daily reports and analyses throughout the conference's work. Despite public declarations in favor of the abolition of the Capitulations, the GKA, which was supposed to represent the entire Greek population in Egypt, expressed its deep concern. Mikès Salvagos, the GKA president, sent a warning letter to Greek dictator Ioannis Metaxas. Highly respected by the community and the Greek state alike, Salvagos was a prominent example of the old bourgeoisie of the community. His father, Konstantinos, was born in Marseille in 1845. The son of a big merchant, Konstantinos moved to Alexandria at the age of twenty to found a branch of the family business, which later became an independent commercial and banking firm in Egypt. His eldest son, Mikès, was born in 1875 and, after graduating from the Averofeio boys' high school of Alexandria, studied law in Paris. He was president of the GKA for almost thirty years and developed significant financial and social activities at the community and Egyptian state level. Apart from serving as GKA president, he was a member of the municipal authority, vice president of the Egyptian industrialists' federation, and president of the board of several companies, including the Alexandria Water Company, the Alexandria & Ramleh Railway Company, Société Egyptienne des Industries Textiles, and the Land Bank of Egypt. The Greek state would have regarded him as "the first Greek of Egypt"[14] because of his position as GKA president. In his letter to Metaxas, Salvagos claimed that unless concrete guarantees concerning the status of Greeks in Egypt were provided, the abolition of the Capitulations would lead to the dissolution of the Greek community through the massive repatriation of its members.[15] This was bound to happen, Salvagos maintained, as the capitulatory privileges constituted one of the main coherent elements of the Greek presence in Egypt.

While foreign diplomats and officials publicly welcomed the signing of the convention in triumphal tones, skepticism prevailed behind these statements about the true intentions of the Egyptian government and the ability of their respective nationals to adjust to the new, nonprivileged environment. Few shared the optimism of Andreas Delmouzos, Greece's ambassador in Cairo, that the equality of foreigners and Egyptians before the law would ensure the security and long-term presence of foreigners in the country.[16] The Egyptian government had achieved its goals at Montreux with the abolition of the privileged status of foreigners. However, despite the guarantees for the transitory period and for treaties of establishment, the post-Capitulations era would require foreigners in Egypt to make radical changes to adjust to the new dispensation. A debate on the future of the Greeks in Egypt and their effort to conform to the new conditions had begun long before 1937.[17] The Egyptians viewed the ending of the Capitulations as a priority from at least the turn of the twentieth century, and their demands for their abolition became more emphatic after the dissolution of the Ottoman Empire and the country's nominal independence. In an article he wrote in the progressive Egyptiot journal *Panaigyptia* shortly before the conference, I. Meletios, an Alexandrian lawyer, illustrated the challenges of the new era:

> Until now, under the Capitulations, we have lived on the margins of Egyptian life; under the new established order, we are called to participate socially and materially in Egyptian life in close connection with the natives; the realization of our new situation in Egypt will, of course, depend on many factors, but arranging from now on the principal points of our contact with local life will greatly facilitate our doubtlessly smooth advancement in the future.[18]

However, neither the community leadership nor the Greek state had a long-term policy on how the Greek population should adjust to the new Egyptian reality. On the contrary, the prevailing idea among the majority of Greek officials and notables was that after the transitional period, the Greeks in Egypt would be able to maintain, through a treaty of establishment, the status of a privileged minority. Moreover, the outbreak of World War II only two years after Montreux postponed all discussions on the readjustment issue.

WAR AND INTROVERSION

Egypt became the main front in the Middle East during World War II. As a result of the 1936 Anglo-Egyptian Treaty, the country came under British military, and increasingly political, control. When the war broke out in 1939, Britain imposed censorship and martial law in Egypt, which was forced to suspend diplomatic relations with the Axis countries. Even though Egypt officially remained neutral, Britain obligated it to make its facilities and resources available to the Allies and to accommodate a British Army numbering more than a hundred—and many more allied forces. As London considered the collaboration with the Egyptian government crucial for the settlement and refueling of Allied forces, it tried to impose control over Egypt.

The British intervention in Egypt's internal affairs provoked the reaction of the nationalists and several other political forces. On the one hand, the government of the Saadist Party, the Muslim Brotherhood, and its antagonistic party New Egypt, nationalist army officers and politicians along with King Farouk viewed Nazi Germany as a power that would help Egypt rid itself of British hegemony. On the other hand, the Wafd, the liberal party of Nahhas Pasha, backed by the Left and antifascist movements, backed the British and their allies. In February 1942, after a long period of political unrest and using the imminent threat posed by German general Erwin Rommel, who was approaching Alexandria from Libya, the British demanded that Farouk appoint Nahhas Pasha as prime minister. When the king refused to conform, the British surrounded his palace with armored vehicles. Nahhas Pasha became prime minister, but his collaboration with the British delegitimized the Wafd and reinforced opposition voices in Egypt.

Because of the steadfast British presence during wartime, the foreign populations in Egypt felt that almost nothing had changed despite the country's independence and the abolition of the Capitulations a few years before. The Egyptiot leadership in particular felt complacent not only because it availed itself of British protection, but also because the Greek government, following the German invasion of Greece in April 1941, settled in Egypt as a government in exile. Thus, while Montreux had sparked a debate about compliance, regularization, or readjustment to the new conditions in Egypt, all discussions on the matter ceased because of the war. Instead, community dignitaries and a large part of the Greek population entered a long period marked by a peculiar introversion—peculiar because the reference point was outside Egypt: the battlefronts in Greece. News from the Albanian front during the Greek-Italian War and later the German invasion provoked a strong solidarity movement within the community, which was expressed in fundraising and in providing various other kinds of assistance to Greece.[19] Even though the overall conditions were favorable for national cohesion, the ideological rivalries in Greece since World War I between liberals and monarchists known as the "national schism" divided Egyptiots and heightened during World War II. They were gradually transformed according to the new political context and created the political balances and correlations that would determine community political life in the postwar era.

On 23 May 1941, the Greek king, George II, and the government disembarked at Alexandria. Almost a month later they continued to South Africa and ended up in London, where most of the Allied exiled governments had gathered. However, the deputy prime minister and naval minister Alexandros Sakellariou, along with the air force and army ministers, remained in Egypt. Upon their arrival, they created the Royal Greek Army of the Middle East, which was placed under British command. One of the characteristics of the Greek force was its strong heterogeneity in terms of the political orientation of the soldiers and officers in its ranks, which included Metaxas dictatorship supporters, Royalists, Liberals, and Communists who had reached Egypt through the Aegean Sea and Turkey. Egyptiots joined the Greek armed force but served in a different battalion from those of mainland Greeks because of the differences among them. After receiving the permission of the Egyptian authorities, the exiled government called up the Greeks of Egypt to the army in December 1941. Overall, 7,063 men enlisted.[20] Since many of them had abandoned their jobs to join the army, community charity associations supported their families morally and financially. The Greek government contributed to this effort only from 1943.

Mobilization was not the only way the community was involved in the war effort. The presence in Egypt of the Greek king, army officers, and Metaxas-era ministers provoked a strong reaction from the community's Liberals—who formed the majority—and Communists. In addition, the British established control over the Greek community, quashing all efforts to revive Greek fascist organizations in Egypt, which Greek nationalist politicians and some members of the Greek Orthodox patriarchate of Alexandria had promoted. In this context, the Prime Minister, Emmanouil Tsouderos, officially abolished the August 4 regime in February 1942, appointing Panagiotis Kanellopoulos, who received the broad acceptance of the majority of the community and the army, as deputy prime minister that May.

The vast majority of Egyptiots stood by the Allied forces. In January 1941, even before the arrival of the exiled government in Egypt, an Anglo-Greek Association was founded, on the initiative of Clifford Heathcote-Smith, British consul general in Alexandria. His aim was to coordinate the actions of the community with British policy. Heathcote-Smith and his Greek counterpart, Konstantinos Valtis, served as copresidents of the association, whose members were all wealthy and prominent members of the community and the GKA, the leadership of which was traditionally liberal and pro-British.[21]

While the struggle in interwar Greece between liberals and monarchists was also fought out within the community, the communist activity of intellectuals and workers was also important. Some of them participated in the founding of the Egyptian Socialist Party in 1921 (which became the Communist Party in 1923) and the antifascist organization Ligue Pacifiste in the 1930s, along with Egyptian Jewish Communists. When the war started in 1939, though, the Egyptiot communists organized themselves in an autonomous way because of the difficult situation facing Greece shortly after: the Greek-Italian War since October 1940 and the German invasion and occupation since April 1941. Until 1942 they strongly opposed the supporters of the fascist regime and were in contact with the EAM in Greece. A strong indication of their shift toward Greece was the renaming of the journal *Aigyptiotis Ellin* (Egyptiot Greek) to *Ellin* (Greek), which became their organ. Theodosis Pieridis ran the journal with a five-member committee, which included Stratis Tsirkas, who later became a well-known novelist, and Stratis Zerbinis, the younger brother of industrialist Dimitrios Zerbinis, who served as GKA and GCCA president in the postwar years.

In January 1943, the National Liberation Association (EAS), which constituted the main mouthpiece of EAM in the community, was established. This was almost immediately followed by the establishment of a sister, purely communist, organization called Antifascist Vanguard (AP), a product of the collaboration between Egyptiot Communists and members of the Communist Party of Greece (KKE), who had reached Egypt. The organization did not employ the term "communist" in its title, in order to avoid prohibition by the Egyptian authorities. Members of the EAS, such as Pieridis and Tsirkas, were also members of the AP. The EAS had branches in Cairo, Alexandria, and Port Said and organized collections and various events in support of Greece. Initially the British tolerated the EAS because of its antifascist character and because many liberal personalities, such as Georgios Roussos, had also joined it. However, the more the relations of the British with EAM deteriorated during the war, the more the EAS found itself in a difficult position.[22]

Sharp tensions emerged in March 1943 after an army mutiny, which provoked the replacement of the deputy prime minister, Kanellopoulos, with Roussos. The appointment of an Egyptiot and liberal ex-minister of Eleftherios Venizelos's government reveals the importance the British and Greek governments attributed to the community's support. More revealing of this is the fact that the government asked the *koinotites,* the fraternities—associations for people with common origins in a particular island or region like Chios or the Peloponnese—and other Greek associations in Egypt to express their loyalty to the king and the Tsouderos government and to deplore all those who provoked and supported the mutiny. After another mutiny in 1944 in which the navy was implicated, the British in Cairo and Alexandria arrested EAS members, whom they set free later the same year. The EAS was required to cease its activity, but the AP became the principal organization around which the Egyptiot Communists gathered in the following decades. The AP continued to be organized in an autonomous way after the war, establishing stronger links with the KKE than with the Egyptian Communist Party.[23] In the postwar period, the AP constituted the basic oppositional voice to the community's conservative leadership, which was mostly represented by the GKA. The GKA would continue to work closely with the Greek consular authorities and Greek state, leading it to be described as "the favored child of the Greek government"[24] and "the first of the Greek *koinotites* abroad."[25]

POSTWAR DILEMMAS AND CERTITUDES

Egyptiot concerns about the future in the post-Capitulations era emerged in 1944, as the war's end was approaching. On 8 September 1944, the GKA's legal advisors convened to examine the issue of the treaty of establishment announced during the Montreux conference. The meeting was held on the instructions of Dimitrios Pappas, Greek ambassador to Cairo, to examine a series of matters that he expected would affect the community after the war. These included the economic conditions of the Egyptiot Greeks and small enterprises in particular, the readjustment of the Greek education system to the new conditions, commercial issues, the patriarchate of Alexandria, and, of course, the treaty of establishment. The meeting was held seven years after Montreux, that is, more than halfway into the agreed, twelve-year transitory period. Due to the undoubtedly special circumstances prevailing in Egypt, no initiative had been taken either to draft a treaty text or to prepare for the oft-cited "readjustment" (*anaprosarmogi*).

In the postwar era, "readjustment," which was seen as necessary to ensure the viability of the Greek presence in Egypt, became something of a slogan. Nonetheless, each section of the community advocating the word invested it with different and conflicting meanings, according to their special interests and ideology.[26] The GCCA and GKA, for instance, especially during the presidency of industrialist Dimitrios Zerbinis (March 1947–January 1949 and 1948–54), underlined the necessity to readjust to the new economic conditions and the changing labor market.[27] This was not new. Since the interwar period, Egyptiot industrialists, in opposition to the traditional group of merchants, were more in favor of a rapprochement with Egyptian society, which would guarantee the long-term future of Greeks in Egypt. The Egyptiot industrialists had made important investments in the country and were part and parcel of the wider industrialization project. Egyptiots had to remain because they constituted for them significant social capital and a labor force.[28] Strongly linked to the labor market was the education of young Greeks, whose schools the *koinotites* generously funded.

Members of the Egyptiot Left, on the other hand, envisaged readjustment more in terms of a cultural and psychological rapprochement with the Egyptians. They considered learning Arabic and developing a new professional orientation as a key element of this effort, which had also a strong political dimension: support for Egyptian national demands.[29] Indeed, AP members embraced the anticolonial struggle throughout the period. They expressed their support in many ways: publications, demonstrations, solidarity committees, and, later, voluntary participation in the Egyptian militia during the 1956 Suez Crisis.[30] After the anti-British riots of February 1946, Theodosis Pieridis, in an article published in the leftist Egyptian journal *Al-Fajr Al-Jadid,* made their position clear:

> We Greeks live scattered amid the Egyptian people, and move within its popular quarters and villages; our interests are tied to Egypt, our struggle is on the side of its struggle and we share with it good times and bad. We are tens of thousands of Greek workers who settled their stock on this native earth and developed their torsos by inhaling its air. Its virtuous dust enveloped them [and] there is no doubt that the great mass of Greeks in Egypt ... stand in strong and firm solidarity with the Egyptian nation in its demand for freedom that it holds sacred.[31]

At the same time, Pieridis also strongly criticized the community leadership in the journal *Ellin,* claiming that the former should stop behaving like "a closed/introvert ... minority of a few hundred people, which tries to defend itself against the overall context."[32] Only closer relations with the Egyptians could ensure the long-term future of the Greeks in Egypt, according to Nikolaos Tsaravopoulos, a progressive doctor from Cairo, who insisted on the vocational dimension of readjustment. In a December 1947 speech, he said, "We should stop cherishing unrealistic illusions about the continuation of our presence as a privileged minority, and we should understand that our future will be judged by our professional abilities and by the degree of friendship we will develop with the Egyptian people and also by the appreciation and respect we will inspire in them as friends."[33]

However, the development of strong links with the Egyptians at the leadership level was often limited to an elitist attitude restricted to formalities or enthusiastic initiatives that fizzled out. One such scheme was the founding of the Greek-Egyptian Association right after the war, which failed to produce any concrete results. Instead, it remained for more than a decade in "suspended animation," as the Greek ambassador noted in 1956.[34] The association was restricted to sending "a telegram on the occasion of Muslim celebrations with anodyne and unnecessary conventional words," according to *Ellin*,[35] or to initiatives that were "taking place miles away from the mass of the Egyptiot people and from the people of this country."[36] Such rather meaningless activities on the part of associations that were supposed to represent the community did little to overcome Egyptian distrust. In any case, before the war, and especially before Montreux, no one was interested in a rapprochement with the Egyptians, as Dimitrios Pappas acknowledged in 1948.[37] His successor as ambassador, Georgios Triantafyllidis, shared the same view: "Greeks here have always kept themselves far from the native element and they did not cultivate close ties with them, as they should have. Now, at the last minute, such an effort cannot possibly have a serious outcome because the Egyptians are not so naïve as not to understand its purpose."[38] In order to support this view, he forwarded to the Foreign Ministry in Athens the following translated article from the Egyptian paper *Al-Assas*, an organ of the Saadist Party:

> It has been recently observed that the ... organizations of the [Greek] community ... have traced a new line which they bring into play against the Egyptians ... in order to gain the affinity of the country in which they reside and to satisfy it. They also maintain such a standpoint in order to inspire in the citizens of the country and its officials the feeling that they are similar to them and that they care about their issues in the same way that they care about their national interests; ... the main aim that they try to achieve using every way and means is securing a foothold and acquiring affinities through a systematic, methodical, and organized course of action.[39]

At a bilateral level, the readjustment was expressed through the backing of the Greek state for Egyptian demands. In that direction, Athens voted for the Arab positions in the general assemblies of the United Nations against the partition of Palestine in 1947 and refused to recognize the State of Israel, despite pressure from its Western allies. This policy did not remain without reward in the UN context, since Egypt and other Arab countries supported Greece's membership in the UN Security Council in 1952–53.

The discussion concerning the Greek presence in Egypt had another dimension, apart from "readjustment." The Greek side, either through the government or through the community leadership, had sought to differentiate itself from other foreigners in Egypt and especially the British. They maintained that Greeks had contributed to Egypt's development and that both Egypt and Greece had strong ties since antiquity. The first argument was almost identical to the one utilized by the colonial powers to justify their intervention and their role as "civilizing" forces of "underdeveloped" societies.[40] The role of the Capitulations and British protection in this "contribution" was carefully excluded from any public discourse because this would equate the Egyptiots' interests with those of the colonial powers. For the same reason, this argument ignored cases of exploitation of Egyptian peasants when initiatives and achievements in agriculture were publicized.[41]

To avoid being equated with the colonial powers, the community leadership focused on the second argument: Egyptian-Greek ties since antiquity. This, in practice, implied that Greek presence in Egypt was much older than the British or French, and therefore, Egyptians should not identify them with the colonial presence. Even though the argument about perennial ties did not necessarily imply ties with modern Egyptian society, it was enthusiastically received by the Egyptian side—especially before 1952. This can be explained by the insistence in the national narratives of both countries on the continuation of the two people's presence from ancient to modern times. This notion of an ancient relationship formed the basis of all arguments calling for a favorable treatment of the community in legislation concerning Egypt's foreign residents. The provision of privileges and tax and legislative immunity constituted a *condicio sine qua non* in the Ottoman world and was at the root of the Capitulations. Seeking exemption from the laws of the Egyptian state is somewhat revealing of the mentality of the Greek government and at least a part of the population—and especially of the institutions representing it. They expressed a clear difficulty in recognizing Egypt's right to exist as a nation-state and the basic mechanisms that such an existence presupposes: the protection of Egyptian citizens and the exclusion of foreigners. In any case, the enhancement of the Greek presence's uniqueness was not necessarily compatible with the readjustment effort.

Despite discussions concerning the uniqueness of the Greek presence or different ways of adjustment, the community leadership and the Greek state but also a part of the Egyptiot Left primarily envisaged the consolidation of the Egyptiot position through a treaty of establishment. Communists and other progressive elements of the community tried to detach the issue of the long-term future from the treaty. They sought rapprochement with Egyptian society, specifying that Greeks should by all means support Egyptian national claims for full independence. Other interventions from the Left, however, showed that "readjustment" was not incompatible with the conclusion of a treaty. For instance, Persis Kitrilakis, an Alexandrian lawyer and president of the progressive League of Demobilized Greeks of Alexandria, wrote:

> The treaty of establishment that will be contracted ... must principally establish the existing vested rights and afterward must trace the exact framework, especially with regards to the Greeks' right to settle in Egypt. ... All the hopes of the tens of thousands of Greeks of Egypt are turning to the official representatives of Greece, as well as to the Alexandrian Koinotita, the strength of which has always been the object of general admiration in the defense of Greek interests.[42]

This ambiguous position is indicative of the contradictions of the Egyptiot Left, which tried to strike a balance between its de facto position as part of a relatively privileged minority and its strategic choice for closer contact with the Egyptian population.[43]

The importance the community leadership attributed to the treaty was lucidly expressed in a memorandum sent by GKA president Mikès Salvagos to the ambassador, Dimitrios Pappas, on 20 September 1944. With it he clearly connected the future of the Greek presence in Egypt with the conclusion of a bilateral treaty: "Protected by a treaty of establishment, the Greeks of Egypt will face the future with more security and will thus be able to continue their activities in the best interest of Egypt and of Greece."[44] The fact that a bilateral agreement was meant to regulate the status of the Greeks in Egypt would de facto increase the role of the Greek state in their affairs. Moreover, the protection of the Egyptiots through a bilateral agreement would offer the community a new, cohesive element for its consolidation and would also enhance its dependence on the homeland.

Greek state officials also attributed the same fundamental importance to a legal framework that would safeguard the Greek position in Egypt. Their desire, as before the war, was to prevent by all means a massive repatriation movement. In this respect, Athens instructed the diplomatic authorities either to keep Greeks in Egypt or to encourage them to migrate to other destinations.[45] Therefore, concluding a treaty before the end of the transitory period would represent the main tool of the Greek state to consolidate the

Greek presence in Egypt. In early February 1944, Ambassador Pappas, in a letter to the prime minister and foreign minister, Themistoklis Sofoulis, predicted that if a treaty of establishment was not signed before the end of the transitory period, "we will ... face the gradual outflow of the poorest [and] ... a vast wave of refugees toward Greece."[46] The consul general in Alexandria pinpointed the importance of maintaining the Greek presence because it was extremely beneficial for Greece. Demonstrating a colonial imperialist spirit, he said, "Egypt's Hellenism constitutes for Greece a colony, which does not constitute a burden for Greece at all. ... It is the natural nucleus for the expansion of Hellenism in the Middle East."[47]

The Greek state was extremely reluctant to receive Egyptiots, especially those who were destitute and unemployed. The reasons for this were numerous. Emerging from Axis occupation and a civil war, Greece had no capacity to accommodate additional population at a time when the Greek state was facing the "new refugee" issue, namely the reception of refugees from Eastern Europe.[48] In addition, the refugee experience of Greeks from Asia Minor and other areas in the 1912–24 period was still fresh in the collective memory.[49] State officials and community dignitaries alike feared that repatriates from Egypt, especially those unemployed and destitute, risked becoming an intolerable "burden" for Greece's economy at the same time that the Greek state was planning an emigration program for its residents to counter overpopulation, unemployment, and the danger of social disorder.[50] The instructions of the Greek Ministry of Foreign Affairs (GMFA) to the Cairo embassy were clear: "We strongly advise against their arrival in Greece, because of the situation in the country and because of the danger of a general refugee influx from Egypt. We would be grateful if you could examine the possibility of finding employment for them in Egypt ... or of preparing their emigration to neighboring countries."[51] Besides, prospective repatriates would be more useful for the Greek economy if they remained abroad and sent remittances. The Greek government could not countenance the immigration of unemployed and destitute Egyptiots, as it feared they could embrace communist ideas at a time when anticommunism was the central ideological tenet of the state.[52]

What the Greek side sought—but could not openly admit—were guarantees that Greek nationals would not be expelled.[53] Where did this fear come from? Even before the abolition of the Capitulations, many Greeks were anxious about their position in the Egyptian labor market, an issue that will be discussed in chapter 3. In April 1944, the ambassador, Pappas, claimed the Egyptiot economic elite was generally pessimistic about the community's future. They believed that the Greeks in Egypt would meet the fate of the Greek populations in Romania, Russia, and the Ottoman Empire, who abandoned these countries in the 1910s and 1920s. The Egyptiots remained one of the few Greek communities in former Ottoman territory. In the interwar period, the Greek minority in Istanbul had come under pressure from Turkish nationalists in the context of the formation of the Turkish nation-state. Conscious of these changes, the community leadership and Greek state officials feared that Greeks would come under the same kind of pressure during the formation of the Egyptian nation-state and be compelled to leave the country.

At another level, the influence of the colonial empires, whose traditional role was to protect the Christian and foreign populations in the Middle East, was dwindling in the aftermath of World War II. In Southeast Asia, the liberation movement in Indochina was challenging the hegemony of France, which definitely lost the Indochina War in 1954. The British left India in 1947 and Palestine in 1948, and the State of Israel was founded the same year. The world was rapidly changing. The superpowers, the United States and the USSR, and the newborn postcolonial nation-states gradually replaced the power of the old colonial empires. In this global context and under an imagined threat of expulsion, the Greek side viewed the accomplishment of a treaty of establishment as a vital issue.

In the meantime, Britain's military presence in Egypt during the war and its often brutal intervention in Egyptian political life encouraged a resurgence of nationalism, and the claim for full independence came strongly to the fore after 1945. The denunciation of the Anglo-Egyptian Treaty of 1936 and the related demand for the immediate withdrawal of British troops from the Suez Canal became major issues. The negotiations during 1946 on the withdrawal of the British from Suez did not produce the anticipated results. In addition, the defeat of the Arabs in the Palestine War and the creation of the State of Israel in 1948 were major disappointments for Egyptian public opinion, which was convinced that the existing political personnel could provide no solution. These circumstances boosted not only support for the nationalists but also the strength of the Communists and the Muslim Brotherhood.

At a socioeconomic level, the demographic boom over the previous decades had raised the importance of the issues of rural land redistribution and unemployment, for which politicians could not provide any viable solutions either. In the postwar period, Greeks, along with other foreigners, like the French and Belgians, had realized that the wartime economic boom was a temporary and extraordinary situation. When the British and their allies departed, the situation reverted to its sluggish antebellum course. It became more and more obvious that after the war, a crisis would arise especially in the labor market. This imminent labor market crisis, according to the Greek ambassador's estimation, would "further weaken the position of foreigners, who are bound to become convenient scapegoats in the hands of an unpopular and unstable Egyptian government in dire need to reassert its legitimacy."[54] Initiatives such as Law 138 of 1947, which increased the minimum percentage of Egyptian citizens that joint-stock companies were required to have in their administration and workforce, worried foreigners but did not bring any solution to the unemployment problem. Out of the gradual destabilization of the constitutional republic, as a result of social inequality, political instability, political assassinations, and massive demonstrations, emerged the Free Officers Movement, which would undertake dynamic initiatives in the 1950s leading to a bloodless coup d'état in July 1952.

In this unstable context, the exploitation and the political use of anti-British popular feeling at times led to the targeting of all foreigners living in the country. After all, as early as 1882, the Egyptian population linked the presence of foreigners in Egypt with Britain's policy in the country. Besides, the vast majority of foreigners, even those who had arrived before the British, had no legal bonds with the country through citizenship, did not send their children to Egyptian schools, and had a poor knowledge of Arabic. Thus, it is not surprising that Theodosis Pieridis would write in 1946 that "these days when, in the mind of the struggling Egyptian people, the term 'foreign force of occupation' is confused with the single word 'foreigners.'"[55] Indeed, anti-British riots in Cairo and Alexandria that year resulted in a few Greek-owned enterprises and residences being damaged.[56] Such incidents seem to have worried the Egyptiots, contributing to the general negative attitude of the majority of foreigners toward Egyptian independence. "The vast majority of the community," wrote Yiannis Anastassiadis in his memoirs of the Egyptiot Left, "did not see with much sympathy and were hostile to the Egyptian struggle for independence. They linked it to the damage of shops and the looting in which almost all demonstrations ended up."[57] Even though such incidents were not very common, they increased the feeling of insecurity among foreigners and were utilized by Western observers and Israel to accuse Egyptian society as a whole of xenophobia and racism. Within this fluid and extremely unstable context, postwar Egyptian governments, which lacked popular legitimacy, were not eager to conclude treaties of establishment with former capitulatory states. This was all the more the case given that the Egyptian public opinion linked the treaties with the Capitulations.

COUNTDOWN

In June 1946, diplomats, jurists, and the presidents of the principal organizations of Greek Alexandria formed a committee to work on preparing a draft treaty of establishment. The committee asked Polys Modinos, a prominent judge in Alexandria's Mixed Court of Appeal, to prepare a draft and submit it to the committee and to Georgios Triantafyllidis, the Greek ambassador. The Modinos draft, which the committee elaborated further, is revealing of how the Greek elite perceived the community's position in Egypt in the post-Capitulations period. Two principles, also dictated by the Montreux Convention, prevailed in the text: (a) equal rights for natives and foreigners in a wide range of issues such as taxation, the right to enter and exit the country, and working rights and (b) reciprocity between the contracting members.[58] Given that very few Egyptians lived in Greece and the interests of Egypt there were rather insignificant, it is evident that reciprocity was of little value for Egypt. This was bound to make a treaty unbalanced, and therefore offsets had to be invented and offered to the Egyptian side. This explains initiatives such as the proposal to build a mosque in Athens at the expense of wealthy Egyptiots or to provide grants to Egyptian students to attend Greek universities.

To achieve the maximum benefits, the Greek treaty committee relied on legal arguments, the development of an atmosphere of cordiality with Egyptian officials, and the close collaboration with British diplomats. It took into account the treaties of establishment already concluded with Persia and Turkey, as well the terms of the Montreux Convention concerning nondiscrimination, personal status, deportation of foreigners, associations' status, and joint-stock companies. The conclusion of a treaty was not a simple bilateral issue between Greece and Egypt but one facing all former capitulatory states. British diplomats held a consultative role in all foreign committees, the Greek included; collaboration was so close that every step taken by the latter had to be first approved by the former. At the same time, to avoid the risk of Egyptiots being targeted because of anti-British sentiment in Egypt, the GMFA recommended to the leadership to distance themselves from the British and French, who were more worried about politics than matters concerning their own citizens. For that reason, the close collaboration between the committee and the British embassy was kept secret, for fear of provoking an Egyptian reaction.

The committee submitted the final Greek draft to the Egyptians on 12 April 1948, but a year later, even though the end of the transitional period was approaching, negotiations between Greece and Egypt had not even begun. In May 1949, a group of Greek notables, under the guidance of lawyer Nikolaos Vatibellas, principal of one of the most prominent law firms in Alexandria, Mikès Salvagos's legal collaborator, and former GKA president for a short period, expressed to the Greek prime minister of Alexandrian origin, Konstantinos Tsaldaris, their "deep concern" at the fact that the transitory period was about to elapse with no treaty having been signed. The notables requested Tsaldaris, who was of Alexandrian origin, to accelerate the process and highlighted two points: the guarantee of the Egyptiots' right to work unhindered in the country and the ability to transfer their property to Greece in the event of repatriation.[59]

In the meantime, the signs from the Egyptian side were not positive. In May 1949, a report by the constitutional review commission of the Egyptian Senate clearly stated that the Egyptian government's obligation to respect the rule of nondiscrimination, as dictated by the Montreux Convention, was limited to the transitional period. This was the first time an Egyptian state body had openly declared that after the end of this period, "Egypt ... will have no other legal obligations toward foreigners [living in Egypt] than those that derive from the principles of international law that are also valid in all other countries."[60]

The Egyptians submitted their counterproposal to the Greek committee on 1 August 1949, two and a half months before the end of the transitional period. The Egyptian text for the treaty of establishment was not tailored to Greek wishes but was the standard draft presented to all foreign delegations. The Greeks, who considered that their needs were different from those of other foreigners, and especially the British, French, and Belgians, were deeply disappointed. They had shared the widespread belief that the "eternal friendship" between the two peoples, the support for Arab claims at the UN, and common interests in the Eastern Mediterranean would be sufficient for the Egyptians to express a different attitude toward them.[61]

Negotiations between the two delegations started on 13 September 1949. The most contentious articles—numbers one, two, three, and seven—were related to the issue of entering, exiting, and residing in Egypt, deportation, and the right of foreigners to work in Egypt. The first round lasted fifteen days, until 28 September, when the final joint draft was prepared.[62] The second round lasted only three days, from 24 to 27 April 1950, with no concrete results. The community leadership eagerly awaited the conclusion of the treaty, on which it pinned almost all hope for a secure future of the Greeks in Egypt. The Greek dignitaries were deeply apprehensive, as is reflected in the reports in the Greek-language press.

Even before the negotiations started, the Egyptian national movement had become stronger and more radical. The Arab defeat in Palestine in 1948 had increased popular dissatisfaction with the political system. Moreover, the consolidation of the USSR, coupled with the parallel decline in the influence of the colonial powers in Africa and Asia, was another factor. In March 1950, negotiations between Britain and Egypt over the abolition of the 1936 Anglo-Egyptian Treaty resumed. In this context, *Al-Ahram* and other Egyptian newspapers intensified their criticism of the proposed treaties of establishment. The French-language newspaper *La voix de l'orient* suggested that these treaties "constitute the way that will lead us straight to the new Capitulations."[63] Given the critical situation in Egypt, which the Anglo-Egyptian rivalry had fueled, the Egyptian Wafd government, in power since early 1950, decided to abandon the plan to conclude the treaties and to promulgate a law regulating the residence of foreigners in the country. The Egyptian ambassador to Athens justified his government's choice thus: Egypt could not grant to a country what it refused to another, and public opinion clearly connected the treaties with the Capitulations.[64] This turn of events had a profound, negative effect on the community leadership. In May 1951, Alexios Liatis, consul general of Alexandria, acknowledged that "the morale of the community ... has reached its lowest point."[65]

Indeed, the fact that a treaty had not been concluded by the end of the transitional period on 15 October 1949, the abolition of the Mixed Courts, and the changes under way in the economy, labor market, and education gave rise to frustration and pessimism among the Egyptiot leadership regarding the future of the Greeks in the country. Triantafyllidis attributed this frustration to the comparisons made by the Egyptiots to the Capitulations era, during which "they constituted a state within a state."[66] According to the ambassador, that period bequeathed them a mentality and habits that they could not abandon. As a result of this mentality, the prevailing idea was that "despite the abolition of the Capitulations ... the country [would] remain forever under foreign control."[67] This view is in line with a remark made after World War II by another observer. A Greek police officer, visiting Egypt in late 1948, claimed that the leadership was very much concerned about the future of the Greeks in Egypt. The situation would calm down only if "English troops come back to Egypt."[68] A year later, the consul general in Alexandria, Harilaos Zamarias, noted that even the most propitious treaty of establishment would disappoint the Greek nationals because it could only guarantee equal rights for foreigners and Egyptians but not the privileges they had enjoyed under the Capitulations.[69]

Despite the leadership's vehement complaints about the Egyptian government's "completely incomprehensible"[70] attitude, which was totally contrary to its commitments at Montreux, Egypt decided to settle the issue of residence the way former capitulatory countries treated foreigners internally.[71] Egyptiot dignitaries and diplomats had believed Egypt would follow its expressed intentions as they were declared in the Monteux Convention, ignoring the fact that the emergence of a nation-state is defined, inter alia, by two parameters: the emergence of a "rule of law" and the distinction between nationals and non-nationals.

The end of the transitional period and the abandonment of a plan for a treaty of establishment in practice signified that the legal position of foreigners and, of course, the Greeks ceased to be a bilateral issue and would thereafter depend on the host country, which had decided to act as a sovereign state. As Hamid Sultan, professor of public law at Cairo University, pointed out:

> Egypt must force its foreign inhabitants to respect its sovereignty, and it must subject them to its laws for a certain period of time. Not in order to take revenge, but simply in order to reaffirm its sovereignty and to enable the state to produce laws that are necessary for the regularization of its interests with those of foreigners, and the protection of Egyptian nationals and their interests.[72]

Egypt had decided to treat foreigners according to its territory under the standards of international law, as did the ex-capitulatory countries, among them Greece. This is what the dramatic chain of events and changes from 1937 imposed on the country. The world of 1950 was very different from that of 1937. The war had decreased colonial influence. In the new postcolonial world, Egypt sought to follow with determination the road to national independence and the consolidation of the nation-state.

A question then arose as to the definition of "foreigner." Egyptian law defined a foreigner as simply anyone who did not have Egyptian citizenship—the issue of Egyptian and Greek citizenship is discussed in chapter 3. However, not many Greeks applied for it during the Capitulations era, and even fewer obtained it. Most of them preferred to maintain their foreign status because, among other reasons, they could take advantage of the privileges provided by the Capitulations. Egyptiots wished to be considered locals and maintain the same privileges, more or less as previously, not by virtue of nationality but by virtue of their long residence in the country. However, such categorizations were common only in premodern societies such as the Ottoman Empire, which categorized the population according to criteria other than nationality. One may therefore observe a rather peculiar scheme according to which the Egyptiots desired to be considered not Egyptians but non-foreigners. It is from this perspective that one may interpret the opinion expressed by Modinos: "A foreigner who has always lived in Egypt and whose ancestors have lived in Egypt for generations is not a foreigner. All his activities are Egyptian, as are his work, his income, and his capital."[73]

Since the Egyptiots lacked the protection provided by a bilateral agreement, the importance of the Greek diplomatic authorities in Egypt was diminished. However, the role that was accorded to them by the leadership remained salient. Losing the privileged status they had enjoyed under the protection of the Greek state, the community now had to emancipate and adjust itself to a new situation. Greek citizens would be legally considered foreigners, as was the case in any other contemporary sovereign nation-state. Readjustment and the policy of rapprochement with the Egyptians seemed to be the only alternative for the consolidation of the Greek presence. The Greek community itself, however, undermined this latter choice. Political cleavages in the Cold War context, which in part had developed during World War II and were reinforced during the Greek Civil War, forced the Egyptiots to perform a balancing act between the anticommunist policy of the Greek state and the reemergence of the Egyptian national movement.

The entrenched belief that the future of the Greeks in Egypt almost exclusively depended on the treaty had become a stumbling block regarding the question of readjustment. The Greeks of Egypt did not use the twelve-year transitional period offered at Montreux as such, namely as a period during which they would readjust themselves to the new Egyptian reality. They used it mainly as a waiting period, at the end of which they hoped they could maintain more or less the same privileges. Whether due to the war or because of inertia stemming from the hope that a treaty would be a light version of the Capitulations, the community undertook little in the direction of readjustment, even in the educational realm, such as in giving Greek schools a technical orientation or introducing the teaching of Arabic. Even if the Greek state did not wish to receive Egyptiots, the gradual departure of many in the immediate postwar period made it clear that more and more Egyptiot Greeks already envisioned their future somewhere else, not in Egypt.

BETWEEN ANTI-BRITISHISM AND ANTICOMMUNISM

The Egyptian government not only retreated on signing treaties of establishment but also, on 8 October 1951, abrogated the Anglo-Egyptian Treaty of 1936 and requested the imminent withdrawal of British troops from the Suez Canal area. A surge of patriotic activity ensued, marked by anti-British demonstrations around the country, in which Egyptian Socialists, Communists, the Muslim Brotherhood, Wafd members, and members of the Free Officers participated. Significant activities took place in all cities, but the biggest protests were in the Suez Canal zone, where a guerilla campaign targeting the British military presence started in October 1951. More than fifty thousand Egyptians and foreign workers and employees abandoned their positions in the auxiliary services of the British base along the Suez Canal, which the Egyptian state considered illegal after the abrogation of the treaty. Employees and workers in factories and enterprises that were connected to the base followed their example, whereas railroad workers and customs and airline company employees stopped serving the base. Economic life came to a halt in Port Said and Ismailia due to the recurring strikes in the Suez Canal Company by Egyptian workers, who were also supported by their Greek and Italian counterparts.[74]

Guerilla fighters, the so-called *fedayyin*, began attacking the British military base. Made up of students, local farmers and workers, radical intellectuals, and army officers, these units initially attacked the installations supporting the barracks (aqueducts, telegraph and post offices) and, depending on the level of active support from local residents and the Egyptian police, inflicted severe damage and human casualties on the British, who then replied with heavy artillery. Ismailia was the most affected, since its prosperity depended on the British presence and the city, along with its greater area, hosted the biggest corps of foreign, and presumably Greek, employees in the region.[75]

A number of Greeks collaborated with the *fedayyin* or supported their action. These were mainly Communists from both Egypt and Greece, some of whom had already fought in the Greek Civil War and offered their services to the anticolonial struggle. For many of the Egyptiots, actively supporting Egyptian national claims was part and parcel of the readjustment process. The Greek diplomatic authorities, however, opposed such collaboration. Information on the issue is fragmentary because the Greek authorities did not have a full picture of communist activity in the area. For instance, a Greek police officer who was in Egypt in August 1952 to monitor communist activity informed the GMFA that "a Greek whose name is still unknown to me, a former ELAS [Greek People's Liberation Army] bandit, is leading the Egyptian *fedayyin* in Port Said."[76]

In Alexandria, for which information is more detailed, the reaction of the different community institutions to local demonstrations provides a clearer picture on how the different sides conceived support for the Egyptian national movement. In view of the mobilization in Alexandria on 14–15 November 1951, El-Maraghi Pasha, the interior minister, asked the GKA and other Egyptiot institutions to participate in the silent demonstration in favor of Egyptian independence, to show that Egyptians and foreign citizens constituted a common front against the British. The GKA initially ignored the invitation because its president, Dimitrios Zerbinis, was in Europe on business, but as soon as he returned, a senior officer in the governorate, who happened to be a friend, emphasized the importance of the GKA's participation in the demonstration. In the event, the most important Koinotita did participate, even if somewhat reluctantly. Other organizations—associations of Greek workers and of students at Farouk University in Alexandria and other progressive Greek organizations—participated in the mass silent demonstrations, the only Europeans in Egypt to do so, according to the educator Panagiotis Xenos.[77] According to the local and international press, several hundred Greeks participated, carrying banners with slogans such as "Our Egyptian brothers: the Greeks have joined you in your struggle."[78]

The position of the consul general of Greece in Alexandria, Alexios Liatis, as he presented it to the representatives of the GKA and the other institutions, was that "the Greek citizens and the Greek organizations do not have a place in such national Egyptian events and actions and their participation in them is incompatible with their Greek nationality."[79] Additionally he threatened to revoke the citizenship of Greek students at Farouk University if they participated in the demonstrations. His effort to convince Greek nationals had also another dimension, as the French-language weekly newspaper *L'Actualité* reported. He warned Greeks that "soon enough the English will reoccupy Egyptian cities and ... the Greeks would then be rounded up in concentration camps if they are found to have participated in the Egyptian national demonstration."[80] We do not know to what extent Athens dictated Liatis's views. It is true, however, that during this period tensions over the recognition of the title of the Egyptian king dominated Greek-Egyptian relations.

This incident is indicative of the limits of Greece's pro-Egyptian policy as it developed in the post-Capitulations period. Athens adopted the British position on the matter, refusing to recognize Farouk's title as king of Egypt and the Sudan. Egypt's addition of Sudan to the royal title came in the wake of the abrogation of the 1936 Anglo-Egyptian Treaty and chronologically coincided with the transfer of ambassador Triantafyllidis. The Greek embassy in Cairo remained headless from spring to August 1952, that is, during a period of high tension that ended in the military coup of 23 July 1952. Filippos Dragoumis, a former vice-consul in Alexandria (in the 1910s) and government minister in Greece, whom foreign minister Sofoklis Venizelos sent to Egypt on a special mission in April 1952, was in no doubt about Greece's position on the matter: "The stance [of the Greek government] is dictated by the close and abiding bond with England."[81]

To return to the November 1951 demonstrations in Alexandria: Liatis felt extremely uneasy and ordered consulate staff to take photographs of the Egyptiots who took part in the demonstration and to prepare detailed lists of them.[82] A few days later, in a communication to the Cairo embassy, he blamed communist intervention for the Greek Alexandrians' action in favor of the Egyptian national struggle and against "British imperialism."[83] The situation was similar in Cairo, according to the city's consul general: "Since October 1951 the leftist elements of the Cairo community, taking advantage of the English-Egyptian dispute, wanted to drag it into activities against the English under the pretext of an alleged solidarity with Egypt."[84]

Early in December 1951, after the Alexandria demonstrations, progressive elements founded the Council of Greek-Egyptian Friendship and Cooperation. The council was in a way a brainchild of Theodosis Pieridis, who in the meantime had been denied entry to Egypt after a trip he made to Cyprus in 1947. Egyptians and Greeks collaborated in the council to support Egyptian national claims and thus to rectify the consulate's attitude. This became even more pressing because the Egyptian press characterized Liatis's activity as "an action in favor of a state which Egypt is fighting against."[85] The council's main aims were to strengthen relations with the Egyptians, to actively support the national struggle of their country of residence, and to actively support Egyptian demands. After the abandonment of the idea of a treaty of establishment, the Egyptiot Left believed this was a concrete way to demonstrate its intention to cooperate with the Egyptians.

How can one explain the reaction of both consuls regarding the participation of Greeks in anti-British demonstrations? In targeting Communists, the diplomatic authorities reflected the divisions of the Greek Civil War and the belief that the Soviet Union was responsible for whipping up the Arab world, the Egyptian national movement in particular, against the Western, colonial forces and, consequently, against foreigners. Regarding the role of the Soviet Union, *Pravda* noted in October 1951 that resistance against British imperialism constituted "a natural duty" of the Egyptians.[86] The Soviet Union indirectly encouraged movements wishing to put an end to Western colonial influence in the Middle East in the late 1940s and early 1950s. It seems though that, especially during the Stalinist period, it did not have direct involvement in the region other than observing the situation and providing moral support.[87] The Egyptian communist movement, even if it emerged strengthened in the aftermath of World War II, faced severe repression not only in the 1940s but also throughout the 1950s and the first half of the 1960s. The above-mentioned declarations of the community dignitaries, though, identified Egypt's foreigners with British policy during the Egyptian anti-British struggle.

In order to prevent communist penetration, the diplomatic authorities, along with the GKA and other community organizations, often took either a repressive or a preventive stance against what they considered to be a communist "threat." First, they systematically kept individual files recording the activities and the evaluation of the political beliefs of Egyptiots suspected of communist involvement. The consulates and the *koinotites* used these files to issue "social belief certificates," which confirmed they were not Communists and were necessary to find employment in Egypt—in Greek and other foreign businesses—and in Greece.⁸⁸ The consulates firmly collaborated with the Athens police, whose officers frequently visited Egypt to update their own files. The evidence would suggest that the consular authorities denounced Greek citizens engaged in communist activity to the Egyptian police. In turn, Egyptian state security either forbade them to enter the country upon their return from foreign trips—as it happened in the Pieridis case—or expelled them. Greeks serving in the Egyptian police also facilitated the "cleansing" of potentially dangerous people from the community.⁸⁹ As an ultimate measure, the consular authorities stripped Greek Communists of their citizenship, using their "antinational" activities as a pretext. In order to protect cohesion within the community, members of its leadership, such as GKA president Dimitrios Zerbinis, often refused to collaborate with the consular authorities or to speak out against their fellow compatriots. The consuls condemned them for this.⁹⁰ This kind of protection, along with kinship and other networks in the community, often made it relatively easy for them to issue social belief certificates, even for persons who were not eligible to receive one. For this reason, from 1952, the Security Division of the Greek Interior Ministry undertook the task of providing information on the beliefs of the Egyptiots when required.⁹¹

The anticommunist drive of the Greek authorities in the 1950s involved imposing political control over the *koinotites* and, especially, the GKA. The local Egyptiot economic elite, whose members were in a position to pay the high subscription fees, traditionally controlled the GKA. The GKA, thanks to its property and the donations of its members, funded the schools and the hospital in the city along with the numerous charities. However, after World War II, the mass registration of new members financed by industrialists who supported different factions led, in a peculiar way, to the gradual democratization of the GKA. Overall its membership increased from 301 in 1937 to 1,510 in 1952, whereas in the meantime the number of members fluctuated depending on when elections were held: 657 members in 1945, 1,044 in 1947, 4,290 in 1948, 997 in 1949 and 3,100 in 1951.⁹² Enrollment usually surged before elections, paid for by well-off Egyptiots in an attempt to influence the result. The tobacco manufacturer Achilleas Koutarellis, for instance, paid the registration fees for 1,600 members in the hope of influencing outcome of the 1952 elections.⁹³

As Liatis acknowledged, the Left faction possessed "the strongest cohesion and discipline, the best organization, and the most effective leadership" of all the community dignitaries. The Communists controlled the faction, which also included Socialists and "progressive people of all kind." In its program, it opposed the old, privileged economic elite. The Left's support for Zerbinis ensured his election as GKA president from 1948 to 1954, and he often covered the registration fees of new members. This gave rise to a peculiar alliance in the late 1940s and early 1950s between Communists and Egyptiot industrialists such as Zerbinis, who wished to push aside the old community elite, mostly embodied by Koutarellis and Konstantinos Salvagos—and to reinforce the position of Greeks in post-capitulatory Egypt. This collaboration did not necessarily mean that the Left fully endorsed Zerbinis's positions and program. As Liatis pointed out, Zerbinis "is availing himself of the support and tolerance of the Communists because, according to their leadership, 'Zerbinis represented a lesser evil to the imminent danger represented by the full subjugation of the GKA to fascists such as Koutarellis and semifascists such as Salvagos.'" This informal alliance was all the more remarkable considering that, in Liatis's words, "as for political beliefs, Mr Zerbinis is more to the right than Salvagos."[94]

This peculiar democratization of the GKA resulted in the Left securing five—out of a total of twenty-four—Koinotita board members in the 1952 elections. Under the main slogan "readjustment," the Communists tried to put forward an agenda to safeguard the long-term residence of Greeks in Egypt. In the 1956 elections, in which 3,377 out of a total 3,795 registered members voted, the Left garnered an impressive 42.4 percent of the vote.[95]

The consulate and the GKA leadership resisted the Left's efforts, and in 1958 they abruptly ended the participation of Communists in the GKA administration. The fear regarding the emergence of the Left in Greece—the United Democratic Left (EDA) became second party in the May 1958 general election—was reflected in Egypt as well. Fearing control of the Koinotita could be lost, the consul general provoked the intervention of Egyptian state security, which annulled the 1958 GKA election and demanded the replacement of candidates elected with communist support.[96] Subsequently, elections would be conducted under the "auspices" of the consulate in order to prevent a communist majority and to consolidate the control of the GKA by nationalist elements.[97] Under these circumstances, the Communists' percentage in the elections of 1959, 1960, and 1961 diminished to 14.3 percent, 16.5 percent, and 17.4 percent, respectively. At the same time, the electorate shrank from a high point of 3,377 in 1956. In 1959, only 1,738 (out of 2,139 registered voters) participated in the election. In 1960, it numbered 1,352 (out of 1,761), and in 1961, it was 996 (out of 1,535). Abstention increased over three years from 11.1 percent to 35.1 percent, which was mostly an indication of the hopelessness of the situation, since the consulate, community leadership, and certain dignitaries prevented the questioning of the communal status quo. At the same time, the Nasserite regime, despite developing links with the Soviet Union and Eastern bloc countries, continued to follow a "constant prosecution of communism and fight against the entire pro-communist movement" in Egypt. [98]

The efforts to maintain political and ideological control included censorship by the Greek authorities of the Greek-language press. "Some Greek diplomats always put obstacles on journalists because they wanted the Greek newspapers to be their organs," wrote Manolis Yalourakis, a columnist for the Alexandrian *Tachydromos,* after his repatriation to Greece.[99] The effort to control the press sometimes took a more aggressive stance. For instance, the Greek embassy managed to close down the communist newspaper *I Foni tou Aigyptiotou Ellinismou* (The Voice of Egyptiot Hellenism) in 1953. The newspaper had begun publication in June 1952, but nine months later the Egyptian authorities shut it down following the intervention of the Greek embassy press office.[100] The ambassador, Michail Melas, decorated the staff of the Egyptian ministry who executed the order.

The anticommunism of the period was also expressed in the effort to consolidate the nationalist feeling of Egyptiots through the use of propaganda in the communal schools, media, newspapers, and radio. An important piece in this propaganda effort was the radio program of Agis Tabakopoulos, justice minister in the Metaxas regime and GCCA legal advisor and representative in Athens. In the late 1940s, Athens Radio broadcasted his propagandistic pro-nationalist discourse every Sunday morning.[101] The reinforcement by all means of nationalist feeling in the community intensified its introversion and the belief in the cultural superiority and uniqueness of the Greek presence in Egypt. Thus, this propaganda undermined whatever efforts might have been made for the readjustment of the community in cultural and political terms.

Apart from any effects on the Egyptiot population, anticommunism influenced its relationship with Egypt. At a very critical time in Egypt, which was on the road to full independence, the anticommunism of the Greek state and community leadership reaffirmed their identification with British policy; community dignitaries even publicly invoked this identification. Without referring openly to communism, since the GCCA statute forbade political discussions, its president, Nikolaos Sakellarios, a major cotton merchant and member of the chamber's board since 1941, told its annual general meeting in March 1952 that

> there is a new factor that has recently penetrated the political life of the country, the identity of which there can be no doubt whatsoever ... the same forces that are involved in subversive activity in other countries have also appeared in Egypt.... If they manage to settle in Egypt then both the ... sea route of the Suez Canal and the control of the whole of Africa will be in danger, the latter being an extremely valuable prey.[102]

The "new factor" he referred to was undoubtedly communism, which Greek diplomatic reports considered a "threat" in the late 1940s and early 1950s. The reference to the Suez Canal, just a few months after the denunciation of a treaty that preserved the British military there, underlines another dimension: that of British protection of Egypt from communism. The logic is simple: since the British defended the canal, they defended Egypt and the entire African continent from communist penetration. This view constitutes a contradiction. Greek state policy involved seeking the cooperation of its Western allies at the same time that it was seeking to support Egyptian national claims against them, at both the state and community level. To the extent that their policies collided, the Greek side found itself in a no-win situation. So, to avoid being identified with the colonial powers, it played the card of the "uniqueness" of the Greek presence in Egypt, which sprang from the eternal links between the Egyptians and Greeks and their contribution to the economic development of the country.

Bearing in mind the alignment of interests between the Greek state and community dignitaries and the British, as confirmed by Sakellarios and Dragoumis, it is not strange that the British military administration in the canal zone a few months later tried, even without any obvious approval from the Greek government, to create a network of people "composed exclusively by Greek nationals or people of Greek origin,"[103] to be trained in British military bases in Cyprus, as Epaminondas Skarpalezos, Greek vice-consul in Zagazig, wrote in a top-secret report.[104] The British sought three or four Egyptiots who would be sent to Cyprus for three months to be trained by the British. Upon their return, they would be used as trainers for a limited number of other trusted Egyptiots to create groups for the protection of the foreigners in the Suez Canal area until the British military took control of the situation.

While some Greeks backed the anticolonial struggle, others collaborated closely with the nationalists' enemy. Such a contradiction reflected the situation in postwar and post-civil war Greece, toward which the official and, to a great extent, the rest of the community was oriented. Regarding its policy toward Egypt, the Greek state tried to balance itself between its ideological affinity with the colonial powers and support for the Egyptian national struggle, in order to protect the Greek presence in Egypt from the communist threat. These contradictions were more vividly manifested—to a greater or lesser extent—throughout the entire period under study and especially during the Suez Crisis, as the next chapter will show.

Returning to the uneasy situation of November–December 1951, while the *fedayyin* groups intensified their action in the Suez Canal area, in January 1952 they attacked the British barracks in Tel el-Kebir, located between Ismailia and Zagazig. The funerals of the Egyptian casualties of the fighting led to rioting, which ended in the destruction of foreign properties. In reprisal, the British attacked the Ismailia police station a few days later, with considerable loss of life on the Egyptian side. When news reached Cairo, unions called a general strike that soon spread across the country. The big demonstrations that took place in the capital ended up with the burning and looting of buildings and companies in downtown Cairo, the modern European center of the city, on Saturday, 26 January 1952. On "Black Saturday" night, 463 shops belonging to foreigners, of which Greeks owned 157, were destroyed and pillaged.[105] The destruction provoked nervousness among foreigners and, of course, among Greeks. Apprehension and uncertainty about their future in Egypt reemerged in full force. While several theories have been put forward about who was blame for this disaster, it is still not clear who provoked this event.[106]

In the meantime, political instability continued to characterize Egyptian political life. In order to reassure foreigners in the aftermath of Black Saturday, the two governments that succeeded the Wafdist government of Nahhas Pasha arrested a number of protesters, paid compensation, and, soon enough, on 26 May, promulgated Law 72/1952, which regulated the matter of foreign residency in the country. But Egypt was moving toward a coup d'état after a long period of political instability and unrest, which had started with the end of World War II, intensified after the Arab defeat in the 1948 Palestine War, and reached its peak in 1951 and early 1952. In these seven years, the Capitulations had been fully abolished—after the Mixed Courts had come to an end in 1949—and the plans for treaties of establishment had been abandoned. Cairo had unilaterally renounced the Anglo-Egyptian Treaty, which foreigners considered another means for their protection. Even in this extremely fluid environment, during which the community did not avail itself of any kind of legal or other external protection, the standpoints of some members of its leadership were remarkably naive. In a speech to the GCCA general assembly in March 1952, Sakellarios, who was also responsible in the GKA for educational issues, not only neglected to mention the issue of "readjustment" but also expressed his hope that the normalization of the political situation would finally lead to the conclusion of a treaty of establishment. "We Greeks do not wish to leave Egypt, where we and our fathers were born and which we love deeply. We will be happy to find again the old, familiar endearing face of Egypt."[107]

NOTES

1. Michail Melas, *Anamniseis enos presveos* [Memoirs of an ambassador] (Athens, 1965), 160.

2. Greek Foreign Ministry Archive (AYE)/Central Service (CS)/1953/51/1/1, 8, Mansoura, 3 January 1953, Korantis to Cairo embassy; AYE/CS/1950/16/1/1, 434, Cairo, 2 February 1950, Triantafyllidis to Greek Ministry of Foreign Affairs (GMFA); *O Paroikos,* 26 May 1957, 1; Themistoklis Matsakis, *To dilimma tou aigyptiotou ellinismou* [The dilemma of Egyptiot Hellenism] (Cairo, 1961), 4, 9.
3. Panayiotis Jerasimof Vatikiotis, *The History of Modern Egypt: From Muhammad Ali to Mubarak* (London: Weidenfield and Nicolson, 1991), 269–70.
4. Evelyn Baring, Earl of Cromer, *Modern Egypt,* vol. 2 (1908; repr., London: Routledge, 2001), 428.
5. For a good summary of the Capitulations in Egypt, Persia, and the rest of the Ottoman Empire, see John E Wansbrough et al., "Imtiyazat," in *The Encyclopedia of Islam,* ed. HAR Gibb (Leiden: Brill, 1986), 1178–95.
6. Yehia Abdel Kader, *Les passeports et la résidence des étrangers en Egypte* (Alexandria: Journal du commerce et de la marine, 1953), 12.
7. Cited in Jasper Y Brinton, "Egypt: The Transition Period," *American Journal of International Law* 34, no. 2 (1940): 208–19, here 218.
8. Nantes Diplomatic Archives Centre (CADN)/Consulat de France à Alexandrie/224, Proceedings of the Montreux conference, 59, cited in Polys Modinos, *Etude sur le projet du Traité d'établissement présenté par le gouvernement égyptien,* Strictement confidentiel, Alexandria, 21 August 1949.
9. Alexander Kitroeff, *The Greeks in Egypt, Ethnicity and Class, 1917–1937* (Oxford: Ithaca Press, 1989), 144–45.
10. Archives of the Greek Koinotita of Alexandria (AGKA)/K136. In a working note of the GKA, the following *koinotites* are mentioned: Abu Qir, Alexandria, Assyut, Aswan, Banha, Beni Mazar, Beni Suef, Cairo, Damanhur, Damietta, Dairut, Faqus, Fayum, Heliopolis, Helwan, Ibrahimia, Ismailia, Kafr el-Zayat, Magana, Mansoura, Marsa Matruh, Mehalla Kebir, Minet el Kamh, Minya, Mit Gamr, Port Said, Qantara, Rahit, Seitoun, Serbin, Sibin el-Kom, Suez, Tahta, Tanta, Velkas, Zagazig, and Zifta. At other times, *koinotites* were active in Kafr el-Dawwar and Ramli.
11. Georgios Mavris, *Ypomnima peri ton en Aigypto Ellinikon Koinotiton* [Memorandum concerning the Greek *koinotites* of Egypt] (Zagazig, 1911).
12. AGKA/K136, 1931, Paris, 18 May 1937, Politis to Metaxas.
13. *La bourse égyptienne,* 20 July 1937.
14. AYE/CS/1952/50/6/1/1, Speech of Alexis Liatis to the GKA general assembly, Alexandria, 9 February 1951.
15. AYE/CS/1937/78/2/1/1-1, Alexandria, 21 April 1937, Salvagos to Metaxas.
16. AYE/CS/1937/31/4/1, 3387, Cairo, 15 November 1937, Delmouzos to Metaxas.
17. G Nikolaou, *O aigyptiotis ellinismos kai i mellontiki autou katefthynsis* [Egyptiot Hellenism and its direction in the future] (Alexandria: Patriarchal Printing House, 1915); A Konstantinidis, *I ekatontaetiris tou aigyptiotou ellinismou kai to mellon tou* [The centenary of Egyptiot hellenism and its future] (Alexandria, 1930); Eugenios Mihailidis, *O aigyptiotis ellinismos kai to mellon tou* [Egyptiot Hellenism and its future] (Alexandria: Grammata, 1927).
18. *Panaigyptia* 14 (416), 3 April 1937, 8–9.

19. Alexander Kitroeff, "I elliniki paroikia stin Aigypto kai o defteros pagkosmios polemos" [The Greek community in Egypt and World War II], *Mnimon* 9 (1983): 4.
20. Manolis Yalourakis, *I Aigyptos ton Ellinon* [Egypt of the Greeks] (Athens: Mitropolis, 1967), 201.
21. AYE/CS/1941/25/B/3/AC, 289, Alexandria, 20 January 1941, Valtis to GMFA.
22. Kitroeff, "I elliniki," 5.
23. Katerina Trimi-Kyrou, "Être internationaliste dans une société coloniale: le cas des Grecs de gauche en Égypte (1914–1960)," *Cahiers d'Histoire, Les Gauches en Egypte, XIXe–XXe siècles* 105–6 (2008): 100.
24. AYE/CS/1951/6/4/1/1, 24063, EK /4, Athens, 28 February 1951, Venizelos to General Consulate in Alexandria.
25. AYE/CS/1952/50/6/1/1, 23, Alexandria, 4 January 1952, Liatis to GMFA.
26. On the issue of the readjustment of the community, see Anthony Gorman, "The Failures of Readjustment (Αναπροσαρμογή): The Postwar Egyptian Greek Experience," *Journal of the Hellenic Diaspora* 35, no. 2 (2009): 45–60; Gorman, "Repatriation, Migration or Readjustment: Egyptian Greek Dilemmas of the 1950s," in *Greek Diaspora and Migration since 1700*, ed. Dimitris Tziovas (Farnham: Ashgate, 2009), 61–72.
27. "The adjustment and the consolidation of our position in Egypt," *Bulletin of the GCCA* 569 (15 January 1948): 1–4.
28. Kitroeff, *The Greeks*, 181.
29. For the issue of the postwar Egyptiot Greek Left, see Anthony Gorman, "Egypt's Forgotten Communists: The Postwar Greek Left," *Journal of the Modern Greek Studies* 20 (2002): 1–27; Trimi-Kyrou, "Être internationaliste," 85–117.
30. Trimi-Kyrou, "Être internationaliste," 107.
31. Cited in Gorman, "Egypt's Forgotten Communists," 6.
32. *Ellin*, 2 March 1946, 1.
33. Nikolaos Tsaravopoulos, *I Egkatastasi ton Ellinon stin Aigypto* [The Settlement of Greeks in Egypt], (Cairo: K Tsouma, 1948), 40.
34. AYE/CS/1957/22/9/1/1, 6857, Cairo, 4 June 1957, Lambros to GMFA.
35. *Ellin*, 16 March 1946, 5.
36. Tsaravopoulos, *The Settlement*, 28.
37. AYE/CS/1948/103/1/6/6, Top Secret, Proceedings of the assembly of the political affairs council of the GMFA, Athens, 27 February 1948.
38. AYE/CS/1948/103/1/6/2/10161, Cairo, 5 February 1948, Triantafyllidis to Pipinelis.
39. Ibid. Translation of article from *Al-Assas* by the Greek embassy personnel.
40. Jürgen Osterhammel, *Colonialism: A Theoretical Overview*, 2nd ed. (Princeton, NJ: Markus Wiener, 2005), 108–10.
41. Kitroeff, *The Greeks*, 92.
42. League of Demobilized Greeks of Alexandria, *Memorandum concerning the Greek–Egyptian treaty of establishment*, Alexandria, 1950, 22–23.
43. Gorman, "Egypt's Forgotten Communists," 8.
44. AGKA/K 547, Memorandum to the Greek Ambassador in Cairo, Alexandria, 20 September 1944, 11.

45. AYE/CS/1948/94/4/4/2, 48431, Athens, 2 December 1948, Kontoumas to Triantafyllidis.
46. AYE/CS/1946/36/5, 1195, Cairo, 4 February 1946, Pappas to Sofoulis.
47. AYE/CS/1944/13/4, 443, Alexandria, 24 October 1944, Valtis to Cairo embassy.
48. AYE/CS/1951/3/2/1, Athens, 9 January 1951, Zaimis to GMFA: The number of these refugees was estimated at 5,500 persons by January 1951 by the Greek Health Ministry, whereas more Greek refugees were expected from Bulgaria, Korea, and China.
49. More than 1.5 million Greek refugees from Asia Minor, Russia, and Bulgaria arrived in Greece from the beginning of the Balkan Wars of 1912 to the defeat of the Greeks in Asia Minor in 1922 and the exchange of population between Greece and Turkey from 1922 to 1924.
50. AYE/CS/1948/92/3/1/1, 4381, Cairo, 17 November 1947, Triantafyllidis to Greek consular authorities in Egypt; AYE/CS/1948/92/3/1/1, 23/48, Alexandria, 6 January 1948, Zerbinis to Tabakopoulos; Lina Venturas, "Greek Governments, Political Parties and Emigrants in Western Europe: Struggles for Control (1950–1974)," *Revue Européenne des Migrations Internationales* 17, no. 3 (2001): 64–65.
51. AYE/CS/1948/94/4/4/2, 48431, Athens, 2 December 1948, Kontoumas to Cairo embassy.
52. AYE/CS/1947/10/1, 21214, Secret, Athens, 17 March 1947, Bensis to Cairo embassy; AYE/CS/1948/103/1/6/3, 1065, Top Secret, Cairo, 15 March 1948, Mavrokefalos to Triantafyllidis.
53. AYE/CS/1948/103/1/6/1, Top Secret. Proceedings of the meeting of the political affairs' council, Athens, 20 June 1948.
54. AYE/CS/1944/40/1, 243, Secret, Cairo, 18 July 1944, Pappas to Papandreou.
55. *Ellin,* 2 March 1946, 1.
56. AYE/CS/1946/36/3, 2398, Cairo, 7 June 1946, Sofianos to Cairo embassy.
57. Yiannis Anastassiadis, *Mnimes apo tin drasi tou aristerou kinimatos tou aigyptioti ellinismou* [Memoirs from the action of the left movement of Egyptiot Hellenism] (Athens, 1993), 25.
58. CADN/Ambassade de France au Caire/29/Projet du Traité d'Amitité et d'Etablishment entre l'Egypte et la Grèce.
59. AYE/CS/1949/42/1/5/2, Alexandria, 12 May 1949, Vatibellas to Tsaldaris.
60. CADN/Consulat de France à Alexandrie/224, *Journal des Tribunaux Mixtes,* 4081, 31 May 1949, cited in Polys Modinos, *Etude sur le projet du Traité d'établissement présenté par le gouvernement égyptien,* Strictement confidentiel, Alexandria, 21 August 1949.
61. Ibid.
62. As it had also occurred at Montreux, probably the most disputed part of the treaty concerned its duration. Egyptians wanted five years, and Greeks insisted on twenty years.
63. *La voix de l'Orient,* 3 May 1951.
64. Archives of the French Foreign Ministry (MAE)/Levant 1944–65/Egypte 1944–52/Dossier 124/Rapport avec les pays étrangers/série k/carton 72/Dossiers 11 à

18/Egypte juin 1947/février 1953/Rapports avec la Grèce/124/Bulletin II, Athens, 16 June 1952.
65. AYE/CS/1951/96/2/1/1, 3610, Alexandria, 4 May 1951, Liatis to Cairo embassy.
66. AYE/CS/1950/16/1/1, 434, Cairo, 2 February 1950, Triantafyllidis to GMFA.
67. Ibid.
68. AYE/CS/1948/94/2/1/1, 135/2/1/90, Athens, 1 December 1948, Vlastaris to GMFA.
69. AYE/CS/1949/42/1/5/1, 515, Alexandria, 21 December 1949, Zamarias to Cairo embassy.
70. AYE/CS/1951/6/4/1/1, 9562, Cairo, 25 July 1951, Triantafyllidis to GMFA.
71. For as long as the Capitulations lasted, foreigners enjoyed practically free movement and residence in Egypt. Under a decree of 23 June 1938, the minister of interior obtained the right to deport foreigners on the basis of the Montreux Convention. A few months later, on 1 September 1938, Law 78/1938 allowed those who refused to leave the country to be imprisoned for fifteen days to six months. The first effort of the Egyptian state to regulate the entry and exit of foreigners in the country was Law 49/1940. No reference to the matter of residence was made, though. Nevertheless, during World War II the law remained a dead letter. The issues of entering, exiting, and residing in the country were finally regulated by Law 72/1952 (see Kader, *Les passeports,* 12).
72. Cited in Kader, *Les passeports,* 18.
73. CADN/Consulat de France à Alexandrie/224, Polys Modinos, *Etude sur le projet du Traité d'établissement présenté par le gouvernement égyptien,* Strictement confidentiel, Alexandria, 21 August 1949.
74. Anne-Claire Kerboeuf, "L'incendie du Caire, 26 Janvier 1952. D'un régime à l'autre" (Ph.D. diss., University of Provence, Aix-Marseille I, 2007), 226–29; Caroline Piquet, *La Compagnie du Canal de Suez. Une concession française en Egypte, 1888–1956* (Paris: Presses de l'Université de Paris-Sorbonne, 2008), 350–53.
75. AYE/CS/1952/49/4/1/1, 332 A/1, Port Said, 29 January 1952, Avramidis to the Greek embassy in Cairo.
76. AYE/CS/1953/51/1/1, 2735/1567bis, Athens, 22 May 1952, Tseberopoulos to GMFA.
77. Papers of Panagiotis Xenos, Hellenic Literary and Historical Archive (ELIA), Athens.
78. *Egyptian Gazette,* 14 November 1951; *The Times,* 14 November and 15 November 1951, all cited in Gorman, "Egypt's Forgotten Communists," 7.
79. AYE/CS/1951/6/4/1/1, 8402, Alexandria, 12 November 1951, Liatis to the Greek embassy in Cairo.
80. *L'Actualité,* 8 December 1951.
81. AYE/CS/1952/1952/48/1/1/1, 6510/Athens, 23 April 52, Bensis to Venizelos.
82. *L'Actualité,* 8 December 1951.
83. AYE/CS/1952/49/4/1/1, 5, Alexandria, 12 January 1952, Liatis to the Greek embassy in Cairo.
84. AYE/CS/1953/51/1/1, 298, Cairo, 18 January 1953, Georgiadis to Melas.
85. AYE/CS/1952/48/6/3/1, 3748, Note, Athens, 11 December 1951.

86. Rami Ginat, *The Soviet Union and Egypt, 1945–1955* (London: Routledge, 1994), 123.
87. Constantin Katsakioris, "The Soviet-South Encounter: Tensions in the Friendship with Afro-Asian partners, 1945-1965," in *Cold War Crossings. International Travel and Exchange across the Soviet Bloc, 1940s-1960s,* edited by Patryk Babiracki and Kenyon Zimmer (Arlington, TX: A&M University Press, 2014), 137.
88. Anastassiadis, *Mnimes,* 149.
89. Ibid.
90. AYE/CS/1953/78/1/1, 11, Alexandria, 14 January 1953, Liatis to Cairo embassy.
91. AYE/CS/1953/78/1/1, 15/6/34, Athens, 14 April 1952, Rentis to GMFA.
92. AYE/CS/1952/50/6/1/1, 4331bis, Alexandria, 10 July 1952, Liatis to Cairo embassy.
93. Ibid.
94. Ibid.
95. AYE/CS/1961/16/1/3/2, 299, Alexandria, 29 March 1961, Kontoumas to Cairo embassy.
96. Anastassiadis, *Mnimes,* 149.
97. AYE/CS/1961/16/1/3/1, 171, Alexandria, 9 February 1961, Baizos to Cairo embassy.
98. Ibid.
99. Yalourakis, *I Aigyptos,* 222.
100. AYE/CS/1953/51/1/1, 7137, Cairo, 10 November 1953, Melas to GMFA and AYE/CS/1953/51/1/1, 6325, Cairo, 4 April 1953, Melas to GMFA.
101. "Speech of Agis Tabakopoulos on the Radio," *Bulletin of the GCCA* 592 (31 December 1948): 6–8.
102. AGCCA/General assemblies, 1952–72, Speech of Nikolaos Sakellarios, GCCA president, to the general assembly on 20 March 1952.
103. AYE/CS/1953/78/1/1, 465, Secret, Zagazig, 15 May 1952, Skarpalezos to the Cairo embassy.
104. AYE/CS/1953/78/1/1, 836, Zagazig, 29 October 1952, Skarpalezos to the Greek embassy in Cairo.
105. CADN/Consulat de France à Alexandrie, 324/Note, 28 February 1952, Une nouvelle conclusion du mouvement panarabe: l'insurrection du 26 janvier 1952 au Caire; AYE/CS/1952/6146, Cairo, 7 February 1952, Mavrokefalos to the Greek embassy in Cairo.
106. Anne-Claire Kerboeuf, "The Cairo Fire of 26 January 1952 and the Interpretations of History," in *Re-Envisioning Egypt, 1919–1952,* ed. Arthur Goldschmidt et al. (Cairo: American University in Cairo Press, 2005), 194–216.
107. AGCCA/General assemblies, 1952–73, Speech of Nikolaos Sakellarios, GCCA president, to the general assembly, 20 March 1952.

Chapter Two

Egypt at the Forefront (1952–60)

In summer 1952, most of the Free Officers were still quite young. Their bloodless coup d'état on the night of 22–23 July surprised the members of the old regime. King Farouk, who was on holidays in Alexandria, sought the intervention of the US ambassador, but within a few hours the army entered the Mediterranean port city. In any case, US officials, along with their British counterparts, who had prior knowledge of the military coup through their intelligence services, approved it, hoping it would bring stability to the country. The Free Officers had reassured the Western powers that their movement was not Islamic or communist in nature but that its members were modernizing military officers.[1] While they lacked a detailed political plan, the Free Officers supported a nationalistic discourse that aimed to achieve full independence, namely the emancipation of Egypt from the British presence. The demand in Egyptian society for a British withdrawal was such that it could function in its own right as a consolidating element for the new regime. Six principles that were part of clandestine manifestos before 1952 and were later enunciated in the preamble of the 1956 constitution became the guiding principles of the new regime: "The eradication of all aspects of imperialism; the extinction of feudalism; the eradication of monopolies, and the control of capitalistic influence over the system of government; the establishment of a strong national army; the establishment of social justice; and the establishment of a sound democratic society."[2]

After Nasser's advent to power in 1954, at the age of thirty-six, Egypt would engage in the anticolonial struggle, the emergence of the Third World, and what would become known later as the Non-Aligned Movement. In contrast, Greece faced the new international context—which was determined by the increasing rivalry between the two superpowers and the decline of the European colonial empires—exhausted and divided after almost a decade of Axis occupation and civil war. Internally the central ideological tenet was anticommunism, whereas the Cypriot Greek claim for unification (*enosis*) with Greece and Cold War alliances largely defined its external policy. In this local and international context, the Egyptiot community leadership sought ways to ensure the long-term presence of Egyptiots without the protection offered by the Capitulations or a treaty of establishment, which in the event was never concluded. This chapter discusses what kind of strategies the Greek state, the community leadership, and the Egyptiot Left developed to safeguard the presence of Greeks in Egypt, from the Free Officers coup d'état until Nasser's visit to Athens in June 1960, just a few months before the exodus started.

TIME OF RAPPROCHEMENT

King Farouk fled the country on 26 July 1952, and General Muhammad Naguib, a respected and popular officer, became the leader of the new regime. From his very first days in power, Naguib tried to reassure foreigners of the government's intentions toward them. A series of laws in this direction settled the issue of their residency in Egypt. Whereas new legislation envisaged the new residence permits would be valid for five years, in February 1953 the interior minister decided to extend this to ten years for those who had been born in Egypt or who could prove more than twenty years' permanent residence in the country. The ministry's new passport and nationality offices started operations on 28 February 1953. At the inauguration ceremony, Naguib himself handed out twenty-six permits to foreigners, among whom were five Greeks.[3] The symbolism of this gesture was evident: Egypt's foreigners now enjoyed the protection of the new regime. Officials in Alexandria adopted the same triumphal tone. The director of the passport office there declared that "Egypt opens its heart and its arms toward its foreign brothers."[4]

After the abandonment of the treaty of establishment and the Cairo events, the military coup presented an opportunity for a rapprochement between the community and the new Egyptian authorities. From the earliest days of the military regime, the *koinotites* and representatives of other foreign groups sent messages affirming their loyalty and their will to collaborate with the new regime. The foreign-language press congratulated the new government and reassured readers of the regime's intentions vis-à-vis foreigners.[5] So did the Greek community leadership, while the Egyptian government underscored the deep friendship between the two peoples on every available occasion.

The Egyptiot Left, loyal to the principle of supporting Egyptian national demands, also congratulated Naguib. However, it toned down this warm welcome for the Free Officers regime after the intervention of the army in the workers' uprising at Kafr el-Dawwar, a textile center fifteen miles south of Alexandria and in the Koutarellis tobacco factory in August 1952.[6] It soon became apparent that notwithstanding the concerns expressed by Greek diplomats about the left-wing affinities of the new regime,[7] the latter was favorably disposed toward foreigners and, particularly, foreign capital. A few months later, on 5 January 1953, the banning of "communist or communist-friendly journals" left few doubts about the real intentions of the new government. The embassy took advantage of this decision to close down the newspaper *Foni,* which they argued "constantly published pictures of Stalin ... [and] promoted the Kremlin's foreign policy,"[8] was following Cominform orders, and was funded by the Eastern bloc embassies.[9]

While receiving journalists from Greece and Egypt in November 1952, Naguib underlined the importance and the positive role of the community in Egypt's development. On the occasion of the Greek national day, on 25 March 1953, he addressed himself to the Greek people, seeking to assure them about the future of their compatriots in Egypt. Beyond any personal sympathies regarding foreign populations, the new regime had many economic and political reasons to be in favor of the long-term presence of foreigners in Egypt. First of all, it needed to keep and increase foreign investments in Egypt. In this respect, it tried to prevent the flight of capital and secure the collaboration of foreigners in development plans in order to attract more investors from abroad. Second, it did not want to be accused of maltreating foreigners or of xenophobia and thus provide a pretext for a British or other Western military intervention, as had happened in the past.

Despite the seemingly cordial atmosphere between the community leadership and the Egyptian authorities, skepticism prevailed among Greek diplomats regarding the future position of the Egyptiots. This skepticism did not only result from the political situation or the left-wing affinities of the government, but was also due to the difficulties Egyptiots faced in the labor market and the unwillingness or incapacity of the leadership to move forward on the matter of adjusting to the changing Egyptian environment. Indicative of these inabilities was the intensification in the early 1950s of the departure movement from Egypt, which had started right after the war. The new political situation, combined with long-term economic problems facing the community, provoked vivid concerns and a feeling of uncertainty about the future within its ranks. The leaders of the Alexandrian Egyptiot Left referred to this feeling during the electoral campaign in 1954. They insisted on the necessity for a rapid readjustment process in many different sectors, which they bemoaned had not been done "when it should have been done—in the old good times—because of inaction, conservatism, or bad predictions."[10]

Israel tried to exploit the increasing skepticism of Egyptiot Greeks and other foreigners about their future in Egypt. Since the 1948 war, the Israeli government and press accused Egypt of anti-Semitism and Nazi-style persecutions of the Jews of the country.[11] Even though these accusations were mostly unfounded, the comparison of Egypt with Nazi Germany found resonance in France and Britain, two Western countries that had little sympathy for the expression of Egyptian nationalist feelings against colonizers. On the contrary, they approached Egyptian nationalism through colonial stereotypes, dismissing it as xenophobic.[12] Israel tried to take advantage of events like Black Saturday for its anti-Egyptian propaganda, which sought to increase the anxiety among the Jewish population and other foreign residents. In July 1954, while Egypt was in parallel negotiations with Israel for a peace treaty and with Britain for the withdrawal of its troops, Israeli secret agents orchestrated a series of bomb attacks aimed to jeopardize the negotiations.[13] Thus, to counter Israeli espionage and other threats, which were linked to the Cold War context, Egypt set up its own intelligence service. A number of spying incidents were revealed, some of which were more real than others. These seem to have had important effects on social and political life. In the late 1950s and early 1960s in particular, newspaper headlines concerning spy cases were so common that they fueled conspiracy theories and general suspicion.

Despite the bombings, negotiations between Egypt and Britain continued. On 19 October 1954, Nasser—who had already marginalized Naguib to become the chief figure of the regime—concluded with Anthony Nutting, the minister of state for foreign affairs, an agreement for the definitive withdrawal of British military forces from the Suez Canal area within twenty months, that is, by June 1956. In February 1955, Israel, which, after the decision for a British withdrawal, tried to present itself as the best advocate of Western interests in the region, launched raids into Gaza. Nasser turned to the United States to purchase arms so he could challenge the incursions. The United States asked Nasser to participate in the Baghdad Pact, the newly founded NATO branch in the Middle East and Central Asia, which grouped Turkey, Iraq, Iran, and Pakistan under Britain's auspices. France, on the other hand, requested Nasser to halt his moral and material support for the armed struggle of the National Liberation Front (FLN) in Algeria, which had commenced in November 1954. Nasser refused the Western requests and turned to the Soviet Union and China.

In this new postwar diplomatic system of alliances, defined by the Cold War and anticolonial context, the new Egyptian policy found affinities with those of Yugoslav president Josip Broz Tito and the Indian prime minister Jawaharlal Nehru, who had adopted the doctrine of neutrality toward the United States and Soviet Union. Nasser confirmed his policy by attending the Bandung Conference of African and Asian countries in April 1955. The main purpose of the summit was to condemn colonialism and underline the necessity of maintaining an independent stance toward the superpowers. The new international context led Egypt to sign an arms deal with Czechoslovakia in September 1955. This deal proved to be crucial for the break with the Western powers and, especially, the United States, since, in the eyes of American secretary of state John Foster Dulles, whoever was not an ally was considered an enemy.

The Egyptiot Left strongly supported Nasser's policy turn and expressed its support on every occasion. To avoid the same fate as *Foni,* the Cairo left-wing daily *O Paroikos,* set up in 1953, followed the Bandung line from April 1955.[14] Nonetheless, apart from the Egyptiot Left, Egypt found an unexpected ally for its anticolonial policy in Greece. Nasser's advent to power and his change of policy coincided chronologically with the emergence of the Cypriot issue and the demand of Greek Cypriots for unification with Greece. Greece decided to internationalize the issue, a fact that brought it into dispute with Britain and, consequently, its Western allies.

The first attempt at a UN resolution for Cyprus in December 1954 did not produce the anticipated results, because of British and Turkish reaction and US neutrality. In April 1955, as the Baghdad Pact took shape and Nasser was in Bandung, the National Organization of Cypriot Fighters (EOKA) started a guerilla war against the colonial British forces. Shortly afterwards a rivalry erupted not only between Greek Cypriots and Turkish Cypriots, but also between Greece and Turkey.[15] The tensions between the two countries led a few months later to the 6–7 September 1955 pogrom against the Greek and other minorities in Istanbul, an incident reported in the Egyptiot press.[16] The incident dealt a mortal blow to the most solid Greek presence within the territory of the former Ottoman Empire—apart from Egypt. On 21 September, the UN General Assembly rejected Greece's demand to place the Cypriot issue on the agenda. In the subsequent period, Greece's relationships with its NATO allies were about to be tested even more.

Konstantinos Karamanlis, whom King Paul appointed prime minister in 1955, won the elections of 19 February 1956. That spring, the British deported Archbishop Makarios, head of the Greek Cypriots, to the Seychelles. Huge demonstrations took place in Athens and Thessaloniki in support of the Cypriot demand for unification with Greece and against the British. The matter reached the UN, and the Greek government sought new alliances. To this end, it sought to activate its traditionally good relations with the Arab countries, which represented a voting bloc in the UN and most of them were traditionally suspicious of Turkey and British colonial policy. In the context of this rapprochement, Minister without Portfolio Grigorios Kassimatis visited Egypt, Syria, and Lebanon in March 1956.[17] Egypt, which wished to see the British deprived of their last base in the Middle East in Cyprus, which was two hundred nautical miles away from Port Said, supported by all means, as did other Arab countries, the Greek claim in the UN. Greece's relations with the Arab countries, and Egypt in particular, improved and further developed across a wide spectrum of activities, from commercial relations to education.[18]

The policy of establishing good relationships with the Arab countries in this period was fueled not only by the necessity to create alliances in the UN context for the Cypriot issue and to protect the Greek presence in Egypt.[19] Following World War II, the Greek merchant fleet sought closer collaboration with the oil-producing Arab countries as well as for unrestricted navigation through Suez. Greece depended on Arab oil, and important construction companies were doing business in Saudi Arabia and Iraq. These links were the key reasons for developing good relations with the Arab countries.[20] At another level, Greek foreign policy sought to ensure its control over the patriarchates of Jerusalem and Alexandria and to prevent any Soviet penetration, especially of the Holy Land, through the Russian Orthodox Church.[21] The Greek governments did not wish to lose the Arabic-speaking followers of the Greek Orthodox Church, who constituted the majority of the Greek Orthodox flock in the region. The loss of the Antioch patriarchate in the late nineteenth century to Arab control was an event that Greece did not want to see reproduced elsewhere. For all these different reasons, Greece remained, until 1990, the only non-Muslim country that did not have diplomatic relations with Israel. This position contributed, according to Egyptian newspaper *Al-Qahira,* to the strengthening of Greece's prestige in the Arab countries, leading them to support Greek claims in the UN.[22]

The Egyptiot press on the whole treated the rapprochement of Greece with Egypt against the British as a factor that would consolidate the Greek presence and guarantee the long-term viability of the community. A consequence of this argumentation was to link the Greek presence in Egypt directly with the Greek state's policy in the international scene. This practically implied that for as long Egypt's and Greece's interests coincided, the community's position would be secure whereas in the event of Greece opposing Nasser's policy, the Egyptiot presence would be in danger. This new era of common anticolonial struggle did not escape the attention of the community leadership. The GCCA president, Nikolaos Sakellarios, despite his procolonial and anticommunist statements in March 1952, claimed in another speech delivered three years later, in March 1955: "The Egyptians ... can rely on their proven friends, the Greeks, whose interests coincide absolutely with theirs. ... In order for this fraternal collaboration between Greeks and Egyptians to fully yield fruit ... it is necessary to keep our community compact and active."[23]

BETWEEN COLONIALISM AND EGYPTIAN NATIONALISM

In line with the terms of the Nasser-Nutting agreement, the last British soldier left Suez on 18 June 1956. A few months earlier, on 16 January 1956, a state committee approved the new constitution of the Arab Republic of Egypt, enabling Nasser's election as the country's president on 23 June of the same year. At that time, the construction of a giant hydroelectric dam in Aswan got under way. The government considered the pharaonic public work symbolizing the new Egypt as indispensable to cover the increasing needs of almost twenty-three million people and the country's development. To fund the dam's construction, Nasser, counting on US assistance, sought World Bank support. However, the gradual deterioration of Egypt's relations with the West after an arms deal with Czechoslovakia caused the United States to change its mind. On 19 July 1956, after intense diplomatic maneuvering, it withdrew support, and the World Bank subsequently refused to fund the project, in a way that humiliated Nasser. The Egyptian president responded a week later. In a famous speech addressed to about two hundred thousand people in Alexandria, he announced the nationalization of the Suez Canal Company (SCC). Almost a month after the British military withdrawal, he took the decision to utilize the navigation's immense profits to fund the construction of the dam.

The SCC was not a simple company. An Egyptian joint-stock company, it was founded by the French diplomat and engineer Ferdinand de Lesseps in 1854 to establish a navigation channel between the Mediterranean and the Red Seas. The opening of the canal started in 1859, and ten years later a waterway that would radically change the way people traveled and traded on a world scale was ready. The company acquired the privilege to exploit the navigation through the canal for ninety-nine years after its opening, that is, until 1968. The SCC was administered by Paris but was under the military protection of London. Despite their opposition in many colonial areas, the British and French business and diplomatic personnel collaborated in administrating the company. After 1875—when Egypt was forced to sell its shares in the company to Britain to relieve a part of its debt—the canal company's shareholders were chiefly the British government, which owned 44 percent of the total shares, and French private investors. Egypt did not receive any of the profits until 1936, and even after that date it received only a very small part of the colossal earnings. In 1955, for instance, Egypt's share of the LE 32 million in profits was no more than LE 900,000.[24] Thus, it is obvious why the SCC became the most powerful symbol of colonial imperialist penetration in Egypt and the Suez Canal region became the field of anticolonial struggle in the early 1950s.

Nasserite Egypt viewed the company's nationalization as a major economic and, principally, symbolic move. The reaction of Conservative British Prime Minister Anthony Eden and his French Socialist counterpart, Guy Mollet, to Nasser's announcement was quick and fierce. Mollet, comparing the Egyptian leader to Adolf Hitler, called him an "apprentice dictator."[25] Nasser's action attracted global media attention. The world's attention turned to Suez, the new front in the anticolonial struggle. In Greece, the nationalization boosted Nasser's popularity to a degree that Athens cinemagoers "applauded with frenzy" when he appeared in newsreels, as the French ambassador observed with clear annoyance.[26]

In Egypt as well as in Greece, Greek and even Egyptian patriotism, with a common anti-British background, fueled the Greek-language press. Even before the nationalization announcement, the press minister, Konstantinos Tsatsos, set the tone in Athens in a message to Cairo in which he identified the "national struggle" of Greece for Cyprus with the "equally hard struggle" of Egypt to get rid of the British.[27] But this rhetoric did not imply that Greece was ready to completely abandon its pro-Western policy and to align itself with Egypt and other neutral countries in all matters. Replying to this demand, which left-wing MPs expressed within the Greek parliament, the Greek government said that "although [we] attach importance to friendship with Egypt [we] do not overrate its value."[28] Thus, the nationalization of the SCC caused the Greek government some embarrassment during the Suez Crisis that started on 26 July and, after several diplomatic steps, ended in the tripartite military intervention in late October 1956.

This embarrassment became obvious especially when Britain, France, and the United States invited Greece to participate in an international conference that was scheduled to take place on 16 August 1956 in London for the purpose of imposing international control over the Suez Canal. Organizers invited states whose financial and maritime interests had been affected by Nasser's initiative, and the importance of the Greek merchant fleet was the reason for Greece's invitation. Athens found itself in a delicate position. On the one hand Britain, France, and the United States—its NATO allies—put pressure on Greece to accept the invitation. In a personal message to

Prime Minister Konstantinos Karamanlis, John Foster Dulles, US foreign minister, "stressed that his government gave great importance to the acceptance of the invitation by the Greek government."[29] On the other hand, as his Greek counterpart, Evangelos Averoff, confided to the US chargé d'affaires, "Egypt had made it known to the Greek government that it would appreciate a rejection" of the invitation.[30] On 11 August 1956, Greece finally decided to reject the invitation. Western diplomats aptly interpreted this choice as "a clear step in the direction of neutrality."[31] Nonetheless, as we will see further on, some of Greece's actions would favor the Egyptian cause. In turn, Nasser, who had already expressed his solidarity for the Cypriot issue, constantly referred to the eternal friendship between the two peoples. In an interview with the Athens daily *I Kathimerini* in September 1956, he referred to the Egyptiot Greeks: "I regard them as Egyptians and I believe they think like Egyptians. They love Egypt and our people reciprocate their feelings. The two peoples are the products of great civilizations. A new era of activity is opening before them."[32]

The most telling illustration of Greek policy during the crisis was an incident regarding the SCC's pilots. The nationalization act stipulated that the former employees of the SCC would automatically become employees of the new Egyptian Suez Canal Authority. In the event of their failing to obey its directions, they faced imprisonment and consequently could be stripped of their jobs and pensions. After a waiting period, on 15 September 1956, France and Britain asked the employees to resign from their posts, especially the navigation pilots. Their severance package would consist of full pay up to 1968, the year when the company concession was due to expire. The colonial powers aimed to show that Egypt was not capable of ensuring the navigation of the canal and thus put pressure on Nasser. This would eventually justify the intervention of Britain and France to restore order, according to the terms of the Convention of Constantinople of 1888, which required that the canal remain open to navigation in all circumstances.

The vast majority of foreign employees—especially the French and British—abandoned their posts and complied with the demands of the Western powers. Most of the Greeks though, who constituted the majority of foreign employees and were mostly employed in mid- to lower-level positions, remained and carried on with their duties, along with their Egyptian colleagues. Seven pilots were among them. For the community, the pilots' decision symbolized the spontaneous alignment of the mass of Egyptiots with the anticolonial struggle of the Egyptian government. However, the Egyptiot reaction was not only spontaneous, because the Greek government, "after an allusion from the Egyptian side,"[33] urged the Egyptiot employees not to abandon their posts. As early as 12 August, the vice-consul in Port Said had called a meeting at Ismailia to inform the company's Greek employees of the Greek government's expectations of them:

> In the name of the consul general of Port Said, I am forwarding to you the instructions received from Athens. Your country's government asks you to closely collaborate with the new administration ... [and] to carry out whatever orders you receive from the Egyptian authorities. Greeks who work in the canal administration are safe, even more so than during their service for the former canal company. The government in Athens thus encourages them to sign their contracts blindly, as Greece puts all its trust in the government of President Gamal Abdel Nasser.[34]

Such a position, which was compatible with the tactics of the community to distance itself from other foreign cohorts, was founded on the good relations that had developed following the emergence of the Cypriot issue. Its main concern, of course, was to protect Egyptiot Greeks from possible retaliation.

Apart from the above exhortation, which may very well be considered an order, the Greek government went a step further regarding the position of the Greek employees. Almost a month later, in September 1956, it threatened them that if they applied to the consulate for an exit visa, the consular authorities would hand their names over to the Egyptian police.[35] The autobiography of a French pilot adds that despite the Greek consulate's efforts to prevent them from leaving Egypt, some Greeks applied to the French consular authorities for visas.[36] The applications submitted by thirty-one Greek citizens, ex-employees of the company, to the Greek embassy in Paris at the end of September for visas for Greece suggests some had succeeded in leaving Egypt in this way.[37]

The Egyptiots' attitude during the Suez Crisis was to some extent determined by Greek government policy and the instructions of its diplomatic representatives, but even so, there was no unanimous acceptance of these instructions. The contradictions of Greece's policy seem to have been central in ensuring there would be dissent. Athens was traditionally a loyal ally of the Western powers, a stance that was reinforced during the intense anticommunist struggle of the late 1940s and early 1950s. As a result of the emergence of the Cypriot issue, Greece gradually decided to play, apparently without much success, the role of a regional power that adopted an anticolonial discourse and sought close cooperation with the Arab states. This hazardous equilibrium between Western/colonial affinities and anticolonial public discourse was also reflected in its nationals in Egypt.

The contradictions of such a policy reflected wider conflicts in the community during the crisis. Almost a month after the nationalization of the canal company, the GKA had issued no official reaction. Even if the vast majority of Egyptiot institutions spoke in favor of Nasser, the largest and most prosperous of the *koinotites* hesitated to take a position in favor of Nasser's action. On 4 August 1956, Sokratis Kalliarekos, Persis Kitrilakis, and Kostas Stamelos, representing the left-wing opposition within the Alexandrian Koinotita, addressed a letter to its president, Anastassios Theodorakis, requesting him to publicly express his solidarity with the Egyptians by saying that the GKA approved of Nasser's action.[38] In a front-page article, *O Paroikos* asked, "Why are they absent?" and called on the GKA to take a position immediately and to also counter the Western accusation about the prevalence of xenophobia in Egypt.[39] Finally, on 21 August, the GKA sent a telegram of support to Nasser, which made no direct reference to the nationalization act. It was more "a telegram for all purposes," according to *O Paroikos,* which also strongly criticized the GKA's behavior in a particularly ironic tone.[40]

O Paroikos viewed Nasser's action as an opportunity for rapprochement with the Soviet camp and intensified its rhetoric aimed at mobilizing the Greeks against the Western powers. According to the newspaper, both Egypt and Greece faced the same imperialist threat.[41] *O Paroikos* also claimed that the Egyptiot Greeks should participate in the pro-Egyptian demonstrations to express their solidarity with the Egyptian people, since the crisis provided them with the opportunity to clearly show that they belonged in the country. An Egyptian response to this position was evident at the 10 August 1956 demonstration in Cairo. Along with the political slogans in favor of nationalization and Nasser, protesters shouted other slogans such as "Hurray for Greek Cyprus" and "Hurray for the Egyptiot Greeks."[42] At the same time, the *Cairo Daily,* in a front-page article, noted the community's backing for the Egyptian people.[43] *O Paroikos* said it was vital to increase the actions in support of the Egyptian position to reassure the Egyptians that they had the backing of the country's Greeks and that this was the only way they would be "rewarded" in the future.[44] The Alexandrian *Tachydromos,* on the other hand, considered protest action useless and dangerous. Without, however, proposing an alternative, it considered it a mistake for Egyptiots to express their solidarity through strikes and demonstrations.[45]

In October 1956, as the UN discussed the issue of control over the canal and diplomatic efforts were ongoing to find a solution, France, Britain, and Israel held secret deliberations in the French city of Sèvres, where they agreed to undertake joint military action against Egypt. The plan foresaw Israel invading Sinai and the two colonial powers intervening to impose a security zone of sixteen kilometers on either side of the Suez Canal. Subsequently, Britain and France would claim that Egypt was not capable of protecting navigation along the canal and would jointly recover control of the canal. The Israeli assault began on 29 October. Egypt defended the canal, and the following day, as they had planned, Britain and France submitted an ultimatum to both Israel and Egypt for the imminent withdrawal of their respective military forces ten miles away from the canal to allow French and British occupation, which would guarantee peace and free navigation. Without any surprise, the Israeli forces complied with the ultimatum, but the Egyptians refused. Egypt's refusal provided the pretext for the British and French intervention. Even though Egypt was staring a humiliating defeat in the face, it resisted. Voluntary groups of army and militia emerged, and the Egyptians sank empty cargo ships in the narrow parts of the canal to block navigation. On 31 October, the British and French bombarded the entire region and the canal cities, which paratroopers captured the following days. The pressure from the United States, where presidential elections were approaching, and the Soviet Union's threats against France and Britain in the event of the two powers not withdrawing their forces, forced Britain to declare a ceasefire on 6 November. Greece's position, as expressed in a meeting at the Defense Ministry in Athens, was "to remain de facto neutral with some flexibility according to our own interests."[46]

Since late August, the GKA, mainly through public statements, had tried to express its solidarity with the Egyptian struggle and to distance the Greek presence from that of other Europeans. Sometimes, however, this strategy provoked the opposite results. A telling example occurred a few days after the tripartite invasion. The GKA, without seeking the permission of the Egyptian authorities, decided that all Egyptiots of Alexandria should wear a badge with both the Greek and the Egyptian flags on it.[47] It was an action that, above all, aimed to distinguish the Egyptiots from other Europeans in the city. In the event, Alexandria's governor intervened to block the initiative. His argument was that such an act might give the impression that Egyptians maltreated the rest of the city's foreigners. Within the context of differentiating the Egyptiot presence from that of other foreigners, one can also place the decision of the Koinotita of Ismailia to remove the name of eight Jews from the visiting members' register because of Israel's participation in the British-French military intervention.[48]

As had happened after the silent demonstration in Alexandria in 1951, the hesitant and often contradictory policy of the GKA led to the creation of a new association: the Greek-Egyptian Cooperation Committee. Its main aims were the coordination of activities in support of Egypt in the anticolonial struggle during the Suez Crisis, the integration of the Greek population, and the cultivation of closer contacts between the two peoples. The committee, which involved many prominent figures of the Egyptiot Left in Cairo and Alexandria, sought to replace the community's historical leadership and to represent the position of the Egyptiot population during the crisis. The main challenge the Egyptiots faced, according to the committee, was to "consider ourselves as Egyptians."[49] *O Paroikos* vividly supported the committee, which, surprisingly enough, was placed under the auspices of the Greek Orthodox patriarch Christophoros II.

The seemingly paradoxical cooperation between the Greek Orthodox patriarchate and the Left deserves some attention. Since the nineteenth century, the relations between the patriarchate and the GKA had faced a number of serious challenges over financial matters and, of course, over the social control of the community. Such a difficult relationship was mostly due to the sidelining of the "See of Mark the Evangelist," namely the Greek Orthodox Patriarchate of Alexandria and All Africa, by the powerful Egyptiot elite that controlled the GKA in the nineteenth century. During the 1950s their relationship was still very tense. In 1951 the patriarchate came under the financial control of a committee that included GKA members. Both bodies were embroiled in litigation over property-related issues in the Egyptian courts until 1960. In these quarrels, the Greek state had sought to mediate, even though the patriarchate often accused it of "a systematic predisposition in favor of the Koinotita dignitaries."[50] Initiatives such as the interview with the patriarch in the pro-communist newspaper *Foni* in January 1953 provoked the intense dissatisfaction of the diplomatic authorities, who blamed it on the patriarch's Communist doctor, Iraklis Maschas, one of the founders of the Council of Greek-Egyptian Friendship and Cooperation.[51] Beyond any influence Maschas exercised over the patriarch, the latter welcomed all voices opposed to the GKA leadership. In any case, the patriarch enjoyed the moral and economic support of the Russian Orthodox Church and the USSR,[52] a position that became even more obvious when the patriarch visited Moscow in 1955 on the occasion of the feast day of Saint Sergey, without prior approval of the Greek authorities and despite the strong objections of members of the patriarchal synod. It seems that the USSR was attempting, as it was doing in Jerusalem, to control the Greek Orthodox patriarchate and to increase its penetration of the community.

To return to the action of the Greek-Egyptian Cooperation Committee, its Alexandria branch collaborated with the Red Crescent in establishing contact with the Egyptiots of the Suez Canal cities, who had been isolated after the tripartite invasion and in taking a firm stance in favor of the Egyptian people.[53] The committee organized lectures in Cairo, engaged in fundraisers, and sought volunteers to participate in the Egyptian resistance and its auxiliary services. From 31 October, the day of the French and British invasion, to 10 November, 223 volunteers signed up—108 in the civil protection service and 115 in the auxiliary service.[54] However, details of the social and ideological profile or the nationality of those who participated in the committee's activities are not available. While it is likely that leftist sympathizers were involved, since the patriarch supported its action, it is possible that people from a wide political and social spectrum participated in it. Similar committees were founded in the Suez Canal cities.[55] In Port Said, the city most affected by the bombardments—during which four Egyptiot Greeks were killed—there were more opportunities for the expression of solidarity.[56] At the same time, rumors circulated that Egyptiots were collaborating with the French and British invaders. Even if these rumors had a solid basis, the Greek Foreign Ministry repeatedly denied that such collaboration existed.[57]

Contrary to the picture painted in the GKA annual report that the Egyptiot Greek population was solidly behind the Egyptian cause from the very beginning of the crisis, the reaction was more diverse.[58] As regards the GKA, its delay in responding to the nationalization act can also be interpreted in another way: the local Greek bourgeoisie, which must not have approved of Nasser's action, controlled this organization. The GKA enjoyed its role as the leadership of the Greek population in Egypt and retained its national character, maintaining close contact with the Egyptian and the foreign bourgeoisie at the same time. Even if the GKA favored maintaining the British presence in the country, it vacillated in the years before the crisis, sometimes backing the British and French, other times backing the Egyptians and distinguishing itself from the colonial powers.[59] Nonetheless, after 1952, the economic interests of its members were more closely aligned with those of the other foreigners of Egypt than those of the new military elite. Additionally, the British presence in the Suez Canal area was of great importance because of the presence of significant numbers of Greek employees and workers there. Naturally, even if it did not publicly admit it, the GKA did not oppose a French-British intervention that could reinstall a colonial-type order on Egyptian territory. Almost ten years after the end of World War II, the memory of the period when the British military presence offered protection and prosperity to the Egyptiot upper class was still vivid. The connected interests are apparent in a declaration that Dimitrios Lambros, the Greek ambassador in Cairo, made after the Egyptianization laws—which will be examined in the following section—and the expulsion of the British and French from the country: "I am afraid ... that the panic of our people, which is reinforced and preserved by the most powerful economically Greeks, will not cease unless the English and French start coming back."[60]

The Suez Crisis ended with the withdrawal of the British and French forces on 22 December and their replacement with UN peacekeepers. By March 1957, the Israelis had withdrawn from Sinai, and the canal reopened to shipping on 27 April. Even though Egypt had suffered a military defeat,

Nasser's diplomatic triumph in Suez made him the undisputed leader of the Arab world and the major advocate of its unification. As regards his position toward Greeks, apart from decorating the pilots who remained at their posts along with their Egyptian colleagues, Nasser satisfied the Greek demand to exclude the country's fifteen thousand or so Greek Cypriots from the sequestration measures that the Egyptian leader had imposed on 1 November 1956, immediately following the British and French intervention.[61] The confiscations affected the properties of British and French citizens and wealthy Jews; members of these three groups were subsequently expelled. What started as a retaliation over the Suez invasion became Egyptian state policy the following year, in the form of legislation and a concrete economic plan giving the state more extensive control over the economy.[62] The sequestration measures also were applied to Cypriots holding British passports, and for this reason Greek authorities petitioned the Egyptian government to have Greek Cypriots and Greek Jews excluded. With Decree 206 of 17 November, Nasser excluded the Cypriot Greeks from the measures targeting British citizens. The departure, however, of British, French, and Jews also prompted a departure movement of Egyptiots toward Greece and other countries, such as France, where arrivals of Greek "refugees from Egypt" were noticed at the port of Marseille in early December 1956.[63]

SEEKING A STRATEGY

After the Suez Crisis, Egypt was a different country. Twenty years after the abolition of the Capitulations—or nine if the transitory period is taken into consideration—on 29 January 1957 the Egyptian government promulgated three laws (22, 23, and 24/1957) that made clear that it intended to control key sectors of the economy, specifically the banking, insurance, and commercial sectors. The laws ordered the Egyptianization of the companies in these sectors, meaning the directors and the members of the administrative boards ought to be Egyptian citizens. In joint-stock companies, all shares were to be registered and to belong to Egyptian citizens. In general and limited partnerships, all partners were to be Egyptians citizens. Even though some would argue that the tripartite military intervention justified such legislation, in reality this was part of the Egyptianization process of the economy, which had commenced in the 1920s and which Company Law 138/1947 systematized after World War II.[64]

Unlike the 1947 law, the new laws did not establish any quota on foreign and Egyptian personnel, only on the administration. They did make a distinction, however, between companies belonging to citizens of friendly and hostile countries, on the basis of their attitude during the Suez Crisis. The first category included British, French, and Jewish companies, which the state sequestered in November 1956. They faced imminent Egyptianization, and the newly established Economic Organization assumed control of these companies. The second category included companies owned by citizens of countries such as Lebanon, Syria, Belgium, Switzerland, Italy, Germany, the United States, and Greece. The law granted these firms a five-year grace period before the law was fully implemented, with the possibility of its being applied at any time before that. The GMFA estimated that if the government implemented the law fully, between a third and a quarter of Greeks would be forced to leave Egypt within those five years.[65]

Several days before the publication of the laws and while rumors circulated in Egypt that they were being drafted, the community leadership in Alexandria and Cairo prepared a letter for Nasser.[66] The dignitaries were somewhat convinced that a letter would be enough to postpone the promulgation of the laws or even to exempt Greeks from them. Even if they did not manage to send it before the laws were promulgated, the dignitaries did not give up. A joint meeting of the GKA, GCCA, the Greek Koinotita in Cairo (GKC), and the Greek Chamber of Commerce of Cairo (GCCC) on 1 February 1957 decided to send a telegram to Nasser, based on the original text with some modifications, and to publish it simultaneously in the Egyptiot press.[67] The telegram was composed in a very emotional style, expressing the authors' bitterness at the fact that the Greeks were being equated with the British, French, and Jews—even though this was not fully justified—and highlighting the usefulness and the positive role of the community in Egypt's development. They also requested, in an indirect but clear manner, the exemption of Greeks from the new legislation.[68] This emotional reaction was part and parcel of a new strategy conceived by Theodorakis and Chryssovergis—presidents of the GKA and GCCA, respectively—and Georgios Roilos, GKC president, all of whom signed the telegram. According to this new strategy, the issues of the Egyptian legislation and the long-term presence of the Egyptiots were slipping from the community's jurisdiction. The community dignitaries considered that the Greek government should deal with the issue from a legal point of view, whereas they themselves should deal with the "emotional" and "philanthropic" dimension.[69]

Thus, in the second half of the 1950s, the Egyptiot leadership allowed the Greek state more space to have a more pronounced role in the matter of the long-term presence of the Greeks in Egypt, even though Karamanlis and Averoff, as they would later claim, had no faith then in the future of the Greek community in Egypt.[70] Various voices in the GMFA considered the community a "burden" for Greece's foreign policy and relations with its

NATO allies. Members of the community leadership, which, even then, two decades after Montreux, had not put into effect a realistic adjustment plan, also shared this lack of faith in the community's future.

Immediately after the promulgation of the laws, the Karamanlis government proceeded to issue strong demarches to the Egyptian government, via the Cairo embassy, and to the Egyptian embassy in Athens, via the GMFA, which directly called for Greeks to be excluded from the new legislation.[71] Almost the entire Greek press strongly criticized the Egyptian government for the new legislation, generally expressing pessimism about the future of Greeks in Egypt. To prevent massive repatriation, the majority of Greek politicians supported the Karamanlis government on this occasion. In a parliamentary session on 12 February 1957, all parties expressed their disappointment at the promulgation of the laws and offered their backing for the government in taking initiatives in order to protect Greeks.[72]

The Greek government tried to cooperate through diplomatic channels with other countries whose interests had been also affected by the new legislation. In this regard, it approached US and Italian diplomats in Egypt to seek a repeal of the laws. Differences, however, between the interests of three countries did not favor a deepening of the cooperation. The United States did not have many citizens in Egypt and its interests were mostly economic and geopolitical. The Italian government, on the other hand, already encouraged and assisted its citizens in leaving Egypt and repatriating, since it had concluded that there was no future for them in the country.[73] Faced with this situation, the Greek government soon realized that it would have to proceed on its own.

Shortly after the promulgation of the laws, Athens summoned Dimitrios Lambros, Greek ambassador to Cairo and an Alexandrian himself, to a government meeting, along with the GKA and GCCA.[74] While the decision to invite the community leadership was unusual, the reaction from within the community was less so. Not only did these reactions come from the Egyptiot Left, which claimed that the leadership had "confirmed in the most provocative way its foreign nature by its pompous journey to Athens," but from other groups as well.[75] The Koinotita leadership of Port Said, the city that suffered the most during the Suez Crisis, sent letters to Greek MPs accusing the Egyptiot delegates of being concerned only with their own interests.[76] As the relevant Foreign Ministry files have not been released, it remains unclear what the Athens meeting discussed. After this meeting, however, Karamanlis sent Nasser a letter on 20 February 1957.

Before we examine this letter in detail, it is necessary to discuss the reaction of the Egyptiot Left to the announcement of the laws. Scientists, educators, novelists, and merchants, all members of the Greek-Egyptian Cooperation Committee, which was founded during the Suez Crisis, sent a memorandum to the Egyptian president but in a completely different spirit from that of the community leadership. They expressed their support for the Egyptianization measures, acknowledging the right of a sovereign state to promulgate laws for its citizens and foreign residents. It ended with three demands: (a) to guarantee the professional rights to those who held a residency permit, (b) to facilitate the acquisition of Egyptian citizenship to all Egyptiots, and (c) to state openly whether Egypt needed Greeks or not, and, in the event the answer was negative, to afford Greek residents in Egypt the necessary time to organize their repatriation.[77] *O Paroikos* claimed that the exclusion of Greeks from the laws would in practice signify their annulment, and thus, they should not seek favorable treatment.[78] Given that the British and the French governments had requested the withdrawal of the laws for their proper citizens, the Egyptian government and public opinion could identify Greeks with the colonial powers. And this would happen even if the Egyptian legislation had already made the distinction between friendly and hostile countries. The journal claimed that Greeks should seek a solution "in the framework of the absolute respect of Egypt's sovereign rights."[79] In this direction, it proposed Egyptian citizenship be granted to those who had a ten-year residence permit.[80]

In the letter he sent to Nasser on 20 February, Karamanlis acknowledged that the laws did not target Greeks. However, he also noted that in the community "a feeling of near panic has developed that may provoke a mass exodus if no measures are taken." He also asked Nasser to make "a public declaration that would reassure Greeks, since the prospects for their settlement in Greece are not at all favorable."[81] Karamanlis aimed to secure favorable treatment for the Egyptiots, and he specifically wanted those who had already worked in Egypt to be exempted from the 1957 laws. Since the Greek government estimated that the repatriation movement could ultimately not be prevented, it concentrated its efforts in gaining time to minimize the consequences for Greece.[82] With his proposals, Karamanlis showed that he wished employed Greeks to be able to stay in Egypt or at least delay their departure for Greece. In his reply, sent on 10 April, Nasser said that Cairo would do what it could to reassure Greeks: "The Egyptian government will do everything possible to dispel the worries of our brother Greeks, for whom I feel the greatest respect and deepest sympathy."[83] The Greek government was satisfied with Nasser's reply, which it considered as a step forward. Indeed, GMFA officials considered that "they will succeed on the strength of the message, in inducing the Egyptians to take [action favorable to Greeks in Egypt] within a few months."[84]

Nasser on almost every occasion provided assurances to the Egyptiot Greeks that they would not be expelled. "They have nothing to be afraid of," he stated in an interview to the Athens daily *Ethnos* just before the promulgation of the January laws.[85] When Lambros visited him on 3 March 1957, the Egyptian leader declared, "It was not, it is not and it will not be the intention of my government to become the instigator of the Greeks' departure from Egypt," a statement that a subsequent meeting of the two men, two and a half years later on 17 November 1959, reconfirmed.[86] Lambros told Nasser that the Egyptianization measures had discouraged large Greek entrepreneurs, such as Aristotle Onassis, who planned to construct a pipeline across the Suez Canal, Prodromos Bodossakis-Athanassiadis, who was involved in the fertilizer industry, and Stratis Andreadis, who aimed to set up a banking venture in Egypt.[87] Nasser replied that he was fully aware of the possible damage because of the Egyptianization laws and added—according to the Greek ambassador—that "Greek employees will not be affected and no law restricting their right to work will be promulgated."[88]

On many other occasions in the late 1950s, and especially after meeting Egyptian officials who were close to Nasser or with Nasser himself, Lambros sought to reassure his interlocutors—in the GMFA and community leadership—that Nasser had friendly sentiments toward the Egyptiots and made references to the services provided by canal employees during the Suez Crisis.[89] Moreover, it seems that soon after the introduction of the 1957 laws, Lambros received a verbal undertaking that despite the law allowing its provisions to be applied within the next five years, in the case of Greeks the five-year period would be fully respected.[90] For commercial representatives especially, Nasser committed himself verbally that they would find a way to continue their businesses until the end of their careers.[91] As for other demands expressed by the Greek side regarding the Greek ownership of the companies, Lambros registered his disappointment, claiming that everybody considered them to be logical but there was great procrastination in taking decisions. He also underlined that Nasser's and his ministers' assurances were restricted to "generous but vague" ones.[92]

Notwithstanding Nasser's declarations in favor of Egyptiots and the fact that there was no immediate threat to their position in the labor market, the Suez Crisis, the expulsion of the British, French, and Jews, the sequestration measures, and the January 1957 legislation intensified concerns about the future.[93] While Egyptiots had already been leaving Egypt since 1945, the number of departures increased during and immediately after the Suez Crisis and the promulgation of the 1957 laws. However, from the end of 1957 to the third quarter of 1960, the rhythm of departure decreased to the precrisis level. Departure rates were more intense in the canal cities, apparently as a result of the tripartite military intervention, and in Alexandria than in other Egyptian cities.[94] The departures from the latter can be explained by the fact that the Alexandrian community was significantly dependent on the Western element in economic and cultural terms. The measures concerning foreigners became more evident in the Mediterranean port than in Cairo, for instance, whose Arabic character was more pronounced. Most of the big Greek companies had their headquarters in Alexandria, and their employees were mostly Egyptiot Greek and often had foreign customers.

The intense concern triggered by the January laws and the increasing number of departures led Lambros to organize a pan-community meeting in May 1957. Its aim was to find ways to deal with the "psychosis of disordered flight from Egypt."[95] On 24 May, thirty institutional representatives of the community—basically presidents of the *koinotites* and the chambers of commerce—gathered for two days in Cairo. The Greek government special envoy, Sotirios Agapitidis, was also present. An economist and lawyer, Agapitidis was a professor at the Athens Polytechnic, president of the GMFA Migration Committee, and later alternate finance minister during the 1967–74 junta. He was a well-known figure in the community, since he had been called to provide expertise on community problems in 1954 and played an active role in organizing a migration program for unemployed and destitute Egyptiots that began in 1951. In 1957 he was appointed head of a committee that would address how repatriation would be prevented, migration to third destinations reinforced, and readjustment in critical sectors—such as education—undertaken.[96]

The Greek-Egyptian Cooperation Committee, along with professional associations, fraternities, educators, and other community bodies, was not invited to the meeting. This did not prevent the committee from sending a memorandum to the meeting with comments on the matters being discussed. Readjustment was required at three different levels: psychological, professional, and educational. As for psychological readjustment, the memorandum mentioned that the Egyptiots should "dismiss all chauvinistic tendencies, so that they can feel Egypt as their real homeland." That would prevent them from feeling dissatisfied with a law whose purpose was to guarantee the security and development of the national economy. As for professional readjustment, the memorandum proposed the mass granting of Egyptian citizenship, promoting the learning of Arabic, and the activation of Egyptiot capital, which it claimed was "idle." Finally, as regards the educational process, the memo proposed the organization of a more extended summit in which educators and other community bodies would also participate. Other reforms included modifying the internal statutes of the associations and *koinotites* in order to stop distinguishing Egyptiot Greeks according to their citizenship, and the merging of associations all over Egypt in order to make them more financially efficient, more effective, and more representative of all Egyptiots, regardless of social strata.[97]

On the last day of the conference, Nasser received the delegates. Lambros invited him to visit Greece, and Sakellarios, who now delivered a speech in Arabic, confirmed the loyalty of Egyptiots to him and the gratitude of the Cypriot Greeks for being exempted from the sequestration measures.[98] The delegation also asked Nasser to support the setting up of an Arab-Greek association under the auspices of the GKA.[99] The Egyptian leader promised to support the initiative and told the Egyptiots that they need not fear for the future: "I hope that you always feel that you are in your country, that you have absolute confidence, and that you look to the future with optimism."[100] It is interesting to note that although a committee already existed, Lambros presented the creation of a new one as a "milestone" in the cooperation between the two peoples.[101] In a report he sent to the GMFA though, he did not fail to criticize the fact that the leadership had made no substantial effort to closely collaborate with the Egyptians over the previous two decades, that is, since the abolition of the Capitulations.[102]

KARAMANLIS IN EGYPT, NASSER IN GREECE

While the Egyptian president had accepted the invitation to go to Athens, before Nasser visited Greece, Karamanlis went to Egypt. The visit took place in August 1957, which is revealing of his government's strong concerns following the passing of the January laws. On the other hand, it was clear that after Nasser's diplomatic victory over Suez and the critical condition in the Middle East, he had different priorities. Nasser emerged after the crisis as the undisputed leader of the Arab world. His external policy was determined by his increasing involvement in anticolonial struggles, the continuous tensions with Israel, and the further rapprochement with the Soviet Union—which undertook to construct the Aswan Dam. The Eisenhower Doctrine, which aimed to reduce Nasser's influence and promised US aid to countries facing a communist "threat," did not prevent the Egyptian president from undertaking the leadership of the pan-Arab movement, which advocated the unification of the Arab people. Confirmation of the latter was the creation of the United Arab Republic (UAR) in 1958, through the unification of Syria and Egypt. At the same time, Nasser provided moral and material support to anticolonial movements. In Algeria, the FLN intensified the war against the French. Morocco and Tunisia gained independence from France in 1956, the same year as Sudan did from the British. The Gold Coast achieved independence as Ghana from the British in 1957, and Guinea from the French in 1958. The Zurich and London agreements settled the Cypriot issue in February 1959, which led to the independence of Cyprus on 16 August 1960. The nationalist movements in Africa would secure independence in most countries in the early 1960s. Nasser played a central role in all these changes, and thus his visit to Athens in the late 1950s was not a priority.

Karamanlis, who shared none of the Egyptian leader's fame or notoriety internationally, visited Egypt in an effort to allay Egyptiot fears. In the meantime, the general sentiment in Greece vis-à-vis Nasser had changed. The fact that Egyptiots were not fully exempted from the January 1957 laws influenced domestic public opinion, which now expressed a more reserved attitude toward the Egyptian leader. This was reflected in the capital's cinemas, where cinemagoers no longer applauded Nasser during newsreels as they had done a year earlier.[103] On the day of Karamanlis's arrival in Egypt, *Tachydromos* addressed an open letter to both leaders under the title "Gentlemen! Save the Greek community."[104] This showed that the press and the leadership now considered the Greek presence in Egypt a bilateral issue.[105] Karamanlis's visit lasted four days (17–21 August 1957) and provided the community with the opportunity to offer an enthusiastic welcome and the Greek delegation the chance to demonstrate that the community was under the protection of the Greek government.

In the deliberations with Nasser, Karamanlis requested that Greek companies be excluded from the January 1957 laws and that Egyptian citizenship be granted to those who fulfilled the criteria—especially to younger people, to facilitate their entrance into the labor market. Nasser replied that he could not exclude Greeks because no decision had been made even for the citizens of other Arab countries residing in Egypt.[106] He underlined, in a joint statement issued by the two leaders, "his appreciation for the loyalty of Greeks residing in Egypt and their contribution to the economy and country's life" and that it was the Egyptian government's intention to "ensure the prosperity of Greeks in Egypt in a spirit of justice and goodwill."[107]

The Egyptian press reported positively on Karamanlis's visit. Writing in the French-language magazine *Images,* journalist Habib Jamati remarked, "Whatever the policy of the new revolutionary Egypt is toward foreigners ... Greeks will be always treated favorably."[108] Indeed, the Cypriot Greeks had been excluded from the sequestration measures against British citizens, and Egyptiot companies had a five-year grace period for the full implementation of the January laws, with assurances that the provisions would not be applied before the end of this period. Besides, the Nasser government treated favorably the Egyptiots regarding the foreign status of their schools, the statutes of the *koinotites,* and the labor legislation and decrees of 1959–60—an issue that chapter 7 will address. While the Egyptian government acknowledged the particularities of community life and facilitated a number of issues that affected the Egyptiot Greeks, it did not have much room to do more, even had it wished. Other countries would have raised similar demands, which would have been impossible for Egypt to satisfy, as concessions would be interpreted as a loss of national sovereignty.

Intense state intervention in the economy characterized Egypt in the late 1950s. Under these circumstances, Nasser's visit to Athens in June 1960 was a key moment for the Greek state and the Greek community residing in Egypt. Athens had high expectations for a definitive resolution to all open issues concerning the community. Nasser reaffirmed his assurances that it was not his government's intention to expel the Greeks from Egypt. Even though he had been in power for six years—four of them as president—it was his first visit to a NATO country, a fact that the Egyptian and Greek press presented as a milestone in the eternal friendship between the two peoples. For Nasser, the position of the Greek government toward Egypt during the Suez Crisis underscored the friendly relationship between the two countries. The Egyptian president made special mention of Athens's refusal to attend the London conference in August 1956 and said the employees and pilots who remained at their posts had contributed to Egypt's victory. In the speeches he delivered and at a press conference in Athens, Nasser himself emphasized the trope of eternal friendship, emphasizing the contribution that Greeks were making to Egypt's development. He also singled out Athanassios Radopoulos, a Greek resident of Mansoura, who had participated in the National Union elections of 1959 and managed to be elected with a vast majority in his district.[109]

Nasser's visit to Athens was another opportunity to deal with the Karamanlis government's requests: that the five-year time limit for the completion of the Egyptianization of the banks, insurance companies, and commercial representations be extended. The community leadership and Greek government saw the bank issue in particular as a major one because Egyptiot prosperity depended on them.[110] There were four Greek-owned banks at that time in Egypt—Bank of Athens, Commercial Bank (N Tepeghiosi & Company), National Bank of Greece, and Commercial Bank of the Near East, which was affiliated with the Commercial Bank of Greece. Although Egyptianization of banks did not directly affect Egyptiot employees, what really concerned the Greek government and the community leadership was that a change in the banks' national character would have a negative impact on the economic activities of Egyptiots.[111] In addition, the government asked Nasser not to put further restrictions related to citizenship on the occupations that Egyptiot Greeks engaged in, but rather to let them exercise freely their ability to seek employment in both countries. Karamanlis finally requested that all Egyptiots who fulfilled the relevant criteria be facilitated in acquiring Egyptian citizenship.[112] While Nasser viewed these demands favorably, he did not commit itself to fully satisfying any of them. In a question during an Athens press conference on whether the leaders had discussed the Egyptianization of banks, Nasser showed some flexibility, stating that "an agreement can be reached without changing the law, because when we take a measure we cannot go back."[113]

NOTES

1. Tewfik Aclimandos, "Regard rétrospectif sur la révolution égyptienne, ou le 23 juillet 1952," *Égypte/Monde arabe* [special issue "L'Égypte dans le siècle, 1901–2000"], 2nd ser., 4–5 (2001): 28.
2. Fayez Sayegh, "The Theoritical Structure of Nasser's Nationalism," in *Arab Socialism*, ed. Sami Ayad Hanna and George H Gardner (Leiden: Brill, 1969), 101.
3. AYE/CS/1953/1028, Cairo, 11 March 1953, Georgiadis to the Cairo embassy.
4. *Journal d'Egypte*, 8 March 1953, 1.
5. *Progrès dimanche*, 27 July 1952, 2.
6. Joel Beinin and Zakaria Lockman, *Workers on the Nile: Nationalism, Communism, Islam, and the Egyptian Working Class, 1882–1954* (Princeton, NJ: Princeton University Press, 1998), 421–26; *Le Phare Egyptien*, 30 August 1952.
7. AYE/CS/1953/78/1/1, 11, Alexandria, 14 January 1953, Liatis to Cairo embassy.
8. AYE/CS/1953/51/1/7, 7137, Cairo, 10 November 1953, Melas to GMFA.
9. AYE/CS/1953/51/1/1, 6285, Cairo, 21 March 1953, Melas to GMFA.
10. Sokratis Kalliarekos et al., *Programma Anaprosarmogis* [Program of readjustment] (Alexandria, 1954), 3.
11. Joel Beinin, *The Dispersion of Egyptian Jewry* (Berkeley: University of California Press, 1998), 91–92.
12. Ibid., 93.
13. Ibid., 90–117.
14. Anthony Gorman, "Egypt's Forgotten Communists: The Postwar Greek Left," *Journal of Modern Greek Studies* 20 (2002): 14.
15. For the Cypriot question, see Kyriacos C. Makrides, *The Rise and Fall of the Cyprus Republic* (New Haven, CT: Yale University Press, 1977); and Alexis Rappas, *Cyprus in the 1930s: British Colonial Rule and the Roots of the Cyprus Conflict* (London: IB Tauris, 2014).
16. *O Paroikos*, 8 August 1955, 1.
17. Konstantinos Karamanlis Archive (KKA)/24, Kassimatis to the ministerial council, 12 April 1956, in Konstantinos Svolopoulos, ed., *Konstantinos Karamanlis, Archio. Gegonota kai Keimena* [Archive: Facts and Documents], vol. 2 (Athens: Ekdotiki Athinon, 1993), 37–39.

18. FO/371/123852/10634/10/56, Cairo, 26 September 1956, Garvey to Lambert.
19. FO/371/123852/10210/1/56, Athens, 4 July 1956, Lambert to Young.
20. KKA/3A/951, Note, Special Greek interests in the Middle East, n.p., n.d.
21. Ibid.
22. Cited in *Le Progrès égyptien,* 16 October 1954, 5.
23. AGCCA/General assemblies, 1952–73, Speech by Nikolaos Sakellarios, Alexandria, 29 March 1956.
24. Robert Tignor, "Foreign Capital, Foreign Communities, and the Egyptian Revolution of 1952," in *Egypt from Monarchy to Republic: A Reassessment of Revolution and Change,* ed. Shimon Shamir (Boulder, CO: Westview Press, 1995), 120.
25. *Le Monde,* 31 July 1956, 1.
26. MAE/Europe-Grèce/1956–60/177/1045/EU, Athens, 20 October 1956, Charpentier to Pineau.
27. FO/371/123852/10210/1/56, Athens, 4 July 1956, Lambert to Young.
28. Ibid.
29. MAE/Levant 1944–65/Egypte 1953–59/Nationalisation du canal/Réactions des puissances/Grèce/493, 581/582, Athens, 6 August 1956, Charpentier to Pineau.
30. Ibid.
31. Ibid.
32. FO/JE 14211/1721, Translation of the text of interview given by Nasser to Eleni Vlachou in Cairo, for the Greek daily *I Kathimerini,* 11 September 1956.
33. Evangelos Averoff-Tositsas, *Istoria hamenon efkairion. Kypriako 1950–1963* [History of lost opportunities: The Cypriot issue, 1950–63] (Athens: Estia, 1982), 137.
34. *Le Progrès égyptien,* 13 August 1956, 5.
35. CADN/Ambassade de France à Athènes/267/AL 19.4, Note, French embassy in Athens, 6 October 1966.
36. Paul Parfond, *Pilotes de Suez* (Paris: France Empire, 1957), 17.
37. AYE/CS/1956/2/1/3/2, 2693, Paris, 26 September 1956, Christodoulou to GMFA.
38. AGKA/Correspondence, 1954–61/Alexandria, 4 August 1956, Kalliarekos, Kitrilakis and Stamelos to Theodorakis.
39. *O Paroikos,* 6 August 1956, 1.
40. *O Paroikos,* 24 August 1956 1.
41. *O Paroikos,* 1 September 1956, 1.
42. *O Paroikos,* 11 August 1956, 1.
43. *O Paroikos,* 3 August 1956, 1; *O Paroikos,* 11 August 1956, 1.
44. *O Paroikos,* 1 September 1956.
45. *Tachydromos,* 22 August 1956, 1.
46. AYE/CS/1956/1/2/1, Athens, 3 November 1956.
47. *Tachydromos,* 6 November 1956, 1.
48. Archives of the Greek Koinotita of Ismailia, Proceedings of the general assemblies, 219, Ismailia, 22 November 1956.
49. *O Paroikos,* 20 September 1956, 6.
50. AYE/CS/1951/6/4/1/1, 24063/4, Athens, 28 February 1951, Venizelos to Consulate General in Alexandria.

51. AYE/CS/1953/51/1/1, 5, Alexandria, 7 January 1953, Liatis to Melas.
52. AYE/CS/1958/2/1/3/2, 259, Alexandria, 31 May 1958, Baizos to GMFA.
53. Panagiotis Xenos papers, ELIA.
54. *O Paroikos*, 11 November 1956, 1.
55. *O Paroikos*, 18 November 1956, 2.
56. FO/371/118910/P.A./769/AFHQ, 21 November 1956, Murray to Lloyd.
57. *O Paroikos*, 14 December 1956, 1-4.
58. Elliniki en Alexandria Koinotis, *Logodosia etous 1956* [Greek Koinotita of Alexandria, Annual report of 1956] (Alexandria: T. Kassimatis, 1956), 17.
59. Alexander Kitroeff, *The Greeks in Egypt, Ethnicity and Class, 1917-1937* (Oxford: Ithaca Press, 1989), 180.
60. AYE/CS/1957/22/9/1/1, 6544, Cairo 29 March 1957, Lampros to GMFA.
61. KKA/3A/1084-87, Note on Egyptianization measures, 9 August 1957.
62. Robert Tignor, *Capitalism and Nationalism at the End of Empire: State and Business in Decolonizing Egypt, Nigeria and Kenya, 1945-1963* (Princeton, NJ: Princeton University Press, 1999), 130.
63. AYE/CS/1956/2/3/3/1, 4906, 9 December 1956, Rafail to GFMA.
64. Ghislaine Alleaume, "La production d'une économie 'nationale': remarques sur l'histoire des sociétés anonymes par actions en Égypte de 1856 à 1956," *Annales Islamologiques* 31 (1997): 1-16.
65. KKA/3A/1084-87, Note on Egyptianzation measures, 9 August 1957.
66. AGKA/Correspondence, 1954-61/40273, Proceedings of the meeting of the GKA committee and the board of the GCCA, Alexandria, 1 February 1957.
67. Ibid.
68. Sofianos Chryssostomidis, "Elliniki paroikia Aigyptou: i exodus" [The Greek community of Egypt: the exodus], *Archiotaxio* 4 (2002): 118-19.
69. AGKA/Correspondence, 1954-61/40273, Proceedings of the meeting of the GKA committee and the board of the GCCA, Alexandria, 1 February 1957.
70. KKA/71B, Konstantinos Karamanlis's narration, in Svolopoulos, *Konstantinos Karamanlis*, 400.
71. GPD/Period 4/Session 2/Meeting 43, 12 February 1957, Speech of Konstantinos Tsatsos, 34.
72. GPD/Period 4/Session 2/Meeting 43, 12 February 1957, 31-39.
73. FO/371/130018/10316/2, 1032/3/57, Athens, 12 February 1957, Peake to Lloyd.
74. AGKA/Correspondence, 1954-61/40273, Proceedings of the meeting of the GKA committee and the board of the GCCA, Alexandria, 1 February 1957.
75. *O Paroikos*, 11 February 1957, 1.
76. GPD/Period 4/Session 2/Meeting 43, 12 February 1957, Speech of Georgios Bourdaras, 610.
77. Chryssostomidis, "Elliniki paroikia," 120-22.
78. *O Paroikos*, 11 February 1957, 1.
79. Ibid., 1.
80. *O Paroikos*, 23 January 1957, 1.
81. KKA/Letter of Konstantinos Karamanlis to Gamal Abdel Nasser, 20 February 1957, in Svolopoulos, *Konstantinos Karamanlis*, 287.

82. Evanthis Hatzivassiliou, *Evangelos Averoff-Tositsas, 1908–1990: politiki viografia* [Political biography] (Athens: Sideris, 2004), 70.
83. KKA/71A/ Konstantinos Karamanlis's narration, in Svolopoulos, *Konstantinos Karamanlis*, 288.
84. FO/371/130018/10316/2A, 1032/4/57, Athens, 12 April 1957, Lambert to Lloyd.
85. Interview of Nasser to the Athenian daily *Ethnos*, cited in *O Paroikos*, 19 January 1957, 1.
86. AGCCA/General assemblies, Speech of Greek ambassador Dimitrios Lambros, Alexandria, 17 December 1959.
87. AYE/CS/1957/22/9/1/1, 6330bis, Cairo, 6 March 1957, Lambros to GMFA.
88. Ibid.
89. AYE/CS/1958/2/1/3/2 6596, Cairo, 2 April 1958, Lambros to GMFA; AGCCA/General assemblies, Speech of Greek ambassador Dimitrios Lambros, Alexandria, 17 December 1959.
90. GPD/Period 4/Session 2/Meeting 43, 12 February 1957, Speech of Konstantinos Tsatsos, 610.
91. KKA/3A/1044-53, 7155, Cairo, 2 August 1957, Lambros to GMFA, in Svolopoulos, *Konstantinos Karamanlis*, 400.
92. AYE/CS/1957/22/5/1/1, 6801, Cairo, 30 May 1957, Lambros to GMFA.
93. AYE/CS/1957/22/9/1/1, 6544, Cairo 29 March 1957, Lambros to GMFA.
94. AYE/CS/1957/22/5/1/1, 36, Alexandria, 6 February 1957, Argyropoulos to GMFA.
95. AYE/CS/1957/22/9/1/1, 6330bis, Cairo, 6 March 1957, Lambros to GMFA.
96. Archives of the Greek Koinotita of Suez/Adjustment of the statuses according to the 384/1956 law, Report of the Agapitidis Committee, June 1957.
97. AGKA/Correspondence, 1954–61/40215, Memorandum of the Greek-Egyptian Cooperation Committee, Cairo, 24 May 1957.
98. *Tachydromos*, 26 May 1957.
99. MAE/Levant 1944–65/Egypte 1953–59/Relations extérieures du pays/Grèce/ 489, 539/AL, Athens, 29 May 1957, Charpentier to French Foreign Ministry.
100. *Tachydromos*, 26 May 1957.
101. *Tachydromos*, 3 June 1957.
102. AYE/CS/1957/22/9/1/1, 6857, Cairo, 4 June 1957, Lambros to GMFA.
103. MAE/Levant 1944–65/Egypte 1953–59/Relations extérieures du pays/Grèce/ 489, 457, Athens, 19 June 1957, Charpentier to FMFA.
104. *Tachydromos*, 17 August 1957, 1.
105. See also Chryssostomidis, "Elliniki paroikia," 130.
106. FO/371/130018/10316/5, 1032/5/57, Athens, 29 August 1957, Allen to Lloyd.
107. KKA, Joint communiqué, 19 August 1957, in Svolopoulos, *Konstantinos Karamanlis*, 403.
108. *Images* 1458, 17 August 1957, 4.
109. *President Gamal Abdel-Nasser's Speeches and Press-Interviews* (Cairo, n.d.), April–June 1960, 127.
110. AYE/CS/1961/16/1/3/1, 171, Alexandria, 9 February 1961, Baizos to Cairo embassy.

111. AYE/CS/1961/21/15/1/1, 574/Alexandria, 13 June 1961, Theodoropoulos to Cairo embassy; AYE/CS/1961/16/1/3/2, 485, Cairo, 14 March 1961, Yiannakakis to Cairo embassy.
112. AGKA/Correspondence, 1954–61, 63/60 Alexandria, 20 May 1960, Theodorakis and Chryssovergis to Lambros.
113. *President Gamal Abdel-Nasser's Speeches and Press-Interviews* (Cairo, n.d.), April–June 1960, 134.

Part II

Change and Adjustment (1937–60)

Chapter Three

The Labor Market

Early on the morning of Monday, 29 October 1951, nineteen-year-old Georgios Valatiadis, a typist in the auxiliary services of the British base in the Suez Canal, returned to work after spending the weekend with his family in Cairo. On his way to Suez city, Egyptians boycotting the base and demonstrating against the British presence in Suez stopped Valatiadis and his colleagues, forcing them to return to the capital. After returning, they all went to the British consulate to report what had happened and receive directions on what to do next. The British told them that as soon as the situation had calmed down, the British would transfer them to Suez in a diplomatic vehicle. Right after this, Valatiadis and his colleagues informed the Greek consul, who considered it unacceptable that Egyptiot employees be transferred in a British diplomatic car. He encouraged them to return to their jobs using their own means; there were far too many of them, and if they lost their jobs, they would not be able to find another. Even though the Egyptian authorities had informed the Greek consulate in Cairo that assaults against Egyptiots were possible and difficult to stop due to the situation, the consul guaranteed the security of the employees and urged them to return to their workplace at the earliest possibility. Believing they had the protection of the consulate, they tried to return to the British base. On their way to Suez, however, Valatiadis was arrested and sentenced to three months' imprisonment because he was considered a spy. It is not clear whether the Greek consulate intervened. Even if there was an intervention, it was fruitless, as Valatiadis was deported a few weeks later to Greece.

This incident illustrates the policy of the Greek authorities in trying to strike a balance between a pro-British attitude, with an anticommunist and pro-Western basis, and the everyday reality, which required solidarity with the Egyptian struggle. Even if the consulate did not approve the transfer of Egyptiot Greek employees by means of a British diplomatic car, it had no objection to these men carrying on their work on the British base. Under these circumstances, it is not surprising that Egyptiots became scapegoats, guilty of collaboration with the enemy in the eyes of many Egyptians. Besides showing the politically ambiguous and inefficient approach of the consular authorities, the incident is also revealing of the unemployment problem that emerged in the community after the war. In this context, the diplomatic authorities preferred to expose Greek citizens to danger than for them to join the ranks of the unemployed.

This chapter discusses the labor issue as a key factor in the Egyptiot Greek presence. Labor questions came to the fore after the abolition of the Capitulations in 1937 and more intensively after World War II. Throughout the period from 1937 to the end of the 1950s, Egyptiots faced major challenges in the labor market and developed strategies to overcome them. The general economic conditions existing in the community put pressure on small- and large-scale private companies to hire workers and to adjust themselves to a radically changing Egyptian economy.

RICH, PETIT BOURGEOIS, AND THE DESTITUTE

At Montreux the Egyptian government undertook not to enact any regulations against the right of foreigners to residence and property and, additionally, not to place any restrictions on labor or commerce during the twelve-year transitional period. The letters exchanged between the foreign delegations that were subsequently annexed to the convention made it clear that Greeks settled in Egypt would enjoy the same professional rights during the transitory period, while those who would settle from that point onward would be subject to Egyptian legislation.[1] However, as the previous chapter mentioned, despite the Egyptian government's assurances of goodwill, skepticism prevailed among the foreign elites during the 1930s with regard to the real intentions of the state, especially concerning the labor market.[2]

This skepticism was due to the Egyptian policy regarding the labor market during the years following nominal independence in 1922. Egypt sought to extend its national sovereignty in individual sectors that foreigners traditionally controlled, such as the joint-stock companies, in terms of capital, administration, and personnel. The ministerial decrees of 18 July 1923 and 31 March 1927 aimed to increase the participation of Egyptian employees and board members in these companies.[3] In August 1936, when the Anglo-Egyptian Treaty was signed, the Finance Ministry decided to increase the required percentage of Egyptian employees in the companies from 25 to

50 percent and set the minimum share of Egyptian workers at 90 percent. However, the Capitulations, which were still in force, did not allow Egypt to promulgate a law on this issue or to monitor whether companies applied the ministerial decrees or not.[4] So, one may assume that since the Egyptian government had hardly any possibility of intervention, it treated the above decrees as merely symbolic. Thus, in the 1930s, the Egyptian government confined its efforts to applying psychological pressure on the foreign joint-stock companies to hire more Egyptian employees and workers.[5] Companies that had signed separate agreements with the Egyptian government were more susceptible to these pressures and new regulations. For example, the Egyptian government made an agreement with the Suez Canal Company to have four Egyptians appointed to the company board and for Egyptians to constitute a third of the entire workforce (administrative and technical).[6]

The Egyptianization of the labor market was the result not only of sterile ideological processes. The demographic explosion—the Egyptian population increased by 25.75 percent from 1917 to 1937 (see table 1)—the improvement of education, economic stagnancy following the 1929 stock market crash, and urbanization increased unemployment rates, especially among the more educated.[7] The emergence of a middle class in Egypt within the framework of the constitutional monarchy from 1922 required the Egyptian government in the interwar period to search for solutions.[8] In this respect, Egypt aimed to increase the employment of Egyptians in banks and foreign companies. The public sector was already overstaffed by the mid-1920s, and the most important private companies, owned by foreigners, did not easily hire Egyptian employees.

In the main, Egyptianization had to do with the transition of the economy and public administration from an imperial to a nation-state framework. A similar process was underway in post-Ottoman Turkey, which constituted, in this respect, a paradigm for nominally independent post-Ottoman Egypt. Following Turkish independence, the government increased the quotas of Muslim employees in foreign enterprises. One result was an increase in unemployment among Orthodox Christians of Greek origin, who began gradually to leave the country. According to estimates, five thousand Greeks had been dismissed by 1926 from European firms in Istanbul.[9] Turkish labor policy in the interwar period and its results provoked intense concern among Greek diplomats in Egypt, even though religion was used to differentiate Turkish citizens. In the event Egypt was simply to follow the Turkish paradigm, the Greek ambassador in Cairo, Andreas Delmouzos, predicted in October 1938 that the majority of Egyptiots would be obliged to repatriate.[10]

Unemployment in the 1930s was a concern not only for Egyptians. It was a reality that foreigners—the Greek community included—had to deal with.

It mostly affected occupations that were not that profitable, such as small shopkeepers, small traders, drivers, and unskilled workers. These were in direct competition with Egyptians and were gradually replaced in the labor market, especially in the interior of the country. In mid-1938, Konstantinos Valtis, the Greek consul general in Alexandria, underlined to Metaxas the urgent need to secure jobs for unemployed Egyptiot Greeks so they could remain in the country: "There is ... the danger that we will find ourselves facing a group departure of all these unemployed to Greece, which would not be the best solution."[11] However, even in cases where there was no concrete reason for their anxiety, Egyptiot Greeks started having "the understandable fears ... for the future career of their children."[12]

In the late 1930s many foreigners became increasingly worried that the distinctions being made between them and Egyptians would lead to a loss of jobs. Soon after Montreux, Greek officials discussed the possibility of Greek nationals acquiring Egyptian citizenship as a means to combat unemployment. In July 1937, Metaxas himself asked Delmouzos to encourage Greek nationals to exchange their Greek for Egyptian citizenship. This was envisaged as a defense line that would prevent the possible hostile treatment of foreigners in the labor market.[13] Delmouzos, in turn, asked the consular authorities in Egypt to treat the matter discreetly so as not to give the impression that the Greek state was abandoning its citizens.[14] Officials were to examine each case separately and to assure those who decided to take out Egyptian citizenship were that in the event of "repatriation," they would automatically regain Greek citizenship. In this case-by-case approach, officials were to pay special attention to the professional status of each person.

The consular authorities did not recommend all Greeks change their citizenship. There was little point in nationals engaged in professions that the ambassador considered "lower," such as "coffee seller, pastry maker, small grocer, florist, shoemaker, etc., and all kind of working-class professions such as servant, carpenter, car driver, blacksmith, cooks, etc.," acquiring Egyptian citizenship, since native Egyptians were increasingly replacing them in the labor market, especially in the interior.[15] Switching citizenship would in no way improve their position, nor would it affect in any way the other end of the social spectrum, namely the Greek industrialists, bankers, and big merchants. Egypt largely depended on foreign capital,[16] and therefore diplomats did not expect that legislative measures would be taken against Greeks in the foreseeable future, at least not until the end of the transitory period in 1949. Officials viewed Egyptian citizenship as an option for the middle- and lower-class self-employed professionals, namely lawyers, doctors, pharmacists, along with the white-collar workers and clerks. In fact, Delmouzos believed that it would be in the best interest of this last category of professionals not only to change their citizenship but also to learn Arabic.[17]

Given that the majority of Egyptiots were engaged in clerical jobs or were self-employed professionals, as shown in table 2, the issue of changing citizenship was of profound importance to the community.

The consulates and vice-consulates in Alexandria, Cairo, Port Said, Mansoura, Zagazig, Minya, Suez, and Tanta collected the data contained in table 2 in the late 1940s. Based on incomplete information, the data therefore provide only an indication of the professional occupations of Greeks in Egypt at that time.[18] Even though there were variations between the different locations in terms of jobs and occupations, these do not greatly affect the overall picture. According to the statistics, the category of "clerks" constituted the majority of the workforce (9,900 persons), which amounted to 33.5 percent of it. They were followed by the technicians (3,900 persons, 13.2 percent), handicraft laborers (3,775 persons, 12.8 percent), and the vari-

Table 2. Occupations of Greek citizens in Egypt, 1950

Occupations	Persons	Percentage
Merchants/industrialists	1,700	5.7
Various businessmen	335	1.1
Landowners/rentiers	285	0.9
Doctors, lawyers, architects, civil engineers, agronomists, chemists, pharmacists.	710	2.4
Schoolteachers	345	1.1
Shopkeepers	2,300	7.8
Clerks	9,900	33.5
Artists	120	0.4
Nurses	145	0.4
Technicians	3,900	13.2
Waiters/barmen	750	2.5
Drivers	710	2.4
Industrial and handicraft laborers	3,775	12.8
Seamen	975	3.3
Unspecified occupations	3,550	12
Total	29,500	100
Dependents	44,500	
Total Greek citizens	74,000	

Source: AGCCA/Statistics and census of the Greek community, Note on the occupations of Greeks of Egypt, Alexandria, 28 December 1950.

ous shopkeepers (2,300 persons, 7.8 percent), while several other professions such as artists, waiters, teachers and professors, drivers, nurses, doctors, and all kind of liberal professions amounted to just over a quarter (26.1 percent, or 8,040 people) of the workforce. Finally, the upper middle class and the big bourgeois of the community—merchants and industrialists, various businessmen, landowners, and rentiers—accounted for 6.6 percent (1,985 people) of the working Greek population in Egypt.

The difference in the total number of Greeks in Egypt between the above census (74,000; see table 2) and the Egyptian state census (57,427; see table 1) at almost the same time demonstrates an important problem faced by all research on the Greek presence in Egypt: the absence of reliable demographic data on the community. The different figures arose due to the uncertainty of census enumerators and other data gatherers about who could be considered Greek. Those of Greek origin? The Orthodox Christian who spoke Greek? Or only those who were citizens of the Greek state? While the next section deals with the citizenship issue, what is important to highlight here is that neither the Egyptian census takers nor the diplomatic authorities and the *koinotites* had a clear picture of the numbers of the Greek presence in Egypt, especially for the lower economic strata. The numbers that surfaced from time to time were based on estimates, which always showed the community to be larger than it appeared in the Egyptian census. Consequently, we can claim that the various censuses are more useful for the examination of long-term demographic trends, since they are not accurate regarding the exact demographic condition at a given moment.

The occupational census of Greeks in Egypt in 1950 raises two interrelated questions: To what extent did occupations reflect the social stratification of the community? And to what extent did this stratification remain unchanged from the late 1930s to early 1960s? There is no detailed data on the incomes of the different occupations or more specific information on the composition of general categories such as "white-collar workers" or "industrialists/merchants." Observing the situation in the Egyptian capital as regards the social stratification of the community in 1948, Georgis Athanassiadis,[19] a progressive educator in the city, wrote, "Five percent are capital holders, thirty-five percent are petit bourgeois, and sixty percent are poor workers."[20] In his annual report for 1951, Alexios Liatis, the consul general in Alexandria, noted that the majority of Greeks comprised "clerks, small entrepreneurs, and those struggling for an existence."[21] From the data presented in the next paragraph, it seems that Anthony Gorman's view, that there was an "exaggerated sense of middle class"[22] in the community, has a solid basis in fact.[23] The situation described by Athanassiadis and Liatis accurately describes the conditions within the community in the 1950s and early 1960s.

In 1956, right before the Suez Crisis, the social welfare office of the Alexandria consulate had registered 2,500 Greeks "confirmed to be destitute."[24] Four years later, according to the same office, 2,420 families, encompassing approximately 10,000 Greeks, independent of citizenship, earned less than LE 3 per month—from which most had to pay rent. Some earned "much less than LE 3 or nothing." Moreover, 938 families—that is, almost 4,000 people—survived on monthly incomes of between LE 3.5 and 6. Referring to the entire community, the consul general, Theodoros Baizos, wrote, "Their standard of living ... is not higher than the level of the fellah or of the Egyptian industrial workers."[25] GKA data for 1960 paints a similar picture. According to its welfare office, of the 30,000 Greek citizens in Alexandria—as estimated by the diplomatic authorities—10,500 were on a monthly income of less than LE 6. Out these, 4,500 persons had an income of less than LE 4, and for that reason, they received extensive assistance from the GKA, funded by the wealthy Alexandrian Greeks, which included free tuition in GKA schools, two meals per day for the pupils, and free medical and hospital care. The other 6,000 received some subsidies. Most of the community members in receipt of subsidies were under forty-five years old. Three in five were workers, and the rest of them were clerks.[26]

In any event, the number of low-earning Greeks was high in the community if we take into account the Egyptian census, which put the total number of Greek citizens in Egypt in 1960 at 47,673 persons (see table 1). Given that half of the Greek population lived in Alexandria (see table 3), it is clear that a significant share of community members had extremely low incomes. Even if we take into account the estimates of the diplomatic authorities, who believed there were 60,000 Greeks in Egypt at that time,

Table 3. Geographic distribution of Greek citizens in Egypt, 1897–1947

Year	Cairo	Alexandria	Suez Canal cities (Port Said, Ismailia, and Suez)	Upper and Lower Egypt
1907	19,419	24,602	6,743	12,160
1917	15,250	25,393	6,307	9,698
1927	20,115	37,106	8,876	9,954
1937	16,949	36,822	7,720	6,842
1947	15,673	30,753	7,157	3,844
1960	13,590	24,609	6,241	3,233

Sources: *Annuaire statistique, 1910* (Cairo: Imprimerie nationale, 1910); *The Census of Egypt Taken in 1917*, vol. 2 (Cairo: Government Press, 1921); *Annuaire statistique, 1927–1928* (Cairo: Imprimerie nationale, 1929); *Annuaire statistique, 1937–1938* (Cairo: Imprimerie nationale, 1939); *Annuaire statistique, 1947–1948* (Cairo: Imprimerie nationale, 1951); *Al-Qiraa al 'ama li soukan: jadawil 'ama* [General population census of Egypt: General tables] (Cairo, 1960).

the percentage still remains high. To contextualize these income levels, a few examples suffice. In 1958 in Alexandria, a graduate of the Salvageios Commercial Greek School received a salary of LE 12 to 18 per month as an office clerk. In the same year, the average salary of workers—who were in the main Egyptians—was LE 2.37 per week (LE 2.45 for men and LE 1.42 for women), according to the International Labor Office. This corresponded to a salary of almost LE 9.50 per month for workers in services, transport, shops, construction, and mining.[27] At the level of consumption, the prices in Port Said in October 1955 were as follows: a pound (0.453 kg) of bread cost five piastres (there were one hundred piastres in the Egyptian pound); a kilo of beef, thirty-four to forty piastres; and a liter of olive oil, sixty piastres. Finally, the average monthly rent for a two-room apartment in the European quarter of the city was LE 15 to 18.[28]

Before we draw general conclusions for the entire period under examination, three different parameters should be taken into account. First of all, after World War II and especially during the 1950s the community underwent a gradual impoverishment for reasons that will be explained in the following chapters. Second, the demographic and social picture of the community in the early 1960s was definitely different from that of the late 1930s or just after the war. This was due to the fact that migration or repatriation during the 1940s and 1950s had led young and educated elements of the community to leave Egypt. Finally, it has to be taken into account that "destitute" is a rather fluid socioeconomic category in the period under scrutiny.

Who was destitute was subject to different interpretations. In January 1962, Vyron Theodoropoulos, consul general in Alexandria, gave a more moderate view of the total number of destitute people in Alexandria, which may correspond better to reality: "If we classify as destitute those who do not have enough capital either to start a small business or to cover their own expenses during a six-month-long period of waiting to find a job, then I think that the number of the poor reaches or even exceeds 25 percent."[29] On the other hand, Athanassios Tsaldaris, the secretary general of Greece's Social Affairs Ministry, noted during a visit to Egypt that same year, "The number of destitute people in the two bigger communities, these of Cairo and Alexandria, is calculated now at 40 percent, with greater rates in Alexandria."[30] Sotirios Agapitidis, when he visited Egypt in 1954 as a special envoy of the Greek government, claimed that within the community whoever was not rich was considered destitute by the *koinotites* and had the proportionate benefits. He also acknowledged though that the number of real destitute people had increased.[31] The Greek ambassador, Michail Melas, was rather scathing with regard to the benefits provided to people who needed them. "In 1952," he wrote in his memoirs, "a shrewd person ... could literally live from birth to death as a burden on the charity institutions: free nursery, free school, soup kitchen, money distribution, hospital, and cemetery."[32] It is certain though that the communal institutions did not provide assistance out of pure generosity. For the elites who controlled and funded the *koinotites*, charity was a means to legitimize their position in the community and a confirmation of their political, economic, and moral hegemony. The *koinotites*, through their services, are somewhat part of the tradition of the Muslim philanthropic institutions (*waqf*) and also played the role of a welfare state. At the same time, they constituted the mechanisms of an introverted and nationally determined self-sustaining system where the economic elites of the community prevailed. This elite, through the control it exerted over the *koinotites*, patronage practices, and clientelistic networks, ensured it maintained the social control of the community.[33]

Given the professional and social profile of the community, the position of Greeks in the labor market was of paramount importance in the postwar period, as it was directly linked with their possibilities of remaining in Egypt in the long term. The privileged Capitulations regime that ensured the unhindered presence of foreigners in Egypt prior to 1937 no longer existed. Foreign citizenship, instead of being an advantage, gradually became an obstacle in the labor market. Under these circumstances, changing citizenship or professional orientation could contribute to adjustment in the workplace. However, despite the warnings of some dignitaries and the discreet encouragement of the Greek state, little was done in this regard in the years following Montreux. One reason for this was the expectation that the anticipated treaty of establishment at the end of the transitory period would represent the Capitulations in a new form, which would perpetuate the privileged position of the community. Another reason had to do with the extraordinary conditions created in the labor market after the outbreak of World War II.

FORMS OF SOLIDARITY AND COMPETITION

The presence of significant numbers of Allied forces in Egypt during World War II boosted local economic activity, to the benefit of the Egyptian and foreign business community. In 1937, 92,021 industries and artisan manufacturers employed a total of 237,467 persons. Within five years, 103,259 industries and artisan manufacturers (an increase of 12 percent) employed 284,589 (an increase of 17 percent).[34] New job opportunities arose, especially in Cairo and Alexandria, particularly in the military's auxiliary services, the production of supplies for the Allies, and catering. The last-mentioned industry mainly attracted Greeks, who constituted the majority of the employees in this sector.³⁵ Some Egyptiots, however, were excluded from the bonanza. The exiled Greek government called up Greek citizens in Egypt. During the war, 7,063 men in all served the Allied army of the Middle East (4,032 in the army, 1,614 in the navy, and 1,417 in the air force), a number of whom did so as volunteers.³⁶

In December 1941, the Egyptian authorities granted the Greek state permission to enlist three classes of Greek nationals living in Egypt. The mobilization provoked the strong dissatisfaction and reaction of some of those called to serve in the army as well as members of the Egyptiot economic elite.³⁷ As the general consul in Alexandria, Konstantinos Valtis, wrote, "Those among the officials who should have set the tone of enthusiasm, even though they claimed at the beginning that they were in favor of mobilization, expressed so many reservations and so little enthusiasm (they abstained from every relevant publicity event) that, with their stance, they contributed to the reluctance that manifested itself and the general tendency to seek exemptions."³⁸ In February 1942, a month before the above lines were written, the presidents of the GKA and GKC, Mikès Salvagos and Parisis Belenis, respectively, along with the GCCA president, Marios Laskaris, and Georgios Roussos, had addressed a joint telegram to the Alexandria consul general. In this letter they asked that Greeks over the age of twenty-five be exempted from their military obligations, pointing out that failure to provide for this would result in serious trouble and jeopardize the Egyptiots' future, since the Egyptian government demanded that Egyptians fill vacancies created as a result of the mobilization.³⁹

Thus, unemployment would endanger the viability of the community because those who would not be able to find a job would abandon Egypt for good. The reaction took the form of a public confrontation, with the circulation of a leaflet opposing mobilization and the deputy premier and defense minister of the exiled Greek government, Panagiotis Kanellopoulos, personally.⁴⁰ Wealthy members of the community who were, according to British diplomats, admirers of the Metaxas dictatorship and friends of Germany promoted this initiative. The leaflet mentioned, among others things, that "the Greeks of Egypt have become the object of the foulest and dishonest exploitation by the fair-weather warlords. ... The new mobilization of three generations is facing a strong reaction from the people."⁴¹

Valtis, dismissing the leadership's request as "exaggerated and influenced by their own interests,"⁴² carried on with the mobilization. He roundly blamed the community leadership for its selfishness and neglect of the national cause. Eventually out of 1,876 individuals called up to enlist in Alexandria, 1,410 were mobilized—almost 75 percent.⁴³ Valtis considered this proportion satisfactory and praised the consulate's efficiency—that is, himself—in securing the recruits, given the leadership's persistent bad will.[44] The mobilization issue, which is characteristic of the conflict between the interests of the homeland and those of the community, is also indicative of the special treatment Greeks living abroad often sought for themselves by invoking the particularities of diaspora life, a practice that became more emphatic when sponsored migration began. It is also indicative, though, of the tendency of the Greek government to exploit diaspora communities according to current interests.

Unemployment, however, did increase after World War II among younger Greeks, a fact that incidentally justified the concerns of the leadership. Those mobilized Greeks who constituted the most dynamic part of the community in terms of age were naturally compelled to leave their jobs. For as long as they were in the army, the *koinotites,* wealthy compatriots, or big companies belonging to the Allies—such as the Suez Canal Company—provided financial assistance to their families. Many recruits received guarantees that they would be reemployed after the end of the war. However, this was not the case for many of the mobilized persons. Greek veterans could not return to their prewar occupations for three reasons. The first was that many companies that had flourished during the war collapsed with the departure of the Allies.[45] The second reason had to do with the political beliefs of the veterans. Many Greek employers helped veterans to find a job quickly, but some "vicious employers," however, refused to do so in cases where veterans lacked the certificate of "good behavior," a kind of criminal record issued by the consulates to those who had not been involved in Greek resistance activity during the war.[46] The third reason is that Egyptians and other foreigners had replaced many of those who went on military duty. In Port Said, for instance, the Greek consul warned in August 1944 that "the uppermost issue will be to find work for the Greek workers who have been dismissed from the army and who are not permanently working for the Suez Canal, whose positions were occupied by natives, Maltese, and foreign citizens."[47] Thus, the new postwar realities in the labor market created serious socioeconomic tensions between the Greeks, other foreign ethnic or national groups, and the Egyptians.

The issue of the demobilization of Egyptiot Greek soldiers in 1945 provides a good example of such tensions. The evidence shows that until early 1946, the British administration unduly delayed the release of the Egyptiots from military duty, despite the repeated protests of the leadership and the fact that the Greek General Headquarters Staff had ordered their demobilization.[48] It seems that the British deliberately delayed the demobilization of the Egyptiots for two reasons. First, they did not want to do so before the war ended on every front, and second, they wanted to release the Cypriots and Maltese first. Indeed, these groups used their status as British subjects to press for immediate demobilization, ahead of the Greeks, in order to have a head start in finding a job.[49] Additionally, the Italians of Egypt, who had been released en masse from internment camps,[50] began returning to their homes, with some of them taking up jobs previously held by Greeks.[51] Thus, many Egyptiot veterans found their prewar jobs taken, and as a result, unemployment rose considerably, especially among young Egyptiots.

A strong sense of solidarity within each national, ethnic, or religious group, which was also based on allegiance, fueled competition for employment. Mechanisms such as education and the labor market bolstered these allegiances. As regards the latter, the mechanism was maintained through the offer of and demand for a job and through professional networks. Writing about the issue of ethnic allegiance in the Egyptian context, Floresca Karanasou mentions that it mainly emerged within the most populous communities with a complete social stratification, that is, the Greeks, Jews, Armenians, or Syrians, and had as its basis the dependence of the lower classes on the upper class of their community for positions in the workplace. Job offers from rich members to fellow members of the community or co-regionalists (of common origin or place of settlement in Egypt) was of vital importance for the preservation of the prestige and hegemony of the economic elite within these communities. On the other hand, members of the lower economic strata sought such services for their own benefit.[52]

How did this mechanism function within the Egyptiot Greek community context? Greek employers mostly hired Greek employees and workers. Manolis Yalourakis, a columnist for *Tachydromos,* wrote at a later date that "big capital has been concentrated in a few people. The big bourgeois and the bourgeois dominate."[53] The Salvagos and Koutarellis companies in Alexandria, which employed eleven hundred Greeks between them in 1957, were two examples.[54] This concentration of capital among a handful of Greek company owners meant they constituted important employers for the middle and lower strata. Christos Petrondas, an educator based in Mansoura and Alexandria, noted that "the Greeks were a chain," which Katerina Trimi interprets the following way: "One Greek was the employee of the other and one was the customer of the other."[55] In a way, there was a kind of moral obligation for employers to offer jobs to community members. This was at the core of a dependence relationship, which was based on clientelistic networks and patronage, a characteristic of traditional societies.

The importance of a shared ethnic or national background in the labor market should not be overestimated, though, since these are socially constructed categories with fluid boundaries.[56] Personal and neighbor relations, local origin, the place of residence in Egypt, friendships, and other family relations played an equally important, if not at times more important, role in finding and being offered a job. However, it is difficult to discern such characteristics in the sources because contemporaries saw them as obvious owing to the common ethnic or national background. The functioning of the labor market on the basis of ethnic or national criteria had often clear limits. This was evident in the intense competition that traditionally developed between Greek professionals in the absence of important professional unions in the postwar years. It was also apparent in the cases of Communists and other people of the Egyptiot Left who were not hired because of their political beliefs and in the cases of employers who preferred to dismiss Greeks and hire Egyptians either because the latter had the formal and substantial qualification of knowledge of Arabic and Egyptian citizenship or because they were paid less. As the economic conditions of the community members gradually worsened in the 1950s and 1960s, the phenomenon of dismissing Greeks in order to replace them with Egyptians became more common.[57]

The limits of the above scheme are also illustrated from the perspective of the employees. These who worked for Greek and other foreign—mainly European—companies were in the majority.[58] Another category of community members existed who were more integrated in the Egyptian economy and society, however. This was more frequent in Cairo or in smaller cities and villages where contact with Egyptians was more intense. It was not usual for Greeks to work in Egyptian companies or to collaborate with Egyptians. However, in certain professional sectors, such as the retail and grocery trade, where Greeks dominated, employers and employees were of the same nationality. However, where Greek patrons were not able to offer jobs, the result was unemployment for their compatriots in the sector. The following quotation from a speech delivered in 1938 by M. Michailidis, general secretary of the Association of Greek Grocers of Alexandria, is indicative: "The ruin [of the Greek groceries] will be devastating not only for Greek grocers but also for Greek employees, who can be sure that if there are no more Greek groceries they will not find work in foreign groceries."[59] There were, however, sectors such as the cultural field where the mixing with Egyptians was visible and of great importance. Greek actors participated in Egyptian productions after the war and were well known to and beloved by the Egyptian public. Egyptiot entrepreneurs, who in 1944 founded the Studio Al-Ahram and produced ten movies in the space of a decade, supported such productions. In the years to follow, Egyptian directors made movies for exclusive distribution in Greece or prepared Greek and Egyptian versions of the same release.[60]

The above divergences were never important enough to supersede the dominant tendency that placed ethnic or national allegiance at the core of an introverted, self-sustaining labor market. This was not an exclusively Greek practice, for minorities work in these ways all over the world and over time. Other communities in Egypt also functioned this way. Solidarity manifested itself not only at the level of labor relations but also in the clientele that stores, companies, and services attracted; these were mostly people of the same ethnic origin or, alternatively, of the same cultural or religious background (for example, foreigners, Europeans, Christians, or Muslims). This was not the case in big department stores, in Cairo for instance, which were foreign owned but attracted a diverse though well-to-do clientele.[61] After World War II, though, ethnic determination in the labor market became more visible, because whenever and for whatever reason a foreign group departed Egypt, those who remained profited.

Two postwar waves of departure of foreigners or non-Egyptian communities from Egypt contributed to the easing of pressure on the labor market and opened up new job prospects for unemployed Egyptiot Greeks. First, a significant number of lower- and middle-class Armenians,[62] Jews,[63] Maltese,[64] and Italians[65] left before 1951. The Italian population in Egypt, for instance, decreased significantly from 1937 to 1947 because of the war. The Italians never managed to recover demographically after 1945—their number shrank gradually until 1960. Those who did not manage to find a job after they were released from internment abandoned Egypt, usually for good. The situation was hard for many because a significant number of Italian stores and companies, which under normal circumstances would have been able to absorb unemployment among Italians, shut down for good during the war. Additionally, most of the Italian banks, which could have rather easily provided credit to them, had also stopped operating in the country.[66]

Egyptiot Greeks often considered the departure of ethnic groups such as the Italians or other communities with similar socioeconomic characteristics as an opportunity to recover the vacancies left in the local labor market. When, for example, heeding Stalin's call, seventeen hundred Armenians departed from Alexandria for the Soviet Union on the night of 3 September 1947, on board the Soviet ship *Pobeda*,[67] GCCA dignitaries saw this as a major opportunity for the Greeks, who could fill the vacancies left by the Armenians: "A new opportunity for a few either exclusively Greek or Greek-Egyptian new businesses has recently appeared with the repatriation from Egypt to the USSR of a significant number of Armenian owners of small businesses and traders ... their ... departure from Egypt will create a vacuum that the Greeks are capable of filling alongside the Egyptians."[68] Around the same time, a number of Maltese, who were British subjects, followed the migration route toward Australia under the auspices of the

British government. When they left their jobs, these became available to other foreigners.[69] From the end of the Palestine War in 1948 to 1954, 15,872 Egyptian Jews—amounting to roughly 25 percent of the total Jewish population in the country—left Egypt for the newborn State of Israel.[70] Even before the Palestine War, a Greek diplomat had observed a change in the behavior of the Egyptian government toward Jews and pointed out in a rather cynical way, "There is a great possibility that the community will manage to survive in the end, and maybe the antipathy that, according to my information, has started to be shown by Egyptian government and financial circles against our biggest rival, the Jews, will help this survival."[71]

After the Suez Crisis, in late 1956 and 1957, approximately forty thousand Jews departed from Egypt, leaving openings in the labor market to be conveniently occupied by those who remained.[72] Along with the Jews, a significant number of "enemy subjects," namely the British and French, as we have seen in the previous chapter, were expelled from Egypt. It is estimated that approximately eight to ten thousand French citizens[73] and roughly all British subjects, including the Maltese, left Egypt, while a considerable number of Greeks, Italians, and other Europeans or members of non-Egyptian communities, mainly Armenians, followed later. In the case of the French and British of metropolitan origin, the departure basically concerned high-ranking company executives, highly qualified technicians, and employees of public organizations of the two respective states that operated in Egypt.

Under these circumstances, the Greek ambassador, Dimitrios Lambros, tried to convince rich Egyptiots to exploit business opportunities created after the departure of the British, French, and Jews. West Germany had already tried to move in, by hastily organizing an exposition with German industrial products in Egypt in March 1957 to fill the gap left after the departure of many Westerners, mainly British and French. As the ambassador informed the GMFA:

> I do not miss underlining to our compatriots who are still in panic because they had got used to living in Egypt as tails of the English and the French and as collaborators of the Jews, that they should take the Germans' activity as an example and try to take advantage of the undisputed opportunities that have been created after the English-French-Jewish exodus from Egypt. Some of the Jews who have not left have begun recover their good temper.[74]

Indeed, Greek entrepreneurs benefited and made considerable profits from the departure of other foreigners after the Suez Crisis. What also needs to be taken into account is that apart from the above-mentioned members of foreign communities, from the end of the war to the Suez Crisis a significant number of Greeks migrated or repatriated for economic reasons, as will be discussed in part 3. Thus, Egyptians and the foreigners who remained, among them Greeks, made gains in the labor market.

Nevertheless, the departure of foreigners could also have adverse consequences in the labor market for those who remained. Despite competition among ethnic groups, the customers of foreign companies and stores were generally foreigners. Thus, we can observe the following paradox: on the one hand, the departure of a portion of foreigners helped those who remained to find a job more easily, but on the other, turnover in these companies decreased in line with the decline in their customer base.

THE SOLUTION OF EGYPTIAN CITIZENSHIP

To return to the end of World War II, the majority of demobilized Egyptiots had encountered difficulties reentering the labor market. Postwar unemployment affected not only Alexandria but also Cairo and the other cities that hosted Greek populations. Despite the departure of foreigners from Egypt in the late 1940s, the demographic explosion, on the other hand, among the Egyptian population (see table 1), their urbanization, and their gradual entry into professional activities, which had up to that point been almost monopolized by foreigners, created pressure in the labor market among foreigners and, of course, Egyptiot Greeks. Additional factors such as legislation favoring Egyptian citizens, connected to the end of the transitory period in 1949, made it imperative for Egyptiots to seek alternative solutions in order to consolidate their position in the local labor market. One possible solution, which emerged after Montreux, was for them to strengthen their political, civil, and social bond with Egypt through the acquisition of Egyptian citizenship.

Until 1950, Law 19/1929, which governed a number of complex issues resulting from the country's transition from the Ottoman Empire to a nation-state and encouraged foreigners to apply for naturalization, regulated Egyptian citizenship. The latter was mainly due to Egypt's desire, in the late 1920s, to reduce the number of foreign nationals benefiting from the Capitulations.[75] The Egyptian state did not recognize dual citizenship, a facility that the Greek state had permitted for its citizens living abroad since 1914. In the event that a foreigner desired to acquire Egyptian citizenship, he had to renounce the one he already held. Regarding foreigners, Article 7 of Law 19/1929 provided that everyone born in Egypt to a foreign father and permanently residing in the country could become an Egyptian national, provided that he renounced his foreign citizenship and officially declared his intention to adopt the Egyptian one.[76] Acquiring Egyptian citizenship was supposed to be a rather simple process, since applicants could opt for it upon reaching adulthood, even without having any knowledge of Arabic. The everyday practice in the mid-1930s, however, showed that Egyptian citizenship was far from easy to obtain. Since the countdown to the abolition of the Capitulations had begun and it was becoming increasingly clear that being an Egyptian citizen would be a privilege, bureaucratic obstacles to acquiring citizenship emerged. Indeed, the Egyptian Interior Ministry accepted very few of the thousands of applications it received from foreigners for Egyptian citizenship.[77]

In the case of ethnic Greeks, the expansion over time of the boundaries and territorial sovereignty of the Greek state at the expense of the Ottoman Empire further complicated the issue of citizenship. Whether the Egyptiot Greeks were legally Greek citizens, Ottoman subjects, or something else mostly depended on the precise moment they settled in Egypt. For example, people who decided to migrate from the city of Thessaloniki to Egypt before 1912 were theoretically moving within the same state, because the city, along with the entire Macedonia region, constituted part of the Ottoman Empire until that year. The case of those who moved after 1912, when the Greek state annexed the city and the entire region, represented a migration movement from one state to another. While there was little difference as regards migration patterns in these cases, in Egypt those who arrived before 1912 had a different legal status from those who came later. The citizenship issue became even more complicated in the case of ethnic Greeks who came from regions governed by a third country. For instance, Italy occupied the Dodecanese during the Italian-Turkish War of 1912. Under the Treaty of Lausanne in 1923, Turkey renounced all claims to the Dodecanese, and Fascist Italy annexed the islands. Greece gained sovereignty over them only in 1947. Consequently, most of the ethnic Greeks from this area migrating to Egypt, especially from 1925 onward, had Italian citizenship. Thus, the question of who was a Greek citizen and entitled to the protection of the Greek authorities was not always clear.[78] Table 4 shows the breakdown of Greek population in Egypt in 1927 according to the different citizenship Egyptiots held. As the table shows, over two-thirds of Egyptiots had Greek citizenship, whereas just over one in ten was Egyptian. About one in four possessed other nationalities: British (7.5 percent), Italian (6.4 percent), Turkish (4.9 percent), French (0.8 percent), other citizenship or stateless (3.6 percent).

Despite the Egyptian government's prewar assurances that the labor rights of foreigners would be protected until the end of the transitory period in 1949, immediately after the war rumors began to circulate that legal measures providing for restrictions or quotas on foreigners along professional

Table 4. Citizenship of people of Greek origin in Egypt, 1927

Citizenship	Number of citizens	Percentage
Greek	63,914	65.7
Egyptian	10,849	11.1
British	7,355	7.5
Italian	6,243	6.4
Turkish	4,809	4.9
French	738	0.8
Other	3,418	3.6
Total	97,326	100

Source: *Annuaire statistique, 1937–1938* (Cairo: Imprimerie nationale, 1939).

lines were imminent.[79] Since Greece had not signed a treaty of establishment with Egypt, it was generally felt that should these rumors turn out to be true, the future position of Greeks in Egypt would be greatly compromised. The anxiety was also fueled by the xenophobic atmosphere that had reemerged in postwar Egypt because of anti-British feeling. Consequently, public statements such as the one by Abdel Megid Ibrahim Saleh Pasha, a Wafd member, who declared that the country's European citizens, apart from accepting the mandatory teaching of Arabic in their schools and the use of the country's language in their correspondence, should employ Egyptian employees and workers, solidified this feeling.[80]

Confirming these rumors, the Egyptian government proceeded to enact laws reinforcing the position of Egyptian citizens in the labor market. This Egyptianization policy, which had started before the war, was primarily a response to the demographic explosion and also to the related socioeconomic impact of the sharp increase in unemployment, which also rose after the departure of the Allied forces. It was in this context that the Egyptian government passed Company Law 138, in July 1947. Its main aim was to secure employment for the ever-increasing Egyptian labor force, which could not be absorbed by either the public or agricultural sector. It also sought to pass control of joint-stock companies to Egyptians.[81] The law stipulated that companies had three years to ensure that 51 percent of the capital, 40 percent of the board of directors, 75 percent of the employees, and 90 percent of the workers of these companies were Egyptian. In parallel, the Egyptian authorities intensified their unofficial pressure on foreign companies to employ Egyptians.[82] According to the estimates of the Greek embassy in Cairo in March 1948, more than twelve hundred Egyptiot clerks were likely to lose their jobs within three years with the full implementation of Law 138/1947.[83]

At the same time the GCCA noted that "good clerks with Egyptian citizenship [were] sought after."[84] Alexios Liatis, consul general of the city, made a similar observation on rising unemployment: "There is demand for Arab-speaking Greek employees with Egyptian citizenship, with more than satisfactory salaries."[85]

Since the distinction between Egyptians and foreigners in the labor market became more of an issue as a result of the law, the acquisition of Egyptian citizenship as a solution for the Greeks wishing to keep their jobs reemerged. In the postwar era, citizenship became a key issue as regards the access of foreign citizens to the labor market. As a GCCA memorandum from the 1940s noted, the unhindered practice by Greeks of their professions in Egypt was directly linked to the citizenship issue: "The prospect for all the branches of Egyptiots, full-time employees and wage-earners, in the near and distant future, is bleak unless a way can be found for many unspecialized craftsmen and upper-class office employees to obtain Egyptian citizenship, which will permit many of them to be absorbed and others to maintain their positions in joint-stock companies."[86]

For its part, the Greek state placed no obstacles on its nationals who wished to change citizenship in order not to lose their enterprises or their jobs in Egypt and also reassured them that in the case of repatriation their Greek citizenship would be restored. This stance had its basis in the fear that unemployment would, sooner or later, raise the dreaded question of mass repatriation. At the same time, however, the Greek state was not in favor of Greeks acquiring Egyptian citizenship en masse, because it considered that a sudden decrease in the number of Greek nationals in Egypt would harm its interests.[87] In this way, the option of changing citizenship returned to the fore after the war as an efficient and immediate way to counter the advantage Egyptians now enjoyed in the labor market. Naturalization was deemed particularly applicable in the case of Egyptiot Greeks in the middle and lower social strata, who were principally engaged in clerical jobs.

While the Cairo embassy believed twelve hundred people were in danger of losing their jobs, only sixty-three applicants sent petitions to the Greek consulates in Cairo, Alexandria, and Tanta requesting that their Greek citizenship be officially annulled, a prerequisite for applying for the Egyptian equivalent.[88]

Even if the Greek state approved all these petitions, we have no data regarding how many citizenship applications were eventually received by the Egyptian state. With the Egyptian press largely opposed to the naturalization of foreigners, it may be assumed that Egyptian attitudes remained mainly negative, as was the case before the war. Only moderate voices in Egyptian society accepted naturalization, but only of those foreigners who had actually proved their will to be assimilated into Egyptian society.[89] However, although legislation was favorable until 1950, in practice bureaucratic obstacles made naturalization a time-consuming and stressful process.

In 1950, a year after the end of the transitory period for the full abolition of the Capitulations, citizenship Law 160/1950 was enacted, which further complicated naturalization.[90] The new legislation, which replaced Law 12/1929, was based on a combination of the principles of blood (*jus sanguinis*) and soil (*jus soli*). As regards the naturalization of foreigners, there were no major differences between the two laws. Both dictated that a foreigner who had resided in the country for at least ten years had the right to apply for Egyptian citizenship. However, this process was no longer automatic under the new law. Article 4 ruled that foreigners born in the country could obtain Egyptian citizenship on the condition that the ministerial council agreed that they met certain criteria, including residence in Egypt upon reaching adulthood, were sane, and had knowledge of Arabic.[91] Thus, naturalization moved from being theoretically a right, which one could request and acquire, to being a favor that might or might not be granted. Additionally, Article 10 stated that even if foreigners acquired Egyptian citizenship, they could not obtain all the rights deriving from it until five years had passed. This delay, however, could be waived provided the new Egyptian citizen served in the country's military forces.[92]

A close look at the applications from Greeks in Egypt wishing to renounce their Greek citizenship is revealing in many ways. Alexandros Kosmatos, a resident of Alexandria, in 1951 sought to renounce his Greek citizenship because he "was notified by the company in which he was employed that [he] had to obtain Egyptian citizenship, otherwise [he] was likely to be dismissed, a fact that would provoke [his] own as well as [his] family's ruin."[93] Periklis Glymenopoulos, a 42-year-old Greek citizen from the Nile delta city of Kafr el-Zayat, who had worked since the age of 26 in Kafr el-Zayat Cotton Company, a Greek company owned by Dimitrios Zerbinis, also invoked the fear of dismissal.[94] In a note addressed to the Greek authorities, he claimed that despite his patriotic feelings, he was forced to renounce his citizenship in order to keep his job.[95] After Cairo resident Christoforos Madikas lost his job as storekeeper at RKO Radio Pictures Near East, he asked for his citizenship to be annulled, "with deep sorrow."[96] His Greek employer had assured him that he would be reemployed if he obtained Egyptian citizenship.[97] Antonios Kaoustos, a 24-year-old Alexandria resident, learned from his employer, an Egyptian joint-stock company, that he would be dismissed if he did not obtain Egyptian citizenship within six months.[98] He wrote, "I take this opportunity to reassure you that obtaining Egyptian citizenship will not affect in any way my patriotic sentiments and that I remain and will remain Greek forever in my soul."[99] Konstantinos Makris described the acquisition of Egyptian citizenship as a prerequisite to his finding a job: "Under the current Egyptian interdictory statutes, it has become completely impossible to find work, and I am obliged to request Egyptian citizenship. ... I have the honor to inform you that I intend to work in an office where the first condition that was placed on me was to have Egyptian citizenship."[100]

The above examples, and the reasons invoked in each case by those seeking to renounce their Greek citizenship, suggest that the new Egyptian legislation regulating access to jobs was certainly behind the bulk of the applications. The low number of applications, though, raises questions about the extent to which the authorities enforced the 1947 company law. Reports from the Greek consular authorities all over the country suggested that enforcement was much stricter in the large urban centers than in the small cities and interior.[101] In the latter cases, as the vice-consul of Zagazig, Ioannis Fragkoulis, reported, legislation was not fully implemented because matters were principally arranged through an "amicable settlement."[102] It seems, though, that Greek, or more generally foreign, employers who desired to keep Greek employees in their service discovered the means to do so. One novel way was for a company to increase the total number of its employees through hiring Egyptians so that the percentage of Greeks remained within the quota.[103] Another was for a company simply not to declare its employees to the Egyptian authorities, whenever possible. National solidarity was also an important factor in this regard. Since employers in general preferred employees of the same ethnic group and vice versa, during the implementation of Law 138/1947 Greek employers opted to dismiss other foreigners when this was necessary.[104] The flip side of this practice was, of course, that companies owned by foreigners preferred to dismiss Greeks and retain their compatriots or Egyptians to keep the local authorities satisfied. Thus, the number of Greek employees in Anglo-Egyptian Oilfields (Shell) fell from forty in 1948 to thirteen in 1953.[105] There were of course cases of Greek employees who lost their jobs, but it seems that the law was more effective in controlling new hirings than in leading to a significant rise in unemployment among Egyptiots. The law definitely had a considerable impact on the general pessimistic mood within the community and fueled uncertainty as regards the future of foreigners in the country. However, as Filippos Dragoumis commented on Law 138/1947 after he visited Egypt on behalf of the Greek foreign minister in April 1952, "It did not bring about the reductions that the foreigners were afraid of and the Egyptians were expecting."[106]

The less than full implementation of the law, though, is not enough to explain the low number of petitions addressed to the Greek consulates, especially when the Greek state from 1937 promoted the option of changing citizenship in response to the likelihood of legislative measures discriminating in favor of Egyptians. How could one explain the reluctance of Egyptiot Greeks to acquire Egyptian citizenship? At this point, it is worth recalling that until 1951 the negotiations concerning the treaty of establishment were still in progress and Egyptiots hoped that the arrangement of their legal status would permanently solve the issue of their residence and unhindered practice of their professions in Egypt. Moreover, Greek nationals feared that a possible change of citizenship would not benefit their professional career, since, even if they were legally considered Egyptian, at a different level, as Christians, they would never be considered as equal to Muslims.[107] One should also mention the corollary obligation to serve in the Egyptian military forces, which would have been a rather dissuasive factor given the length and harshness of conscription in Egypt.[108] But these were not the only reasons.

Sofianos Chryssostomidis, an activist in the Egyptiot Left and chief editor of *O Paroikos,* mentions that psychological reasons deterred Greeks from changing citizenship.[109] In trying to explain these psychological factors, it is worth mentioning the comments of Nikolaos Sakellarios, GCCA president in 1952, on the matter. He observed that "the change ... in citizenship often brings on an emotional detachment from Greece."[110] Egyptiots viewed the acquisition of citizenship as a binding element with the host country. If they became naturalized, they feared that they would be obliged to remain in Egypt for good. The prevailing fear was that Egyptian citizenship would constitute an obstacle in the event of leaving Egypt for good, because it might hinder the transfer of personal assets.[111] Even though the GMFA sought to reassure Greeks that they would automatically regain their old citizenship if they repatriated, many remained hesitant. This reluctance on the part of Egyptiot Greeks leads to the assumption that a rather substantial number of Greek nationals must have considered their presence in Egypt as provisional or that they had a long-established suspicion toward promises of the Greek state. In addition, the possibility of acquiring five- or ten-year residency permits from 1953 made the acquisition of Egyptian citizenship less pressing, at least for those whose professional status was not endangered.[112]

The community considered Greek citizenship to be an important element for internal coherence since the Capitulations era and legally confirmed a link with the homeland. It is worth bearing in mind that the capitulatory privileges derived from this relationship. If they lost citizenship, the Egyptiot Greeks feared that this might incite a sentimental distance from the metropolis and, consequently, the dissolution of the community. Besides, for them, taking out Egyptian citizenship could result in losing the entitlements they enjoyed from *koinotita* membership, since some of the *koinotites* statutes clearly stated that certain benefits and privileges were reserved for Greek citizens.[113] Moreover, even if the Greek state never admitted it publicly, it seems that it considered people of Greek origin with Egyptian citizenship to be second- or even third-rate Greeks. Athens's instructions were clear as regards the administrative positions that people of Greek origin holding Egyptian citizenship could acquire: "From now on, it is necessary to provide for the Greek institutions—schools, hospitals, national associations, and others—that constitute legal entities and are of Greek character, which must absolutely be preserved, so that the majority of the members who are Greeks will not be forced to renounce their Greek citizenship."[114] Behind this decision lay the fear that Greek control of these institutions might be contested by the Egyptians in the future through the placing of an Egyptian citizen, a "Trojan horse," who could take control of the above-mentioned bodies. Even in 1961, when the mass departure movement had started and many Greek nationals were either emigrating or repatriating, the GMFA enquired of consul general Theodoros Baizos whether there was any objection in assigning the position of director of the city's Kotsikeio Greek Hospital to a Greek with Egyptian citizenship.[115] The government in Athens warned against the appointment: "It is necessary that the Koinotita puts every effort into finding a Greek citizen for this position, because for reasons of convenience it is essential to avoid the possibility of creating a precedent of employing an Egyptian citizen in this post," replied foreign minister Evangelos Averoff.[116]

We must also take into account that Egyptiots had lived for years—during the Capitulations era—in an environment that galvanized a feeling of superiority of Europeans over the "underdeveloped" Egyptians. Indeed, unlike Egyptian citizenship, citizenship of a European state might lend prestige and sometimes privileges, such as the protection of a powerful state in a crisis situation. Before World War II, when the Greek personnel of the British military had to make the choice between British and Egyptian citizenship, the Greek state promoted the British solution, which it considered preferable "by all means."[117] Moreover, in some cases Egyptiots considered Egyptian citizenship something of a "stigma,"[118] which also explains why, in their applications for the annulment of their Greek citizenship, applicants were emphatic, almost apologetically, that this in no way affected their national feelings. Finally, the preservation of Greek citizenship was one of the key elements that differentiated Egyptiots from other Greeks living abroad as, for example, in the United States, who had "surrendered" to the assimilating power of Western countries and had ruptured their legal bonds with Greece.

The citizenship issue surfaced in the life of the community when labor legislation distinguished between Egyptians and foreigners once again, thus placing restrictions on a number of professionals. After the Suez Crisis and

January 1957 laws, the daily *O Paroikos* strongly urged Greeks to apply en masse for Egyptian citizenship in order to be able to remain in the country and practice their profession unhindered.[119] In Athens, Prime Minister Karamanlis told MPs that the Egyptian government seemed willing to discuss the issue of double citizenship. His comments followed a meeting in New York between Averoff and his Egyptian counterpart, Mahmoud Fawzi, where the former suggested Egyptian citizenship should be afforded to those Greeks who wished to have it.[120] Karamanlis, however, was reluctant, because "the issue has not been completely resolved because then there is a danger of making the distinction between those who were born in Egypt and those who were not."[121] However, during his visit to Egypt in August 1957, he resubmitted the request. But nothing concrete emerged from it. Since the Egyptian side was not eager to accept double citizenship and Egyptiot Greeks never really showed any particular interest in acquiring Egyptian citizenship en masse, this path was no longer seen as a solution. Changing citizenship was a tool that Egyptiots in general used individually, and rather reluctantly at that. Consequently it did not provide a solution to the unemployment issue. It was only one of the paths pursued after World War II—another envisaged solution that revealed the limits of an introverted community and labor market.

THE LIMITS OF SELF-SUFFICIENCY

Unemployment in the postwar period mostly affected unskilled workers, low-level technicians, and white-collar workers who held foreign citizenship.[122] Many of them were World War II veterans. There are no accurate statistics as to unemployment rates within the Greek community in the immediate postwar years. An indicative picture can be gleaned from data collected by the Cairo and Alexandria consulates. In 1948, for instance, the number of unemployed Egyptiots in the Cairo area was 419, with the expectation that this number would increase in the following period.[123] In 1953, in the Alexandria area the number of unemployed was estimated at between 600 and 1,000.[124]

In the immediate postwar years Greeks faced difficulties in finding a job even with small manufacturers, while the provisions of Law 138/1947 constrained the joint-stock companies. Even for those who worked, wages were often lower in comparison to the interwar period or wartime. The fall in earnings was the result of the smaller profit margins compared to the interwar period and, especially, wartime, a fact that undoubtedly had repercussions on employers' ability to hire additional personnel. The reduced profits were due to, first, the imposition of income taxes and general taxes, from which they had been exempted under the capitulations; second, price controls on essential goods, which the government introduced in the 1940s; third, the limited profit margins from both domestic and imported products; and fourth, the limited purchasing power of people in the middle and lower strata.[125] This limited purchasing power was the result of Egypt's economic stagnation in the immediate postwar years, the departure of well-off foreigners, and the abrupt increase in the cost of living by 193 percent from August 1939 to 1952.[126] During the same period, wages remained stagnant or were reduced, a fact that intensified economic difficulties, especially for those on lower to medium incomes. These relatively low wages resulted mainly from the massive entry into the labor market of Egyptians, who as a general rule were paid less than the Europeans,[127] and secondly from the difficult economic position of small- and medium-sized enterprises, which, especially after the war, did not increase but reduced salaries.

The above situation apparently had a negative impact on the overall economic activity of small- and medium-sized enterprises and forced their owners either to use the capital they had accumulated during wartime in order to preserve their standard of living[128] or to seek investment opportunities in other countries and migrate. Since small- and medium-sized enterprises in Egypt made only limited investments to increase the turnover, community networks were not sufficient to provide a solution to the unemployment problem.[129] When Egyptiot Greeks needed to hire someone, they preferred candidates who had a substantial knowledge of Arabic, which in 1942 became obligatory in all business dealings. Nevertheless, the vast majority of Egyptiot Greeks were unable to read and write in Arabic. Thus, when the stock exchange closed in 1952, very few of the traders who became unemployed were able to find jobs at the newly founded Egyptian Cotton Committee, which was under state control, "because they don't have sufficient knowledge of Arabic [and the] necessary skills for a public service."[130]

Within the framework of a self-sustaining job market, the employment offices run by community organizations provided some relief for unemployed Egyptiots in the late 1940s and early 1950s. Their existence confirms not only the unemployment problem but also the unsuitability of traditional ways of finding a job to meet their needs. Set up by the GCCA, the GCCC, the Greek Orthodox patriarchate, and the League of Demobilized Greeks of Alexandria, the employment offices tried to facilitate people of Greek nationality or origin to gain access to the labor market. These organizations kept lists or published job advertisements in the daily Greek-language press of every city.

In the postwar years the GCCA was heavily preoccupied with the unemployment problem, setting up an employment office to help tackle the problem. The chamber of commerce was a place where employers and unemployed could meet each other. Usually the GCCA published job advertisements in the Alexandria daily press, and people interested in the advertisement would then contact the GCCA. Unemployed individuals or people wishing to change jobs could also contact the GCCA on their own accord, without necessarily replying to an ad. In 1947, for example, Nikolaos Vatsakis referred to his father's involvement in the chamber in a letter to GCCA director Evmolpos Viscovitch: "My father happens to have been a member of your chamber of commerce for years. Therefore, I thought I would address you, to make use of one of the many advantages that having the aforementioned role entails. Specifically, I am interested in the employment office."[131] The fact that many GCCA members were big merchants and industrialists drawn from the community encouraged some unemployed Greeks to apply to its employment office with the hope of finding a position in a business belonging to a member. As Vatsakis continued, "I wish to work as an assistant chemist ... given that many of the esteemed members of the GCCA happen to be factory owners and manufacturers, it would probably be easy for you to place me somewhere."[132] A similar case is provided by Michail Maschas, who addressed a letter to Dimitrios Zerbinis himself, owner of the Kafr el-Zayat Cotton Company and GCCA president: "I ask of you that you look into finding a suitable job for me in the Kafr el-Zayat Cotton Company. ... My only wish is to work for your company, in whatever position."[133]

According to the resumes submitted to the chamber, almost all the unemployed applications were Greek males; out of eighty cases, there was only one woman, of relatively young age.[134] Indeed Greek employers who contacted the chamber seeking employees of Greek origin preferred those with Egyptian citizenship and a substantial knowledge of Arabic.[135] Such candidates, however, were rare in the postwar years, when Egyptian citizenship became the basic "qualification" for someone to find a job.[136] Besides, many of the applications to the employment office were not unemployed but simply desired to improve their income, since, in the postwar period, the wages were not enough to cover the ever-increasing living costs.

In the late 1940s, when the job requests increased, the employment office contributed to restraining unemployment. This was not the case, though, in the following decade. In 1953, for example, the employment office failed to find any jobs for the unemployed who sought its help.[137] It was during this period that the GCCA systematized the emigration of Greeks from Egypt, and leaving the country became a far more viable option for many destitute and unemployed Greeks, as will be discussed in chapter 6. The employment office ceased operations in the early 1960s, when the exodus reached its peak. In effect, the employment office succeeded in preserving the clientelistic networks within the community and recycling the Greek labor force within the same self-sustaining job market, putting unemployed Greeks in contact with Greek employers, most of whom were GCCA members.

After World War II, the most innovative but also risky solution to unemployment was provided by the auxiliary services of the British base along the Suez Canal. The base became the biggest recruiter of unemployed Egyptiots, especially war veterans who had left their jobs during wartime. The Egyptiot leadership, along with the Greek diplomatic authorities, promoted the recruitment to the base as an eminent solution to unemployment.[138] Thus, they fulfilled the instructions received from Athens, namely to find jobs for unemployed and destitute Greeks in order to prevent a repatriation movement.[139] More than a thousand Egyptiots were immediately hired in low-paid positions, such as radio and telegraph mechanics, Morse operators, telephone switchboard mechanics, and touch typists.[140] These employees earned an average of LE 8 to 15 a month, which was particularly unsatisfactory, especially for those employees whose family did not live in the Suez Canal area, a situation that obliged them to maintain two different households. In the main, those Greeks who accepted these jobs saw them as a stopgap measure until they would have to leave the country.[141]

While the auxiliary services alleviated unemployment, the main problem was that these jobs were specifically designed to meet the needs of the British military and not the Egyptian labor market; a British withdrawal was bound to mean that the Greeks employed in the base would be condemned to unemployment. These jobs provided immediate, but short-term, unemployment relief, but they were not a definite solution. Aware of the problem, Greek diplomats and leading community members feared that a British withdrawal would create "an emergency situation," characterized by a sharp rise in unemployment rates within the community.[142] The work at the base constituted the "last resort" for unemployed war veterans who wanted to remain in Egypt, as the consul in Port Said pointed out.[143] Another benefit, from the point of view of the Greek authorities, was that the employment opportunities at the base constrained internal migration and protected the main urban centers from increased unemployment rates for some years. The collaboration, though, with a colonial power in a period when the Egyptian national movement was in the ascendance proved to be not only shortsighted but also dangerous, as indicated by the Valatiadis case mentioned at the beginning of the chapter.

In such an economic environment, marked by the increasing number of destitute Greeks[144] and the existence of a restricted labor market with strong ethnic characteristics, one solution might have been for the Egyptiot upper class to invest the considerable capital it had accumulated during the war. Harilaos Zamarias, who arrived in Alexandria after the war to serve as consul general, compared the situation he found then to the one he had known fifteen years earlier, when he served as vice-consul in the same place: "I found Egypt's Hellenism to be in much better economic condition than it was fifteen years ago."[145] Nevertheless because of the political situation in the postwar years, those who possessed such capital were extremely skeptical about investing in the country. They were equally self-restrained when it came to donating to the *koinotites* and the community in general,[146] a practice that was extremely common before the war.[147]

Despite the GCCA's recommendation to the most affluent members of the community to invest "their abundant savings ... that add up to many millions of Egyptian pounds"[148] in order to create new businesses in collaboration with Egyptians or to establish subsidiary companies in the interior in order to deal with unemployment, so as to restrain the internal migration movement from the small cities toward the main urban centers, it undertook no organized initiatives in this regard.[149] Inaction and a reluctance to invest were also reflected in the economic condition of the *koinotites,* which deteriorated in the postwar years. The economic problems of the *koinotites* dated to their commercial heyday in the late nineteenth and early twentieth centuries. However, thanks to benefactors and other dignitaries, the budget deficit was usually covered.[150] In the postwar years, though, the tradition of large-scale philanthropy "had been forgotten," as Manolis Yalourakis mentions: "Rich people asked that the budget deficits be covered through cuts and the nouveau-riche of the war did not participate in community life, and others contribute to the impoverishment of the clerks with mooted salaries."[151] Political instability, negative economic circumstances, legislation in favor of Egyptian citizens, the failure to conclude a treaty of establishment and the increasing tension in the Middle East after the creation of the State of Israel led most Greek big entrepreneurs not only to stop making big donations but also to gradually remove their capital from the country, in the search for "new horizons," that is, new markets, elsewhere.[152] The Egyptiot big-business community was not unique in this regard. As Filippos Dragoumis notes, the Greek capital that had been accumulated during the war followed the rest of the foreign capital in leaving the country.[153]

Even though the 23 July 1952 military coup brought political stability and the new government's officials regularly underlined the importance of foreign capital for Egypt's development, the investment of private foreign and local capital remained low during the first years of the new regime.

One of the main priorities of the new regime upon consolidating its power was Egypt's industrialization, in which it envisaged a role for foreign investors.[154] In May 1953 the Egyptian government announced its intention to ease the requirements for obtaining a residence permit for foreigners willing to invest more than LE 20,000, either in a new industry or in an existing firm.[155] To encourage private capital investments, a set of laws was promulgated in 1953 and 1954, and Nasser exhorted Greek businessmen to invest in industry, a move that could also ease unemployment. Even since the end of the war, the demand for highly qualified technicians and scientists had increased, as Nasser needed them to support the army and boost industry. This need was even greater after the Suez Crisis, when Nasser sought replacements for the French and British technicians he had expelled.[156] However, only a small number of highly qualified Greek technicians existed.[157]

Egyptiot businessmen were, generally speaking, reluctant to make large investments in industry. Overall, foreign and Egyptian businessmen did not respond positively to the new regime's efforts to encourage investment. Company Law 138/1947 and the mines and quarries law, which concerned the Egyptianization of big foreign oil companies, had created a potentially dangerous legal precedent.[158] The agrarian reform of August 1952 did little to boost the confidence of private capital holders in the new regime. A new law limited the amount of land that an individual could own to 200 *feddans* (84 hectares). At that time less than 6 percent of the population owned 65 percent of the land in Egypt. Under that law, the state took over any holding in excess of 200 *feddans,* paying for it with long-term bonds, and distributed it to landless peasants.[159] In addition, Nasser's decision to participate in the Bandung Conference in April 1955 and the rapprochement with the Soviet Union, confirmed by the Czech arms deal of September 1955, did not contribute to the establishment of trust between the new regime and foreign big businessmen. This was also visible in the everyday contact between them. As Robert Tignor points out, "The day-to-day relationships between the most powerful foreign firms and the Egyptian government bureaucrats produced countless examples of distrust and mutual recrimination."[160] The investment of private Egyptian and foreign capital fell by up to 65 percent from 1950 to 1956, while the increasing intervention of the state in the economy is evident in the increase in large public investments, which tripled during the same period.[161]

In such an economic environment, the introverted Egyptiot labor market disintegrated because it did not create enough new jobs for Greeks. The main reasons why unemployment did not skyrocket in the mid-1950s was the departure of foreigners, which created openings for others, and the departure of the Egyptiots in particular.

ON THE ROAD TO THE EXODUS

The Suez Crisis had a direct and indirect impact on the labor market. The departure of French, British, and Jews swayed a number of Greeks to leave Egypt as well, further destabilizing the local economy and, as a consequence, the labor market. The military intervention and the resulting uncertainty pushed companies into restricting investments even further. As a result, some Greeks lost their jobs, and the anxiety within the community about its professional future in Egypt intensified. Many of the unemployed, who now encountered even greater difficulties in finding a job, sought ways to migrate. Moreover, the sequestration of British, French, and Jewish companies, coupled with the January 1957 Egyptianization laws, shattered the confidence of the community leadership, even though the Egyptian government had shown signs of flexibility and understanding.

The law regarding the banks did not imminently affect the Greek capital or employees. About two hundred Greeks were employed in the four Greek banks, the shares of which would have to be transferred to Egyptian ownership after five years. The leadership and GMFA were less concerned about the employees than the long-term consequences of the Egyptianization of the banks on the community. Small- and medium-sized businesses preferred to deal with Greek banks because they were more accommodating than Egyptian or other foreign institutions in extending credit and debt repayment.[162] The community leadership and diplomats were suspicious that the Egyptian boards that would replace the Greek ones would be less cooperative. They were also concerned that big Egyptiot capital holders would have to turn increasingly to the Greek banks, since up to the Suez Crisis most of them preferred to deal with the large Western banks, which provided generous credit at relatively low interest.

The five-year deadline set for Egyptianization also included insurance companies, where Greek involvement was limited to just two small companies. The sale of insurance policies in Egypt, however, had hitherto provided employment for many Greek nationals, who constituted the majority of insurance agents. Although the law did not directly threaten the jobs of foreign employees of banks and insurance companies, at the end of the five-year period they would be obliged to work under a different hierarchy. The Egyptiot leadership and Greek government were most concerned about the law concerning the commercial representation of foreign firms and with the import of their products. According to the Alexandria consul general, around three hundred Greeks were commercial representatives, employing about three thousand Greek employees.[163]

The economic difficulties of the small- and medium-sized Greek enterprises, which had emerged in the 1940s and early 1950s, persisted after the Suez Crisis period. Turnover fell gradually. A main reason for this was the departure of many foreign customers in the aftermath of the crisis. However, in a 1958 report, the GCCA mainly blamed Egyptian state intervention in commercial activities.[164] It mentioned the ban on the imports of certain products and that free trade terms were constantly modified for the worse. The state monopoly on the import and distribution of certain products, such as pharmaceuticals, tea, and coffee, also resulted in falling profit margins and increased operating costs. Greek coffee-grinders, for instance, protested that they were provided with less coffee than their Egyptian counterparts by the relevant state agency and, therefore, were forced to supplement their needs via the black market at much higher prices.

The unfavorable terms for retail trade had a serious impact especially on groceries, a sector that the Greeks had monopolized before World War II.[165] The price controls on many products, which the government imposed from the late 1940s and more vigorously after September 1952, had considerably limited the profit margins for Greek grocers. In parallel, inflation made imports from Greece difficult, whereas imports from other countries with weak currencies, such as the drachma, were restricted.[166] In the Alexandria district alone, the number of groceries gradually fell from 218 in 1936 to 62 in 1958 (–71.5 percent) (see table 5). In Cairo, on the other hand, the decline was less severe, falling from 67 in 1950 to 46 (–31.4 percent) in 1961.[167] During the same period other small stores, such as barbershops, bakeries, and tobacco stores, ran into economic difficulty, and their number in Alexandria fell considerably over twenty years (see table 5). Their turnover had fallen as their clientele dwindled. At the same time, small Egyptian shopkeepers profited from the rise in their standard of living and the increasing purchasing power of their compatriots, allowing them to offer the same products at lower prices.

According to the GCCA report, the position of the small and medium traders was hindered in many sectors because not only did their profits fall, but also tax increases forced them to use their accumulated capital to remain in business.[168]

In restaurants, bars, and liquor stores, the situation was equally unpleasant, particularly because licenses to serve alcohol became personal and nontransferable from 1951. Consequently, after a licensee passed away, the bar ceased to exist.[169] In addition, the departure of foreigners, the main alcohol consumers in Egypt, contributed to the fall in the number of these enterprises, as is evident from table 5. The contraction in turnover prevented entrepreneurs from investing and hiring additional staff. Under these circumstances, the basic concern of many of them was to transfer their capital abroad.

Self-employed professionals and scientists also faced difficulties because Egyptian graduates from Egyptian universities were successfully applying

Table 5. Greek businesses and professionals in the Alexandria district, 1936 and 1958

Profession/business	1936	1958	Difference in Percentage
Self-employed professionals			
Engineers	32	15	–53.1
Lawyers	85	28	–67
Doctors	109	76	–30.2
Dentists	21	18	–14.2
Shopkeepers			
Bakeries	58	15	–74.1
Dairies	11	5	–54.5
Tobacco shops	46	12	–73.9
Coffee shops	175	75	–57.1
Barber shops	43	24	–44.1
Butchers	6	1	–83.3
Liquor stores	64	12	–81.2
Groceries	218	62	–71.5
Restaurants/bars	61	24	–60.6
Services			
Maritime agencies	21	19	–9.5
Pawnshops	17	2	–88.2
Small manufacturers			
Furniture makers	14	4	–71.4
Confectioners	25	16	–36
Tailors	45	17	–62.2
Shoemakers	22	3	–86,3
Bookbinders	5	6	+ 20
Tanners	4	4	–
Trade			
Cotton merchants	59	5	–91.5
Leather traders	12	3	–75
Total	1,245	497	–60

Source: AGCCA/30b/Laws concerning foreigners' employment in Egypt, Note (n.d., n.p.).

for positions, which up to that point Greeks and other foreigners had covered.[170] Legislation also helped the Egyptians in this regard. From 1954, all new doctors or dentists, for example, had to be Egyptian citizens who had graduated from an Egyptian university or had their degrees recognized by the state.[171] The tendency for Egyptiots to study in Greece or other Western countries complicated their access to the labor market. This undoubtedly explains the decrease in the number of Greek doctors from 109 in 1936 to seventy-six in 1958 (–30.2 percent) in the Alexandria district (see table 5). In Port Said their number fell from 22 in 1950 to fourteen (–36.3 percent) in 1961.[172] A possible indication of the better adaptation of the Greek residents of Cairo to the postwar Egyptian reality is the fact that the number of doctors in the postwar era increased slightly, from sixty in 1950 to sixty-three in October 1961.[173]

To practice their profession after the closure of the Mixed Courts in 1949, lawyers and jurists, on the other hand, had to either cooperate with Egyptian lawyers or have an excellent command of the Arabic language. Additionally, in order to practice legally, they had to be graduates of an Egyptian university and to have trained in a lawyer's office for two years. Egyptiots who required legal services preferred to engage Egyptian lawyers, who were more aware of the situation in the country. Egyptiots who managed to learn Arabic properly or to be employed by joint-stock companies were not affected, but these must have been in the minority, as can be seen in table 5: of the eighty-five lawyers in the district of Alexandria in 1936, only twenty-eight (–67 percent) remained in 1958, while in Cairo the number decreased from fifty-five in 1947 to twenty-one in 1961 (–61.8 percent).[174]

The GCCA report also mentioned that only a few of the Egyptiot civil engineers, building contractors, or architects left in Egypt could still work satisfactorily. This was partly due to the lack of investment in real estate by foreigners. The Egyptian state, on the other hand, which was the main funder of public works in the second half of the 1950s, preferred to employ Egyptians. Consequently, the number of Egyptiot civil engineers fell from 32 in 1936 to 15 in 1958 (–53.1 percent) in the district of Alexandria alone (see table 5). In Cairo, on the other hand, where there was more interaction with the local element, the number of people practicing these professions increased from twenty in 1950 to twenty-six in 1961 (an increase of 23 percent).[175]

From the above data, it is evident that the same legislation and economic conditions affected the Greek labor market in various cities in different ways. If we assume that most of those who lost their jobs also left Egypt, it is clear that Alexandrian Greeks departed more easily. The Greeks of this port city were definitely more influenced by the departure of other foreigners, while in Cairo they proved to be more resilient. In the case of Port Said, the bombardment of the city during the Suez Crisis and the particular conditions created by the nationalization of the Suez Canal Company should also be taken into account.

A point worth noting is that the loss of a job by an individual did not necessarily lead to his or her departure from Egypt, since the newly unemployed person could change career or move to another Egyptian city. The reduction in the number of professionals is also due to the fact that the deceased were not replaced by younger people from the community in their business activities. There were a number of reasons for this. Either their business licenses had become personal and nontransferable, as in the case of liquor stores, or new legislation restricted the entrance into certain professions to Egyptian citizens. The latter applied to the medical, dental, stock-broking, and some other professions.[176]

Nevertheless, unlike small- and medium-sized enterprises or self-employed professionals, large Greek enterprises and industries did not suffer major losses during the same period. Rather, the opposite was the case. As we have seen, the expulsion of the British, French, and Jews after the Suez Crisis did create business opportunities for Greeks. The creation of the United Arab Republic in 1958 also had a positive effect, since the inclusion of Syria created a wider market for businesses. Despite the difficult economic conditions for the rest of the community, in 1959 the GCCA president, Yiagkos Chryssovergis, was able to tell its annual general meeting that big business was booming: "Not one important Greek company closed, was sold, or stopped functioning. On the contrary, most of them increased their capital."[177] The fact that large Egyptiot entrepreneurs and industrialists increased their profits during the 1950s is also confirmed by another source. Nikos Katapodis, the Greek embassy's second in command in the early 1960s, noted in his memoirs that "in contradistinction to what they claimed in order to get compensation from the Greek state, most wealthy Greeks actually made more money by remaining in Egypt."[178] This leads us to the assumption that the majority of those who remained in Egypt until the late 1950s were principally employees of the big Greek companies, which had not been affected by the wider economic difficulties and Egyptianization. Indeed, there were numerous such employees: almost 1,100 Greeks worked for the Salvagos and Koutarellis companies alone in early 1957 in Alexandria.[179]

However, the capital made by large Egyptiot businesses in the late 1950s was not invested in the country; rather, they sought to transfer it outside the country. The continuous lack of investment and the export of capital suggest that despite the increasing profitability of their ventures, the Greek business community was seemingly ready to depart, especially after the Suez Crisis. Writing after his "repatriation" in 1967, *Tachydromos* columnist Manolis Yia-

Iourakis describes the motivation of the Egyptiot upper class: "For as long as the Egyptian state did not 'touch' them, they were happy to remain in Egypt. ... Their logic was quite simple: 'We will remain as long as we earn money. While we remain we export our foreign currency and savings out of the country in order to find it intact when we are obliged to leave the country.'"[180] Egyptiot capital and those on high incomes began, however, to be affected by a number of concrete measures enacted from 1959 in the context of Nasserite socialism. In that year, the shares of joint-stock companies lost 40 percent of their value as a result of a law passed on 10 January 1959 that restricted the dividends to 10 percent of those of 1958.[181] Moreover, the value of these shares had already decreased because of regulations ordering the distribution of 25 percent of the profits to the workers and the increasing taxation of high incomes.[182]

The government's economic policy was based not on ethnic criteria but on political, economic, and social principles. Nasserite socialist policy did not target foreign but mainly private Egyptian capital. In this respect, the Economic Organization, which the state set up in January 1957, absorbed a significant number of private enterprises by mid-1960.[183] The Misr Bank, which controlled the country's twenty-four biggest industrial consortiums, was nationalized in February 1960. Additionally, the main media organizations and the pharmaceutical industry were nationalized in May and July 1960, respectively. This practice, combined with the nationalization of Belgian assets in January 1961, deeply worried big business. The constant appearance of new legislation concerning capital unsettled the foreign business community. They felt they were living in "a state of gloom, wondering where the axe would fall next," as one foreign journalist reported from Cairo,[184] while large Egyptiot Greek entrepreneurs in particular feared that "sooner or later their turn will come."[185] The state's continuous intervention in the private sector in 1959 and 1960 gradually reduced turnover in the larger private companies and industries to such a degree that, as Tignor notes, "even before ... the socialist laws of July 1961, big business had been rendered catatonic."[186]

NOTES

1. AGKA/K 136, 1931, Paris, 18 May 1937, Politis to Metaxas.
2. AYE/CS/1937/31/9/1, 1337, Cairo, 7 June 1937, Delmouzos to Metaxas.
3. Hossam M Issa, *Capitalisme et sociétés anonymes en Égypte. Essai sur le rapport entre structure sociale et droit* (Paris: Librairie générale de droit et de jurisprudence, 1970), 158–59.
4. Floresca Karanasou, "Egyptianisation: The 1947 Company Law and the Foreign Communities in Egypt" (Ph.D. diss., Oxford University, 1992), 32–33.

5. AYE/CS/1937/31/3/1, 328, Cairo, 15 Feb 1937, Delmouzos to Metaxas.
6. Caroline Piquet, *La Compagnie du Canal de Suez. Une concession française en Égypte, 1888–1956* (Paris: Presses de l'Université de Paris-Sorbonne, 2008), 132–33.
7. Al El Amary, "La crise du chômage en Égypte et ailleurs, ses causes et ses remèdes," *L'Égypte contemporaine* 164 (May 1936): 478.
8. Lucie Ryzova, "Egyptianizing Modernity through the 'New Effendiya': Social and Cultural Construction of the Middle Class in Egypt under the Monarchy," in *Re-Envisioning Egypt, 1919–1952,* ed. Arthur Goldschmidt et al. (Cairo: American University in Cairo Press, 2005), 124–63.
9. Alexis Alexandris, *The Greek Minority of Istanbul and Greek-Turkish Relations, 1814–1974* (Athens: Centre for Asia Minor Studies, 1992), 110; Ayhan Aktar, "Turkification Policies in the Early Republican Era," in *Turkish Literature and Cultural Memory: "Multiculturalism" as a Literary Theme after 1980,* ed. Catharina Dufft (Wiesbaden: Harrassowitz, 2009), 29–62.
10. AYE/CS/1939/B/10/AC, 2344, Cairo, 5 October 1938, Kapsalis to GMFA.
11. Ibid.
12. AYE/CS1937/31/9/1, 1337, Cairo, 7 June 1937, Delmouzos to Metaxas.
13. AYE/CS/1937/31/9/1, 14637, Athens, 12 July 1937, Metaxas to Delmouzos.
14. AYE/CS/1937/31/3/1, 1989, Cairo, 18 October 1937, Delmouzos to the Greek consular authorities of Egypt.
15. AYE/CS/1937/31/9/1, 1654, Cairo, 27 July 1937, Delmouzos to Metaxas.
16. Robert Tignor, *State, Private Enterprise and Economic Change in Egypt, 1918–1952* (Princeton, NJ: Princeton University Press, 1984), 188–93; Jean Ducruet, *Les Capitaux Européens au Proche-Orient* (Paris: Presses Universitaires de France, 1964), 305.
17. AYE/CS/1937/31/9/1, 1654, Cairo, 27 July 1937, Delmouzos to Metaxas.
18. AGCCA/Statistics and census of the Greek community, 1949–50, list of occupations in the consular districts, Alexandria, 28 December 1950.
19. Athanassiadis was director of the Xenakios School of the GKC from 1929 to 1944 and of the French High School in Cairo from 1944 to 1948.
20. Giorgis Athanassiadis, *O paroikiakos ellinismos kai i paideia tou* [The Hellenism of the community and its education] (Cairo, 1948), 23.
21. AYE/CS/1952/49/4/1/1, 5, Alexandria, 12 January 1952, Liatis to the Cairo embassy.
22. Anthony Gorman, "Repatriation, Migration or Readjustment: Egyptian Greek Dilemmas of the 1950s," in *Greek Diaspora and Migration since 1700: Society, Politics and Culture,* ed. Dimitris Tziovas (Farnham: Ashgate, 2009), 62.
23. Ibid.
24. AYE/CS/1957/22/5/1/1, 29, Alexandria, 28 January 1957, Argyropoulos to the Cairo embassy.
25. AYE/CS/1961/16/1/3/1, 171, Alexandria, 9 February 1961, Theodoropoulos to Lambros.
26. Archives of the Intergovernmental Committee for European Migration (AICEM)/Egypt 1959–65, Note, Emigration of Europeans from Egypt, Alexandra Ioannides, Athens, 13 March 1961.

27. International Labour Office, *Yearbook of Labour Statistics, 1960* (Geneva: International Labour Office, 1960), 278.
28. CADN/Consulat de France à Port Said/78, Coût de la vie dans la circonscription de Port Said, Port Said, 29 October 1955.
29. AYE/CS/1962/30/4/1, 139, Alexandria, 16 January 1962, Theodoropoulos to GMFA.
30. AYE/CS/1962/43/5/1/1, Report on the mission of the general secretary of the Ministry of Social Affairs in Egypt (n.d., n.p.).
31. *O Paroikos,* 3 October 1955, 3.
32. Michail Melas, *Anamniseis enos presveos* [Memoirs of an ambassador] (Athens, 1965), 163–64.
33. Alexander Kitroeff, *The Greeks in Egypt, Ethnicity and Class, 1917–1937* (Oxford: Ithaca Press, 1989), 144–51.
34. *Annuaire statistique 1937–1938* (Cairo: Imprimerie nationale, 1939); *Annuaire statistique 1947–1948* (Cairo: Imprimerie nationale, 1951).
35. AYE/CS/1946/36/3, 2398, Cairo, 7 June 1946, Sofianos to Triantafyllidis.
36. Manolis Yalourakis, *I Aigyptos ton Ellinon* [Egypt of the Greeks] (Athens: Mitropolis, 1967), 201.
37. AYE/CS/1941–43/24, 891, Alexandria, 5 March 1942, Valtis to Pappas.
38. Ibid.
39. AYE/CS/1941–43/24, 7177, Alexandria, 12 February 1942, Valtis to Pappas.
40. Alexander Kitroeff, "I elliniki paroikia stin Aigypto kai o defteros pagkosmios polemos" [The Greek community in Egypt and World War II], *Mnimon* 9 (1983): 15.
41. Panagiotis Kanellopoulos, *Imerologio 31 Martiou 1942–4 Ianouariou 1945* [Diary 31 March 1942–4 January 1945] (Athens: Kedros, 1977), 149, cited in Kitroeff, "I elliniki paroikia," 15.
42. AYE/CS/1941–43/24, 7177, Alexandria, 12 February 1942, Valtis to Pappas.
43. AYE/CS/1941–43/24, 891, Alexandria, 5 March 1942, Valtis to Pappas.
44. Ibid.
45. AYE/CS/1946/36/3, 2398, Cairo, 7 June 1946, Sofianos to Triantafyllidis.
46. Yiannis Anastassiadis, *Mnimes apo tin drasi tou aristerou kinimatos tou aigyptioti ellinismou* [Memoirs from the action of the left movement of Egyptiot Hellenism] (Athens, 1993), 127.
47. AYE/CS/1944/40/1, 1888, Port Said, 14 August 1944, Negrepontis to Pappas.
48. AYE/CS/1945/15/4, Alexandria, 24 April 1945, Salvagos to Voulgaris.
49. AYE/CS/1945/15/4, 4900, Cairo, 6 July 1945, Pappas to Voulgaris.
50. Marta Petricioli, *Oltre il mito: L'Egitto degli Italiani, 1917–1947* (Milan: Bruno Mondadori, 2007), 421–22.
51. AYE/CS/1945/15/4, Alexandria, 3 November 1944, Salvagos to Pappas.
52. Karanasou, "Egyptianisation," 327.
53. Yalourakis, *I Aigyptos,* 454.
54. AYE/CS/1957/22/5/1/1, 29, Alexandria, 28 January 1957, Argyropoulos to Cairo embassy.

55. Katerina Trimi-Kyrou, "The Big Decision: Literary Narrative as a Historical Source," *Journal of the Hellenic Diaspora* 35, no. 2 (2009): 76.
56. Howard E Aldrich and Roger Waldinger, "Ethnicity and Entrepreneurship," *Annual Review of Sociology* 16 (1990): 131–32.
57. AYE/CS/1961/16/3/2/1, Cairo, 21 November 1961, Yiannakakis to Cairo embassy.
58. For Greeks and other groups of foreigners working for foreign companies, see Nancy Y Reynolds, "Entangled Communities: Interethnic Relationships among Urban Salesclerks and Domestic Workers in Egypt, 1927–61," *European Review of History* 19, no. 1 (2012): 113–39.
59. AGCCA/I Melissa, Association of Greek Grocers of Alexandria, 1938–42, Speech of M Michailidis delivered to the general assembly, 5 June 1938.
60. Viola Shafik, *Popular Egyptian Cinema: Gender, Class and Nation* (Cairo: American University in Cairo Press, 2007), 20.
61. Nancy Y Reynolds, *A City Consumed: Urban Commerce, the Cairo Fire, and the Politics of Decolonization in Egypt* (Stanford, CA: Stanford University Press, 2012).
62. Anne Le Gall-Kazazian, "Les Arméniens d'Egypte (XIXe–XXe): La reforme à l'échelle communautaire," in *Entre reforme sociale et mouvement national. Identité et modernisation en Egypte, 1882–1962*, ed. Alain Roussillon (Cairo: CEDEJ, 1995), 501–17, here 516–17; Le Gall-Kazazian, "Etre Arménien," in *Alexandrie 1860–1960. Un modèle éphémère de convivialité: communautés et identité cosmopolite*, ed. Robert Ilbert and Ilios Yannakakis (Paris: Autrement, 1992), 68–80, here 80.
63. Michael Laskier, *The Jews of Egypt, 1920–1970* (New York: New York University Press, 1992), 164–297; Gudrun Kramer, *The Jews in Modern Egypt, 1914–1952* (London: Tauris, 1989), 205–21; Joel Beinin, *The Dispersion of Egyptian Jewry* (Berkeley, CA: University of California Press, 1998), 70–72, 156–63, 181–85.
64. Karanasou, "Egyptianisation," 345–54.
65. Petricioli, *Oltre il mito,* 443–79.
66. AYE/CS/1944/40/4, Alexandria, 26 October 1943, Maxouris to Tsouderos.
67. CADN/Consulat de France à Alexandrie/367, 509/AL, Alexandria, 8 September 1947, Filliol to French Ministry of Foreign Affairs (FMFA).
68. "The Greek Idle Capital," *Bulletin of the GCCA* 584 (31 August 1948): 3.
69. Karanasou, "Egyptianisation," 345–51.
70. Kramer, *The Jews,* 218.
71. AYE/CS/1948/94/4/4/2, 230, Alexandria, 11 October 1947, Zamarias to Triantafyllidis.
72. Kramer, *The Jews,* 221.
73. Colette Dubois, "La nation et les Français d'Outre-Mer: Rapatriés ou sinistrés de la décolonisation?," in *L'Europe retrouvée: Les migrations de la décolonisation,* ed. Jean-Luis Miège and Colette Dubois (Paris: L'Harmattan, 1994), 86; Jean-Jacques Jordi, *De l'exode à l'exil. Rapatriés et Pieds-Noirs en France* (Paris: L'Harmattan, 1993), 21–23.
74. AYE/CS/1957/22/9/1/1, 6544, Cairo, 29 March 1957, Lambros to GMFA.
75. Iskandar Assabghy Bey, *La nationalité égyptienne. Etude historique et critique* (Cairo, 1950), 31.

76. Egyptian Law 19/1929, Article 7.
77. AYE/CS/1937/31/9/1, 1654. Cairo, 27 July 1937, Delmouzos to Metaxas.
78. Robert Ilbert, "Qui est Grec? La nationalité comme enjeu en Égypte (1830–1930)," *Relations Internationales* 54 (1988): 139–60.
79. AYE/CS/1946/36/3, 24505, Confidential note of the GMFA (n.p.), 1946.
80. AYE/CS/1946/36/2, 7233, Cairo, 8 October 1945, Pappas to Politis.
81. Ibid., 96–125.
82. AGCCA/57, Royal Consulate General of Greece in Alexandria, 1947–55, Confidential note on various issues concerning the Consulate General of Greece for the review of the year 1948 (n.d./n.p.).
83. AYE/CS/1948/94/1/1/1, 917, Cairo, 11 March 1948, Triantafyllidis to GMFA.
84. AGCCA/57, Royal Consulate General of Greece in Alexandria, 1947–55, Confidential note on various issues concerning the Consulate General of Greece for the review of the year 1948 (n.d./n.p.).
85. AYE/CS/1951/95/2/3/3, 21, Alexandria, 29 January 1951, Liatis to Triantafyllidis.
86. AGCCA/57, Royal Consulate General of Alexandria, 1947–55, General observations on the community life during 1949 and on the Greek-Egyptian commerce during the year, Alexandria, 29 November 1949.
87. Ibid.
88. AYE/CS1951/95/2/3/1, 2233, Cairo, 8 July 1951, Triantafyllidis to GMFA.
89. AYE/CS/1948/59/3/3/2, 2859, Cairo, 13 August 1948, Triantafyllidis to GMFA.
90. AYE/CS/1950/14/4/1, 178, Cairo, 2 March 1950, Sevastopoulos to Greek Press Ministry.
91. Mohammed Hanafi, *Loi No 160 du 1950 sur la Nationalité Egyptienne* (n.d., n.p.), 4–5.
92. Ibid., 5.
93. AYE/CS/1951/6/1/6/2, 52668, Application of Alexandros Kosmatos or Mazarakis, Alexandria, 15 January 1951.
94. See Dimitrios Zerbinis, *Histoire d'une entreprise industrielle. The Kafr-el-Zayat Cotton Company SAE: 1894–1956* (Alexandria: Société de publications égyptiennes, 1956).
95. AYE/CS/1951/6/1/6/2, 52664, Application of Periklis Glymenopoulos, Tanta, 14 December 1950.
96. AYE/CS/1951/6/1/6/2, 52662, Application of Christoforos Mantikas, Cairo, 4 January 1951.
97. Ibid.
98. AYE/CS/1951/6/1/6/2, 52661, Application of Antonios Kaoustos, Alexandria, 8 August 1950.
99. Ibid.
100. AYE/CS/1951/6/1/6/4, 3908, Application of Konstantinos Makris, Alexandria, 15 May 1950.
101. AYE/CS/1949/159/6/1/1, 418, Cairo, 2 February 1949, Triantafyllidis to GMFA; AYE/CS/1948/94/4/4/2, Information bulletin of the vice-consulate of Minya, attached to a document dated 1 October 1948.

102. AYE/CS/1948/94/4/4/2, 350, Zagazig, 3 September 1947, Fragkoulis to Triantafyllidis.
103. Karanasou, "Egyptianisation," 119–20.
104. AGCCA/57, Royal Consulate General of Greece in Alexandria, 1947–55, Confidential note on various issues concerning the Consulate General of Greece for the review of the year 1948. (n.d./n.p.); Karanasou, "Egyptianisation," 340.
105. AYE/CS/1954/131/1, 149, Suez, 28 January 1954, Papaioannou to Cairo embassy.
106. AYE/CS/1952/48/1/1/1, Secret, Athens, 21 May 1952, Report concerning the position of Greeks in Egypt, Dragoumis to Venizelos, 17.
107. AYE/CS/1948/94/4/4/2, Suez, 23 September 1947, Igglesis to Pappas; AYE/CS/1952/48/1/1/1, Secret, Athens, 21 May 1952, Report concerning the position of Greeks in Egypt, Dragoumis to Venizelos, 19.
108. Ibid.
109. Sofianos Chryssostomidis, "Elliniki paroikia Aigyptou: i exodos" [The Greek community of Egypt: the exodus], *Archiotaxio* 4 (2002): 120.
110. AGCCA/40/Actions of the GCCA concerning the diplomatic authorities, 777/52, Alexandria, 10 September 1952, Sakellarios to Smyrniadis.
111. Anastassiadis, *Mnimes,* 23.
112. AYE/CS/1952/50/1/1/1, 2437, Cairo, 29 September 1952, Melas to GMFA.
113. For example, this occurred in the case of the GKA. See Statute of the GKA, 1961, Article 2.
114. AYE/CS/1947/10/1, 11767/E/2, Athens, 7 April 1947, Melas to Triantafyllidis.
115. AYE/CS/1961/16/1/3/1, 174, Alexandria, 21 February 1961, Baizos to Averoff.
116. AYE/CS/1961/16/1/3/1, DAD 42-11, Athens, 23 February 1961, Averoff to Baizos.
117. AYE/CS/1939/B/3/AC, Cairo, 17 January 1939, Kapsalis to GMFA.
118. Kostas Tsagkaradas, *Ta provlimata tis xeniteias* [The troubles of living abroad] (Alexandria: S. Grivas, 1946), 99–100.
119. *O Paroikos,* January/February 1957.
120. Chryssostomidis, "Elliniki paroikia," 120.
121. GPR/Period 4/Session 2/Meeting 43, 12 February 1957, Speech of K Tsatsos, 37.
122. AYE/CS/1948/94/4/4/2, 177/48, Alexandria, 9 February 1948, Pandelidis to Triantafyllidis; AGCCA/62/Commercial and financial information on Argentina, 1540/49/8, Alexandria, 13 September 1949, Pandelidis to Kapsabelis.
123. AYE/CS/1948/94/4/4/2, 307, Cairo, 20 February 1948, Mavrokefalos to Cairo embassy.
124. AYE/CS/1954/131/1, 92, Alexandria, 25 February 1954, Argyropoulos to Melas.
125. AGCCA/57/Royal Consulate General of Alexandria, 1947–55, General observations on the *paroikia* life during 1949 and on Greek-Egyptian commerce during the year, Alexandria, 29 November 1949.
126. Nantes Diplomatic Archives Centre (CADN)/Consulat de France à Port-Saïd/78.
127. Karanasou, "Egyptianisation," 342.

128. AYE/CS/1952/48/1/1/1, Secret, Athens, 21 May 1952, Report concerning the position of Greeks in Egypt, Dragoumis to Venizelos, 18–19; "The Greek Inactive Capital," *Bulletin of the GCCA* 584 (31 August 1948): 1–4.
129. Karanasou, "Egyptianisation," 341.
130. AYE/CS/1952/49/3/1/1, 9086, Alexandria, 4 December 1952, Liatis to Cairo embassy.
131. AGCCA/73/Employment office, Talha, 2 July 1947, Vatsakis to Viscovitch.
132. Ibid.
133. AGCCA/73/Employment office, Talha, 6 May 1948, Maschas to Zerbinis.
134. AGCCA/73/Employment office, Ibrahimia, 19 December 1947, Papadopoulou to GCCA.
135. AGCCA/73/Employment office, Kafr el-Zayat, 14 April 1947, David to GCCA.
136. AGCCA/73/Employment office, Alexandria, 19 April 1947, Viscovitch to David.
137. AYE/CS/1954/131/1, 92, Alexandria, 25 February 1954, Argyropoulos to Melas.
138. AGCCA/73/Employment office, 7176, Alexandria, 24 August 1948 Zamarias to GCCA; AGCCA/73/Employment office, 2066/48/35, Alexandria, 2 September 1948, Zerbinis to Zamarias; AYE/CS/1948/94/4/4/2, 177/48, Alexandria, 9 February 1948, Pandelidis to Triantafyllidis.
139. AYE/CS/1948/94/4/4/2, 48431, Athens, 2 Decebmer 1948, Kontoumas to Triantafyllidis.
140. AGCCA/73/Employment office, 623, Cairo, 30 November 1948, Eliopoulos to GCCA.
141. AYE/CS/1950/2227/D/1, 949, Suez, 10 January 1950, Tsourkas to Triantafyllidis.
142. AGCCA/Rearrangement of situation related to the migration of Greeks from Egypt under the auspices of the WCC/ICEM. Notes of a conversation between A Liatis, Greek consul general to Alexandria, D Cosmadopoulos, vice-consul to Alexandria, N Sakellarios, GCCA president, E Viscovitch, GCCA director, and MC King, representative of the WCC Service to Refugees, at the Greek Consulate General in Alexandria. Alexandria, 11 October 1952.
143. AYE/CS/1952/49/4/1/1, 332 A/1, Port Said, 29 January 1952, Avramidis to the Greek embassy in Cairo.
144. *O Paroikos,* 3 October 1955, 3.
145. AYE/CS/1946/36/3, 22061, Alexandria, 20 June 1946, Zamarias to Cairo embassy.
146. AYE/CS/1952/48/1/1/3812, Cairo, 10 July 1952, Georgiadis to the Greek embassy in Cairo.
147. Kitroeff, *The Greeks,* 144–46.
148. "The Greek Inactive Capital," *Bulletin of the GCCA* 584 (31 August 1948): 1–4.
149. Ibid.
150. Euthymios Souloyannis, *I thesi ton Ellinon stin Aigypto* [The position of Greeks in Egypt] (Athens: ELIA, 1999), 220.
151. Yalourakis, *I Aigyptos,* 454–55.
152. In a letter addressed to the Greek Finance Ministry, Ioannis Kontoumas, a GMFA official, wrote about the "tendency" of the Egyptiot business commu-

nity, namely big merchants and industrialists, to transfer their business to other countries. See chapters 4 and 5 for more details on the matter of exporting capital (AYE/CS/1949/159/5/2/2, 8378, Athens, 21 January 1949, Kontoumas to Greek Finance Ministry).

153. AYE/CS/1952/48/1/1/1, Secret, Athens, 21 May 1952, Report concerning the position of Greeks in Egypt, Dragoumis to Venizelos, 18–19.
154. Robert Mabro, *The Egyptian Economy, 1952–1972* (Oxford: Clarendon, 1974), 107.
155. Robert Tignor, "Foreign Capital, Foreign Communities, and the Egyptian Revolution of 1952," in *Egypt from Monarchy to Republic: A Reassessment of Revolution and Change,* ed. Shimon Shamir (Boulder, CO: Westview Press, 1995), 108.
156. Judith Cochran, *Education in Egypt* (London: Croom Helm, 1986), 50.
157. AGKS/Readjustment of the statutes according to Law 384/1956, Agapitidis Committee report, June 1957.
158. Tignor, "Foreign Capital," 107.
159. Mabro, *The Egyptian Economy,* 58–61.
160. Robert Tignor, *Capitalism and Nationalism at the End of Empire: State and Business in Decolonizing Egypt, Nigeria and Kenya, 1945–1963* (Princeton, NJ: Princeton University Press, 1999), 113.
161. Jean Ducruet, *Les capitaux européens au Proche-Orient* (Paris: Presses Universitaires de France, 1964), 326.
162. AYE/CS/1961/21/15/1/1, 574, Alexandria, 13 June 1961, Theodoropoulos to Cairo embassy; AYE/CS/1961/16/1/3/2, 485, Cairo, 14 March 1961, Yiannakakis to Cairo embassy.
163. AYE/CS/1957/22/5/1/1, 29, Alexandria, 28 January 1957, Argyropoulos to Cairo embassy.
164. AGCCA/30b/Laws concerning foreigners' employment in Egypt, Report draft for the Greek Consulate General of Alexandria concerning the Egyptian economy and the situation of Hellenism in Alexandria in 1958 (n.d., n.p.).
165. Kitroeff, *The Greeks,* 126–28.
166. AYE/CS/1951/143/4/2/1, 2, Secret, 17 October 1951, Pechlivanos to Stefanou.
167. AGCCA/Statistics and census of the Greek community, List of the occupations of Greeks per district based on the note on the occupations of Greeks of Egypt, Alexandria, 28 December 1950; AYE/CS/1961/21/15/2/2, Census of the occupations of the Greeks in Cairo (n.d., n.p.).
168. Ibid.
169. AYE/CS/1951/143/4/2/1, 2, Secret, 17 October 1951, Pechlivanos to Cairo embassy.
170. Ibid.
171. AYE/CS/1963/44/5/2/1/2, 553, Cairo, 18 December 1961, Yiannakakis to Cairo embassy.
172. Ibid.; AGCCA/Statistics and census of the Greek community, List of the occupations of Greeks per district based on the note on the occupations of Greeks of Egypt, Alexandria, 28 December 1950; AYE/CS/1961/21/15/1/1, 1641, Port Said, 8 June 1961, Daratzikis to Lambros.

173. AGCCA/Statistics and census of the Greek community, List of the occupations of Greeks per district based on the note on the occupations of Greeks of Egypt, Alexandria, 28 December 1950; AYE/CS/1961/21/15/2/2, Census of the occupations of the Greeks in Cairo (n.d., n.p.).
174. Ibid.
175. Ibid.
176. AGCCA/Correspondence, 1960–63, Confidential note on labor issues of the Greeks in Egypt, May 1962; GPR/Period 4/Session 2/Meeting 43, 12 February 1957, Speech of G Kartalis, 36.
177. AGCCA/General assemblies, 1952–73, Speech of the GCCA president Yiagkos Chryssovergis delivered to the general assembly on 17 December 1959 in Alexandria.
178. Nikos Katapodis, *Skorpia fylla tis diplomatikis mou zois* [Aspects of my diplomatic career] (Athens: Potamos, 2004), 32–33.
179. AYE/CS/1957/22/5/1/1, 29, Alexandria, 28 January 1957, Argyropoulos to Cairo embassy.
180. Yalourakis, *I Aigyptos*, 212.
181. AGCCA/12/Various statistical data, Note GCCA, 1.
182. AYE/CS/1961/16/3/2/2, 745, Secret, Alexandria, 26 July 1961, Theodoropoulos to Lambros.
183. Tignor, *Capitalism*, 158–59.
184. Patrick O'Brien, *The Revolution in Egypt's Economic System, from Private to Socialism, 1952–1965* (London: Oxford University Press, 1966), 126.
185. AYE/CS/1961/16/1/3/1, 171, Alexandria, 9 February 1961, Baizos to Lambros.
186. Tignor, *Capitalism*, 159.

Chapter Four

Education

"The Greeks of Egypt, deprived of any substantial knowledge of Arabic, which they have always disregarded, and mainly employed in clerical and not technical professions, do not have the required skills to fully and successfully participate in the Egyptian economy that is under transformation."[1] At the peak of exodus of Egyptiots from Egypt in 1962, this is how Harilaos Zamarias, Greece's ambassador to Cairo, explained the mass departure to his foreign minister, Evangelos Averoff. Having served as vice-consul in the early 1930s and consul general in the second half of the 1940s in Alexandria, Zamarias was very familiar with the Egyptiot reality. The matter of Arabic knowledge and professional orientation he mentioned did not suddenly emerge in the early 1960s. The community leadership and the public sphere had openly discussed these issues since the interwar period, especially after the abolition of the Capitulations, and they were strongly related to the Egyptiot educational system in the communal schools.

This chapter discusses the issue of education as another structural element—along with labor—of communal life. After an examination of the possibilities offered by the Egyptian educational system, it focuses on the way Greek communal education was structured, its targets, the educational outlets associated with other foreign communities, and the issues of readjustment that emerged in view of and after the abolition of the Capitulations. Education was a mechanism that could have created the contact points between the community and the professional and cultural Egyptian context that was under transformation. Education had an inherent disadvantage when it came to encouraging change, though: it required time to bear fruit. Its role, however, in the adjustment process emerged as a major issue during the period under scrutiny, for two reasons: first, in regard to the connection of the curriculum with the Egyptian labor market, and, second, in regard to the teaching of Arabic. Both parameters were a prerequisite for better career prospects and closer links with Egyptians. In this light, this chapter examines if and to what extent the Egyptiot curriculum undermined the long-term prospects of the Greeks in Egypt.

EGYPTIAN EDUCATION FOR A FEW

In 1927, the illiteracy rate of the Egyptian population was 87.35 percent (78.2 percent for men and 96.5 percent for women).[2] This extremely high percentage is not surprising given the fact that at the beginning of the twentieth century, the government allocated little more than 1 percent of the annual state budget to education.[3] This fact prompted the reaction of the Egyptian intelligentsia in the interwar period, as they perceived this British-inspired policy as evidence of the intention of the colonial power to keep the local population, almost in its entirety, uneducated to justify its presence in Egypt and to indirectly force them into engaging with agriculture. The latter choice was linked to the development of the cotton industry, the cultivation of its raw material being promoted during the second half of the nineteenth and beginning of the twentieth centuries at the expense of industrial development. Education funding increased to 3.4 percent of the annual budget in 1910, to gradually reach 7.3 percent in 1930.[4] Egyptian educational policy was marked by the new Egyptian constitution of 1923, which first mandated that primary education be free and compulsory for all children from the age of six to twelve.

In the interwar period, an increasing percentage of the young Egyptian population passed through the educational system, which heightened their job expectations and prospects. Greeks and other foreigners considered the much-cited "awakening" mentioned in the sources as one of the main causes for the pressures that they began to face in the labor market. The notion of "awakening" complemented, in a way, the Egyptiots' idea about their contribution to Egypt's development. In reality though, it referred to the transition of the Egyptian economy and society from traditional structures to a capitalist-type economy. This economy had as its epicenter the urban centers, where industrial activities were concentrated. A characteristic of this transition was the urbanization of the Egyptian population and its increasing access to education, especially from the 1920s. The "awakening" argument, though, is revealing of the colonial way of thinking of members of the community and the Greek state. It reflects the mentality of cultural and, partly, class superiority that they had toward the indigenous residents of the country, which many Egyptiots called their "second" home. Thus, they painted the picture of a lazy, dormant East, which they helped emerge from lethargy, to an "awakening" and progress. Through the use of such orientalist stereotypes, the colonial powers monopolized their action across the globe. In Egypt, their use was also linked to the attribution to Egyptians of characteristics "as less civilized, potentially fanatical, and usually unreliable."[5] In parallel, this very same logic suggested that Egypt did not have the right to legislate as a sovereign nation-state and, consequently, distinguish between Egyptian and foreign citizens.

Initially, Egyptians with a primary education could expect to have a career in occupations in which lower-class foreigners and, especially, Greeks were also engaged: as small shopkeepers, chauffeurs, small-scale traders, and so on. This social group of Greeks was the first to recognize the emerging competition from the Egyptian lower class. Egyptians who continued to the secondary level could hope for a clerical career, as the education system was oriented to preparing personnel for the state bureaucracy or private enterprises. For Egyptians, this path represented the entry into the world of professional security, tenure, and pension rights as well as a chance to advance to the upper levels of the social hierarchy.[6] The Egyptians found themselves in an advantageous position in comparison to foreign citizens because of, first, the ethnic solidarity that developed among them and, second, their way of life, which was frugal in comparison to that of the mainly urban-based foreigners. The quality of education provided by Egyptian schools never reached the level of the foreign establishments. In 1956, illiteracy among Egyptians was still high, at 75 percent,[7] and the Nasser regime emphasized the right of education for all.[8]

The Egyptian education system had little appeal for the majority of foreigners residing in the country. However, 771 pupils with Greek citizenship attended Egyptian schools in the 1948–49 school year according to scholar statistics.[9] If we add persons of Greek origin with Egyptian citizenship, this number would undoubtedly be greater, but no statistics exist for that specific group. Attending an Egyptian school usually meant integration in Egyptian society. These Greeks probably came from the lower class, who mostly lived in smaller cities in the interior, where Greek education was not so organized at all levels and where contact with natives was more frequent and intense than in cities such as Alexandria, Port Said, or even Cairo.[10] Parents who sent their children to such schools did not envisage a future for their children outside Egypt; on the contrary, they aimed to achieve a form of "readjustment," which was tantamount to integration or assimilation into Egyptian society, a path that Greek state representatives frowned upon.[11]

The contempt with which members of the community elite referred to those who sought to integrate themselves is indicative of the mentality of a part of the community and how it viewed its links to Egypt. Kostas Tsagkaradas is an example.[12] Born in Zagora in the Pilio region, he moved to Asyut in 1914, where he became involved in the cotton trade. A literary man and community dignitary in Upper Egypt, he was president of the Greek Koinotita in Asyut (1920–31) and representative of the Minya vice-consulate. In his 1946 book *Ta provlimata tis xeniteias* (The troubles of living abroad), he referred to those Greeks condescendingly as "prisoners with life sentences in Upper Egypt."[13] According to him, most of them were of Greek origin, usually holders of Egyptian citizenship, and basically lived in the cities of Upper Egypt. They spoke Arabic more fluently than Greek, which is why he contemptuously called them "Greek-speaking Egyptians." They had chosen to marry Egyptians, either Christians or Muslims, a choice that relegated them to the margins of the community, if not excluding them from it altogether. There are no reliable statistics on the exact number of those who chose to integrate in Egyptian society through the local educational system. It seems that they stayed outside the Greek educational system and Egyptiot Greek reality and thus, in Tsagkaradas's eyes, could not be considered pure Greeks:

> They have chosen to be educated in the Egyptian educational system and to acquire the baccalaureate of a secondary school or to have the diploma of a commercial or technical school of the country in order to be appointed as civil servants or to a bank. They did not spend one single day learning Greek. They placed their children from the age of five or six in Egyptian state or propaganda schools with the deliberate intent to safeguard them from being ever racially "decontaminated." Needless to say, these children speak an undefined form of Greek. Their parents not only obtained Egyptian citizenship, but they have worked hard to erase whatever may remind them their racial origin.[14]

From the Egyptian perspective, Greeks who sought to integrate in the political, cultural, and social life of Egypt were very much welcome. Such was the case of Athanassios Radopoulos, who was elected in the local and provincial elections for the National Union in July and November 1959. Radopoulos was born on the island of Syros in 1912 and migrated as a child with his family to Mansoura. He graduated from a Greek school and then studied agronomy at Cairo University and received Egyptian citizenship. His local fellows called him Khawaga Thanasi (Thanasi the Lord/European), and it was under this name that he contested the 1959 election, in which he topped the poll in the Abu El Matamir region, where the Tsanaklis estate, of which he was director, was located. According to an article in *Images*, he spoke Arabic more fluently than Greek.[15] His election was proof, according to an Egyptian journalist, that the Egyptian people rejected any racial discrimination once foreigners proved their strong links with Egypt. Nasser himself, when he visited Greece in June 1960, referred to the elected politician "with the Greek name."[16] The cases of Radopoulos and the "Greek-speaking Egyptians" are indicative of the different narrations of members of the community elite and Egyptian society as regards the issue of integration/assimilation of Greeks in Egypt.

Let's return to the decision of some parents to send their children to Egyptian schools. This choice was determined not only by the willingness of "Greek-speaking Egyptians" to send their children to Egyptian schools, but also by the unwillingness of some Greek schools to accept these children as pupils. For instance, the Greek schools run by the GKA accepted pupils of Greek origin with Egyptian citizenship only in 1960, when the mass departure movement had already begun and threatened the viability and the existence of these institutions.[17] In any case, integration through education concerned only a rather marginal part of the Greek presence in Egypt. The majority of Greek pupils attended Greek institutions. The choice of their parents to send them to Greek schools was never intended to lead to integration in, not even readjustment to, Egyptian reality.

SUFFICIENCIES AND INSUFFICIENCIES OF KOINOTITA EDUCATION

Given the low quality of the Egyptian education system and the strong national character of the community, the majority of Greek pupils attended Greek schools. The orientation of these institutions, however, not only prevented integration but provided little or no assistance to pupils to adjust to the Egyptian context. Establishing a school was a top concern for Greeks wherever they settled. Their establishment and operation principally depended on the *koinotites* of each city. In 1955, the *koinotites* controlled fifty-seven out of the eighty-three Greek schools functioning in Egypt.[18] The *koinotita* educational committees were concerned with ensuring the smooth running of the schools, but they also paid special attention to the curriculum, the character of the education, and its connection to the labor market. Donations from wealthy Egyptiots, especially from the nineteenth to the early twentieth centuries, helped find sites for schools and equip classrooms. Alexandria, in particular, could boast of much better schools than in Greece and other centers of the Greek diaspora. Even though tuition fees existed, many pupils were exempted, as their parents were incapable of paying. In 1957, for instance, out of 1,167 pupils of the GKA schools, only fifty-seven, that is, less than 5 percent, paid full tuition fees.[19] A telling figure of the importance given to education by the *koinotites* is the relatively low illiteracy rate within the community. In 1927, while 18.2 percent of the Egyptiot population (9.2 percent of men and 27.2 percent of women) was considered illiterate,[20] in Greece the rate was as high as 50.7 percent (36.23 percent for men and 64.04 percent for women).[21]

The Egyptiot educational system largely drew its strength from the freedom of activity provided by the Capitulations. The Egyptian state had no right to intervene in the running of schools or to interfere with the curriculum or any other issue concerning not only the Greek but also all the foreign schools in the country. This began to change gradually in the 1930s. At the end of the transitional period, the operation of the schools was to come gradually under the jurisdiction of the Egyptian state. The Egyptian prime minister and chief of the Egyptian delegation at Montreux, Nahhas Pasha, in a letter to the president of the Greek delegation in Montreux, guaranteed that the state would not interfere in the running of the Greek schools until 1949, unless a treaty of establishment determined otherwise in the meantime.[22] After the end of the transitional period, Laws 583/1953 and 160/1958 on foreign education sought to Arabize and impose state control on the foreign schools. The latter law, promulgated in the aftermath of the Suez Crisis, provided for the appointment of an Egyptian director to each foreign school and an Egyptian representative for them in the Education Ministry. According to the second law, the owners, directors, and personnel of foreign schools were to be Egyptian citizens. In addition, foreign teachers could be hired with the approval of the Education Ministry. The Greek schools, though, since they did not depend on a colonial power, were exempted from the legislation and managed to maintain their autonomy.

In the 1950s, state intervention was limited to the curriculum and, especially, the teaching of Arabic. Under the direct control of the *koinotites* and, consequently, the local Egyptiot elite, the Greek education system served two main objectives: the first was ideological, since it constituted the main mechanism for the consolidation of the pupils' Greek national identity; the second was more practical, to ensure that the skills acquired by pupils corresponded to the needs of the labor market. As the vast majority of pupils were Greek citizens (in the 1948–49 school year, 92.9 percent of the 9,188 enrolled pupils were Greek citizens),[23] the teaching of the Greek language and history, along with the promotion of the Greek civilization, had a central place in the educational process.

At times, progressive educators openly contested the educational policy of the *koinotites,* particularly concerning the language issue. In Alexandria and other cities like Kafr el-Zayat inspiring educators promoted the use of the modern vernacular (*demotiki*) over archaic for official and formal purposes (*katharevousa*).[24] The *koinotites,* however, supported use of *katharevousa,* which remained dominant. Similarly, even if there were calls for the reorientation of the education system to the Egyptian environment in the interwar period, its strict Grecocentric character remained completely uncontested at least until the end of World War II.[25] Given the different local origins outside Greece of the Egyptiots, the consolidation of the national identity meant symbolic and natural links had to be forged with what was for many an imaginary country in a way to paper over all local sentiment of belonging. The implementation of a Grecocentric curriculum made this objective possible, while at the same time the education of children was complemented through a variety of rituals and practices, such as parades on Greek national holidays and visiting Greece on an annual basis, all of which were meant to forge the national spirit.

Greek schools in Egypt followed the same curriculum as schools in the homeland. Only slight modifications were made, especially concerning foreign languages. The teaching of other foreign languages, mainly French and English, constituted a basic feature of Greek education in Egypt. Within the multicultural environment of many Egyptian cities, knowledge of foreign languages was necessary for daily communication and one's professional career, since many companies that employed Greeks belonged to French, British, Belgian, or other Western interests. Besides, until the war, French was effectively the lingua franca of commerce and communication between foreigners in Egypt. The teaching of Arabic was not introduced systematically to Greek schools until the 1920s.

Until 1961, secondary schools followed essentially the Greek state curriculum of 1935, which placed emphasis on classicism and the reproduction of the values of the "glorious" Greek past.[26] Greek dictator Metaxas also adopted this curriculum, which he slightly modified in 1939. Even after World War II, elementary schools continued to follow the 1913 Greek curriculum. Even as late as the early 1960s, when the Greek exodus from Egypt was taking place, the curriculum basically remained that of interwar Greece. The emphasis was on the teaching of the Greek language, ancient and modern, and the inculcation of the Greek Orthodox religion, while the Egyptian context was deliberately neglected. It is not accidental that Egyptiot schools first introduced courses in Egyptian geography in 1926, almost at the same time as courses in Arabic.[27] Moreover, modern Egyptian history was officially introduced into the curriculum of elementary schools in 1946.[28]

The total dependency of the Greek educational system in Egypt on that in the homeland, in theory as well as in practice, was almost undisputed by the community leadership. The Greek state recognized *koinotita* schools and required that their teaching staff meet the standards specified by Greek law. Primary and secondary schoolteachers from the 1930s onward were in the main Egyptiots who had studied in Greece and then returned to work in the Greek schools.[29] The Greek Education Ministry also sent teachers, whom the *koinotites* paid. The role of the Greek state was considered fundamental in practical terms. It controlled the running of the schools by sending inspectors. It also provided an important part of the educational material and, in addition, published the operational instructions for the schools.

The Greek state, through its inspectors and diplomatic representatives, sought to supply Greek educational institutions in Egypt with instructions and inspiration, which GKA dignitaries as Nikolaos Vatibellas warmly approved.[30] At another level this reliance translated into a complete intellectual orientation toward Athens, which led to the creation of a community almost entirely focused on Greece, which was an "imagined homeland" for most.[31]

Especially in the postwar years, the consolidation of nationalistic feeling was also in tune with the ideological struggle of the Greek state against communism. As the diplomatic representatives in Egypt admitted, the communal education system constituted the central mechanism for the repression of communist influences in the community.[32] The role of the Greek state was central to this effort, as it also provided the propaganda material and monitored the social and political beliefs of teaching staff. In January 1950, for example, the Greek ambassador, Triantafyllidis, asked Zerbinis, the GKA president, to show the propaganda film *Grammos* in the elementary schools of Alexandria.[33] The aim of the film, which the Greek military had provided, was to demonstrate the achievements of the national army against the Communists during the civil war.[34] Zerbinis refused to give his permission on the grounds that "the civil war had ended," to which Triantafyllidis replied, "Moral values never go out of date."[35] Harilaos Zamarias, consul general of Alexandria, suggested showing the movie in other Egyptian cities, but the ambassador refused and asked him to put pressure on Zerbinis.[36] While it is not clear what eventually happened, in any case Zerbinis's reaction should be considered an exception to the rule and was apparently dictated by his decision to align with Communists in the late 1940s and early 1950s in order to secure control of the GKA.

In general, the leading members of the community collaborated with the Greek state in maintaining ideological control of the schools, since Greek officials monitored all teachers and professors for their nationalist feelings, and if they suspected them of communist sympathies, they transferred or simply fired them. One example is the case of Ioannis Pikos, a teacher at the Averofeio boys' high school in Alexandria. Some parents, whom the consulate general considered "trustworthy persons," denounced him to the diplomatic representatives (but not to the GKA) for pursuing communist activities.[37] In a letter addressed to the consul general in Alexandria, Alexios Liatis, they mentioned, "In the fourth year of high school, the teacher, Mr Pikos, often elaborates on his pet subject of the contrasts and struggle of the social classes and, by comparing the poor to the capitalists, ridicules by name and in front of the whole class some students because of their comfortable financial position and the lifestyle of their parents."[38] After receiving this letter, the consular authorities recommended to the general inspector of Greek schools abroad, Anastassios Atsaves, to transfer Pikos from Alexandria: "He happens to behave like a Communist ... the continuation of his detachment abroad is definitely not recommended," the consular authorities noted.[39] Later in the period under scrutiny, when the consulate intervened in 1960 to suppress communist activity in the GKA, the consul general, Theodoros Baizos, declared with satisfaction that "the Communists' activity in the schools has been significantly reduced thanks to the watchful eyes of the director, Mr Chatzianestis."[40]

The fear of the communist "threat" ensured that the Greek education system preserved a highly Grecocentric outlook, which in turn never really encouraged contact with Egyptian society. Consequently, the question whether Egyptiot Greeks should be considered foreigners or not reemerged. As *O Paroikos* pointed out, "Egypt is the homeland of the Greeks of Egypt. Those who do not adapt themselves and those who have not yet realized that it is no longer possible to constitute a state within a state will remain foreigners in the eyes of the Egyptians."[41] This dimension became more evident after the Suez Crisis, when Egypt emerged as one of the leading countries in the anticolonial movement. Despite the cordiality between Egyptian and Greek state officials, the Greek education system directly clashed with official Egyptian educational policy, since it was characterized by a clearly Eurocentric view. This bias was more obvious in geography and history textbooks, where the Egyptian population was called "non-European."[42] In a series of articles in *O Paroikos* in 1957 on the matter of Greek education in Egypt, Panagiotis Xenos, an Alexandria-based educator, provided an example of the Western-friendly educational bias. He mentioned that the geography textbook used in the third class of high school and published in Athens in 1951, still in 1957 stated that Palestine was under British occupation and the British were there as "overseers" of order and as the "protectors" of the Holy Land.[43] Xenos accused the community leadership of a serious "oversight" in such a sensitive period. Greek schools taught pupils that the entire world should be under the influence of the West and that it was considered important for the colonial forces to maintain their power.[44]

In the late 1950s, Egyptian inspectors of the Arabic language urged the GKA educational committee to assist Greek pupils in developing closer contact with Egypt. One, Abdel Ghelil Halifa, maintained the Greek school should "instill the love toward the UAR in its pupils so that a salute to the flag takes place in the morning, and it should work instilling Arabic nationalism in the souls of the pupils at every opportunity provided by national events."[45]

Such a rapprochement was not feasible because Greek schools were actually designed, as we have seen, to consolidate Greek national feeling and prevent the population from assimilating into Egyptian society.[46] For Egyptiots and especially the *koinotites,* education constituted "the cornerstone" on which the survival of the community largely depended. This was even clearer in smaller cities like Port Said, where the operation of Greek schools seemed to constitute the main means for the preservation of the Greek population. In the early 1960s, for instance, the local consul mentioned that a possible mass departure movement could be triggered by the Arabization of the city's Greek schools:

> If the Greek schools ... turn Arabic ... the major part of the Greeks will leave ... almost all of the Greeks in Port Said and Ismailia belong to the middle and working class. Indeed, if they do not have the financial means to send their children to Greece or elsewhere for useful future studies, they will most probably consider leaving as soon as possible.[47]

The geographical distribution of the educational establishments was linked to the distribution of the population in the consular districts in Egypt. Only one elementary school operated in each one of the eight consular districts. However, in only ten of the thirty-three cities were pupils able to progress to the secondary level,[48] mostly in Alexandria and Cairo. In other places, the post-elementary schools could support only three or four classes.[49]

Table 6 illustrates the number of Greek educational establishments in Egypt, per consular district and per level of education. The absence of high schools was due to the low numbers of Greek population in some cities, which could not support such schools. The *koinotites* in these cities did not enjoy anything like the economic support of the GKA or GKC. The lack of schools was also due to the fact that many pupils did not complete high school. In 1931 for instance only 27 percent of the pupils attending the first or second year of high school finally graduated. This suggests that almost three-quarters (73 percent) of Greek pupils left school early; they either dropped out or left Egypt.[50]

Greek pupils moving from one city to another had to adapt to the small differences in the curriculum of different schools, which complicated the learning process.[51] This is indicative of the prevailing localism among Egyptiots in different Egyptian cities. The issue of the lack of cooperation between the *koinotites* had preoccupied members of the community even before World War II. For instance, an article published in the progressive journal

Table 6. Greek schools in Egypt per consular district and per level of education, 1955

Consular district	Primary education	Secondary education	Total
Cairo	11	9	20
Alexandria	18	12	30
Port Said	5	2	7
Suez	4	1	5
Minya	6	–	6
Tanta	5	1	6
Zagazig	4	1	5
Mansoura	2	2	4
Total	55	28	83

Source: Leonidas G Markantonatos, *Ta en Aigypto ellinika ekpaideftiria* [The Greek schools in Egypt] (Thessaloniki: Society for Macedonian Studies, 1957), 15.

Panaigyptia in July 1937 condemned the absence of any collective policy concerning the problems and continued residence of the Greeks in Egypt: "At times when the new local conditions demand a general consolidation of our powers on a firm basis, capable of supporting the collective social structure, we are scattered in ten small states, and we gamble our luck and the luck of our offspring."[52]

It would not be an exaggeration to say that the type of education offered by *koinotita* schools in a way encouraged those who passed through them to leave Egypt.[53] In the postwar period, school graduates who left Egypt rarely returned to work there. If they did, it was for a short period, given that their career prospects and the anticipated income outside the country were much more promising. By offering grants, the *koinotites* encouraged people to study in Greece. There was no provision, though, for these university graduates to find a job in Egypt, not even in the *koinotita* institutions if they returned. When Filippos Dragoumis visited Egypt in early 1952 on a Greek government fact-finding mission to examine the problems of the community, he found that most high school graduates wished to leave the country.[54] The brain drain jeopardized the long-term prospects of the community. As Leonidas Markantonatos, a Greek diplomat, observed in 1961, "The community is being constantly transformed into a society of old and uneducated people, since the most educated ones generally leave Egypt for good."[55]

The fact that the school curriculum in Egypt was so closely linked to that of Greece afforded pupils easy access to the universities of the homeland. Those who could afford it continued with their studies either in Greece or in other Western European countries. It was not rare for Greek secondary-level graduates to continue their studies at Egyptian universities, at least until the early 1950s. In the 1945–46 academic year, thirty-two students with Greek citizenship attended Egyptian universities, a figure that rose to forty-nine by 1948–49.[56] The *koinotites* offered grants to study at Egyptian universities from 1952, when third-level education in Egypt was democratized through the reduction of tuition fees and the founding of new universities.[57] In 1961 though, only twenty graduates of Cairo's Greek schools were studying at the city's Egyptian universities.[58] Even in the case of those who remained in Egypt to continue their studies, the final objective for most was to continue their studies in Greek universities after a subsequent transfer or by taking the equivalent of the Egyptian degree in order to avoid the ordeal of the competitive matriculation examination to Greek universities.[59]

Data from the Averofeio boys' high school in Alexandria—a school with an academic orientation—shows that graduates from 1955 to 1959 who remained in Egypt continued their studies in an Egyptian educational institution or started working. The steady decrease in the number of graduates during that time suggests that many families left the country before their children had completed high school. Out of the forty-four members of the class of 1955, only twenty remained in Egypt: fourteen to study and six to work. At the same time, twelve graduates continued their higher education in Greece and three in Western Europe. Four years later, in 1959, the number of graduates had fallen to thirty-six, and only eleven stayed in Egypt, while fourteen continued their studies in Greece and three in Western Europe. During the second half of the 1950s, most of this school's graduates decided to leave Egypt and continue in a Greek or other Western European university, mainly British, French, or German.[60]

THE "GERM OF COSMOPOLITANISM"

A significant number of Greek pupils went to other foreign schools, mainly those dependent on Western countries. While it was somewhat bothered about the attendance of Greeks at Egyptian schools, the community leadership took a more serious view about attendance at Western European schools, which operated with the cultural penetration of Egypt in mind. In 1948–49, more than a fifth of Egyptiot pupils (22.9 percent) attended such establishments (see table 7). Western European schools, especially those that belonged to ethnic groups with similar characteristics to the Egyptiot entity, catered to more or less the same target group as Greek ones. The Italian education system in Egypt, which was determined by the Italian government,

Table 7. Distribution of pupils of Greek citizenship per nationality of school, 1948–49

Nationality of school	Greek pupils		
	Boys	Girls	Total
American	23	24	47
British	142	155	297
Egyptian	364	407	771
French	697	1,090	1,787
German	7	39	46
Greek	4,782	3,750	8,532
Italian	137	185	322
Other	17	13	30
Total	6,169	5,663	11,832

Source: *Statistique scolaire, 1948–1949* (Cairo: Imprimerie nationale, 1951).

aimed, on the one hand, to offer Italian youth the means to develop itself, to enter the labor market, and to be competitive in it and, on the other, to increase the prestige of the Italian community and nation.[61] The French and British, in addition to these ideals, served the cultural policy of their states through the extension of the use of their respective languages.[62]

A variety of reasons led Egyptiot pupils to attend schools associated with Western countries. Many were from mixed families, so the choice of school corresponded to the cultural and linguistic orientation of the family. Second, studying in a foreign school facilitated the learning of a foreign language. Since the medium of education was in a particular foreign language, pupils acquired a more substantial knowledge of it than they would in the Greek institutions. Alongside that, one could interpret the tendency of a considerable number of Egyptiot families to send their children to Western schools as part of what Hervé Georgelin appropriately called "la xenomanie levantine."[63] Robert Tignor also observed accordingly: "The more successful the foreign residents became, the more they drew themselves away from Egyptian ways and toward a European style of existence. Even Jews, Greeks, and Syrians, despite long-distance attachments in the Arab East, behaved in this fashion."[64] This is what contemporary observers called the "germ of cosmopolitanism," which infected those who adopted this behavior, expressed in a feeling of social and cultural superiority toward Greeks and Egyptians of a lower class.[65] The "sickness" had to do with the danger of dehellenization, and the "cure" required attendance at Greek schools. Greek pupils, especially in smaller Egyptian cities, sometimes attended foreign Western schools when there were no local Greek alternatives. The inspector of Greek schools abroad, Anastassios Atsaves, considered it extremely important to have Greek schools in the interior in order to prevent pupils attending Western alternatives, since, as he noted, "We must keep our youth near the nuclei of ethnicity."[66]

Since there was no exemption from tuition fees, as was often the case in *koinotita* schools, the pupils who attended Western schools were mostly drawn from middle- and upper-class families. This provoked the particular ire of the community dignitaries. Since they held that the mission of the economic elite was, in a way, to become the leaders of the community institutions, the dignitaries considered that their education should be purely Greek. Otherwise, not only the national character of the *koinotites* and the schools would be in danger, but that of the community itself. Male pupils, in particular, were expected to receive a national education, because it constituted a central element in their identity and thus ensured their future involvement in *koinotita* affairs.[67] For female pupils, it was easier to opt for the French education model or others, and their families were ready to pay handsomely for this. This mentality is reflected in the number of Greek female pupils attending foreign schools. In 1948–49, for instance, Greek girls (1,090) greatly outnumbered Greek boys (697) in the French schools.[68]

The relatively high number of Greek pupils attending Western schools was a cause of deep concern for the Greek diplomatic representatives and the community leadership because they feared the pupils' patriotism was at stake. As the GCCA's *Bulletin* commented, "When the Greek children in their preadolescent years are placed in foreign schools as external or boarding students ... foreign mentalities will affect them due to the teachings and the majority foreign environment, hence their national character will be weakened. This will also result in the weakening of their natural interest in and their love toward their motherland."[69] Nonetheless, where Greek pupils did not attend Greek schools, other means were sought to consolidate their national consciousness and the learning of the Greek language. Scouting, for instance, offered a powerful addition, or indeed alternative, to the basic purpose of the schools. Nikolaos Sakellarios, given his dual role as head of the GKA education committee and GCCA president, not only insisted on this option but also proposed that the chamber undertake a more active role and, eventually, finance private lessons in Greek language and civilization for these pupils.[70]

Western institutions also attracted Egyptiots whose needs were not covered by the Greek educational system. Foreign technical schools such as the Italian Don Bosco, which was organized and equipped to a very high degree, offered a complete vocational education, covering both theoretical and practical aspects.⁷¹ Fees for this school were as high as LE 35 per year, and the GKA granted scholarships to some students. In 1951, almost one-third of Don Bosco's three hundred students were Greek,⁷² a percentage that increased in the following years.⁷³ The Egyptiots' interest in technical education remained limited in comparison to classical studies, for reasons that will be now discussed.

TECHNICAL OVER CLASSICAL EDUCATION

The Egyptiot Greek population considered national self-realization through the consolidation of the Greek national identity a prerequisite not only for its self-definition but also for its definition in relation to the "other," be it on ethnic or religious grounds. The "other" in this case refers not only to Egyptians but also to other foreign residents in the country. Contacts with other groups developed on terms that were antagonistic, since all foreign groups put a premium on national identity and the sense of "national belonging" as the main factors of self-definition and in the settlement of business relations in the labor market. This constituted a relatively closed, introverted system, where Greek employees often had Greek employers. The local Greek bourgeoisie was the main employer. In an introverted labor market, economic gain provided a fundamental motive for promoting Greek culture within the community. By exercising control over the schools, the local Greek bourgeoisie aimed to reproduce "the nationalist bourgeois ideology."⁷⁴ The schools thus functioned as a mechanism of social control, penetrating all the different levels of the socially stratified community. By controlling the *koinotites* and the running of schools, the Egyptiot Greek upper class principally served its own economic interests. The curriculum and the type of schools were adapted to its own economic needs, since they mass produced white-collar workers for their companies. So, apart from any ideological expediencies, the nation-oriented education also "waterproofed" Greeks, consolidated ethnic allegiance within the community, and ensured the existence and continuous production of law-abiding employees and customers.

During the 1950s, the Grecocentric classical or commercial education constituted the main choice for Greek pupils. On the other hand, the education system largely neglected technical training, which could provide solutions to the postwar unemployment problem. Despite the fact that the need to develop technical education was identified in the late nineteenth century, the take-up among Greek students was small. In the 1945–46 school year, only 7 percent of the total number of the pupils in the community attended the country's only technical-vocational school for Greeks, which was in Cairo.[75] In 1949, the GKA, under Zerbinis's presidency, established a vocational night school in Alexandria. Initially, it hosted classes for electricians and mechanics, albeit providing theoretical knowledge mainly.[76] The monthly tuition fees were LE 1, but a grant of up to 80 percent was given to some students. The GKA and donations supplied the school with equipment. The educational staff of the schools consisted mainly of volunteers, who received no salaries.[77] However, technical education required significant investment, which was hard to source because the schools did not correspond to the interests and needs of the elites. In this regard, the benefactors of the community stood idly by. The French technical school in Port Said, for example, cost LE 1 million, a sum that the Suez Canal Company covered in its entirety.[78] Filippos Dragoumis aptly summed up the situation of Greek technical education in Egypt when he visited Egypt in spring 1952 on behalf of the Greek government: "This effort is wonderful as a plan, but, of course, it is inadequate."[79]

Technical education, which could provide a solution to unemployment, only began to develop in the postwar era, and it was available only in Cairo and Alexandria. The distribution of pupils according to the type of school and the level of education are illustrated in table 8. The majority of those pupils who continued their education after the primary level entered the high school with an orientation toward classics, whereas the technical schools, despite their ostensibly high enrollment numbers, did not succeed in their mission, namely the training of highly qualified technicians. One of the reasons why the high number of pupils in technical schools did not correspond to an equally high number of graduate technicians is that the technical

Table 8. Distribution of Egyptiot pupils per school type, 1954–55

Consular district	Elementary schools	Secondary education	Technical schools	Total	Percentage
Cairo	2,192	634	492	3,318	29.3
Alexandria	3,635	1,135	982	5,752	50.79
Port Said	878	280	—	1,158	10.22
Suez	365	116	—	481	4.25
Minya	84	—	—	84	0.75
Tanta	153	8	—	161	1.43
Zagazig	43	8	—	51	0.45
Mansoura	164	156	—	320	2.38
Total	7,514	2,337	1,474	11,325	100

Source: Leonidas G Markantonatos, *Ta en Aigypto ellinika ekpaideftiria* [The Greek schools in Egypt] (Thessaloniki: Society for Macedonian Studies, 1957), 30.

schools had two different sections: one for vocational education and another for foreign languages. Pupils were almost equally divided between the two different sections. In 1955, for instance, 56 percent opted for the vocational option, whereas 44 percent took foreign languages.[80] The number of pupils in the technical schools constantly decreased from 1952 to 1955 despite the fact that the labor-market demand for highly qualified technicians increased in the postwar era, especially, after Nasser's advent to power. This decrease was directly linked to the general fall in the Egyptiot Greek population in the same period.

In periods of important political, economic, and social change in Egypt, when the very future of the Greeks was at stake, the educational issue became prominent on the agenda of the community leadership. Education was considered the main mechanism that could contribute to the development of contact points between the community and Egypt. Even in the 1930s, at a teaching conference in Alexandria, different views were expressed on the future direction of education. The titles of some presentations are indicative of the issues that preoccupied the conference: "The practical impetus that should be given to our schools," "Adjustment of the elementary school to the needs of Egypt," "The teaching of foreign languages in elementary school," "Language courses in secondary schools," and "How to be more successful in foreign languages."[81] It was obvious that the institutions would need to provide convincing responses to the social, economic, and political transformation taking place in Egypt. Thus, technical education and foreign languages should have remained at the heart of the community's readjustment efforts. However, as the Cairo educator Giorgis Athanassiadis observed:

> Our schools prepare [pupils] mainly for a white-collar career, precisely where the openings for employment and success are diminishing. No serious attention is being paid to the practical professions in our educational programs. We ignore them; worse, we systematically cultivate contempt for them through the hollow, pseudoclassical ideas we hand down to the young.... Naturally, there is the occasional reference to technical education, or schools and evening classes! At ceremonies, on speech days, at general meetings, and in the pompous public appearances of certain individuals [we hear] announcements of grandiose plans, which, of course, never materialize.... With the path we follow today lurks the danger that a big part of the community will remain professionally useless and socially unable to adjust.[82]

The readjustment to the local labor market required more focus on a technically oriented education, according to Zerbinis, who in 1948 linked the issue to that of the social stratification of the community: "The Koinotita

... must principally deal with the issues that concern the majority of the community and not the few wealthy ones that have the means to send their children to study in private high schools to obtain a classical education."[83] Education needed to be clearly oriented toward new professional realities; only this could ensure that the majority of Greeks would remain in Egypt. Greeks had to distance themselves from classical education and take a clear turn toward a more professionally oriented education, which would be more closely associated with industry.[84] In this respect, as GKA president, Zerbinis, founded the Vocational Night School in Alexandria in 1949, but this effort fell far short of expectations, since the school lacked the laboratories to efficiently support technical education, as was mentioned above.[85] Diplomats and other members of the community leadership also highlighted the need to reorient Greek education toward the technical professions.[86] Even if the contribution of technical schools was considered an important step in this direction, no significant investment was made in equipping them.[87]

Educational readjustment was the key issue for the left-wing party in the run-up to the GKA elections of 1954. In its program, Sokratis Kalliarekos, Persis Kitrilakis, and Kostas Stamelos, representing the left-wing opposition within the Koinotita, emphasized the need for a long-term plan to readjust Egyptiot education to the new needs of the Egyptian labor market: "The new necessities for readjustment demand the implementation of a long-term and bold educational policy for the general elevation of the cultural level of the community, so that our young men and women become not only useful but also indispensable to Egypt. With its modernized industry, new Egypt is in need of skilled scientists and technicians."[88] The trio proposed: (a) adjusting the Greek school curriculum to the new Egyptian reality, as the existing curriculum was destined to serve the needs of another country; (b) making pupils fluent in Arabic and teaching them the history and civilization of the Egyptian people (they made a direct link between this matter and the psychological rapprochement with the Egyptians); (c) encouraging Greek pupils to continue their studies at Egyptian universities; and (d) connecting the educational process with the labor market. To this end, they suggested the development of more efficient technical schools as well as the establishment of day technical schools in Alexandria.[89] Providing an example of what form this technical education could take, a Cairo educator, Pandelis Paidousis, referred to the Italian community, which did not face the same difficulties, since a great number of Italians were excellent technicians due to the Don Bosco technical school, which explained the Egyptians' high regard for them.[90]

The Greek state, on the other hand, not only was unable to contribute economically,[91] but also did not have the required know-how either. The

1935 curriculum, which in the postwar era served anticommunist propaganda, restricted the educational system in Greece. After the end of the Greek Civil War, anticommunism justified the emphasis in education on the Greek Orthodox tradition and the values of the past.[92] In this respect, "the one-dimensional focus of the basic education in the national, religious, and moral instruction ... became especially powerful ... immediately after the civil war. Technical education ... did not interest the Greek state."[93] The postwar reform of Greece's education system started in 1957, under a committee set up by the Karamanlis government, whereas Decrees 3971 and 3973 first introduced technical-vocational education in 1959.[94] In 1961, the first overall reform of the Greek curriculum since 1935 took place.

Since Greek education in Egypt also served anticommunist propaganda, it did not succeed in overcoming the ideological guidelines of the post–civil war Greek state. On the contrary, it remained more committed to the logic of an educational process that had as its main target the reinforcement of "national" education and combating the "communist danger." In the 1950s, the classicism in Greece's education system came in for criticism.[95] In view of this reality and because of the danger that the community would miss the opportunity to readjust, *O Paroikos* repeatedly called on the *koinotites* to free themselves from the Greek Education Ministry and for the Egyptiot Greek school system to be reevaluated on the basis of the Egyptian reality.[96]

Apart from the cost and ideological stakes involved, the initiative to support technical schools was faced with another obstacle: the aversion of Egyptiots to technical education. The mentality of the second- or third-generation Egyptiot immigrants was opposed to it: these new petite bourgeoisie, who grew up in an environment that promoted upward social mobility, found it inconceivable to revert to the status of a blue-collar worker.[97] Egyptiot Greeks severely criticized Ambassador Triantafyllidis, who tried to sponsor the establishment of technical schools, accusing him of trying "to turn the Greeks from petite bourgeoisie into workers."[98] The "white-collar dream," as Michail Melas, a subsequent ambassador, described the professional ambitions of the Egyptiot family, proved to be very resilient.[99] Greek children from the lower classes had the opportunity to be educated and acquire skills, a chance that was not available to their parents when they first migrated to Egypt. In this respect, they had managed to become office clerks instead of small shopkeepers and workers.[100] Dragoumis also wrote about the related disinclination toward technical education: "The tendency of most of the parents is to have their children obtain a high school education, so that they can preferably get a bureaucratic position that will supposedly elevate them socially, rather than being armed with initiative and creative abilities to face the difficulties of life in Egypt, either by continuing their parents' work or by going their own way."[101] Five years later, in 1957, Greek government special envoy Sotirios Agapitidis proposed the promotion of technical education among Egyptiot Greeks in order to safeguard their future: "We must cultivate the idea that the turn to professions of a lower social level [constitutes] a realistic treatment of the situation and a better guarantee for the future, something that does not usually happen with the ordinary classical formal training."[102]

In August 1957, after Karamanlis's visit to Egypt, the Greek Education Ministry allowed the Greek schools in Egypt to modify their curriculum without raising the issue of the recognition of their school certificates.[103] A more concerted effort to establish vocational schools was made in 1958. At a joint meeting in Cairo, the GKA and GKC agreed to set up a vocational school in the capital with a boarding facility to cater not only to the needs of the Greeks of Egypt, but also to those Greeks living in neighboring countries.[104] In order to succeed, the meeting called on the Greek government to contribute and Greek universities to cooperate. However, despite the goodwill shown by all participants, the initiative did not lead to any concrete results.

The initiatives and efforts undertaken in the post-Capitulations period for the reorganization of the community's education system, which would place special emphasis on technical training, were gradually neutralized. The leadership proved incapable of responding efficiently and on time. The Greek nationalist mentality, promoted by a classicist curriculum and consolidated by many different means in the Greek schools of Egypt, was never disputed in practice. On the contrary, the Grecocentric agenda remained the backbone of Greek education in Egypt, to the neglect of technical education. So, the strong connection of the majority of pupils of the community with the Greek educational system led them steadily to hover between two nationalisms: the Greek and Egyptian.

LEARNING ARABIC

The community leadership was slow to deal with the question of teaching Arabic at Greek schools in Egypt. Courses in Arabic were more regularly studied since the 1920s, just a few years after Egypt's nominal independence, when the future of the Greek presence in Egypt had already become an issue.[105] Later, Law 40/1934 mandated that all students in foreign schools, regardless of nationality, were required to learn Arabic, even if they did not intend to take the state exams.[106] In the interwar period, it had become quite clear that knowledge of Arabic would largely determine the future of the Greeks in Egypt. As early as November 1927, the GCCA *Bulletin* commented:

The discussions that have been held for a while on the vital issue of our position in Egypt show clearly that ... knowledge, serious and full knowledge, of the Arabic language is absolutely ... necessary. This ... is essential, not only for the wider Greek activities, development, and prevalence here, but it is utterly crucial if we want to live and work; if, simply, we want to keep on living in Egypt.[107]

Writing on the issue in 1946, Nikolaos Vatibellas, GKA vice president and head of its education committee, noted in the run-up to the Koinotita elections that "for us education aims to ... create good Greeks who will keep and propagate a high standard in the Greek language, the Christian religion, the Greek spirit, tradition, and virtues of our race."[108] This view contrasted with that of Dimitrios Zerbinis, GCCA president and GKA presidential hopeful. In a study, he expounded a new approach to the issues concerning the educational orientation of the Greek schools. He suggested, "the education of Greek students must be Greek-Egyptian and pay particular attention to the foreign languages (above all Arabic)."[109] Ambassador Triantafyllidis also insisted on the importance of increasing the hours of Arabic instruction because, otherwise, the graduates would face many difficulties in their efforts to find a job.[110] Even in the early 1950s, however, there was no unanimity on the orientation that the education system needed to take, even though Anastassios Atsaves observed that the majority favored change: "Almost everyone is almost in accordance that the Greek education in Egypt should prepare the Egyptiot youth for Egypt."[111]

However, it was only in the postwar era that a more systematic effort for the teaching of Arabic was undertaken in some schools, especially in Alexandria. However, this push did not bring the anticipated results.[112] The teaching of Arabic remained problematic and did not lead to effective learning.[113] This was mainly due to the difference between classical Arabic, which is the written form of the language and the language of business, and the colloquial language used in daily transactions. The majority of Greeks in Egypt possessed a very basic knowledge of colloquial Arabic, but only a few of them could write and work in it. For instance, in a sample of forty different resumes received by the GCCA employment office in the late 1940s and early 1950s for various jobs, only ten specified that the applicant had a working knowledge of Arabic. Fifteen candidates declared that they only spoke it, while an equal number did not specify whether they had any knowledge of the language.[114] Thus, three out of four people seeking a job were in a disadvantaged position when it came to finding a job in Egypt. Thus, it was reasonable to expect that the gradual expansion of the language as the official and sole language of the state would marginalize Greeks in the labor market and weaken their position within Egyptian society, since they were unable to "talk" to the Egyptian state.

Even before the Greek schools integrated Arabic language courses into their curriculum, the GCCA started night classes in Arabic in 1923.[115] The school had three classes, attended mainly by white-collar workers and bank employees. Despite some initial enthusiasm, this experiment was unsuccessful. The number of students steadily decreased from 192 in 1923–24 to forty-six in 1924–25 and to only twenty-five in 1927–28.[116] When in 1942 the use of Arabic became compulsory in public administration and private business, knowledge of it was a prerequisite for finding a job. In 1947 the chamber restarted its intensive evening classes in Arabic for adults, but again the city's Greek residents demonstrated little enthusiasm. This reluctance to learn Arabic annoyed the school staff and GCCA dignitaries, who reacted vigorously through the pages of the GCCA *Bulletin:* "The students of our Arabic school currently number twenty. It seems that it has not become sufficiently clear among the Egyptiots how terribly important and how much it is in our interest to know the language of this place. ... Those of us who insist on ignoring this language will inevitably encounter difficulties at every turn, and we will constantly be facing more and more of them."[117]

After 1953, Arabic lessons in foreign schools became more demanding because the Arabic-language syllabus in Greek schools was to follow to the letter the curriculum in force in Egyptian schools. This situation increased the number of teaching hours of foreign languages, and students had to spend more time learning languages, including Arabic. English and French also were taught, as they were still widely used, and knowledge of one or both of them greatly facilitated migration. For this latter reason, Greek students, even in the mid-1950s when they had a choice, preferred to learn English or French over Arabic. The diplomatic authorities promoted the learning of English in the postwar period at the expense of French because prospective emigrants tended to go mainly to Commonwealth countries, especially Australia but also toward British East Africa colonies.[118] The number of pupils learning the three languages in the technical schools in Egypt is indicative in this regard: out of 639 pupils, 344 (53 percent) had chosen English, 220 (34.4 percent) French, and only 75 (11.7 percent) Arabic.[119]

The efforts made in almost every *koinotita* school in theory aimed to equip students with a high standard of Arabic. There were of course pupils who learned Arabic and thus managed to enter the city's university in departments where the language of instruction was Arabic and, also, to find jobs. For instance, the GKA annual report for 1957 mentioned that graduates of the Salvageios commercial school "found jobs because of their knowledge of Arabic."[120] Nevertheless, the overall results proved rather disappointing, especially in Alexandria. In the same year, the director of the Girls' Secondary Schools in the same city, Alkmini Petronda, attributed the low level of proficiency in Arabic to her students' lack of contact with educated Egyptians:

> The Arabic lesson as it is taught in the Greek schools typically corresponds to the curriculum of the Egyptian schools. In reality, though, our pupils are not as good as they should be ... they are not good enough in pronunciation, writing, reading, orthography, and, generally speaking, the expression of their ideas. ... All of the above is a normal consequence of their complete ignorance of the language and their poor vocabulary, which is already distorted because of their daily contact with uneducated elements of Egyptian society (servants and people from the market). They are not good enough at forming oral expression because they have no daily contact with educated Egyptians as is the case in the smaller cities of the interior. ... Even if they knew the Egyptian dialect well enough, that would not solve the problem because teaching is in classical Arabic. ... Ninety-nine percent of our children have no help from their parents because they too are completely ignorant of the language of the country.[121]

The lack of knowledge of Arabic was even greater in cities that had been developed after the arrival of Europeans in the nineteenth century, such as Alexandria, Port Said, and Ismailia, than in cities of the interior, Cairo or Suez. In the first case, the Arabic neighborhoods were often isolated from the European ones, which did not facilitate everyday contact. In the second group of cities, the Egyptiot Greeks were better integrated in the urban space, and in general, they were less introverted and isolated, which also affected the language they spoke. Apart from the lack of everyday contact, there were other reasons why Greeks failed to learn Arabic properly. Many of them must have felt that their time in Egypt was temporary, and there was a delayed awareness of the practical need to have knowledge of the language of the country hosting them. Another matter emerging from Petronda's statement was Alexander Kazamias's description of the "highly parochial social life which many Greeks led, avoiding closer relations outside the narrow circle of their churches, clubs, and societies," especially in cities such as Alexandria.[122]

Up to the early 1960s the efforts of the *koinotites* and other Egyptiot Greek organizations to encourage the learning of Arabic were not as successful as they had hoped. Gradually the imperative to use Arabic in business no longer enabled Greek entrepreneurs to give Greeks preferential treatment when it came to hiring staff.[123] When they recognized the true extent of the problem, it was too late to devise a solution that would help the Greeks to learn Arabic in order to readjust to the new conditions. On the occasion of the 1961 GKC elections, Themistoklis Matsakis, a leading figure in the Cairo Greek Left, wrote:

We have been in Egypt for three and four generations. We have schools with remarkable organization. Despite that, neither our fathers nor we—not even our children—have benefited from any creative encouragement or help to acquire in a substantial way the language of the country, which is spoken by people that we declare to love and want to live with. However, which Greek would ever imagine, let alone justify, that Greeks, permanently settled in France, Italy, or America, would refuse or avoid learning the language of their host country? This inadmissible situation is happening here, in our case. And it has not happened by accident, but as a result of unacceptable mentalities and, of course, at the expense of the needs and interests of the majority of the community.[124]

NOTES

1. AYE/CS/1962/36/5/3/3, 6391, Cairo, 19 March 1962, Zamarias to Averoff.
2. *Annuaire statistique 1937–1938* (Cairo: Imprimerie nationale, 1939).
3. Afaf Lutfi Al-Sayyid Marsot, *A History of Egypt: From the Arab Conquest to the Present* (Cambridge: Cambridge University Press, 2007), 113.
4. Judith Cochran, *Education in Egypt* (London: Croom Helm, 1986), 35.
5. Alexander Kazamias, "The 'Purge of the Greeks' from Nasserite Egypt: Myths and Realities," *Journal of the Hellenic Diaspora* 35, no. 2 (2009): 23.
6. Marsot, *A History of Egypt*, 114.
7. Georgie DM Hyde, *Education in Modern Egypt: Ideals and Realities* (London: Routledge and Kegan Paul, 1978), 7.
8. Cochran, *Education*, 50.
9. *Annuaire statistique, 1937–1938*.
10. AYE/CS/1952/48/1/1/1, Secret, Athens, 21 May 1952, Report concerning the position of Greeks in Egypt, Dragoumis to Venizelos, 42.
11. Alexander Kitroeff, *The Greeks in Egypt, Ethnicity and Class, 1917–1937* (Oxford: Ithaca Press, 1989), 25.
12. Manolis Maragkoulis, *"Kairos na syngronisthomen": I Aigyptos kai i aigyptiotiki dianoisi, 1919–1939* [It's time to modernize ourselves: Egypt and the Egyptiot Greek intelligentsia, 1919–39] (Athens: Gutenberg/University of Cyprus Press, 2011), 456–67.
13. Kostas Tsagkaradas, *Ta provlimata tis xeniteias* [The troubles of living abroad] (Alexandria: S Grivas, 1946), 89–106.
14. Ibid., 99–100.
15. *Images* 1558 (18 July 1959): 17.
16. *President Gamal Abdel-Nasser's Speeches and Press-Interviews,* April–June 1960, 127.
17. AYE/CS/1961/16/1/3/1, 171, Alexandria, 9 February 1961, Baizos to Lambros.
18. Leonidas G Markantonatos, *Ta en Aigypto Ellinika Ekpaideftiria* [The Greek schools in Egypt] (Thessaloniki: Society for Macedonian Studies, 1957), 16. Not all Greek schools in Egypt depended on the *Koinotites*. In 1955, for instance, of the eighty-three Greek schools, fifty-seven depended on the *Koinotites,* four on the Greek Orthodox Church, six on private support, fourteen on various orga-

nizations, and two were run by parents. This chapter examines the case of the schools dependent on the *Koinotites,* which actually educated the vast majority of the Egyptiot Greek pupils.

19. Elliniki en Alexandria Koinotis, *Logodosia etous 1951* [Greek Koinotita of Alexandria, Annual report of 1951] (Alexandria: T. Kassimatis, 1951).
20. *Annuaire statistique, 1937-1938.* (Cairo: Imprimerie nationale, 1939).
21. *Statitistika apotelesmata tis apografis tis Elladas tou 1928* [Statistic results of Greece's 1928 census], vol. 2 (Athens: National Printing House, 1935).
22. AYE/CS/1939/B/2/AC, Montreux, 8 May 1937.
23. *Statistique scolaire 1948-1949* (Cairo: Imprimerie nationale, 1951).
24. Kitroeff, *The Greeks,* 172; Katerina Trimi-Kyrou, "Être internationaliste dans une société coloniale: le cas des Grecs de gauche en Égypte (1914-1960)," *Cahiers d'Histoire, Les Gauches en Egypte, XIXe-XXe siècles* 105-6 (2008): 110.
25. Nikolaos Vatibellas, *To kathikon tou aigyptiotou ellinismou ke ta scholia mas* [The duty of the Egyptiot Hellenism and our schools] (Alexandria: Typografeio tou Emporiou, 1945), 43.
26. Haralambos Noutsos, *Programmata mesis ekpaidefsis kai koinonikos elenchos, 1931-1973* [Curriculum of secondary education and social control, 1931-73] (Athens: Themelio, 1999), 265.
27. Kitroeff, *The Greeks,* 173.
28. AYE/CS/1951/7/2/1/1, Syllabi of the Greek schools in Egypt.
29. Euthymios Souloyannis, *I thesi ton Ellinon stin Aigypto: Apo tin akmi stin parakmi kai tin syrriknosi* [The position of Greeks in Egypt: From prosperity to decline and decrease] (Athens: Politismikos Organismos Dimou Athinaion, 1999), 90.
30. Vatibellas, *To kathikon,* 46.
31. Hervé Georgelin, *La fin de Smyrne* (Paris: Editions du CNRS, 2005), 95.
32. AYE/CS/1951/95/2/3/1, 9778. Cairo, 23 November 1951, Stefanou to GMFA.
33. AYE/CS/1950/16/2/4/4, 136, Cairo, 13 January 1950, Triantafyllidis to Zamarias.
34. Ibid.
35. Ibid.
36. Ibid.
37. AYE/CS/1954/131/1, 61923, Athens, 21 September 1954, Argyropoulos to Greek Ministry of Education.
38. Ibid.
39. AYE/CS/1954/131/1, 211, Alexandria, 21 April 1954, Alexandrakis to GMFA.
40. AYE/CS/1961/13/1/3/1, 171, Alexandria, 9 February 1961, Baizos to Cairo embassy.
41. *O Paroikos,* 26 May 1957, 1.
42. Ibid.
43. Ibid.
44. Ibid.
45. Archive of the Averofeio Boy's high school of Alexandria, Inspection of Arabic, 30 October 1958, Inspector Abdel Ghelil Halifa.
46. Yalourakis, *I Aigyptos,* 386.

47. AYE/CS/1962/36/4/2/1, 376/EMP/E.F., Secret, Port Said, 25 January 1962, Megalokonomos to Zamarias.
48. Markantonatos, *Ta en Aigypto*, 16.
49. Ibid.
50. Kitroeff, *The Greeks*, 174.
51. AYE/CS/1951/10/4/1/1, 120, Cairo, 12 January 1951, Triantafyllidis to GMFA.
52. *Panaigyptia*, 3 July 1937, 18.
53. Hyde, *Education in Modern Egypt*, 4.
54. AYE/CS/1952/48/1/1/1, Alexandria, 9 May 1952, Dragoumis to Greek journalists in Egypt.
55. AYE/CS/1961/21/15/2/1, Athens, 1 June 1961, Markantonatos to Consulate General in Alexandria.
56. Floresca Karanasou, "The Greeks in Egypt: From Mohammed Ali to Nasser, 1805–1961," in *The Greek Diaspora in the Twentieth Century*, ed. Richard Clogg (London: Macmillan, 1999), 55.
57. Hyde, *Education in Modern Egypt*, 4.
58. AYE/CS/1962/36/6/2/1, 6698. Cairo, 31 October 1961, Yiannakakis to Lambros.
59. Ibid.
60. Archive of the Averofeio boys' high school of Alexandria, General statistics and census.
61. Marta Petricioli, "Italian Schools in Egypt," *British Journal of Middle Eastern Studies* 24, no. 2 (1997): 186.
62. Frédérick Abécassis, "L'enseignement étranger en Égypte et les élites locales, 1920–1960. Francophonie et identités nationales" (Ph.D. diss., Aix-Marseille University I, 2000), 215–20.
63. Georgelin, *La fin*, 103.
64. Robert Tignor, *State, Private Enterprise and Economic Change in Egypt, 1918–1952* (Princeton, NJ: Princeton University Press, 1984), 247.
65. Giorgis Athanassiadis, *I proti praxi tis ellinkis tragodias. Mesi Anatoli: 1941–1944* [The first act of the Greek tragedy: Middle East, 1941–44] (Athens, 1975), 14.
66. Interview of the general inspector of Greek schools abroad, Anastassios Atsaves, *Tachydromos*, 29 November 1949.
67. Abécassis, "L'enseignement," 796.
68. *Statistique scolaire, 1948–1949*.
69. "The Position and the Destination of the Greek Educational Establishments in Egypt," *Bulletin of the GCCA* 581 (15 July 1948): 1–3.
70. AGCCA/95/Greek education of Greek pupils of foreign schools, 121/31, Alexandria, 15 February 1951, Sakellarios to Anastassiadis.
71. AYE/1951/95/2/3/2, Note, Alexandria, 15 January 1951, Kambiotis to Liatis.
72. Ibid.
73. AYE/CS/1952/48/1/1/1, Secret, Athens, 21 May 1952, Report concerning the position of Greeks in Egypt, Dragoumis to Venizelos, 36.
74. Konstantinos Tsoukalas, *Eksartisi kai anaparagogi. O koinonikos rolos ton Ekpaideftikon michanismon stin Ellada, 1830–1922* [Dependence and reproduction: The

social role of the educational mechanisms in Greece, 1830–1922], trans. I Petropoulou and K Tsoukalas (Athens, 2006 [1st edn 1975]), 347.
75. Karanasou, "The Greeks," 46. A similar school would open in 1949.
76. Elliniki en Alexandria Koinotis, *Logodosia etous 1952* [Greek Koinotita of Alexandria, Annual report of 1952] (Alexandria: T. Kassimatis, 1952), 23.
77. AYE/CS/1952/48/1/1/1, Secret, Athens, 21 May 1952, Report concerning the position of Greeks in Egypt, Dragoumis to Venizelos, 35.
78. AGKC/Secretariat/153, Anastasios Atsaves's report, "Concerning the Greek Schools of Egypt," Cairo, 15 April 1952, consul general of Cairo to Roilos.
79. AYE/CS/1952/48/1/1/1, Secret, Athens, 21 May 1952, Report concerning the position of Greeks in Egypt, Dragoumis to Venizelos.
80. Markantonatos, *Ta en Aigypto,* 29.
81. *Ta pepragmena tou A en Aigypto ellinikou didaskalikou synedriou* [Proceeding of the first Greek teachers' conference in Egypt] (Alexandria, 1931), 9–11.
82. Giorgis Athanassiadis, *O paroikiakos ellinismos kai i paideia tou* [The Hellenism of the community and its education] (Cairo, 1948), 17, 27.
83. Zerbinis, *To kathikon,* 69.
84. Ibid., 69.
85. AGKC/Secretariat/153, Pandelis Paidousis report, Cairo, 15 May 1953.
86. AYE/CS/1951/95/2/3/2, Note, Alexandria, 15 January 1951, Kambiotis to Liatis.
87. AGKC/153/Secretariat, Pandelis Paidousis report, Cairo, 15 May 1953.
88. Sokratis Kalliarekos et al., *Programma Anaprosarmogis* [Program of readjustment] (Alexandria, 1954), 12.
89. Ibid.
90. Ibid.
91. AYE/CS/1951/95/2/3/2, 19606, Athens, 25 January 1951, Melas to Stefanou.
92. Konstantinos Tsoukalas, *I Elliniki tragodia. Apo tin apeleftherosi os tous syntagmatarches* [The Greek tragedy: From the liberation to the colonels] (Athens: A Livanis, 1981), 106.
93. Haris Meletiadis, "I politismiki diastasi tis ekpaideftikis politikis stin Ellada kata tin proti metapolmiki periodo (1945–1967)" [The cultural dimension of educational policy in Greece during the first postwar period (1945–67)], in *I elliniki koinonia kata tin proti metapolemiki periodo (1945–1967)* [Greek society during the first postwar period (1945–67)] (Athens: Sakis Karagiorgas Foundation, 1994), 442–56.
94. Noutsos, *Programmata,* 269.
95. Ibid., 270.
96. *O Paroikos,* 26 August 1957, 1.
97. See also Trimi-Kyrou, "Être internationaliste," 86.
98. AYE/CS/1951/10/2/1/1, 507, Cairo, 8 February 1951, Triantafyllidis to GMFA.
99. AYE/CS/1951/95/2/3/2, 19606, Athens, 25 January 1951, Melas to Stefanou.
100. Karanasou, "The Greeks," 45.
101. AYE/CS/1952/48/1/1/1, Secret, Athens, 21 May 1952, Report concerning the position of Greeks in Egypt, Dragoumis to Venizelos, 35.

102. AGKS/Readjustment of the statutes according to Law 384/1956, Agapitidis Committee report, June 1957.
103. *O Paroikos,* 26 August 1957, 1.
104. AGKC/282/Secretariat/Sent mail, 1981/1047, Pierrakos to Greek Ministry of Industry.
105. Kitroeff, *The Greeks,* 173.
106. Cochran, *Education,* 29.
107. *Bulletin of the GCCA,* November 1927, 12.
108. Vatibellas, *To kathikon,* 41.
109. Dimitrios Zerbinis, *To kathikon ton ithynonton tis paroikias* [The duty of the dignitaries or our community] (Alexandria: I Proodos, 1946), 69.
110. AYE/CS/1948/92/3/1/1, 4381, Cairo, 17 November 1947, Triantafyllidis to the Greek consular authorities in Egypt; AYE/CS/1951/10/4/1/1, 120, Cairo, 12 January 1951, Triantafyllidis to GMFA.
111. AGKC/153/Secretariat/Report concerning the Greek schools in Egypt by Anastasios Atsaves (n.d., n.p.).
112. Zerbinis, *To kathikon,* 69–70.
113. Pandelis Lekkou, "To Averofeio Gymnasio Alexandrias apo tis idryseos tou eos to 1960" [The Averofeio high school of Alexandria from its foundation to 1960] (Ph.D. diss., Aristotle University of Thessaloniki, 2001), 173.
114. AGCCA/Employment office.
115. Athanassios Politis, *O Ellinismos kai i Neotera Aigyptos* [Hellenism and modern Egypt], vol. 1 (Alexandria: Grammata, 1928), 387–88.
116. Ibid.
117. *Bulletin of the GCCA,* 15 September 1947, 2.
118. AYE/CS/1949/42/1/5/4, 3908, Cairo, 31 October 1949, Triantafyllidis to Pappas.
119. Markantonatos, *Ta en Aigypto,* 34.
120. AGKA/Correspondence, 1954–61, Report, The teaching of the Arabic language in the schools of the GKA, Alexandria, 3 March 1958.
121. AGKA/Correspondence/Inbox/1957–62, Alexandria, 11 March 1957, Petronda to Theodorakis.
122. Alexander Kazamias, "The 'Purge of the Greeks' from Nasserite Egypt: Myths and Realities," *Journal of the Hellenic Diaspora* 35, no. 2 (2009): 23.
123. AGKS/Readjustment of the statutes according to Law 384/1956, Agapitidis Committee report, June 1957.
124. Themistoklis Matsakis, *To dilimma tou aigyptiotou ellinismou* [The dilemma of the Egyptiot Hellenism] (Cairo, 1961), 10–11.

Part III

Leaving Egypt before 1960

Chapter Five

Mobility, Migration, and Repatriation

"The situation of the Greeks in Egypt is dire and it will soon get worse ... it is our duty to advise them to take the necessary measures now, in order to reduce their businesses, sort out their properties, and find other places, which have not yet been arranged, where they will prosper by following methods that bitter past experiences have taught them."[1] These thoughts were not expressed during the period under study, but appeared in the Alexandrian daily *Efimeris* on 23 February 1914. Even before World War I, a public debate was in progress regarding the future of Greeks in Egypt after a long period of economic recession. The anonymous author, a "prominent Greek lawyer" who went under the initial "R," urged the Greeks to leave Egypt and to emigrate, once again, in order to be able to "thrive." In his view Greece was then an attractive destination because the new territories annexed after the Balkan Wars had to be populated with Greeks. It was a view broadly in accordance with the line of the consul general of Alexandria, who recommended, through the pages of the same daily, repatriation as the best option for those facing economic difficulties.[2]

Leaving Egypt, and moving to Greece in particular, constituted a central choice for Egyptiots in periods of economic crisis. We may draw the same conclusion when we consider the mass applications for repatriation that the Greek consulate in Port Said received in May and June 1919 at the time of the Egyptian revolution and in the aftermath of the recurring strikes at the Suez Canal Company.[3] This behavior is not surprising because the community was never a static settlement. On the contrary, it was always determined by intense mobility to and from Egypt and also in its interior. The interwar period witnessed considerable mobility between Greece and Egypt as well as diverse options on where to settle inside the country and whether to repatriate entirely. In this period, the community lost—according to the Egyptian censuses—more than 30 percent of its demographic strength, since the Greek population decreased from 68,559 in 1937 to 47,673 in 1960. In the same period, the Egyptian population increased from 15.73 to 25.98 million people, that is, by over 65 percent (see table 1).

The departure of Greeks in the postwar period was not an isolated phenomenon. Most of the European and non-European communities in Egypt lost much of their demographic power in the postwar years. For the French, British, and Jews, the reasons for their departure are more or less clear. The Suez Crisis was decisive for the fate of the first two groups in the country. In the case of the Jewish population, the creation of the State of Israel in 1948 was a watershed. Many Armenians, on the other hand, responded to Stalin's call to resettle in the USSR, with many departing for good immediately after the war. As for the Italians, they never recovered from their wartime demographic loss.

INTERWAR MOBILITY

In the 1930s, the mobility of the Greek population between Egypt and Greece was intense as well as continuous. This population movement was due, as it is illustrated in table 9, to a variety of reasons: tourism, business, studies, commerce, and family reasons. The available data show that within this decade, there were 78,814 registered visits of Greek nationals from Egypt to Greece. Not only may travelers have visited more than once, but they also may have traveled for none of the above reasons, but rather to repatriate. Given that the total number of Greek nationals in Egypt, according to the official Egyptian censuses of 1927 and 1937, was 76,264 and 68,559 persons, respectively (see table 1), one could safely assume that in the 1930s over 10 percent of the Greek population in Egypt may have visited the motherland annually. Compared to other important centers of the Greek diaspora, such as Australia and the United States, there were more regular visits made by the Greeks of Egypt to the metropolis up to World War II.[4] Only 190 Australian Greeks visited Greece from 1931 to 1940 (8,337 Australian Greeks declared Greece as their birthplace in the 1933 Australian census), and 6,506 Greek Americans visited the homeland in the same period (163,252 Greek Americans gave Greece as the country of their birth in the 1940 US census). These numbers do not imply that Egyptiots were more interested than the Greeks of Australia or the United States in the motherland, but rather that traveling to Greece was cheaper and easier. It is obvious that

Table 9. Visitors with Greek citizenship from Egypt to Greece and the purpose of visit, 1931–40

Year	Tourism	Health reasons	Studies	Commerce	Family affairs	Other	Total
1931	4,227	61	50	155	734	23	5,250
1932	5,540	76	121	532	795	8	7,072
1933	8,225	22	158	252	290	28	8,985
1934	8,606	12	151	154	282	21	9,226
1935	7,754	36	134	161	377	43	8,505
1936	7,845	36	136	98	480	32	8,627
1937	11,133	35	28	151	237	23	11,607
1938	9,339	19	79	170	434	14	10,055
1939	7,839	28	275	114	307	8	8,571
1940	617	13	123	62	96	5	916
Total	71,125	348	1,255	1,849	4,032	205	78,814

Source: Tableaux analytiques du mouvement migratoire et touristique de la Grèce avec l'étranger pendant les années 1931–1940 (Athens: National Statistical Service of Greece, 1946), 231–41.

the proximity of Greece and Egypt facilitated close contact. Proximity and intense mobility created a distinctive diaspora identity in Egypt compared to other Greek diaspora settings, since contact with the metropolis and repatriation were accessible options.

The increase in the Greek population in Egypt, as shown in the 1917 and 1927 censuses, which was mainly due to the movement of refugees from Asia Minor toward Egypt, was followed by a decrease in the following two censuses, conducted in 1927 and 1937. According to the latter, the number of Greek citizens in Egypt decreased by 7,705 persons (see table 1). This decrease could be a hint that the departure had actually begun in the interwar period.[5] However, as we shall see, this would only partially apply, since the statistics indicate that there was movement in both directions. According to table 10, in the 1930s a total of 19,453 Greek citizens repatriated from Egypt. This possibly led to the creation of the Association of Greeks from Egypt and Sudan in Athens in December 1933. The reasons behind this movement are not clear, but as the diplomats noted, many Greeks, after they made their fortune in Egypt, decided to return to Greece.[6] Additionally, a considerable number of them remained in Egypt until they retired, when they then decided to spend the rest of their lives in Greece. However, in this case, the Egyptian census should have recorded a much greater reduction in the number of Greek citizens than 7,705 people. How can one explain this difference? As table 10 illustrates, 10,670 Greek citizens emigrated for the

Table 10. Repatriation and migration of Greek citizens from and to Egypt, 1931–40

Year	"Repatriates" to Greece from Egypt	First-time emigrants from Greece to Egypt
1931	1,882	649
1932	1,665	1,408
1933	1,925	956
1934	2,147	1,771
1935	2,119	1,229
1936	2,011	1,378
1937	2,499	1,012
1938	1,917	1,212
1939	1,874	823
1940	1,414	232
Total	19,453	10,670

Source: *Tableaux analytiques du mouvement migratoire et touristique de la Grèce avec l'étranger pendant les années 1931–1940* (Athens: National Statistical Service of Greece, 1946), 100–11.

first time from Greece to Egypt during the 1930s. This means that during this decade Egypt constituted one of the main destinations for prospective emigrants from Greece. The United States, where 11,878 Greek emigrants moved for the first time, remained another important destination.[7]

Greek emigration to Egypt was due to the economic opportunities, but also to the easy, uncomplicated entry procedures, the economic crisis prevailing in the West after the 1929 crash, and the closure by the United States of its borders to immigrants in 1924. An additional reason, though, was proximity. The intense mobility and the physical presence of the Egyptiots in Greece undoubtedly contributed to the attractiveness of Egypt as a migrant destination. To have a better understanding of the close distance we should bare in mind that the port of Irakleio in Crete is 366 nautical miles from Alexandria, and 349 nautical miles away from Thessaloniki, in northern Greece. Thus, despite the fact that a considerably high number of Greek citizens repatriated, the Greek population in Egypt was continuously "provided" with first-time immigrants until World War II. This explains why the Greek population of Egypt did not decrease significantly during the 1930s in spite of the departure of 19,453 people. World War II blocked the movement of people, and mobility was mostly limited to refugees and soldiers moving between Greece and the battlefronts of the Middle East and Africa. In the other direction, the overall number of migrants from Greece to Egypt fell from 1937 to 1940, whereas departures for other destinations remained high.

Bearing in mind the above elements, the reduction of the Greek population in Egypt by 20,886 persons, as illustrated in the Egyptian censuses of 1937 and 1960 (from 68,559 to 47,673, respectively), seems less impressive. Leaving Egypt was a choice Egyptiots made even before the abolition of the Capitulations. After World War II though, Greek migration to Egypt was reduced to a trickle. The arrivals of new immigrants from Greece ceased or were extremely low. Of course, after 1937 the Egyptians did not wish to see the number of foreigners, Greeks included, increase. This desire was expressed in the strong opposition of the Egyptian government to the possibility that Greek soldiers from mainland Greece would be demobilized while still in Egypt.[8] This is also clear in the fear among Egyptiot soldiers that in the event of their being demobilized outside Egypt, the government might not allow them to reenter the country.[9] Thus, the war brought an end to the boosting of the Egyptiot population with external elements. Greece's prospective emigrants followed the route toward Australia and other countries that constituted popular destinations in the postwar migration market. In the main, Egyptiot Greeks would leave Egypt for the same destinations.

INTERNAL MIGRATION

The intense mobility of Egyptiot Greeks took them not only from Egypt to Greece and back but also around the Egyptian interior. One of the main characteristics of the Greek presence in Egypt was the settlement in almost every corner of the country. The newly arrived Greeks not only settled in Cairo and Alexandria but also inhabited the cities across the Suez Canal area and penetrated the Egyptian interior, moving into the cities and the villages of the Nile delta, such as Mansoura, Tanta, and Zagazig, and into Upper Egypt. According to the official 1907 Egyptian census, the Egyptiots were the largest foreign population group settled in the Egyptian interior: 19 percent of the entire Greek population in Egypt was living outside Cairo and Alexandria, whereas 11 percent of the French population, 9 percent of the British, and 6 percent of the Italian population. Of the non-European communities in Egypt, 23 percent of the Syrians lived in the hinterland and 10 percent of the Armenian population.[10]

The Greek presence outside Cairo and Alexandria reached its demographic peak during the first two decades of the twentieth century. Beginning in the 1920s, Greeks living in these areas began moving to Alexandria and Cairo and the Suez Canal cities, following in a way the respective movement of Egyptians.¹¹ Gradually but steadily urbanization altered the map of the Greek population. In small cities like Mit Ghamr in the center of the Nile delta, the Greek community numbered around 600 persons before World War II. By 1952 this number had fallen to 82.¹² That same year, Damanhur, a town located seventy kilometers southeast of Alexandria, had 50 Greek residents, a far cry from the 375 Greeks who resided in the city twenty-five years earlier.¹³

Greeks' mobility in Egypt not only followed the urbanization movement of Egyptians, but it was also influenced by the special conditions prevailing in each location. In Damanhur, for instance, the proximity to Alexandria played a decisive role. With the development of public transportation and motor cars, a Greek teacher could live and work in different cities, as Liatis learned after a visit to the town in 1952: "The only Greek stores [of Damanhur] are two old bakeries, a grocery and a liquor store—which was closed for Ramadan. The rest of the community are clerks of medium economic status. Some of the working country fellows there, the teacher of the Greek school included, have their residence in Alexandria."¹⁴ Proximity to Alexandria must have also played a role in the case of Kafr el-Dawwar, which is halfway between Alexandria and Damanhur. The economic activity of Greeks in this small town was halved in twenty-eight years. "In the town there are fourteen Greek stores—eleven groceries, two coffee shops, and a bakery—compared to thirty stores that existed in 1924."¹⁵

Moneylending had been a source of wealth for Greeks in the interior under the Capitulations and, especially, in the nineteenth century. The gradually reduced profits from it also contributed to the gradual departure from the hinterland. Some of these moneylenders, and others who traveled from Alexandria to the interior for this purpose, lent to peasants at extremely high interest. Even the banker Andreas Syngros was amazed at the dimension of this usury when he visited Egypt in 1867:

> Many people, especially middle-class Greeks, came to Egypt bringing small capital—some of them not even this—but they acquired it in Alexandria, and as representatives of big capital holders moved to the interior to lend this. ... There is no point to describe these actions in detail. Suffice it to say that they lent with 30 to 36 percent interest per year, on the peasant's and debtor's harvest. And they were paid back in produce that was undervalued by 20 to 30 percent.¹⁶

As the Alexandrian literary critic Timos Malanos writes in his autobiography, "some unscrupulous ones among us" were usurers and operated also in the cities during the 1930s. In the interior, however, they had "plundered the villages of Egypt." He wrote also, "Some of them (Jews, Syrians, Greeks) had literally run riot and consequently many of the real estate fortunes were created from the unpaid loans, the savage compound interest rates, and the seizure of fields."[17]

In the Egyptian "collective memory," the image of the moneylender/grocer, who sold products to peasants for part of the cotton harvest and lent money at extremely high interest, was linked in the early twentieth century with the Greeks of Egypt.[18] Evgenios Michailidis, a theologian and Arabic-language teacher, wrote with indignation in 1927, "The current generation of Egyptians unfortunately only knows the name *bakal* from the great civilizing activity of Hellenism across Egypt. This name literally means grocer but figuratively means trickster, adventurer, cunning one, and thief!"[19] The exploitation of the Egyptian peasant *fellahin* sometimes led to retaliation against Greeks. For instance, from 1931 to 1934, fourteen Greeks were murdered in the Egyptian interior, a fact that provoked the strong reaction of the Cairo embassy.[20] Insecurity and the extension of the banking system drove the moneylenders to abandon the hinterland.[21] The gradual creation of the Egyptian nation-state and the control it exerted even in the remotest of areas no longer permitted Greeks to engage in illicit activities, such as a Dr Valsamakis in Minya who "distilled alcohol and engaged in the wholesale retail trade in pharmaceutical products, as well as dealing in antiquities."[22]

Various sources indicate that the turnover of Greek businesses fell constantly in the interwar period, a process that accelerated after 1945. As a result, many shopkeepers closed their stores and left. The movement of Egyptians into professions that thus far Greeks and other foreigners had mainly conducted contributed to this shrinkage and, also, the movement of Greeks from the interior. The native Egyptians had sidelined them to such a degree that contemporary observers were pessimistic not only about the future but also about the current conditions of the Greeks in the interior. Some said they were witnessing "the Greek village grocer, the then king of the rural areas, being wiped out for good, and along with him, the cotton merchants and the others are also being wiped out."[23] In order to maintain the Greek population in Egypt, the existence of Greek companies was a prerequisite. Investment was limited after the war, though. However, wherever company branches opened up, new residents replaced those who had already left, and the Egyptiots' internal migration did not lead to the demographic downfall of a community. In Tanta, for instance, the local community benefited from the opening of branches of the Salvagos, E&B Houri, Yieha, and Fargali companies and a Coca-Cola factory. The firms recruited "about sixty Greek employees from other areas of Egypt, whose families settled here and in the surrounding areas."[24]

As was often the case, Greeks preferred to leave Egypt even if there were vacancies. Unemployed people from Alexandria and Cairo could not be lured into moving to the interior even with the offer of a job. Thus, there is some paradox in the fact that while Greek consuls and vice-consuls were constantly sending reports on the internal migration of Greeks from the interior and smaller cities to Egypt's main urban centers,[25] presumably on account of unemployment, at the same time they were informing the GCCA that "there are enough vacancies for unemployed young Greeks" in restaurants, hotels, bakeries, nightclubs, and cinemas in Upper Egypt.[26] Similar messages came from the delta region/Lower Egypt, which was "suffering from a lack of manpower."[27] The vacancies were mostly in the manual occupations, for which Egyptiot Greeks showed no particular predilection. Greek ambassador Georgios Triantafyllidis thought that younger Greeks were also attracted to the urban lifestyle, which they also linked to increased possibilities of upward social mobility and economic opportunities without having to leaving Egypt. His successor in the embassy post, Michail Melas, made a similar observation in October 1952: "Unfortunately ... there is a reluctance among young Greeks in Egypt, who are now used to big-city life, to abandon them and move to Upper Egypt, even in order to have a secure job."[28]

Another important push factor was the insecurity in the hinterland created by war. Marsa Matruh, a coastal town 240 kilometers west of Alexandria, is an example. With a Greek population of over three thousand people in the 1920s, the town had a *koinotita* and an elementary school. The town, however, was evacuated in May 1940, because of the German advance, but after the war less than half of the town's former Greek population returned. In 1952, almost a hundred Egyptiot Greeks lived there, including four families in the villages of Sidi Barrani and Sallum. As the Alexandria consul general Liatis pointed out:

> Inside this little town there are five Greek hotel-pensions, three coffee shops, three bakeries, two restaurants, and a grocery. Moreover, half of the Shell and all the Socony-Vacuum diesel and petrol stations are in Greek hands. The only cinema in the city is half-Greek. Greeks also run the largest and most luxurious hotel (Lilo). Finally, there are two Greek fishermen, who are more or less struggling. There is only one Greek businessman, who deals with broader commercial activities and is also the owner of the biggest coffee shop in town. In Sidi Barrani, there are three Greek stores dealing with small-scale trade. In Sallum only one Greek family of fishermen resides.[29]

The activities of *fedayyin* guerrillas in the early 1950s gave rise to particular conditions in the delta region, which neighbored the Suez Canal and the British base barracks along the isthmus. Joining the existing Greek communities in the area in the late 1940s was a significant number of Greeks who came to work for the auxiliary services of the British Army. The principal centers that hosted the British military services in Egypt were in Fayid, Tel el-Kebir, Kasfareet, and Suez. In the early 1950s approximately seven hundred Greeks worked in Fayid and almost four hundred in the other three places.[30] Two categories of workers and employees existed: those who moved to the canal zone from other areas and cities and those who lived in cities close to the canal area. Quite a lot of people in the first category brought their families with them. Around the military bases, Egyptians and foreigners, including Greeks, developed and engaged in various economic activities; for example, the branch office of the Salvagos Company, which operated in Fayid, maintained an unknown number of Greek employees. When Cairo denounced the Anglo-Egyptian Treaty, many of the employees and workers left their jobs in and around the bases and moved to Cairo and Alexandria. It seems, however, that the tense atmosphere affected other residents of the area, too.

Even though consuls and vice-consuls in the region usually stressed the good relationships between Greeks and Egyptians and, especially, the local authorities, it seems that the struggle between the Egyptians and British in the area generated insecurity, as the consul reported from Mansoura:

> Since the differences with England have accentuated, the fanaticism of the Egyptian elements has increased and has turned not only against the English, but also against the Europeans in general. A lot of incidents have been registered in which the Egyptians have expressed hostility toward Europeans without distinction. The word *khawaga* [master, European] is expressed in a hostile way and meaning.

But, he continued, "In any case, the relationship of Greeks with the Egyptians is always good, especially with the local authorities."[31] Epaminondas Skarpalezos from Zagazig, who also confirmed the good relations of Greeks with the Egyptian authorities, denounced the behavior of some lower-ranking policemen: "Despite our participation in the public demonstration against England, despite our generous contribution to the struggle (LE 500 in Zagazig and LE 700 in Faqus), no Greek dares to leave his house; the stores remain with the door half-closed under the controversial protection of the armed guard (meaning blackmailer) in front of it."[32] From the above, one may conclude that the anticipation of a British departure might have contributed at a psychological level to insecurity and, consequently, the movement to big urban centers in the 1950s.

Another reason for the movement from the interior to urban centers was the geographical distribution of Greek schools, an issue mentioned in the previous chapter. The matter preoccupied the community leadership given that the lack of primary and secondary education pushed Egyptiots into moving to urban centers.[33] For instance, in areas with an important Greek presence, such as Upper Egypt, there was no high school in the 1950s. Kleovoulos Tsourkas, vice-consul in Suez in the early part of the decade, highlighted this complex situation and the link between education and internal migration. To encourage Greeks to remain in the small cities of Upper Egypt, he proposed a number of measures to Ambassador Triantafyllidis. He called for, first, the establishment of a boarding school in the Upper Egypt city of Minya and, second, for Greeks to be exempted from tuition fees to all Greek schools on the understanding that Greek parents would not send their children to foreign schools unless it was absolutely necessary.[34] The only boarding school was in the delta city of Mansoura, but it was not easy for children to leave home at such a young age, not to mention the prohibitive cost that such an alternative represented for the average Egyptiot family.[35] An incident indicative of the importance given to Greek education in smaller cities comes from the Greek Koinotita of Tanta, where the education committee warmly welcomed the establishment of a sixth class in the high school. The Koinotita leadership deemed the addition of another class as necessary "to prevent the 'outflow' of the Greek community from here and to avoid Greeks studying in foreign propaganda schools."[36] For the small *koinotites,* the departure of even a few members could have devastating effects. Since they could no longer keep schools open, parents who wished to send their children to a Greek school saw no option but to move.[37] Thus, the migration of families to seek a Greek school for their children or for other reasons provoked chain reactions.

Because of these simultaneous departures, the *koinotites* in other smaller cities and villages could no longer continue operating and began to close down in the 1950s and 1960s. A Greek-Egyptian agreement of 1949 dictated that whenever a *koinotita* ceased to operate, it should merge with the GKA, GKC, or Mansoura Koinotita, depending on which was nearest. If one of these three closed, the property would pass to the remaining two. The last operating *koinotita* would gain all the property. In the event it closed as well, its assets would be transferred to the Greek state, which had the obligation—which it still retains—to distribute the assets to projects for destitute Egyptiots. Examples are the Zifta and Mit Gamr Koinotites, which both merged with the Mansoura Koinotita on 20 February 1962.[38] In 1963 the Qantara Koinotita merged with the GKA.[39] On 12 December 1965, the GKC general assembly approved the absorption of the Sibin el-Kom Koinotita.[40] On 25 June 1965, the Mehalla Kebir Koinotita joined that of Mansoura,[41] and on 27 July 1965 the Heliopolis (Ain Shams) Koinotita merged with the GKC, although the decision had been made a year before.[42] In 1966 and 1967, respectively, the Zagazig and Tanta Koinotites merged with the GKC.

TOWARD NEW POSTWAR HORIZONS

The movement of Egyptiots after the war was not limited only to within Egypt. As had been the case in the interwar period, they were also leaving Egypt for various destinations.[43] Greek consular and other reports noted that this departure movement involved the destitute and unemployed, usually war veterans, who, relying on kinship networks, had decided to leave.[44] Along with them, a number of small and medium capital holders and small shopkeepers who were affected by the postwar economic recession decided to transfer their savings to another country and invest there. The departure of lower-class members of the community did not particularly worry its leadership; on the contrary, leaders welcomed the removal of the poor as a solution to rising unemployment. Chamber dignitaries assumed that many Greeks would leave the country given the problems that had developed in postwar Egypt.[45]

Right after the war, and especially after the promulgation of Law 138/1947 on joint-stock companies, the GCCA considered possible destinations for those who were in a position to pay the cost of migrating. The chamber, given its involvement in commercial activity, was de facto the most extroverted Egyptiot organization. It is important to bear in mind that GCCA board members were often members of the GKA board and, thus, constituted the community leadership. There is a paradox here. While the leadership theoretically had as its objective to support Greeks in remaining in Egypt, in practice it dealt with ways of how to leave it. This contradiction can be explained by the fact that the leadership believed it could serve its own ideological and economic goals through migration. Migration provided them with the chance to convert the departure of Egyptiots into a business opportunity. Indeed, they used migrants as nodes in extensive commercial networks around the Greek diaspora to promote their business activities, as we will now show. While small capital holders sought ways to get their money out of Egypt and invest it, the GCCA investigated the possibilities for their resettlement. It gathered information on possible destinations and presented them in the GCCA *Bulletin*.[46] Prospective migrants from all over Egypt consulted the chamber's office to get more information about the advertised destinations, the terms, and the necessary administrative steps involved in emigrating and settling in these countries. In 1948, 146 people visited the GCCA to obtain further information about the opportunities to migrate to the French protectorates in North Africa and to Australia.[47]

The chamber's leaders activated unofficial networks that were based on established personal relations with Greek diplomatic officials who had already served in Egypt. Given the absence of a central coordinating state body for facilitating the migration of Egyptiot Greeks, the GCCA often engaged directly with Greek diplomats to collect information on possible destinations. A telling illustration is the correspondence from March 1949 to February 1950 between the chamber president, Ioannis Pandelidis, and Georgios Kapsabelis, then a diplomat in the Greek embassy in Buenos Aires. Kapsabelis was well-known in the community, as he had served for four years (1931–35) in the consulate general of Alexandria and for a few months in 1943 in the Greek embassy in Cairo. During his stint, he had obviously developed some social contacts, which he maintained. Before moving to Argentina in 1948, he had served as consul general in Jerusalem (1946–48), a period during which he stayed in contact with a number of Alexandrians, mainly members of the local Egyptiot elite.[48]

Pandelidis's main aim, as expressed in his correspondence, was the development of commercial relations through the activation of diaspora organizations (communal institutions, chambers of commerce, associations) for the common benefit. The chamber dignitaries saw the Greek diaspora from a global perspective as a transnational entity, or as Pantelidis expressed it a "unified commercial space," that could boost commercial activity.[49] In fact, the commercial networks of the Greek merchant diaspora that dominated the Eastern Mediterranean in previous times continued to operate on a much larger scale following the developments in technology and means of transportation. While the form changed, from the Mediterranean to a global level, the mechanisms seemed to have remained the same.

Later, in September 1949, Pandelidis requested Kapsabelis to provide him with information about the required formalities for people wishing to migrate to Argentina.[50] This "unified commercial space" provided economic and social opportunities for those who wished to emigrate. Even if their activities did not always coincide with the particular commercial occupations of chamber members, the chamber's dignitaries considered it useful in promoting commercial interests the fact that they had lived in Egypt and were familiar with the Egyptiot situation and mentality. The aim of the chamber was to maintain communication with the migrants once they had reached their destination. In turn, they were expected to send back information about job opportunities, migration prospects, and other commercial or business opportunities.[51]

No organized migration program could possibly rely exclusively on these unofficial networks to produce satisfactory results; should any one of the two interlocutors in the correspondence change, the network collapsed. In the case of the communication between Pandelidis and Kapsabelis, it was interrupted after the former stepped down from the presidency of the chamber and the latter was transferred to Chicago, as consul general, in early 1950.[52] In 1952 Kapsabelis was appointed ambassador to Rio de Janeiro, and Sakellarios, the new GCCA president, reactivated the contact to facilitate the migration of Egyptiot Greeks to Brazil.[53] In early 1954, though, Kapsabelis moved again, returning to Buenos Aires.

Another factor contributing to the failure of such networks, which forestalled the migration of Greeks from Egypt to other destinations, was the unwillingness of the Greeks who had already settled in diaspora settings, as well as of the local Greek diplomatic representatives, to receive more Greeks from the diaspora, as Konstantinos Salvagos pointed out in a letter to Pappas, a former ambassador in Cairo and now a high-ranking GMFA official:

> One of the main obstacles to the penetration of new members of our community in different countries is the lack of interest or goodwill on behalf of the Egyptiots who are already settled there but also of the representatives of our state. It is necessary to find a way to change this ... negative spirit ... and to ensure a spirit of national solidarity if we wish to broaden the horizons of the activities of the Greeks abroad which are always valuable for the nation.[54]

This opposition stemmed from the belief that newly arrived migrants would increase competition in the local labor market. As Marc Choate has identified in relation to the Italian diaspora, people already settled in the diaspora were distrustful toward the newcomers because they "could also undermine and fragment their local community and change the colony's relationship with host societies."[55]

Those who left Egypt in the late 1940s preferred migration to repatriation. A basic criterion was the existence of a Greek settlement and a program for receiving immigrants in the intended host destination. After 1947, Australia was a favored area. The existence in this country of a considerable Greek presence even before the war and the establishment of a program for receiving migrants in 1947 served as a magnet for many Greek migrants from Egypt. Moreover, Greeks in Egypt regularly received positive feedback on living conditions and career prospects from Egyptiot Greeks who had migrated to Australia. Australia's immigration policy was extremely open; the only prerequisite until October 1952, when individual migration was temporarily halted, was that prospective immigrants should already have relatives or friends who could cater to their needs and assist them in settling in the country.

Australia was the first choice for most Greek migrants from Egypt. This is hardly surprising, since Australia was a popular destination for many European immigrants in the postwar era. Egypt was on the sea route from Europe to Australia. Ships full of European migrants anchored in the ports of Alexandria and Port Said for refueling and then passed through the Suez Canal. People living on the coast around the canal area, and especially in the cities of Port Said, Ismailia, and Suez, were in daily eye contact with ships heading from the Mediterranean to the Indian Ocean, with Australia as their final destination. Besides, when people wished to migrate, they did it in all possible ways. Eleftherios Mavromatis, who departed from Cairo to Egypt, "managed to get on the British trade ship *Agamemnon* as an oiler." He informed the GKC in order to receive a destitute certificate and have his new passport issued without delay, as his ship was due to depart three days later from Port Said to Melbourne.[56]

Apart from Australia, other popular postwar destinations were Canada, the United States,[57] Argentina, and Brazil. Egyptiot Greeks also moved to Western Europe, mainly France and Britain. Another significant factor was the language spoken in the destination country and also its proximity to and accessibility from Egypt. Following this route, some migrants tried to move to the French colonies of North Africa (Morocco, Tunisia), to British territories in East Africa, and to the Belgian Congo. The colonial environment in these countries, which protected European citizens, also influenced this choice, since immigrants found an integration mechanism that had similar characteristics with capitulatory Egypt. Ambassador Melas acknowledged that the Western powers had a vivid interest in attracting Greek migrants to the colonies: "Given that the countries that have colonies realize that Greeks will be their natural allies in the event of a revolt of the local population, there may be possibility in the future to increase individual migration of Greeks on the condition that this is done discreetly."[58] Decolonization, though, prevented this movement from developing a mass character. It is also worth mentioning here the case of the Greek Jews, a number of whom moved from Egypt to Israel after 1948.[59]

Potential migrants based their decision to move to particular destinations on the expectations and information about work and opportunities they received from their networks as well as the support that they believed was available to them after their arrival in the host country. The role of the GCCA in this process, as we shall see in the next chapter, proved to be crucial. Of equal importance was the fact that some Greek companies specifically sought Egyptiot Greek employees. Such was the case, for instance, in the Belgian Congo, Morocco, Saudi Arabia, and South Africa. It is also worth mentioning that migrants often undertook a short, exploratory trip to a particular destination in order to see conditions for themselves, before returning to Egypt. In some cases, they traveled a second or even a third time to find the most favorable living conditions and job opportunities. Usually men left first, and, if the conditions in the chosen country were encouraging, the rest of the family members followed.

Even if Australia constituted the most popular destination, GMFA officials had other ideas regarding the migration of Greeks from Egypt. They considered neighboring countries to Greece and Egypt to be ideal destinations. At a meeting of the cabinet of the exile government in London in November 1941, the prime minister in exile, Emmanouil Tsouderos, raised the idea that Greeks should colonize North Africa; other politicians would subsequently repeat this proposal.[60] The settlement of Greeks from Egypt in the Eastern Mediterranean was then considered to be of major importance for the reinforcement of Greece's political and economic influence from Istanbul to Cyrenaica.[61] These diplomats still conceived the Greek community, against all odds, as a bulwark for the "expansion of Hellenism" in the Eastern Mediterranean.[62] The issue seemed to be, as Hadziiossif plausibly puts it, "the peaceful and permanent reestablishment of the Mediterranean diaspora as a territory of national, nonstate expansionism."[63] It is interesting, though, to underline this attitude of fake imperialism in this regard at this particular juncture: it was shortly before the creation of the Israeli state in 1948 and more than two decades after the collapse of Greece's "Great Idea."[64]

The idea of migrating to the neighboring countries had another "advantage": it reduced the danger of the possible assimilation of the Greeks living abroad—as had happened in the United States and other Western countries—since Greek diplomats considered these areas to be inhabited by peoples of "inferior civilization."[65] Thus, strong links with the motherland—and consequently remittances to Greece that would boost postwar development—would not be jeopardized. In the early 1950s, the migration of Greeks to the Middle East, the Eastern Mediterranean coast, or to Eastern and Central Africa became a central political aspect in the official Greek migration policy for metropolitan Greeks as well as for Egyptiots.[66]

Migration to Australia and other destinations continued throughout the 1950s. The wave was sometimes reinforced and other times it was reduced following the general trend to leave Egypt. For instance, departures increased before the evacuation of the Suez Canal by the British and especially in the first months of 1957 after the Suez Crisis. From 1 January to 31 March, 1,500 Greeks left Egypt for good; of these, 800 went to Greece and the rest to various destinations.[67] To the departing Greeks we must also add about 170 families who left for Gaza in 1957 as members of the UN mission there.[68] The departures continued in the following months, but at a slower pace. According to consular data for 1957, 1,779 persons departed from Cairo—the destination is not provided. In 1958, that number was 582; in 1959, 398.[69] Even if overseas migration was the first choice for the Egyptiots right after the war, it was not the main one in the 1950s. As the destitution certificates issued by the GKC show—this document exempted the bearer from passport application fees—repatriation was the principal motivation; returning to an imaginary—or not—country was considered by many the most logical choice when the question of leaving Egypt was set. Of the 664 certificates issued from 1947 to 1961, 224 concerned repatriation and 117 emigration to Australia or other destinations, whereas in 323 cases the destination was not specified, probably because the applicant had not decided on one.[70]

UNAVOIDABLE REPATRIATION

Repatriation was not a realistic option in the latter half of the 1940s because of the situation in Greece due to the Greek Civil War (1946–49).[71] Egyptiot repatriates, especially unemployed and destitute ones, were considered to be an intolerable "burden"[72] for Greece's economy at the same time that the Greek state was planning an emigration program for metropolitan residents to counter unemployment and the danger of social disorder.[73] Besides, these prospective migrants from Egypt would be more useful for the Greek economy if they remained abroad and sent remittances to the homeland.[74] Given the economic difficulties facing the Egyptiots, the representatives of the Greek state urged them to keep a cool head, as they did before the war, and proposed that they stay in Egypt or to move to other destinations, but not Greece.[75] But not everyone was dissuaded from repatriation. Already in 1947 the Greek ambassador, Triantafyllidis, asked the consular authorities to encourage those who wanted to transfer their capital to Greece and, thus, create new job opportunities there, to repatriate.[76] There is also evidence that immediately after the end of the civil war, wealthy members of the community moved to Greece.[77] As the GCCA annual report for 1949 pointed out, this was "because of the encouraging information from Greece that there are opportunities for medium- and large-scale businesses."[78]

Despite the Greek state's instructions to diplomats to prevent the repatriation of those facing economic difficulties, a significant number of Egyptiot Greeks went to Greece. After the war, they resumed their visits to Greece for pleasure, business, health reasons, studies, and family reasons. At the same time, fewer people than in the previous decades migrated to Egypt.[79] It was not complicated for an Egyptiot looking for a job to find one in Greece and remain there. Despite the difficult situation in Greece in the late 1940s because of the civil war, hundreds of Egyptiots moved to the metropolis annually.[80] Observing this increasing trend, which he attributed to unemployment and the other difficulties faced by Egyptiots, journalist Dinos Koutsoumis, from the Alexandrian *Tachydromos,* proposed the creation of a special service, with the participation of community dignitaries and the Greek state, to facilitate this movement.[81]

Even people who had made some arrangement to secure a job before moving to Greece faced difficulties. The case of Panagiotis Xenakis, a young Greek from Cairo with family origins in Ikaria, is revealing in this regard. Twelve days after his arrival at the port of Piraeus, he wrote to his father describing his first days in Greece: "All day long I walk around like a wandering Jew. Life in Athens is very hard and extremely expensive."[82] During these twelve days, he had the time to apply for a job at the airline company, TWA, on the recommendation of an Egyptian family friend, who apparently had a connection with the company's office in Cairo. Besides, the choice for this type of company is also explained by the fact that a basic advantage of the Egyptiots was their polyglotism, which was a much sought-after skill in any airline company.

In his letter, Xenakis asked his father to send him his school-leaving certificate and a social belief certificate, which the airline company had requested. In turn, his father asked the GKC president, Georgios Roilos, to issue the latter and to highlight that his son was "a law-abiding person, of healthy and pure nationalist feelings, not a Communist."[83] Roilos consulted with the Greek consul of Cairo, Eleftherios Mavrokefalos, who noted that the father, Aristotelis Xenakis, was "an old resident of Cairo and a member of the Koinotita" and recommended that the consulate issue the certificate for Panagiotis even if, as one may assume from the tone of the letter, he was probably not entitled to it.[84] This correspondence reveals the methods that the *koinotites* and the Greek state employed as they collaborated in the aftermath of the civil war to control repatriation.

In spite of the efforts to bar repatriation and the fact that the community organizations and the Egyptiot press, on Athens's instructions, recommended that Egyptiots emigrate to third destinations,[85] their emigration in all possible ways was a reality in the early 1950s, as table 11 illustrates.

Table 11. Exit visas issued by the Greek consulate general in Alexandria, 1951–53

	Destination					
Year	Greece	Israel	Australia	African countries	Other countries	Total
1951	157	94	258	–	–	509
1952	165	–	207	24	56	452
1953	127	30	143	22	11	341
Total	449	124	608	46	67	1,302

Sources: AYE/CS/1952/49/4/1/1, 5, Alexandria, 12 January 1952, Liatis to Greek embassy in Cairo; AYE/CS/1953/78/1/1, 11, Alexandria, 14 January 1953, Liatis to Greek embassy in Cairo; AYE/CS/1954/131/1, 92, Alexandria, 25 February 1954, Argyropoulos to Melas.

The data in table 11 show that 30 percent of the departing Egyptiot Greeks moved to the homeland in 1951. This percentage increased to 36 and 37 percent in 1952 and 1953, respectively, in the years following the end of the civil war. This increase, despite the decrease in the overall number of departing Egyptiot Greeks, is also confirmed by other sources.[86] The decrease in the number of Greeks departing from Alexandria in 1952 is due, to a certain degree, to the stabilization of the political situation after the Free Officers coup. In Cairo, on the other hand, the consul general predicted that ten to fifteen people a month were bound to leave in 1950.[87] Among them were many Greek Jews, who were ready to depart for Israel. From the incomplete data regarding Cairo contained in table 12 for the years 1950 to 1952, a quarter of those who departed in 1952 moved to Greece. The increase in the number of Greeks departing from Cairo in 1952 is most probably linked to the Black Saturday events, described in chapter 2.

While the figures in tables 11 and 12 do not provide the exact numbers of people who departed, they are indicative of the cohort of Greeks who left Egypt during that period. Many of them left on exit visas, without declaring that it was their intention to leave permanently. Egyptiots used this tactic to avoid long and troublesome formalities with the Egyptian authorities[88] but also to keep open the possibility of returning to Egypt at a later stage.

Despite the increase in repatriation in the early 1950s, in 1956 the flow to Greece seems to have stabilized, as suggested by the number of applications for destitution certificates. Moreover, membership in the Association of Greeks from Egypt in Athens increased rapidly in 1957, a year after the Suez Crisis. Before 1956 new registrations were practically nonexistent. Fifteen new members were recorded in 1956, and in the following year, 378. Membership subsequently grew, to reach a peak in 1963, when 1,354 new members joined.[89] In its findings, the Agapitidis Committee, established in May 1957 to evaluate the situation of Greeks in Egypt and suggest solutions, noted the atmosphere of near panic that prevailed among the community in the months after the Suez Crisis: "The first thought that comes to the Greek

Table 12. Exit visas issued by the Greek consulate general in Cairo, 1951–53

Year	Destination		Total
	Greece	Australia	
1950	—	—	129
1951	—	—	221
1952	62	180	242
Total	—	—	592

Source: AYE/CS/1953/51/1/1, 298, Cairo, 18 January 1953, Georgiadis to Melas.

of Egypt who encounters ... hardship ... is repatriation. This wish ... becomes stronger when he's informed that the security has been established in the motherland and the economy is clearly improving."[90] It also mentioned that there was a clear tendency toward repatriation, with the rate fluctuating depending on developments in both Egypt and Greece.[91] It concluded with the remark that the official Greek policy against repatriation should be eased. "The situation should be left alone to develop by itself so that repatriation can represent an outlet," it noted, pointing out that it was an issue affecting few people apart from the Greek residents of the Suez Canal.[92]

According to the committee, Egyptiots left out of concern for their children's future. In this respect it also suggested measures for those who desired to transfer more than the permitted amount to Greece in the event of repatriation (which was then set at LE 5,000 per household), as well as how to exempt transferred assets from import duties upon arrival in Greece, and to facilitate integration into the domestic labor market.[93] Alexios Liatis, who was among those who advocated setting up a migration program for Egyptiot Greeks in 1951 and who later became the head of the GMFA's political affairs department, seemed to agree with the idea of a more flexible policy regarding repatriation but disagreed with almost all of the proposed measures. In practice, the Greek state remained reluctant, as it feared a massive arrival of Egyptiots. As regards migration, the committee's report felt emigration was bound to continue, despite the problem presented by the closure of the Australian embassy in retaliation for the Suez Crisis. Even if the Greek state were to continue to support overseas migration, it was stated that each prospective migrant should feel free to choose his or her preferred destination. Egyptiot Greeks dispersed so widely around the world that it is almost impossible to reconstruct the full migratory pattern. The destinations sometimes corresponded with the wishes of the Greek state and community leadership, sometimes not. The variety of destinations, the different means migrants used to reach them, and the time span of this migratory movement mirrored the multifaceted characteristics of the community.

TRANSFERRING ASSETS—EVEN AFTER 1960

Money, in the form of remittances to the homeland, capital transfers for investments, or donations, always circulated freely between Egypt and Greece during the Capitulations era. In the 1930s the Greek Foreign Ministry estimated that Egyptiots sent LE 1 million in remittances annually to Greece.[94] Under the Montreux Convention and the subsequent legislative restrictions on transferring money, these transfers were increasingly conducted in an illicit way through illegal currency exchanges and the smuggling of valuables—a practice that the GMFA was aware of at least as early as 1950.[95] In one case, an Egyptiot smuggled a large amount of gold sovereigns. While the importation and sale of sovereigns was not illegal in Greece, this individual was put on trial because he failed to declare the sovereigns to the Greek customs. Even though he was found innocent, an Egyptiot residing in Egypt blackmailed him, threatening to denounce him to the Egyptian authorities unless the individual paid him to keep his silence.

Because of the increase in illegal money transfers to Greece in the early 1950s, the Egyptian Foreign Ministry sent intelligence service agents to the Egyptian embassy[96] in Athens to investigate which Egyptiots had transferred their assets to Greece illegally. The action of the agents in Athens continued throughout the 1950s and intensified in the 1960s during the exodus.[97] The Egyptian agents monitored the investments by Egyptiot Greeks in real estate or their businesses. According to a Greek Central Intelligence Service (KYP) report, the agents engaged in the "systematic tracking of the arrival of capital coming from members of the community in Egypt and of purchases of real estate." They relied on "the relevant data from the mortgage registrar's office in Athens and on information obtained from a wide network of Greek informants in Athens and Egypt."[98] Clearly, some Greeks were prepared to disregard any sense of ethnic solidarity that they might have had to collaborate with the Egyptian authorities. Some of them blackmailed their compatriots by threatening to denounce them to the Egyptian authorities.[99] According to a classified KYP report from September 1959, the cases of denunciation among Greeks had significantly increased:

> A worrying increase in the number of the members of the community in Egypt who cooperate with the Egyptian secret services has been observed. [They] act as informants against their compatriots there, who try to secretly export their capital despite the current prohibitive rules concerning capital transfers. ... The motives behind these anti-Greek acts ... are cons[idered] to be ... poverty ... danger of deportation ... envy and personal disputes. The Greek informants ... seek to gain the trust of the Egyptians, which will come in handy for them during their time there.[100]

The implication of both the Greek and Egyptian intelligence services is indicative of the importance the two governments attributed to this issue. Smuggling savings and valuables out of the country constituted a provocation for the Egyptian authorities and confirmed their fears that foreigners were exporting the capital that they had accumulated in Egypt in order to invest it elsewhere.

Smuggling cases increased after the Suez Crisis, proving that a significant number of Egyptiot Greeks were preparing themselves for every eventuality. Given that repatriates could take only LE 5,000 in cash with them, the capital export limits mainly concerned those community members who had substantial savings and had amassed fortunes, that is, those in the middle and upper social strata. They used all possible means to spirit money out of the country. For instance, from 1958 to 1960 diplomatic routes were abused for this purpose, as Lambros confirmed in a report:

> The diplomatic bags were systematically used for the transfer of capital and values. ... I consider it imperative to give explicit instructions to the ... attaché to refuse on any occasion the transfer of money through the bags. I'm putting forward this recommendation not because I have the slightest suspicion that the officials that serve the embassy would ever export money for their own purposes, but because it is not out of the question that they sometimes get carried away by a willingness to help out members of the community with whom they are friends.[101]

In the early 1960s, when the mass departure movement began in earnest, incidents of Egyptiot Greeks trying to transfer currency and other valuables illegally sharply increased. In the 1961, the consul general to Cairo expressed to the GMFA his deep concern about the issue, declaring, "The Egyptian authorities have the capability to strike crushing blows at any time against the community, due to the clandestine transfer of capital."[102] The Egyptian state had multiplied the inspections at the country's ports and airports. At the same time the Egyptian police placed under surveillance the shipping agents and the homes of people who were preparing to leave the country. From 1961, the Alexandria customs service implemented a new way of inspecting the luggage of departing Europeans: furniture and other household effects now had to be packed at the customs office under the watchful eye of officials, and not in the home, as had been the case.[103]

In other cases, foreigners were arrested for smuggling currency. One of them, Dolly Zarifi, was detained when she tried to transfer "120 shares in the Bank of Athens and many gold and silver objects."[104] She was released on bail of LE 50, but her efforts to leave Egypt before the investigation started were unsuccessful. According to Vyron Theodoropoulos, consul general in Alexandria, members of her family had previously attempted to export currency and other valuables illegally. Zarifi herself often withdrew cash from her bank accounts and transferred it to Greece.[105] The Zarifi affair and other similar cases preoccupied the foreign and Arabic-language press in Egypt. The resulting publicity inflicted serious collateral damage on those who were ready to depart or had chosen to remain in Egypt,[106] not only because the legislation on this matter became stricter, but also because it weakened the negotiating position of the Greek diplomatic authorities.[107] As a consequence, the diplomatic staff warned the community that it would cease to intervene in cases of illegal currency transfer,[108] and particularly in cases involving those who practiced currency smuggling as a profession.[109] As the Greek ambassador, Harilaos Zamarias, pointed out, the "senseless acts of our citizens in Alexandria, and even of respectable ones, endanger all of our policies that we have been implementing in the UAR; they weaken our position toward the Egyptian authorities and make them take measures that in the end are mostly against the majority of the poorer Greeks."[110]

As the Greeks came up with more inventive ways to hide money and other valuables, custom controls were stepped up. An indicative case was that of Lilika Moutselou, the wife of the director of the National Bank of Greece branch in Alexandria, whose pastries were "destroyed" by customs, as Theodoros Baizos, the Cairo consul general, noted: "During her departure at the airport, her luggage was thoroughly inspected, and she was led to a private room where she underwent a full body search. The search became so intense that some of the sweets that Mrs Moutselou was carrying with her were crushed in order to confirm that there were no gold coins or jewels in them."[111] Baizos blamed the inspection on Moutselou's pastries on an unsigned, anonymous denunciation. Such a denunciation could be made to the financial prosecutor, the exchange control office, or the tax evasion service. The authorities could deem the information to warrant a ban on the suspect from exiting the country until the case was fully investigated.[112] The fastidiousness with which the Egyptian authorities controlled departees was striking; according to a classified GMFA document, a gynecologist examined some women before they boarded ships in order to prevent the illegal transfer of jewels and money.[113]

The Greek state was not completely uninvolved in the issue of smuggling currency. For some intending repatriates, the LE 5,000 limit imposed by the Egyptian government was considered too low. Sometimes though, the "repatriates" found it difficult to transfer even this sum of money because it had to go through Egyptian-Greek clearing, where the Egyptian side had a deficit.[114] In simple terms, for the Egyptiot Greeks to transfer LE 5,000, Greece had to import the equivalent in products from Egypt.[115] In most cases the departees received their money several months after their repatriation, a delay that created additional, unpleasant situations for them. Despite the continuous requests from the GCCA from 1954 for the normalization of the clearing system, no serious efforts were undertaken in this regard. When the exodus started, these efforts intensified in order to facilitate the repatriation of Egyptiots, but not much was achieved. The Greek state did not have the financial means to settle the issue definitively and, of course, did not want to facilitate repatriation. In addition, industrialists and businessmen in Greece were understandably reluctant to see huge amounts of unwanted products imported from Egypt just to enable the transfer of savings of Egyptiots.[116]

In any case, Egyptiot capital that had been accumulated in Egypt from business activities was not invested usually in Egypt; big businessmen and industrialists sought to move it abroad.[117] The most common way they used to transfer money was through a kind of arbitrage, a practice the Egyptian authorities were aware of.[118] A Greek diplomat describes another way, however: under Egyptian law, the exchange rate between the Greek and Egyptian currencies for companies importing machinery or other equipment for modernization purposes was eighty-six drachmas to the pound, instead of fifty-three to fifty-five drachmas, which was the exchange rate for Egyptian currency at Swiss banks.[119] Consequently, many entrepreneurs arranged with their suppliers to hike the price of equipment and to transfer the difference to another country. The ways to transfer assets from Egypt to Greece were many, but not all of them were illegal. For example, some merchants in Alexandria and Mansoura expressed their wish to exchange blocks of flats they owned in Egypt with *waqf* buildings in Muhammad Ali's native city in Kavalla, northeastern Greece.[120]

The possibility of transferring assets determined to a certain degree the departure rate from Egypt during the 1950s and 1960s. It is almost certain, though, that were the Egyptian policies on currency transfer less strict, the departure movement in the early 1960s would have been larger. One of the reasons Greeks did not declare their definitive departure was to avoid settling the tax affairs.[121] When from May 1962 those traveling abroad were obliged to submit a tax clearance certificate, an obligation existing at that time in almost all European countries, some Egyptiots protested vigorously. The consul general in Cairo, Ioannis Yiannakakis, justified their reaction in the following way: "The ... discontent of the Egyptiots is mostly due to the impunity they enjoyed in the past."[122]

Transferring assets obviously concerned those who had assets to transfer. The community, though, contained in its ranks a significant number of destitute people who were not concerned with clearance and smuggling. Many of them had expressed their wish to leave Egypt in the late 1940s and early 1950s. While the Greek state had no objections to repatriates transferring assets, it did not wish to receive those who had no financial means. The Greek state not only prevented the Egyptiots from moving to Greece, as Sofianos Chryssostomidis pointed out with justified bitterness,[123] but in collaboration with the community and international organizations, it also created a mechanism to push the unemployed and destitute to other, remote destinations—a process referred to as the "decongestion" of the community.

NOTES

1. Cited in G Nikolaou, *O aigyptiotis ellinismos kai i mellontiki autou katefthynsis* [The Egyptiot Hellenism and its direction in the future] (Alexandria: Patriarchal Printing House, 1915), 4.
2. Ibid., 3.
3. Angelos Dalachanis, "Internationalism vs. nationalism? The Suez Canal Company strike of 1919 and the formation of the International Workers' Union of the Isthmus of Suez," in *Social Transformation and Mass Mobilization in the Balkan and Eastern Mediterranean Cities 1900–1923*, ed. Andreas Lyberatos (Iakleio: Crete University Press, 2013), 352.
4. *Tableaux analytiques du mouvement migratoire et touristique de la Grèce avec l'étranger pendant les années 1931–1940* (Athens: National Statistical Service of Greece, 1946), 231–41.
5. Alexander Kazamias, "The 'Purge of the Greeks' from Nasserite Egypt: Myths and Realities," *Journal of the Hellenic Diaspora* 35, no. 2 (2009): 15.
6. AYE/CS/1952/48/1/1/1, Secret, Athens, 21 May 1952, Report concerning the position of Greeks in Egypt, Dragoumis to Venizelos, 13.
7. *Tableaux analytiques du mouvement migratoire*, 100.
8. AYE/CS/1944/40/3 2860, Cairo, 17 August 1944, Pappas to GMFA.
9. AYE/CS/1944/40/3, Cairo, 8 July 1944, Erskine to all Greek units.
10. Floresca Karanasou, "The Greeks in Egypt: From Mohammed Ali to Nasser, 1805–1961," in *The Greek Diaspora in the Twentieth Century*, ed. Richard Clogg (London: Macmillan, 1999), 54.
11. Alexander Kitroeff, *The Greeks in Egypt, Ethnicity and Class, 1917–1937* (Oxford: Ithaca Press, 1989), 13.
12. AYE/CS/1952/49/4/1/1, 367, Mansoura, 5 June 1952, Korantis to Cairo embassy.
13. AYE/CS/1952/49/4/1/1, 4164, Alexandria, 6 June 1952, Liatis to Cairo embassy.
14. Ibid.
15. AYE/CS/1952/49/4/1/1, 4478, Alexandria, 19 June 1952, Liatis to Cairo embassy.
16. Andreas Syngros, *Apomnimonevmata* [Memoirs] (Athens: Estia Bookstore, 1908), 103.
17. Timos Malanos, *Anamniseis enos Alexandrinou* [Recollections of an Alexandrian] (Athens: Boukoumanis Publishing, 1971), 176–77.
18. Sayyid 'Ashmawi, "Perceptions of the Greek Money-Lender in Egyptian Collective Memory at the Turn of the Twentieth Century," in *Money, Land and Trade: An Economic History of the Muslim Mediterranean*, ed. Nelly Hanna (London: IB Tauris, 2002), 244–78.

19. Evgenios Michailidis, *O aigyptiotis ellinismos kai to mellon tou* [Egyptiot Hellenism and its future] (Alexandria: Grammata, 1927), 4.
20. Kitroeff, *The Greeks*, 87.
21. Ibid., 87, 127.
22. Athanassios Politis, *O ellinismos kai i neotera Aigyptos* [Hellenism and modern Egypt], vol. 1 (Alexandria: Grammata, 1928), 165.
23. AYE/CS/1948/94/4/4/2, Report of vice-consul Igglesis, Suez, 23 September 1947, Igglesis to Cairo embassy.
24. AYE/CS/1952/49/4/1/1, 2195, Tanta, 15 December 1951, Igglesis to Cairo embassy.
25. AYE/CS/1952/49/4/1/1, 22 D/1, Mansoura, 9 January 1952, Papadakis to the Greek embassy in Cairo; AYE/CS/1953/51/1/1, 35, Zagazig 13 January 1953, Skarpalezos to Melas; AYE/CS/1952/48/1/1/1, Secret, Athens, 21 May 1952, Report concerning the position of Greeks in Egypt, Dragoumis to Venizelos, 14.
26. AYE/CS/1952/50/6/1/1/2481, Cairo, 31 October 1952, Melas to GMFA.
27. AYE/CS/1952/48/1/1/1, Secret, Athens, 21 May 1952, Report concerning the position of Greeks in Egypt, Dragoumis to Venizelos, 11.
28. AYE/CS/1952/50/6/1/1/2481, Cairo, 31 October 1952, Melas to GMFA.
29. AYE/CS/1952/49/4/1/1, 4695, Alexandria, 28 June 1952, Liatis to Cairo embassy.
30. AYE/CS/1950/2227/D/1, 949, Suez, 10 January 1950, Tsourkas to Triantafyllidis.
31. AYE/CS/1952/49/4/1/1, 22 D/1, Mansoura, 9 January 1952, Papadakis to Cairo embassy.
32. AYE/CS/1952/50/6/1/1, 71, Zagazik, 25 January 1952, Skarpalezos to Cairo embassy.
33. AYE/CS/1951/89/4/1/1, 1439, Tanta 15 December 1950, Igglesis to Cairo embassy.
34. AYE/CS/1951/10/2/1/1, 131 D/1, Suez, 31 January 1951, Tsourkas to Triantafyllidis.
35. AYE/CS/1952/48/1/1/1, Secret, Athens, 21 May 1952, Report concerning the position of Greeks in Egypt, Dragoumis to Venizelos, 14.
36. Archives of the Greek Koinotita of Tanta/Correspondence/Tanta, 11 May 1945.
37. AYE/CS/1950/89/4/1/1, 1439, Tanta, 15 December 1950, Igglesis to Cairo embassy.
38. AYE/CS/1963/44/5/2/1/2, 254 D/1, Mansoura, 20 February 1962, Kouzopoulos to Cairo embassy.
39. AYE/CS/1963/44/5/2/1/2, 685, Port Said, 8 February 1963, Megalokonomos to Cairo embassy.
40. AYE/CS/1965/46/2/1/1, Sibin el-Kom, 18 December 1965, Triantafyllou to Horafas.
41. AYE/CS/1965/46/2/1/1, 607, Mansoura, 30 June 1965, Kouzopoulos to Cairo embassy.
42. AYE/CS/1965/46/2/1/1, 4406, Cairo, 27 July 1965, Horafas to GMFA.
43. AYE/CS/1947/10/1, 135/2/1/27, Piraeus, 22 March 1947, Karamouzis to Foreigners Department; "On Migration," *Bulletin of the GCCA* 569 (15 January 1948): 10–11.

44. AGCCA/57, Royal Consulate General of Alexandria, 1947–55, General observations on the community life during 1949 and on the Greek-Egyptian commerce during the year, Alexandria, 29 November 1949.
45. AGCCA/57, Royal Consulate General of Greece in Alexandria, 1947–55, Confidential note on various issues concerning the consulate general of Greece for the review of the year 1948 (n.d., n.p.).
46. "Concerning Migration to South Africa," *Bulletin of the GCCA* 573 (15 March 1948): 1–4; "Concerning Migration," *Bulletin of the GCCA* 569 (15 January 1948): 10–11; "Concerning Entrance and Settlement in the Union of South Africa," *Bulletin of the GCCA* 571 (15 February 1948): 6; "Migration Possibilities for Greeks to Ethiopia," *Bulletin of the GCCA* 551 (15 April 1947): 8–11.
47. AGCCA/Book of provided services.
48. AGCCA/62/Commercial and financial information about Argentina, 1421/B/12, Buenos Aires, 23 May 1949, Kapsabelis to Pandelidis.
49. AGCCA/62/Commercial and financial information about Argentina, 463/49, Alexandria, 28 March 1949, Pandelidis to Kapsabelis.
50. AGCCA/62/Commercial and financial information about Argentina, 1540/49/8, Alexandria, 13 September 1949, Pandelidis to Kapsabelis.
51. AGCCA/Migration fund, Alexandria, 18 September 1951, Miliarakis to GCCA.
52. AGCCA/62/Commercial and financial information about Argentina, 321-A/9, Chicago, 15 February 1950, Kapsabelis to Pandelidis.
53. AYE/CS/1954/131/2/1, 55, Rio de Janeiro, 12 January 1953, Kapsabelis to Sakellarios.
54. AYE/CS/1951/7/3/2/2, 1267/49/9, Alexandria, 8 July 1949, Salvagos to Pappas.
55. Mark Choate, *Emigrant Nation: The Making of Italy Abroad* (Cambridge, MA: Harvard University Press, 2008).
56. AGKC/55/Secretariat/Certificates, 1944–52, Cairo, 1 August 1951, Mavromatis to Roilos.
57. Those Egyptian Greeks who migrated to the United States did so on their own initiative and not through sponsored migration programs. See Alexander Kitroeff, "The Greeks of Egypt in the United States," *Journal of the Hellenic Diaspora* 35, no. 2 (2009): 117–32.
58. AYE/CS/1952/48/6/3/3, 7013, Cairo, 30 September 1952, Melas to consulate general in Alexandria.
59. AYE/CS/1950/16/1/1, 17, Cairo, 16 January 1950, Mavrokefalos to Triantafyllidis.
60. Giorgis Athanassiadis, *I proti praxi tis ellinikis tragodias. Mesi Anatoli: 1941–1944* [The first act of the Greek tragedy: Middle East, 1941–44] (Athens, 1975), 106.
61. AYE/CS/1944/The Cairo Government, 443, Alexandria 24 October 1944, Valtis to Pappas.
62. AYE/CS/1944/The Cairo Government/D/1, 243, Cairo, 18 July 1944, Pappas to Papandreou.
63. Christos Hadziiossif, "Apopseis gyro apo ti viosimotita tis Elladas kai to rolo tis viomixanias" [Views concerning the viability of Greece and the role of indus-

try], in *Afieroma sto Niko Svorono* [Tribute to Nikos Svoronos], ed. Vasilis Kremmydas, Chrysa Maltezou, and Nikolaos M. Panagiotakis (Rethymno: Crete University Press, 1986), 330–68.
64. The Great Idea was an irredentist doctrine advocating the expansion of the Greek state so as to encompass all ethnic Greeks settled in the territory of the Ottoman Empire.
65. AYE/CS/1948/25/3/1/1, Athens 27 July 1948, Koutsalexis to Dendramis.
66. AYE/CS/1951/7/3/2/2, 24247 AP/1/Africa, Athens, 26 April 1950, GMFA to Greek embassies in Washington and London.
67. AYE/CS/1957/22/9/1/1, 6857, Cairo, 4 June 1957, Lambros to GMFA.
68. Manolis Yalourakis, *I Aigyptos ton Ellinon* [Egypt of the Greeks] (Athens: Mitropolis, 1967), 388.
69. AYE/CS/1961/16/1/3/3, Cairo, 9 May 1961, Yiannakakis to Cairo embassy.
70. AGKC, Destitution certificates.
71. AYE/CS/1948/92/3/1/1, 4381, Cairo, 17 November 1947, Triantafyllidis to consular authorities in Egypt.
72. AYE/CS/1948/92/3/1/1, 4381, Cairo, 17 November 1947, Triantafyllidis to Greek consular authorities in Egypt; AYE/CS/1948/92/3/1/1, 23/48, Alexandria, 6 January 1948, Zerbinis to Tabakopoulos.
73. On the role of the Greek state in postwar Greek emigration, see Lina Venturas, "Greek Governments, Political Parties and Emigrants in Western Europe: Struggles for Control (1950–1974)," *Revue Européenne des Migrations Internationales* 17, no. 3 (2001): 64–65.
74. AYE/CS/1948/92/3/1/1, 23/48, Alexandria, 6 January 1948, Zerbinis to Tambakopoulos.
75. AYE/CS/1948/94/4/4/2, 48431, Athens, 2 December 1948, Kontoumas to Cairo embassy.
76. AYE/CS/1948/92/3/1/1, 4381, Cairo, 17 November 1947, Triantafyllidis to Greek consular authorities in Egypt.
77. AYE/CS/1949/42/1/5/1, 58979/3, Athens, 9 January 1950, Pappas to Financial Affairs Department of the GMFA.
78. AGCCA/57, Royal Consulate General of Alexandria, 1947–55, General observations on the community life during 1949 and on the Greek-Egyptian commerce during the year, Alexandria, 29 November 1949.
79. National Statistical Service of Greece, *Statistical Directory of Greece* (Athens: National Printing House, 1958), 61.
80. *Tachydromos,* 9 October 1949.
81. *Tachydromos,* 21 August 1949.
82. AGKC/Secretariat/55/Certificates, 1944–52, Piraeus, 9 October 1948, P Xenakis to A Xenakis.
83. AGKC/Secretariat 55/Certificates, 1944–52, 732, Cairo, 25 October 1948, P Xenakis to Roilos.
84. AGKC/Secretariat 55/Certificates, 1944–52, 889, Cairo, 3 November 1948, Roilos to Mavrokefalos.
85. *Kyrix,* 16 June 1949.

86. AYE/CS/1954/131/2/1, 775/53, Alexandria, 1 October 1953, Sakellarios to Tabakopoulos.
87. AYE/CS/1950/16/1/1, 17, Cairo, 16 January 1950, Mavrokefalos to Triantafyllidis.
88. AYE/CS/1954/131/1, 92, Alexandria, 25 February 1954, Argyropoulos to Melas.
89. AGKC/Secretariat/155/2nd World Congress of Egyptian Greeks, Athens, 1992.
90. AGKS/Readjustment of the statutes according to Law 384/1956, Agapitidis Committee report, June 1957.
91. AGKC/Secretariat/155/2nd World Congress of Egyptian Greeks. Krystallo Trimi, general secretary of the Association of Egyptiots in Greece, [presentation "Statistics of the SAE" to the 2nd World Congress of Egyptian Greeks, Athens, 1992].
92. AGKS/Readjustment of the statutes according to Law 384/1956, Agapitidis Committee report, June 1957.
93. Ibid.
94. AYE/CS/1944/13/4, 443, Alexandria, 24 October 1944, Valtis to Pappas.
95. AYE/CS/1951/143/4/2/1, 7507, Top Secret, Cairo, 12 October 1950, Triantafyllidis to Koutsalexis. The incident concerned the illegal transfer of gold sovereigns from Egypt to Greece.
96. AYE/CS/1964/44/3/1/1, E-505107, KYP, Athens, 18 August 1964, Report on the activities of the UAR intelligence services in Greece, Giorgos Agoros, lieutenant general/director.
97. AYE/CS/1954/131/1/150, Cairo, 16 June 1954, Pantermalis to GMFA.
98. AYE/CS/1964/44/3/1/1, E-505107, KYP, Athens, 18 August 1964, Report on the activities of the UAR intelligence services in Greece, Giorgos Agoros, lieutenant general/director.
99. AYE/CS/1964/43/7/1/1, 5601, Cairo, 18 December 1956, Roussos to GMFA.
100. Information bulletin, from 15 September 1959 to 21 September 1959, Top Secret, cited in Manos Iliadis, *To aporrito imerologio tis KYP gia tin Kypro* [The classified journal of KYP concerning Cyprus] (Athens: I. Sideris, 2007), 141.
101. AYE/CS/1961/21/4/1/1, 6259, Cairo, 15 February 1961, Lambros to GMFA.
102. AYE/CS/1962/36/4/2/2, Note, Top Secret, Athens, 30 December 1961.
103. AYE/CS/1961/21/17/2/2, Secret, 22448, Athens, 13 December 1961, Nikitakis to GMFA.
104. AYE/CS/1964/43/7/1/1, 527, Alexandria, 11 June 1962, Theodoropoulos to Zamarias.
105. AYE/CS/1964/43/7/1/1, 6785, Cairo, 11 June 1962, Zamarias to GMFA.
106. *Tachydromos,* 9 November 1962; fifty-one Greeks were accused of smuggling currency.
107. AYE/CS/1964/43/7/1/1, 6785, Cairo, 11 June 1962, Zamarias to GMFA.
108. Ibid.
109. Cases of people earning money through currency smuggling were common in the late 1950s and early 1960s. See *O Paroikos,* 14 April 1955, 1, 6; Kazamias, "The 'Purge,'" 22.

110. AYE/CS/1964/43/7/1/1, 6785, Cairo, 11 June 1962, Zamarias to GMFA.
111. AYE/CS/1961/16/1/3/1, 193, Alexandria, 24 February 1961, Baizos to Lambros.
112. AYE/CS/1964/49/4/1/1, 679, Cairo, 28 January 1963, Yiannakakis to Zamarias.
113. AYE/CS/1961/21/17/2/2, Secret, 22448, Athens, 13 December 1961, Nikitakis to GMFA.
114. Elliniki en Alexandria Koinotis, *Logodosia etous 1958* [Greek Koinotita of Alexandria, Annual report of 1958] (Alexandria: T. Kassimatis, 1958), 30–33.
115. Yalourakis, *I Aigyptos,* 219.
116. AGCCA/Correspondence, 1960–63, Summary note for the administrative council on the occasion of the visit of the Greek trade minister, Leonidas Dertilis, Alexandria, 6 April 1961.
117. Yalourakis, *I Aigyptos,* 212.
118. Nikos Katapodis, *Skorpia fylla tis diplomatikis mou zois* [Aspects of my diplomatic career] (Athens: Potamos, 2004), 32.
119. Ibid.
120. *Le Progrès égyptien,* 14 September 1954, 3.
121. AYE/CS/1962/65/7/1/1, 591, Cairo, 21 May 1962, Yiannakakis to Zamarias.
122. Ibid.
123. Sofianos Chryssostomidis, "Elliniki paroikia Aigyptou: i exodos" [The Greek community of Egypt: the exodus], *Archiotaxio* 4 (2002): 131.

Chapter Six

Decongestion

"Mr Viscovitch, we arrived after a nice and pleasant trip and excellent service on the ship. We are leaving this afternoon for Sydney. ... I will write to you with more news from there. Love. Eleftherios Miliarakis."[1] He wrote his message on a postcard sent from Melbourne to the GCCA director, Evmolpos Viscovitch, on 17 January 1952. Miliarakis, an unemployed carpenter "from Smyrna, one of the ex-employees of the British Suez Canal zone,"[2] had not reached Australia by his own means. He had requested and received a loan of LE 60 from the GCCA migration fund, which the chamber set up in Alexandria in late 1951, because he had no other way of purchasing his ticket and migrating to Australia. In exchange, apart from repaying the loan, he sent back information about the traveling conditions and the situation in the destination country after his arrival. The fund was an initiative of the consular authorities and community dignitaries to "decongest" the community; in other words, to promote migration to countries away from Greece of destitute and unemployed Egyptiots in order to ease social pressures in Egypt and prevent them from repatriating to Greece.

For reasons discussed in this chapter, the migration fund fell well short of meeting expectations. The effort to promote migration continued, however. By the early 1970s, the migration process involved international, community, and Greek state organizations. Through twenty years of organized migration, thousands of unemployed and destitute Egyptiots abandoned Egypt for distant places, mostly Australia, Africa, and North and South America. This chapter discusses migration mechanisms, the organizers, and the motivations of the leavers. Despite the "readjustment" efforts in the labor market and education, and migration or repatriation undertaken by individuals, the Greek state, in conjunction with community and international organizations, found ample space in which to operate and develop migration strategies for Egyptiot Greeks.

SPONSORING MIGRATION

After World War II, increasing numbers of Egyptiots decided to leave their adopted country and move to Greece. This was the case to an even greater degree for the destitute and unemployed, who could not afford the fare for an overseas voyage.[3] Writing in *Tachydromos* in late 1949, journalist Dinos Koutsoumis pointed to unofficial data showing that about 160 destitute Greek were "repatriated" in June, July, and August of that year.[4] Given the fact the traffic between Greece and Egypt usually increased in the summer months, this number may be exaggerated. As the same author admitted, there had always been cases of poor members of the community deciding to live out their remaining years in Greece. In many cases, old people left on the invitation of a relative who had promised them food and accommodation. Others were unemployed, desperate because of failed efforts to find a job in Egypt. In such cases, the consulate often issued the passport free of charge, whereas the patriarchate and the religious fraternities paid for the tickets. There were also cases of people who had to beg in order to pay for tickets.[5]

Tachydromos republished an article from an Athens daily warning of the difficulties some "repatriates" had in Greece. The story concerned Vassilios Kanelidis, a sixty-year-old man from Alexandria who had killed himself in the Byron Hotel on Eolou Street, in downtown Athens. In a suicide note found at the scene, Kanelidis complained that he could not find a job after his repatriation. Regardless of the validity of the published information, what is worth noting is that the journalist urged potential departees to weigh their options carefully before leaving Egypt for Greece. Kanelidis's suicide was a warning to destitute people considering repatriation, for he suggested that the Greek mutual assistance organizations in Egypt could provide them with better assistance.

After the war, the community leadership considered the level of unemployed and destitute Greeks to be a "burden" on the community's charitable organizations, which were already facing economic difficulties, and a constant threat to the social order. This perceived threat became intensified as the anticommunist stances of Greek state representatives in Egypt increased because of the civil war in Greece.[6] In the early 1950s, Greek diplomats clearly expressed their concern at the presence of increasingly unemployed and destitute Greeks. Deeming them a permanent threat to the social order because the destitute constituted a fertile ground for the development of communist ideas, the diplomats concluded that the community had to be "decongested."[7] The promotion of the departure of destitute and unemployed Greeks shows that beyond any internal differentiations linked to the citizenship status, origins, or even religion of Egyptiot Greeks, the community often distinguished among its members on the basis of wealth. Such considerations caused leaders of the community to determine who was worthy to remain in Egypt and who should be encouraged to leave. The poor were pressured to leave. Egyptian state officials were allies in the "decongestion" effort, for they not only viewed communism with disdain, but also encouraged Greek diplomats to remove unemployed and destitute elements of the community from the country in order to make more jobs available for Egyptians.[8]

In this context, the Alexandria general consul, Alexios Liatis, and the GCCA established a migration fund on 12 December 1951.[9] The main reason behind this move, apart from the ineffectiveness of the informal networks to facilitate migration, described in the previous chapter, was the uncomfortable situation created when a significant number of Greek ex-employees of the auxiliary services of the British military left the Suez Canal area and flocked to Alexandria. The fund would not promote wholesale Egyptiot migration. Its main target was to provide assistance through loans to fifty to a hundred destitute persons per year. Liatis considered this number to be "a drop in the ocean" to tackle an ever-increasing problem, since the real number of departing Greeks was estimated to be almost a thousand per year.[10]

As the applications of those who approached the fund show, they could not afford even half of the rather expensive ticket to Australia (LE 114 per person from Port Said to Perth on the *Hellenic Prince*) or for any other destination, not to mention the minimum amount of cash they needed to gain entry to the country. As the monthly salary of an employee in a truck transport company in Alexandria was LE 20, many of those who wished to leave could not afford overseas tickets, particularly when they wanted to bring their family with them. The fund operated under the auspices of the GCCA, which continued to provide information to prospective migrants about the formalities and career prospects in destination countries. At the same time, it offered evening English lessons to people planning to migrate to Australia or to other African countries that were still under colonial rule. With a rather limited capital at its disposal and relying on the financial support of wealthy Egyptiots and local Greek companies, the fund granted interest-free loans to destitute people. Since the attempts to arrange migration options through direct contact with the Greek diplomatic authorities in the host countries did not bear the anticipated results—such as the Pandelidis-Kapsabelis case discussed in the previous chapter—the goal now was to create a self-sustaining Egyptiot network that could assist destitute prospective migrants from Egypt by providing information, invitations from people who were settled in the host country, and money through loans, the repayment of which would finance the departure of more migrants. The idea was that every new migrant to Australia or Africa would serve as a bridge for the settlement of at least one more relative or friend.

According to Liatis, Alexandrian Greeks reacted positively to the plan.[11] The city's daily *Tachydromos* tried to drum up more funding so that the plan would be more effective. The only voices critical of facilitated migration were the Communists, who at the GKA general assembly in 1951 argued that the main issue should be "readjustment" or "repatriation" and not migration. Liatis believed the Communists had a selfish motive: to keep destitute Greeks in Egypt in order to prevent "the space where they hunt for clients and victims from shrinking."[12] As he pointed out in his speech concerning the establishment of the fund:

> This limited effort at decongestion of the community was strongly opposed by the Communists and their leftist allies, who took every opportunity to raise a voice of protest against the so-called planned dissolution of the community. Because in the eyes of the Communists, the departure of Egyptiots who lead an idle existence here represents a clear loss of expected listeners to their preaching.[13]

In the following years, the Communists maintained their opposition to sponsored migration. *O Paroikos* was the main voice opposing migration, leading to strong conflict between it and the GCCA, or the "Mr Sakellarios's migration agency," as the Cairo daily ironically called it.[14] Of course the embassy did not view the newspaper with approval and sought to close it down, as it had previously done with *Foni*.[15] Despite the opposition it faced, *O Paroikos* continued its criticism of migration and the GCCA. As Sokratis Kalliarekos wrote in May 1954:

> A community body has been placed at the head of this effort; its role must be the stabilization of the community and the development of Greek businesses through the readjustment of the working Egyptiots, in a way that they become suitable for and useful to the Egyptian economy. ... As long as there is the escape of migration, we will not be able to use all of our powers.[16]

He referred to the loans given to potential migrants as a "cash bonus" from the GCCA, which promoted migration for its own interests. The "soul of the community is getting frustrated and poisoned" as a result, since migration undermined the community's effort regarding readjustment.[17] The *O Paroikos* campaign claimed that the GCCA engaged in propaganda by painting foreign destinations as "promised lands" in the pages of its *Bulletin*.[18] *O Paroikos* published stories of migrants who were "misled" by the GCCA and returned to Egypt "after spending all their savings for tickets and other expenses"[19] and carried letters from abroad from "disappointed immigrants."[20] Another author wrote in the same issue: "Emigration is not a solution. If we, the young people, want to see a better day, we must adjust to the second homeland." Also indicative for this opposition was a series of articles published in the newspaper in April 1956 entitled "Behold the Australian paradise,"[21] in which letters detailing the negative experiences of Egyptiot Greeks in Australia were published alongside reproductions of articles from the Australian and Athens press that discredited the migration destination.[22]

Returning to the fund's establishment in 1951, a rather small number of around twenty people, mainly from the Suez Canal area, were the first to benefit from it and left the country in the first months of its operation.[23] An indicative case is that of Eleftherios Miliarakis, who requested and received a loan in order to leave for Australia. On 7 December 1951, some days before the official establishment of the fund, he visited the GCCA and discussed with Evmolpos Viscovitch, the GCCA director and officer responsible for the fund, the possibility of receiving a loan to reach Australia. When Miliarakis submitted his funding request, he already had a visa from the Australian embassy in Cairo. A landing permit, issued on the strength of an invitation from a relative or a friend in Australia who could financially vouch for the applicant, was a prerequisite for obtaining an Australian visa.[24] Greeks in Egypt found landing permits hard to obtain, since relatively few of their "compatriots" had already settled in Australia. Moreover, an immigrant who managed to settle in Australia had himself to wait for a long period of time before being allowed to send, in turn, invitations to friends and relatives in Egypt.[25] Some days later, on 18 December, Miliarakis submitted a written application, which the GCCA approved.

A month later, on 17 January, Miliarakis sent from Melbourne the postcard to Viscovitch that opened this chapter. After reaching Sydney, he proceeded to Canberra. From there he wrote once more to Viscovitch, on 17 February, making an initial assessment of his migratory experience and confirming that he had already repaid the first part of the loan. He also wrote that the major concern for someone arriving in Australia as an immigrant from Egypt was to find accommodation.[26] He also provided information about the Australian labor market and the necessary steps to find a job quickly.[27] Almost a year later, after making the first reimbursement payment of his loan, Miliarakis wrote again to the GCCA, responding to Viscovitch's request for an update on the Australian situation.[28] On 20 March 1953, Miliarakis responded from Sydney, where he had gone for medical treatment. This letter contains extremely interesting information about the job prospects of Greeks from Egypt in Australia. For immigrants with technical skills, finding a job was much easier than for those aiming for white-collar positions. Many who belonged to the first category and who had experience in and knowledge of English managed to find well-paid jobs in technical professions. By contrast, unskilled workers and prospective clerical or office employees faced great difficulty in finding positions.[29]

Miliarakis also detailed the difficulties migrants were likely to encounter upon arrival in Australia. In early 1952, Greeks from Egypt who had settled in Sydney had formed a mutual assistance association for their newly arrived "countrymen." Within the very first months of its operation, the Association of Greeks from Egypt organized cultural events, dances, and excursions and even formed a basketball team to bring Egyptiots together. Georgios Thalassinos, another Egyptiot Greek who arrived in Melbourne thanks to the GCCA's financial assistance, reported that he had encountered quite a number of people from Alexandria who had become members of the Association of Greeks from Egypt in Melbourne, founded in 1950.[30] Both organizations sought to safeguard the Egyptiot Greek identity in Australia, and the efforts to keep it distinct from both the Australian culture and the non-Egyptiot Greek immigrants were remarkable. The fact that Egyptiots attempted to create a self-sustaining network based on information provided by migrants from Egypt who had already settled in the destination countries is indicative of their identity. As members of a diaspora community, they were conscious of their differences and defended them. As another fund beneficiary, Antonios Kokkinos, wrote from Sydney, the "ethnicity and kindness of the Greeks of Australia are not at all the same with that of Greeks of Egypt, not even a quarter of it."[31]

Feeling different from other Greek communities abroad was not an Egyptiot specificity. Georgios Kokkinidis, who had asked for a loan to reach the French Cameroons to work as a teacher in a Greek school, kept Viscovitch informed from Douala: "No Greek in Cameroon wishes any Greek who comes from abroad unless it is a relative."[32] Kokkinidis also claimed that the best way for someone to migrate to that or any other African country was through the mediation of the patriarchate of Alexandria, which had jurisdiction over the whole continent. Indeed, the church preferred to see Greeks leaving Egypt migrating to other countries in its jurisdiction. As Kokkinidis admitted, his choice of destination was related to his "patron," Archimandrite Nikodimos.

The GCCA and consulate general set about organizing a support chain with émigrés for Egyptiot migration, based on the regular provision of money and up-to-date information. In practice, though, this support chain was not foolproof, as a number of migrants faced difficulties upon arrival at their destination. Mostly they were unable to find a job and were therefore in no position to honor their debt to the GCCA. One hapless migrant was Dimitris Leriou, a mechanical engineering graduate who, because of the 1947 Company Law, could not find a job in Egypt in a Greek or foreign-owned firm.[33] After receiving a loan, he departed about a month after Miliarakis, embarking on a ship from Port Said on 26 February 1952. In his agreement with the fund, he pledged to repay his loan in three installments. The first was due fifteen days after his arrival in Sydney, at about the end of March. On 4 April he sent a letter from his ship, which was anchored in Melbourne. An unpredictable incident had occurred. As a result of an epidemic that had broken out in Italian agriculture, the ship, which was full of Italian peasants, was put in quarantine for fifteen days, and no one was allowed to disembark. As a result, Leriou could not repay the fund on time.[34]

Nevertheless, even after he eventually landed in Sydney, on 18 April, further difficulties prevented him from clearing his debt. He described his predicament in a letter on 23 October, six months after his arrival in Australia.[35] He assured Viscovitch that he would settle his debt as soon as he possibly could. But there is no evidence that he actually did; on the contrary, on 22 April 1953, Viscovitch wrote a very curt and quite ironic letter to Leriou demanding the immediate reimbursement of the loan.[36] The archives provide no evidence that Leriou ever replied. His example was not the only case of an immigrant who, upon arriving in the host country, ignored his debt. Such cases were rather common and jeopardized the efforts to fund more migrants from Egypt. The increasing number of potential migrants made it clear that it would be impossible to finance the operation solely from donations. By March 1952, donations amounted to LE 590, enough for just eight Egyptiots to migrate to Australia. The fund committee considered that it needed more than the envisaged LE 3,000 to provide assistance to a sufficient number of migrants.[37] It also seems that not all migrants who had traveled with the fund's assistance—or without it—were satisfied with their choice, and indeed some returned. Planning and implementing decongestion was not an easy task. There were no detailed statistics available on unemployment rates in the community or the number of people wishing to migrate.[38] The Cairo fires of January 1952 and the increased number of unemployed people compelled Liatis and the GCCA to appeal to the GMFA for assistance. A new period of collaboration between the GCCA and two international organizations, the World Council of Churches (WCC) and Intergovernmental Committee for European Migration (ICEM), began.

THE OTHER SUEZ CRISIS

After the conclusion of the evacuation agreement on 19 October 1954, the problem of the Egyptiots who were directly or indirectly affected by the departure of the British military forces greatly concerned the diplomatic authorities and GCCA. The area would become the epicenter of the "decongestion" effort. Indeed, the migration fund had been founded mainly with a view to catering to the needs of the unemployed who flocked to Alexandria from the canal cities and the British military base after the Egyptians denounced the Anglo-Egyptian Treaty in October 1951. Despite the solidarity available through the employment offices and social networks, only a third of the unemployed managed to find a satisfactory job, since the economic conditions were extremely difficult and, in many cases, the salaries on offer were lower than the already low salaries (LE 10–15) paid by the auxiliary services of the British Army.[39] By January 1952, of the two hundred people registered with the GCCA employment office, only sixty managed to find to job.[40] When the situation in the Suez Canal gradually normalized in April and May 1952, some employees returned to their positions.[41] It had become more than obvious, though, that when the British would leave for good, unemployment among the Greeks would again rise.[42] Even if the Egyptians were to maintain the base so that it could be reoccupied in the event of a global conflict, it seems that the Egyptian government would employ a limited number of them. *O Paroikos* estimated that the withdrawal of the British military in June 1956 could cost 1,141 Egyptiot employees and workers their jobs and would also affect another 2,000 people working in businesses with direct or indirect links to the British military presence.[43] Including families, the number affected by the closures came to some 10,000 people,[44] a rather high number given the demographic strength of the Egyptiot population.

To deal with the problem, the Greek consular authorities, in collaboration with the Egyptian minister of social affairs, promoted two possible solutions: the employment of those Greeks in enterprises owned by their compatriots or their placement in companies that would undertake the maintenance of the bases after the departure of the British.[45] The first solution was difficult to apply because of the difficulties faced due to economic stagnancy but also because of the 138/1947 Company Law. The second solution seemed to be the most appropriate because these companies were not subject to the laws on joint-stock companies.⁴⁶ Thus, some of the unemployed managed to find a job in Egypt, but for the majority of them departure seemed to be the only realistic solution.⁴⁷ Michalis Germanos, a GCCA representative in Port Said, kept Viscovitch informed about the situation in the canal cities and the plans of local Greeks to migrate. In January 1954, three to four hundred residents of Ismailia (employees and families) were concerned about their jobs and, according to a member of the local Koinotita, were potential migrants.⁴⁸ The GCCA's aim was to deal with the issue on site in order to prevent these prospective migrants from heading to Egypt's major cities. In August 1954, Viscovitch visited Ismailia and Suez to inform Greek workers about the facilities provided by the GCCA and WCC/ICEM.

Germanos's predictions were surpassed. During his visit, Viscovitch gathered information on more than two hundred workers of the Suez Canal area, the majority of whom declared that they had no objection to accept "unskilled work in factories or in rural centers as fruit pickers."⁴⁹ When the families of these workers were included, the number of potential migrants reached five to seven hundred people, all of whom were ready to depart immediately. However, the system of migration based on personal invitations that had hitherto been practiced no longer corresponded to the new requirements of speed and efficiency. Only the ICEM was in a position to handle the massive relocation of the Greeks from Suez, but because of bureaucratic complications, the Greek government did not submit any request for assistance to the ICEM.⁵⁰

The sudden increase in the number of Egyptiots who wished to migrate provoked an unanticipated turn of events when the ICEM headquarters in Geneva decided that Egyptiot Greeks could no longer be financed by the organization. The decision was also due to a leaked document showing that they had received beneficial treatment from the ICEM compared to other Europeans living in Egypt and elsewhere. The Italian delegation to the ICEM, for instance, demanded equal treatment for the Italians of Egypt. In the event, the ICEM decision did not significantly disrupt the migration process because the Greek government stepped in to finance the migration of Egyptiots as if they were "moving from Greece."⁵¹ Thus, no change occurred in the migration process in practice. In theory Greeks from a diaspora setting were treated on equal terms with those from the homeland. On 14 January 1956, the cabinet in Athens decided that 5 percent of the total number of financially assisted migrants a year should be Egyptiot Greeks,⁵² which corresponded to approximately 550 individuals.

Meanwhile the situation of the unemployed Greeks of the Suez Canal area continued to deteriorate as the deadline for the evacuation of Suez approached. In February 1956, Mollie Rule, the chief resettlement officer of the WCC in Athens, claimed that the allocation for assisted migration set by the government in Athens for the Greek migrants from Egypt was far too low to meet demand: "I realize that the figure of 500 to 600 persons to migrate from Egypt is very far below the needs for that country, however, all I can say is that 500 to 600 is better than nothing."[53] She also pointed out that it was futile to request an increase in numbers because Greece was about to hold general elections. GCCA dignitaries also asked that the allocation be increased to 10 percent.[54]

The critical situation resulting from the increase and concentration of the number of destitute Egyptiots worried Greek officials, who still believed that social disorder in Egypt or in Greece was likely to erupt because the mass of destitute people would adopt subversive, communist ideas. For this reason, the Greek state rejected all calls for repatriation, despite the critical situation and relevant appeals from some community leaders.[55] After a visit to Egypt, Sotirios Agapitidis, the Greek government's special envoy for matters concerning the community in Egypt, returned with the same impression, according to Alexandra Ioannides, second in command in the ICEM Athens office. Agapitidis

> is under the impression that the Migration Committee's decision concerning the insignificant amount of 5 percent proves to be wrong following the impressions that he formed in Egypt. Mr Agapitidis believes that it is necessary to set the percentage at 10 percent at the lowest, because if the migration of the Greeks is not increased, the people who do not manage to leave will follow subversive ideas, to the detriment of all the Greeks in Egypt, or they will come to Athens as refugees seeking state support.[56]

The decision to include intending migrants from Egypt in the Greek postwar migration program in early 1956 also had another dimension. A competition of sorts had developed between prospective Greek migrants from Egypt and from Greece because the latter country constituted a priority for Athens.[57] Once again the community leadership promoted the superiority of the Egyptiot Greek migrant.[58] The GCCA maintained contact with the diplomatic authorities of all possible destinations to facilitate migration and to advance its own economic interests. In this respect, the council tried to make the most of the fact that the Greek ambassador to Australia in the early 1950s was one of their own. Born in Alexandria in 1903, Dimitrios Lambros had studied law at Athens University. On 19 March 1953, the career diplomat was appointed Greek ambassador to Canberra and used his position to promote Egyptiot migration. In a memorandum sent to the Australian government's immigration department in 1956, he requested special treatment for the unemployed Greeks of the Suez Canal area:

> A category worthy of attention are those who were, until recently, or still are employed at the various British military establishments of the Suez Canal. They are about 2,000 and many of them had expressed the wish to settle in Australia, when their employment with the British would come to an end. Most of them have a good knowledge of English; some of them are administrative clerks and storekeepers while others are wireless operators, radio technicians, electricians, fitters, etc.[59]

To increase the number of Greek migrants from Egypt, Lambros also asked for the invitation procedure to be bypassed in their case, since "very few of them have friends or relatives in Australia" and because mass migration through the ICEM services "would be difficult to apply in Egypt because it might give rise, among the hard-pressed Greeks of Egypt, to undue expectations."[60] The ensuing Suez Crisis restricted sponsored migration. Meanwhile, in October 1956, the GMFA transferred Lambros from Canberra to his new post, as ambassador to Cairo. From there, he continued to work his contacts in Australia to facilitate the relocation of Egyptiot Greeks. Following the established practice of the GCCA, he set out to advertise the Egyptiots' many purported qualities. He also tried to take advantage of his warm, personal relationship with Alexandra Ioannides of the ICEM Athens office. This acquaintance proved to be crucial after the Australian embassy in Cairo ceased to operate after the Suez Crisis, thus blocking the main migration channel. Lambros, however, sought to circumvent this difficulty by approaching the Australian immigration authorities in Canberra directly.[61]

In early 1957, significant numbers of unemployed and destitute Egyptiots left the Suez Canal cities for Alexandria and Cairo. Many approached the Red Cross in Cairo, who complained about the ever-increasing number of Greeks seeking their assistance by pretending to be stateless:

> Our delegates have noticed since some time, and not without concern, that the number of applicants of Greek nationality or origin has been continuously rising. ... At the moment they make up about half of all the individual cases that we have to deal with. ... We are afraid that in very many cases these Greeks have tried to conceal their true nationality, since the status of stateless persons would give them more rights to receiving our assistance.[62]

The Red Cross also sought the collaboration of the Greek consul in Cairo to establish who was actually entitled to the assistance of the international organizations.

In Ismailia, 203 families of unemployed Egypiots, amounting to 509 people, who had no income, had "started selling their furniture and their clothes in order to survive."[63] According to the consul in Port Said, of these

509 people, 285 wished to repatriate to Greece, 184 to migrate elsewhere, while 40 were seafarers who wanted work on ships.[64] In a letter to Lambros, a committee representing the unemployed in Ismailia described the difficulties they faced in finding a job, especially after the Suez Crisis, and the wish of many to leave Egypt. For that reason, they appealed for free tickets to Greece and economic assistance from the Greek state to find a job in the motherland. They also requested economic aid from the embassy, recommendations to find a job in Greek companies in Egypt, and assistance to migrate to Australia, Canada, Venezuela, Brazil, or Belgium.[65] Given the crucial situation in the Suez Canal area, the Alexandria consulate fund provided financial assistance to Greek citizens of Ismailia who wanted to depart.[66] At the same time, the cabinet in Athens decided, on 10 January 1957, to double the percentage of Egyptiot Greeks who could participate in the ICEM migration program from Greece from 5 to 10 percent.

NEW CHALLENGES, NEW DESTINATIONS

Up to the beginning of the 1960s, the GCCA, in collaboration with the WWC and ICEM, continued to provide assistance to destitute Greeks wishing to migrate. In 1961, the consulate general of Alexandria raised the issue of transferring the WCC office from the GCCA to its offices.[67] The Egyptian authorities did not grant the WCC official recognition during the 1950s. This gave rise to problems and left both the GCCA and WCC exposed in a period when Israel and Western countries were exploiting the departure of foreigners for anti-Nasserite propaganda. Therefore, all actors involved needed to take more precautions. When the exodus began in earnest, the Greek state placed Egyptiot Greek migration under its direct control. Ambassador Lambros did not condone this solution, as it would have embarrassed the Egyptian authorities and made the Greek government ultimately responsible for all the actions of the WCC. Instead, he recommended housing the WCC office in the GKA, but this never materialized.[68]

The GCCA's involvement with the WCC/ICEM in migrations ended in 1962, the year the exodus reached its peak. From that point, the Greek state assumed responsibility for migration, and an ICEM office was created in the consulate general of Alexandria. The GMFA sent Konstantinos Papantonopoulos, an ICEM executive, to Egypt as a migration attaché. Having previous experience in Australia, where he worked for five years in facilitating European immigration to the country, Papantonopoulos arrived in Alexandria in June 1961 to coordinate migrations so that they would proceed alongside the repatriation movement in the following years. The Greek state's collaboration with the ICEM in the migration of Egyptiot Greeks ended in 1973.

There is no concrete data for the total number of people who migrated after World War II at their own expense, that is, without requesting GCCA assistance. There is, however, data for those migrating under the auspices of the GCCA/ICEM/WCC scheme from 1952 to 1961. Table 13 illustrates the number of destitute Egyptiots who emigrated with their support. Overall, with the assistance of these organizations, 3,340 destitute Egyptiots migrated, the largest numbers of whom went to Australia and Brazil. It is interesting to note that 52.7 percent of the total number of destitute Egyptiots who migrated came from the Alexandria district. This number neatly corresponds to the demographic distribution of ethnic Greeks in Egypt, as just over half of them were settled in Alexandria.[69] The table also confirms that the majority of Egyptiot destitute migrants chose to leave for Australia.

The Suez Crisis seems to have had an indirect impact on the migration movement because of the closing of the Australian embassy. Despite this setback, Lambros activated his contacts with the ICEM and the Australian government. The latter approved a special program for the movement of 250 Egyptiots on condition that the WCC would find the necessary people to act as guarantors for their settlement in the country.[70] The ICEM offered to cover the costs of traveling from Egypt to Greece for potential migrants, provided they passed the necessary exams and made the necessary preparations for migration. Then, they either departed for Australia from Greece or returned to Egypt and embarked on ships passing through Port Said.[71]

Table 13. Migration of destitute Greeks from Egypt under the auspices of the WCC/ICEM, 1952–61

Year	Australia	Brazil	Canada	Argentina	Other countries	Total	From Alexandria district
1952–54	404	–	–	–	4	408	170
1955	418	–	–	1	3	422	312
1956	377	–	–	–	19	396	274
1957	796	89	3	–	4	892	549
1958	397	120	–	–	44	561	219
1959	82	105	–	6	23	216	105
1960	56	127	–	4	18	205	108
1961	100	200	–	10	30	340	78
Total	2,630	641	3	21	145	3,440	1,815

Sources: AICEM/Egypt/1959–65, 2513, Athens, 4 January 1961, Alexandraki to Veinoglou; AYE/CS/1961/21/17/2/1/2, 990, Secret, Alexandria, 11 October 1961, Theodoropoulos to Lambros.

This pattern covered the numbers migrating to Australia from 1957 to 1960, when the Australian embassy in Cairo reopened. While the exodus was in full swing in the early 1960s, the ICEM asked Australia to receive more Egyptiots, and another 250 Egyptiots departed. In 1963, the migration program included Cypriot Greeks as well as repatriated Egyptiots, namely those who decided to emigrate after they had reached Greece.[72]

By 1963, most of the migrants from Egypt had gone to Australia (see table 14), mainly thanks to the collaboration of the GCCA, ICEM, and WCC.[73] While it was also possible to move to Latin America—Brazil was preferred—as a destination it only really came into play after the Suez Crisis, when migrants encountered difficulties in moving to Australia. The percentage of people who moved to Greece steadily increased in the early 1950s. Table 14 shows the distribution of the Greeks who left Egypt from 1945 to January 1963, according to "fairly reliable sources and estimates" that Papantonopoulos said he had accessed.[74]

Egyptiots in general orientated toward English-speaking countries. Given British involvement in Egypt, they were familiar with the common administrative and cultural background, and many spoke English. These countries were more receptive to immigrants, offered more opportunities for accommodation, and had developed their labor legislation and created a welfare state. However popular Australia might have been, had the United States been accessible, it would have proved the most desired destination. When demand increased in 1961, Canada and New Zealand emerged as new options. Egyptiots deemed the former a very good choice, as evidenced by the fact that when the country agreed to receive 1,320 people in mid-August 1961, 440 prospective migrants applied within a matter of a few days.[75] New Zealand attracted less interest because the country was unknown to many people and, in any case, even farther away than Australia.

Table 14. Dispersion of the Greeks who left Egypt, 1945–January 1963

Destination	Percentage
Greece	55
Australia	18
African and Middle Eastern countries	10
Brazil	2
Other countries, including Canada	15
Total	100

Source: AICEM/Egypt/1959–65, Report on migration services in Egypt, Alexandria, 9 January 1963, Konstantinos Papantonopoulos.

Another country where English was spoken that began to gain in popularity among migrants was South Africa. However, as it was located in Africa, Egyptiot Greeks feared that the local population might expel white residents, as had already happened elsewhere in countries emerging from colonial rule. But the encouraging information arriving in Egypt from migrants already settled there helped quell these fears. The Greek Orthodox patriarch of Alexandria, Nikolaos VI, who wished to see his flock increase in other parts of Africa, also promoted South Africa.[76] The ICEM, which in 1962, at the request of the Greek state, stood in to organize the migration of Egyptiot Greeks to South Africa because Pretoria had no diplomatic representation in Egypt, also promoted the country. More and more Egyptiots gradually moved there, making South Africa one of the most popular destinations by the mid-1960s. In the summer 1963, the Association of Greeks from Egypt in South Africa was created.[77] This increase is also depicted in ICEM data for 1966, according to which there were 136 applications for South Africa, compared to 147 for Australia. It is also interesting that Greeks from Alexandria preferred to move to Australia, whereas those from Cairo selected South Africa.[78]

One of the Greek government's main political policies from the 1940s to 1960s was ensuring that destitute and unemployed Egyptiots would migrate elsewhere rather than repatriate to Greece. This policy was even more visible in periods of crisis. Even if the Greek state eased its opposition to repatriation in the immediate aftermath of the Suez Crisis, this never really concerned the destitute and unemployed. Even in 1961, when the exodus was in progress, destitute Greeks were practically barred from repatriating. The Greek state's policy was still the same: destitute Egyptiots should either migrate to other destinations or remain in Egypt. Greek diplomats and GCCA dignitaries were quite cynical in this regard, as they openly admitted that it would be far less expensive for the Greek state to have destitute Greeks remain in Egypt than have them come to mainland Greece and seek assistance.[79]

NOTES

1. AGCCA/Migration Fund, Melbourne, 17 January 1952, Miliarakis to Viscovitch.
2. AGCCA/Migration Fund, Alexandria, 18 December 1951, Miliarakis to GCCA.
3. AGCCA/57, Royal Consulate General of Alexandria, 1947–55, General observations on the community life during 1949 and on Greek-Egyptian trade during the year, Alexandria, 29 November 1949.
4. *Tachydromos,* 9 October 1949.

5. *Tachydromos,* 21 August 1949.
6. AYE/CS/1947/10/1, 21214, Secret, Athens, 17 March 1947, Bensis to Cairo embassy; AYE/CS/1948/103/1/6/3, 1065, Top Secret, Cairo, 15 March 1948, Mavrokefalos to Cairo embassy.
7. AYE/CS/1951/95/2/3/1, 8972, Alexandria, 18 December 1951, Liatis to Cairo embassy.
8. AYE/CS/1947/12/6/1, 1915, Cairo, 17 May 1947, Triantafyllidis to GMFA.
9. AYE/CS/1951/95/2/3/1, 8972, Alexandria, 18 December 1951, Liatis to Cairo embassy.
10. AYE/CS/1954/131/2/1, 1292/51/3, Alexandria, 20 November 1951, Argyropoulos to Sakellarios; AYE/CS/1951/95/2/3/1, 8972, Alexandria, 18 December 1951, Liatis to Cairo embassy.
11. AYE/CS/1951/95/2/3/1, 8972, Alexandria, 18 December 1951, Liatis to Cairo embassy.
12. Ibid.
13. AYE/CS/1952/50/6/1/1, Liatis's speech to the GKA general assembly, Alexandria, 9 December 1951.
14. *O Paroikos,* 21/2/1955, 1.
15. AYE/CS/1953/51/1/7, 7137, Cairo, 10 November 1953, Melas to GMFA.
16. *O Paroikos,* 5 May 1954, 1.
17. Ibid.
18. *O Paroikos,* 29 March 1956, 6.
19. *O Paroikos,* 5 May 1954, 1.
20. *O Paroikos,* 1/2/1956, 4.
21. *O Paroikos,* 22–24 April 1956.
22. *O Paroikos,* 27 October 1954.
23. AYE/CS/1953/78/1/1, 11, Alexandria, 14 January 1953, Liatis to Cairo embassy.
24. AICEM/Egypt/until 1958, Athens, 3 July 1952, Ioannidou to Liatis.
25. AICEM/Egypt/until 1958, 381/52/2, Alexandria, 8 April 1952, Sakellarios to Goutos.
26. AGCCA/Migration Fund, Canberra, 17 February 1952, Miliarakis to Viscovitch.
27. Ibid.
28. AGCCA/Migration Fund, 3/53, Alexandria, 5 January 1953, Viscovitch to Miliarakis.
29. AGCCA/Migration Fund, Sydney, 20 March 1953, Miliarakis to Viscovitch.
30. AGCCA/Migration Fund, Melbourne, 1952, Thalassinos to Viscovitch.
31. AGCCA/Migration Fund, 1951–58, Sydney, 19 April 1952, Kokkinos to Viscovitch.
32. AGCCA/Migration Fund, 1951–58, Douala, 25 September 1952, Kokkinidis to Viscovitch.
33. AGCCA/Migration Fund, 1000, Alexandria, 30 November 1951, Leriou to Sakellarios.
34. AGCCA/Migration Fund, 106, Melbourne, 4 April 1952, Leriou to Viscovitch.
35. AGCCA/Migration Fund, Melbourne, 23 October 1952, Leriou to Viscovitch.
36. AGCCA/Migration Fund, Alexandria, 22 April 1952, Viscovitch to Leriou.

37. AGCCA/Migration Fund, 1951–58, Meeting of the committee, Alexandria, 6 March 1952.
38. AICEM/Egypt/until 1958, 6239, Alexandria, 20 August 1952, Liatis to Goutos.
39. AYE/CS/1951/95/2/3/1, 8972, Alexandria, 18 December 1951, Liatis to Cairo embassy.
40. AYE/CS/1952/50/1/1/1, 99/52, Alexandria, 25 January 1952, Sakellarios to Bensis.
41. AYE/CS/1953/51/1/1, 298, Cairo, 18 January 1953, Georgiadis to Cairo embassy.
42. AYE/CS/1953/51/1/1, 35, Zagazig, 13 January 1953, Skarpalezos to Cairo embassy.
43. *O Paroikos,* 3 March 1955, 5.
44. AICEM/Egypt until 1958, Athens, 24 March 1955, Ioannides to Cairo embassy.
45. *O Paroikos,* 28 February 1955, 1, 6; *O Paroikos,* 7 March 1955, 1.
46. *O Paroikos,* 28 February 1955, 1, 6.
47. AGKC/Secretariat/153, Cairo, 20 December 1954, Roilos to the Cairo embassy.
48. AGCCA/Correspondence on the issue of migration from Ismailia, Port Said, 28 January 1954, Germanos to Viscovitch.
49. AGCCA/Correspondence on the issue of migration from Ismailia, 269/55, Alexandria, 18 February 1955, Viscovitch to Rule.
50. AICEM/Egypt/until 1958, Athens, 24 March 1955, Ioannidou to Cairo embassy.
51. AICEM/Egypt/until 1958, Athens, 20 June 1955, Ioannidou to Cairo embassy.
52. AICEM/Athens, 14 January 1956.
53. AGCCA/Correspondence on the issue of migration from Ismailia, R-28, Athens, 16 February 1956, Rule to Viscovitch.
54. AICEM/Egypt/until 1958, 29 June 1956, Mamopoulos to ICEM.
55. AYE/CS/1954/131/2/1, 150/75, Cairo, 29 January 1954, Roilos to Cairo embassy.
56. AGCCA/Rearrangement of situation related to the migration of Greeks from Egypt under the auspices WCC/ICEM, Athens, 24 February 1956.
57. AGCCA/Rearrangement of situation related to the migration of Greeks from Egypt under the auspices WCC/ICEM, 5855, Athens, 9 February 1956, Rallis to ICEM.
58. AICEM/Egypt until 1958, Athens, 29 June 1956, Mamopoulos to ICEM.
59. AICEM/Egypt until 1958, Memorandum, Canberra, 30 August 1956, Lambros to Heyes and Holt.
60. Ibid.
61. AICEM/Egypt until 1958, Cairo, 4 April 1957, Lambros to Heyes.
62. AICRC/B-AG/232/065-001.07.08.09/Citoyens grecs en Égypte, 22 November 1956–2 July 1957, 622, Cairo, 26 June 1957, De Muller to Gaillard.
63. *O Paroikos,* 1 February 1957, 3.
64. AYE/CS/1957/22/5/1/1, 177, Port Said, 19 January 1957, Hatzoudis to Cairo embassy.
65. AYE/CS/1957/22/5/1/1, note, Ismailia, 18 January 1957.
66. AYE/CS/1964/43/8/1/1, Port Said, 9 October 1957, LE 100 receipt.
67. AYE/CS/1961/21/17/2/1/2, 990, Alexandria, 11 October 1961, Theodoropoulos to Cairo embassy.

68. AYE/CS/1961/21/17/2/1/2, 2821, Cairo, 16 October 1961, Lambros to Theodoropoulos.
69. AICEM/Egypt/1959-65, 00623, Note, Emigration of Europeans from Egypt, Alexandra Ioannides, Athens, 13 March 1961.
70. AICEM/Egypt/1959-65, note, Emigration from Greece to Australia, Athens, May 1961.
71. AICEM/Egypt/1959-65, 515, Cairo, 27 May 1960, Dimopoulos to Cairo embassy.
72. AICEM/Egypt/1959-65, 4115, Athens, 28 November 1963, Alexandraki to Kostopoulos.
73. AICEM/Egypt/1959-65, Report on migration services in Egypt, Alexandria, 9 January 1963.
74. AICEM/Egypt/1959-65, Report on migration services in Egypt, Alexandria, 9 January 1963, K Papantonopoulos.
75. AICEM/Egypt/1959-65, Alexandraki's report after her visit to the UAR, which ended on 25 September 1961.
76. AICEM/Egypt/1966-73, 6815, Athens, 6 February 1971, Alexandraki to Pattakos.
77. AICEM/Egypt/1959-65, Athens, 21 August 1963, Gould to Papantonopoulos.
78. AICEM/Egypt/1966-73, Migration movement to South Africa through 1966, Alexandria, 19 April 1967.
79. AYE/CS/1961/21/15/2/2, 1075, Alexandria, 2 November 1961, Theodoropoulos to Cairo embassy; AGCCA/Correspondence, 1960-63, Confidential note on labor issues concerning the Greeks in Egypt, May 1962.

Part IV

The Exodus

Chapter Seven

A Fulfilled Prophecy?

Our Alexandrian community is in steep decline. This is not due to the anti-foreigner, let alone anti-Greek, policy of the Egyptian government or to any Arabic or Muslim chauvinism. On the contrary, we have much tangible proof of the favorable treatment our community receives from government officials. At the same time, I see how harmonious the coexistence is at the popular level between our people and the Arabs, who honestly respect and appreciate us. However, what is pushing us out of Egypt is the unavoidable economic and social evolution of the country. We can neither suspend this evolution nor expect that Egyptians will slow it down for our sake.[1]

For Vyron Theodoropoulos, consul general in Alexandria, the writing was already on the wall when he filed this report on 18 July 1961, just a few days before the announcement of the nationalization laws, which are commonly accepted as the trigger for the exodus of Greeks from Egypt. The report however reveals two important issues: (a) that the Greeks were viewed in a favorable way and (b) that the Greek exodus was already under way.

The prophecy the title of the chapter refers to is the prediction expressed for decades that Greeks would one day be expelled from Egypt. It's worth reminding here that "exodus" is not used in its biblical sense but simply describes the mass departure movement from Egypt that was triggered in the final months of 1960. Twenty-three years had passed since the abolition of the privileges (or eleven taking into account the twelve-year transitory period after 1937). During this long period, characterized by intense fluidity at the local and international level, the Greek state and leadership of the Greek community in Egypt tried to develop policies—which often proved to be ambiguous—to ensure the long-term presence of Egyptiots. During this period many Greeks abandoned Egypt, using their own means or after receiving assistance from international and community organizations and the Greek state. And while the departure rates were relatively normal in 1958 and in 1959 after the increase following the Suez Crisis, in the last few months of 1960, "in a period usually low when it comes to definite departures," these significantly increased in the Alexandria and Cairo consular districts.[2]

SIGNS OF MASS DEPARTURE

The significant increase in departures—including repatriation and unassisted emigration—in the final months of 1960 ensured that the numbers of Greeks leaving Egypt that year were significantly higher than in the previous one. According to data from the Alexandria consulate general, the number of passports issued to applicants intending to leave Egypt for good increased by 16.9 percent, from 391 in 1959 to 457 in 1960.[3] The Cairo consulate issued 414 passports in 1959 and 485 in 1960, an increase of 17.1 percent. Neither district provided information on the intended destination. It is important to bear in mind that these numbers do not accurately reflect the actual number of departures, since many leaving the country exited on open-return visas, in case they wished to return. Moreover, the fact that there had been an increase in late 1960 in the number of Egyptiots seeking to arrange all the necessary bureaucratic formalities associated with leaving the country—such as seeking military service documents—led the consul general in Alexandria to predict that "the number of definitive departures will increase significantly throughout 1961."[4] His forecast proved correct. But how can this sudden increase in departures before the promulgation of the July 1961 nationalization laws be explained?

The reasons that had always pushed Greeks into leaving did not cease to exist; rather, other factors emerged. Egyptiot employees and workers were greatly concerned by Law 19/1959 on the employment conditions of foreigners. Enacted in October, it came into effect almost a year later, in November 1960, on the basis of Decrees 260 and 263. This law obliged all foreign residents working in the country to obtain a work permit from the labor force directorate. Once acquired, this work permit had to be renewed every year. Work permits would be issued to residence permit holders but only for the period of validity of the latter. After the labor permit expired, it could be renewed only on the condition that the country of which the applicant was a citizen respected the clause of reciprocity, that is, mutual exchange of privileges between the UAR and the applicant's country. In addition, no business was permitted to have more than 15 percent of foreign personnel among its total staff, regardless of the category. Nor could the salaries of these personnel exceed 25 percent of the total payroll. The *koinotites* and the chambers of commerce in Cairo and Alexandria asked the Foreign Ministry in Athens to issue a decision on the reciprocity clause. Athens asked the ambassador in Cairo, Dimitrios Lambros, to look into the matter, and Prime Minister Karamanlis raised the issue in his deliberations with Nasser, when the latter visited Athens in June 1960, but the two leaders reached no concrete solution. Thus, when the law came into force in November 1960, it gave rise to strong concerns in the community.

With this particular law "the foreign communities in Egypt ... reached a state of near alarm," according to Alexandra Ioannides, second in command in the ICEM Athens office, who visited the country in March 1961.[5] The Cairo consul general, Baizos, in turn, also confirmed the impact of the law on the community: "The decision 263/1960 of October seriously upset the community, more than ... any other measure."[6] The GCCA expected Decrees 260 and 263 to have disastrous effects, since Greek employers would be forced to fire their principal executives and employees, who would then be compelled to leave Egypt for good.[7] Kalliarekos, Kitrilakis, Stamelos, and Georgiadis, as representatives of the Egyptiot Left in Alexandria, also noted the panic provoked by the decrees.[8] They urged the community leadership to face up to its responsibilities, accusing it of "superficiality," "indifference," "dangerous immobility," "inertia," irresponsibility, and co-ordinating too closely with the Greek state. "It is now urgent that we send out a clear alarm signal once more; but this will be the last," these members of the Egyptiot Left wrote.[9] From Cairo, Themistoklis Matsakis added, "It is a fact that no other decree implemented so far provoked so much concern and panic among foreigners—and of course among Egyptiots— as Decree 263."[10] He also denounced the inertia of the Egyptiot bodies after the promulgation of Law 19 and Decrees 260 and 263.[11] Faced with the imminent threat that Greece would be hit by a mass wave of repatriates, the Greek state activated its diplomatic authorities.

At a meeting with the labor and social affairs minister, Hussein el-Shafei, in October 1960, Lambros highlighted the "importance of a sense of security" among employees, something that the recent decrees had not helped. The minister agreed and requested Lambros to inform the community leadership that he had no intention of forcing Greeks to leave Egypt. He maintained that the purpose of the law was not to make matters difficult for those who had been settled for many years in Egypt, but to standardize the Egyptian legal framework with Syria's. Shafei reassured Lambros that the law regarding the workplace percentages for foreign employees would not apply to Greeks who were born in Egypt before 1932 and to those who had arrived in the country before 1937.[12] According to Greek diplomats, that category included 90 percent of the Greek workforce in Egypt.[13] In January the minister promised that permanent Greek residents would be exempt from the foreigner quotas decreed for all kinds of companies. Additionally, the law collectively exempted employees of the *koinotites,* schools, and charitable associations. Yet, despite this preferential treatment, the great uncertainty about the future among Egyptiots intensified.

The feeling of uncertainty had built up over the 1950s for a wide variety of reasons. A treaty of establishment had not been signed, and the community had made no substantial progress in readjusting following the abolition of the Capitulations. A long economic recession had hit many professional sectors, while the Suez Crisis resulted in the departure of many compatriots and the expulsion of British, French, and Jews. Greeks in Egypt also noted the persecution of the Greeks of Istanbul and the departure of millions of Europeans from former colonies. All of these events fueled the belief that the fate of Greeks was more or less linked to the international political situation, especially decolonization and the Cold War. So as the UAR assumed a more central role in the anticolonial movement and Nasser's socialistic measures and rapprochement with the Soviet Union intensified in the late 1950s, Egyptiots increasingly asked themselves the following question: what would happen in the event of Greece, as a NATO member, and Egypt falling into a dispute?

This question became more pertinent in late 1960 and early 1961, following the sequestration of Belgian assets and the deportation of Belgian citizens from the UAR as a result of the critical situation in Congo.[14] On 1 June 1960, the Congo declared its independence from Belgium. Because of the Belgian efforts to retain its predominant position in the country and the protests against the Belgians in Leopoldville (now Kinshasa), the UAR severed diplomatic relations with Belgium on 1 December 1960. The following day, Nasser nationalized the Banque Belge et Internationale en Égypte, the Egyptian Electric Company, and the Cairo Tramway Company, all of which were of Belgian interests. In retaliation for the assassination of Patrice Lumumba, Nasser also sequestered forty-nine Belgian companies and the properties of 407 Belgian residents in Egypt, on 27 February 1961.[15] Banned from making any commercial or financial transactions, almost all Belgian citizens were given twenty-four hours to leave the country.[16]

Almost at the same time, a spy affair came to light, in which the authorities accused Egyptiots and the Greek diplomatic authorities of involvement. In September 1960, the Egyptian police arrested twenty-seven Greek citizens and accused them of espionage.[17] The suspects included members of the administrative staff of the Port Said consulate and Suez vice-consulate, the Cairo manager of the Greek airline carrier Olympic Airways, and the archivist and secretary of the military attaché of the Greek embassy in Cairo.[18] The charges concerned the monitoring of Egyptian naval movements in the

Suez Canal area. Upon receiving this information, the military attaché of the Greek embassy informed Athens, through the diplomatic bag, for NATO's benefit.[19] As soon as the espionage became public, the Egyptian authorities declared the Greek consuls of Port Said, Suez, and Alexandria as personae non gratae and ordered them to leave Egypt immediately. The Greek authorities had transferred the military attaché, who was considered the head of the network, a short time before the affair was uncovered.[20]

At first, the consuls denied any connection with the spy ring but not its existence. Replying to the Greek embassy's initial reaction to the arrest of the Greek nationals, General Salah Nasr, the head of the Egyptian counterintelligence service, disclosed to Lambros the well-founded basis of the charges,[21] which the arrested Greeks admitted.[22] In addition, the embassy archivist was also accused of being a double agent, because from 1958 to September 1960 he had allowed the Egyptian authorities to photograph the content of the diplomatic bag in exchange for cash.[23] By 10 February 1961, all those implicated had been deported from the country without being put on trial. Evidence in the GMFA archives indicates that Lambros and his ministry were not aware of the network until it was discovered.[24] The Greek ambassador believed that non-state-controlled circles close to the Greek Defense Ministry and Central Intelligence Service (KYP) were behind the spy ring, which they set up on behalf of NATO.[25] This belief is indirectly supported by Nikos Katapodis, the second-in-command in the Cairo embassy.[26] This affair seriously worried the GMFA and the embassy, which tried to keep it secret so as not to create panic within the community. When the deportation of the three consuls came to light, rumors spread, especially in Alexandria, of an impending purge of the Greeks on a Belgian scale.[27]

At this particular time, such rumors found fertile ground because there was little public confidence in the mainstream Egyptian or Egyptiot media, which were under strict state control or the heavy influence of diplomats, respectively. Where uncertainty exists, rumors spread easily, offering answers to ambiguous situations.[28] According to Lambros, the rumors in this case had three different sources: the Communists—the usual suspects—who sought a mass repatriation of the Egyptiots to provoke social disorder in Greece; those who were systematically involved in the illegal transfer of foreign exchange to Greece; and minorities and foreign groups such as the Copts, Lebanese, and Syrians,[29] who hoped to benefit in the local labor market from the departure of the Greeks.[30]

The fact that Lambros was asked to remain in Cairo to handle the issue, despite serious personal health problems, underlined the gravity of this affair. Finally, Nasser himself brought an end to the investigation.[31] As a goodwill gesture he invited the Greek crown prince, Konstantinos, to Egypt in

March, and the visit took place a month later. Lambros believed that Nasser ordered an end to the investigation because he did not wish to further alienate himself from NATO.[32] But the ambassador also had a second theory: Nasser proved that he had no intention of persecuting Egyptiot Greeks, since, as he pointed out, he could have easily exploited the spy affair so as to "draw down the wrath of the Egyptian people" on the community.[33] In a meeting with the Greek trade minister, Leonidas Dertilis, in April 1961, Nasser declared that he had shelved the case but that if it had reached the level of a court-martial, he would not have been able to intervene.[34] This affair, which unfolded almost in parallel with the sequestration of Belgian assets and deportation of Belgian nationals, shows that, for whatever reason, Nasser did not want to purge Greeks, even though he had the chance. It is undeniable, however, that the arrests and the deportation of Greek nationals and, particularly, the consuls had a negative psychological impact on the community.[35] At the same time, rumors that tougher economic socialist measures would follow Decrees 260 and 263 burdened morale even more.[36] Thus, uncertainty about the future increased, pushing more and more Greeks into taking the decision to leave Egypt for good.

In this context, the readjustment issue came to the fore again. Ioannis Yiannakakis, the consul general in Cairo, claimed that exempting the Greeks from the decrees would give them the necessary time to accomplish readjustment.[37] His counterpart in Alexandria, Theodoropoulos, however, was extremely skeptical of the Egyptiots' capacity to readjust to the new socialist economic framework. He pointed out that even if it were achieved, it would be an "extremely painful" process whose results would be "inconclusive." In his view, "the Greek element of Alexandria matured and bloomed as a product of private initiative par excellence and especially in a framework of international exchange."[38]

The representatives of the Alexandrian Egyptiot Left, who had led calls in the early 1950s for readjustment and had been marginalized by the consulate in Koinotita affairs, highlighted the strong contradiction between the dynamic Egyptian context and the sluggish community leadership. "In contrast to the rapid evolution in all aspects of public and private life that characterizes the UAR, our community leadership displays a dangerous [level of] stagnation and inertia. Our *koinotites* are subject to obsolete anachronisms and are focused on outdated habits, following roads lined with illusions."[39] Themistoklis Matsakis from Cairo claimed that increasing uncertainty about the community's future derived not from Law 19 and Decrees 260 and 263, but "from our own unrealistic tactics … the classical inertia and indifference to the issue of readjustment."[40] Offering a general evaluation of the situation shortly before the July nationalization laws, he added:

Many old and new incidents prove the Greek state's carelessness. Our leadership, though, never realized its huge responsibilities deriving from its status. ... The responsible and active behavior was replaced by the wish of most of our leaders to align themselves with the orders of the national center. ... It is not at all inexplicable how we ended up at the critical point we are at today. We lacked a really responsible leadership and coordinated program. Missing out on the necessary psychological, educational, and technological readjustment could have been avoided, and we now find ourselves faced with new conditions without perspective, without orientation, and most significantly, without any concrete official care. Undoubtedly, this truth—possibly the bitter truth—is the source of confusion and turmoil characterizing the community majority today.[41]

THE SECOND REVOLUTION OF 1961

In this context of "confusion and turmoil," two pieces of new legislation confirmed the rumors about upcoming socialist measures. On 9 July 1961, the Egyptian government enacted Law 110 concerning the cotton sector, which placed cotton production under the partial control of the state through the newly founded Egyptian Cotton Commission. The state took control of 35 percent of the shares of joint-stock companies, and it nationalized four raw cotton pressing and baling companies.[42] The Egyptian government was responsible for the evaluation of the share price and paid for them using public bonds bearing 4 percent interest redeemable after fifteen years. Passed later in the week, Law 107 on the import-export trade compelled import-export firms to exchange 0.25 percent of their share capital for the equivalent amount in public bonds bearing 4 percent interest redeemable after fifteen years. With this law Nasser sought to strengthen state control over foreign exchange.[43] Greek diplomats expected the nationalization of exports to further shrink the profits of Egyptiots engaged in wholesale and other types of trade. Besides, most of them, by early 1960, were already facing economic difficulties and had reduced their staff, which increased unemployment rates within the community.[44]

The laws fueled the anxiety and pessimism among the community about their future. In Alexandria, "the prevailing ambience was extremely pessimistic both among the wealthy merchants and manufacturers of the community, as well as the disadvantaged owners of small businesses and tradesmen," noted Theodoropoulos, in his first overall report for Lambros on the general situation of the Greek population of Alexandria.[45]

The next day, on the basis of a presidential decree, the Alexandria stock exchange suspended its operations. Other presidential decrees issued the same day ordered the distribution of a quarter of all company profits to employees. The labor force would also be represented in the administrative boards of all private or national companies and establishments. Moreover, the salaries of board members (including the chairman and the chief executive officers) and all employees of every private or public company were capped at LE 5,000 per year. Finally, a new tax bracket was introduced, fixing the tax-free threshold at LE 1,000 and introducing a rate of 90 percent for incomes above LE 10,000. The above measures, which targeted the middle to upper class, constituted the necessary means for the "crystallization of the democratic socialist cooperative society," according to Mohammed Abdel Kader Hatem, minister without portfolio in the Egyptian government.[46] In other words, they were part of the "second revolution" of 1961.[47]

Next morning Theodoropoulos contacted Lambros to express his deep concern about the speed with which the economy of the country was taking a socialist shape.[48] Just a few hours later, on the night of 20 July 1961—a couple of days before the ninth anniversary of the 1952 military coup—the minister of the presidency, Ali Sabry, announced the promulgation of Laws 117, 118, and 119.[49] Law 117 nationalized banks and insurance companies that had remained under private control, along with forty-four industries, including those involved in electricity, cement, and transportation. With Law 118, the state took control of half of the shares in commercial and light industry companies. Finally, Law 119 capped the holdings of 147 companies at a market value of LE 10,000 for legal and natural persons. The state would automatically take control of any amount above this limit.[50] All these laws compelled shareholders to exchange their share capital for an equivalent amount in public bonds, bearing 4 percent interest redeemable after fifteen years.

The decision to nationalize was Nasser's himself and the announcement surprised even members of his government.[51] The evening after the new legislation was announced, the interior minister, Zakaria Mohieddin, was in Garden City, Cairo, with Dimitrios Zerbinis, whose industry had been just nationalized, to inaugurate the Arab-Greek League, whose creation had been announced in May 1957. The four-year delay in setting up such an important body is maybe indicative of the community leadership's sluggishness regarding its relations with Egypt.

The July laws made no distinction on the basis of the nationality of the owners or shareholders. Egyptians and foreigners were equally affected, and consequently the Greek diplomatic authorities could not seek an exemption for the Egyptiots. Of the private capital nationalized under Law 117, 17 percent was European; with Law 118 this reached 25.2 percent, whereas the share of foreigners' property nationalized under Law 119 was only 8.5 percent.[52] Table 15, which is based on official Egyptian estimates from early 1962, provides the market value of nationalized capital for non-Egyptians and

Table 15. Market value of nationalized foreign capital under the July 1961 laws (in LE)

	117/1961	118/1961	119/1961	Total	Percentage
Greek	1,343,000	1,195,000	2,395,000	4,933,000	37.5
Italian	1,453,000	146,000	493,000	2,092,000	15.9
French	600,000	215,000	560,000	1,375,000	10.4
Belgian	720,000	–	–	720,000	5.4
British	586,000	2,000,000	556,000	3,142,000	23.9
Swiss	372,000	–	493,000	865,000	6.5
Total	5,074,000	3,556,000	4,497,000	13,127,000	100

Source: AYE/CS/1962/36/4/2/1, 6139, Cairo, 29 January 1962, Theodoropoulos to GMFA.

the percentage for each national group. It is obvious that the Greeks were the hardest hit ethnic group, even if the community leadership estimated the amount of the nationalized capital to be much higher, at LE 11 million.[53]

Shortly after the promulgation of the laws, state administrators took over the nationalized companies. Theodoropoulos claimed that most of the previous directors of the companies were excluded from management, even in cases where they still held half of the company shares.[54]

The type of company selected for semi-nationalization suggests the government sought only to partially control certain economic activity where the state lacked the know-how. The finance minister, Abbas Zaki, confirmed the government's intention in a meeting with Lambros in early September. According to the latter, the former mentioned "that the UAR government, which has very good information on the majority of the Greek manufacturers and businessmen, wishes to use them under the new financial regime, too."[55]

Alexandria's Egyptiot business community was affected to a much greater extent economically than that of Cairo, as is illustrated in table 16.

Table 16. Market value of the capital belonging to Greek citizens nationalized in the aftermath of the July 1961 laws in Alexandria and Cairo (in LE)

Law	Alexandria	Cairo	Total
110	473,000	28,000	501,000
117	1,175,000	181,000	1,356,000
118	809,000	27,000	836,000
119	3,936,000	640,000	4,576,000
Total	6,393,000	876,000	7,269,000

Source: AYE/CS/1962/36/8/2/1, Table of financial damage experienced by Greek nationals as a result of the 1961 laws.

Laws 117 and 118 fully or partially nationalized the main Greek industries. Some of them, though, such as the tobacco industries, which were partially nationalized, had already lost their place in the market because of changing consumer habits after the war. The major hit for the Greek industry was the nationalization, which was partial in some cases, of the cotton industry, in which the Egyptiots had played a prominent role for many decades, although many businesspeople left the trade or emigrated in the 1950s as a result of the decline in the sector.

According to Kazamias, thirty-eight firms belonging to an equal number of Greek families were nationalized.[56] In Alexandria, the Zerbinis, Theodorakis, Salvagos, Pialopoulos, Nanopoulos, Lagoudakis, Koutarellis, Sarpakis, and Charitatos families were the most affected by the nationalization measures, according to Theodoropoulos.[57] Members of these families were leading community members; most of them were at that time (or had been) on the boards of the GKA and GCCA. Dimitrios Zerbinis, whose name has surfaced throughout this study, was a past president of the GCCA (1947–49) and GKA (1949–54). Anastassios Theodorakis had been GKA president since 1954 and GCCA board member in 1960. Konstantinos Salvagos, the son of Mikès Salvagos, was the first GKA vice president and a former GCCA vice president (in the early 1950s). Simon Pialopoulos was a GKA board member and chairman of the city's Kotsikeio Greek Hospital in 1960. Konstantinos Nanopoulos was a GKA board member, on its bonds and investments committee, and second GCCA vice president, while Faidon Lagoudakis was also a GCCA board member.

Apart from these businessmen, the nationalizations affected a considerable number of Egyptiots who had invested in shares of Greek (in particular the cotton press companies, which were nationalized by Law 110)[58] and other companies that were placed under state control. These persons saw their investments vanish, since the government bonds offered in exchange did not match the anticipated share profits. About 1,255 Greek nationals (individuals and legal entities) were later estimated to have lost shares in companies that were nationalized.[59] In any case, a total of 1,352 Greek citizens sought compensation from the Egyptian state for their losses in the nationalization program from 1961 to 1963.[60] If we take into account the total number of Greek citizens in Egypt in 1960 according to the official census, it would appear that less than 2.8 percent of the community suffered direct financial losses under the laws. However, nationalization did not only affect individuals; shareholding institutions such as companies, community institutions, foundations, associations, and *koinotites* were also hit.

The impact of the nationalizations on the economic situation of the *koinotites* was very serious. The economic problems that they had been facing since the end of World War II were bound to worsen because they had invested a large proportion of their savings in private company shares, particularly in Greek firms. The GKA predicted a loss of LE 4,500 in annual income.[61] Within a year its deficit had increased by 58.8 percent, from LE 39,625 in 1960 to LE 62,930 in 1961.[62] At the same time the GKC's deficit exploded from LE 250 in 1960 to LE 9,751 in 1961, a fact that was due, according to its annual report, to the nationalizations and the increase in living costs.[63] The reduced incomes would, in turn, affect the charitable services offered by the *koinotites* to members. Consequently, the *koinotites* were obliged to sell some of their property to meet their economic needs. The first major asset to be sold off, in 1965, was the Kotsikeio Hospital in Alexandria, which was the biggest hospital in the Middle East when it was built.[64]

NATIONALIZATION AND EMPLOYEES

In a meeting held in Alexandria a few days after the promulgation of the nationalization laws in July 1961, the community leadership and the local consular authorities discussed the fate of the Egyptiot personnel of the nationalized companies. While there are no concrete figures on the number of Greeks employed by the nationalized companies, the occupations of Egyptiots and the characteristics of the labor market would suggest that they employed a considerable percentage of the Greek workforce. Those attending the meeting heard that after the laws were announced, many of the Greek employees wished to resign and depart immediately for Greece.[65] Those who would remain, the leadership feared, would be completely replaced by Egyptian Muslims in the near future.

Theodoropoulos pointed to two different incidents that had occurred in Alexandria even before the July laws were introduced as not auguring well for Greek employees. The Egyptian Employment Office in Alexandria not only rejected the recruitment of Greek employees to the Nanopoulos and Salvagos companies, but also put pressure on them to hire Egyptian Muslims, despite the fact that there were still vacancies for foreigners.[66] In the case of Salvagos, it was said that the owner was asked to sign a statement confirming he would no longer hire Greek citizens. He refused. While these claims are difficult to verify in the Egyptian archives, it would seem that there were cases where employers were pressured into not employing foreigners and employees pushed into resigning. This practice, though, as we shall see, was not official Egyptian state policy, nor was it witnessed in all nationalized companies. It was mostly the fault of low-ranking government officials who were not always easy to control. It is certain, though, that nationalization did not lead to the massive replacement of Greeks with Egyptians, as the leadership had feared.

What almost all the available diplomatic reports claim is that the community was demoralized under the psychologically negative impact of the socialist measures. These progressively fueled the pessimistic mood and consolidated the strong sense of uncertainty among the community in Egypt regarding its future. As early as March 1961, the consul general in Cairo underlined the lack of composure of community members: "The Egyptiot Greeks, addicted to the lawlessness and their carefree life in the recent past, do not possess the necessary sangfroid to face developments.... They do not exaggerate the problems; they simply do not deal with them with the proper collectedness."[67] A day after the July laws were passed, Lambros expressed his deep concern that a "flight psychosis" would ensue.[68] This was to be expected given that the movement of Greeks out of Egypt for good had already intensified in the last quarter of 1960. In August, Theodoropoulos warned Athens to be prepared to receive an increased number of arrivals from Egypt.[69] In a message to Lambros, he described "the psychological state of our community [as] not far from blind panic,"[70] to which the ambassador replied, "Try to dispel the fears ... in order to avoid creating panic."[71] The July laws fueled the feeling of uncertainty not only among wealthy owners and investors in firms that were nationalized, but also among white-collar workers and the rest of the community. The idea that there was no future for the Greeks in Egypt was gaining ground within community circles.[72] Thus, along with seeking to protect Egyptiot capital, preventing a mass repatriation became a preoccupation for the Greek government and its diplomatic authorities in Egypt. The diplomats were certain that even if the measures did not concern the vast majority of employees and workers, these groups would be greatly affected.[73]

The desire of the Greek government to keep the Greeks in Egypt led the foreign minister, Evangelos Averoff, to make a five-day visit to Cairo in early August 1961. The aim of this visit, as Laurens-Castelet, the French ambassador to Athens, described it, was to gain time and to prevent the Greek population from leaving en masse for Greece.[74] Averoff wished to evaluate the situation together with the community leadership and the Egyptian authorities and to reassure the Egyptiots of the good intentions of the Egyptian government toward them. He sought to exploit the friendship that had developed between the two countries in order to obtain from the Egyptian government a good word that could reassure Egyptiots. In his meetings with Nasser, his counterpart, and the ministers of labor and social affairs, Fawzi and Shafei, respectively, Averoff requested that Greek employees and workers of the nationalized companies be retained in their posts, that small-scale professionals be allowed engage in their work unhindered, and that those affected by the nationalization laws be compensated.[75] Leaving the presidential palace after his meeting with Nasser on 9 August, Averoff conveyed the Egyptian leader's assurances that "the Greeks that work in the Land of the Nile, either as workers or as employees, can continue their work without any problems, as long as they do not exceed the percentage set out in Law 26 of 1959 in the companies where they work." He added, "I also observed with great pleasure that even the ones who are involved in small commercial businesses will not need to give up their jobs."[76] The message was clear: Egyptiots had nothing to worry about. As regards compensation for those affected by nationalization, Nasser accepted Athens's proposal that the Greek state pay out compensation and Egypt would then repay Greece through exports.[77]

However, despite Nasser's and others' assurances given to Averoff, August 1961 saw mass resignations of Greek employees, especially senior managers, from the nationalized companies.[78] Theodoropoulos asked the Greek employers and entrepreneurs to use their influence to stop the resignations,[79] with the ultimate aim of convincing these individuals to remain in Egypt.[80] In many companies, the new Egyptian directors refused to accept the resignations, as they needed these employees' know-how to run these firms in the new era.[81] In addition, a considerable number of small- and medium-scale manufacturers and professionals expressed their will to leave Egypt.[82] Significantly, resignations increased also in enterprises that were by no means affected by the nationalizations.[83] In this context Yiannakakis, the Cairo general consul, "revealed" that many Greek employers availed themselves of the new Egyptian legislation in order to sack Greek employees and hire native-born Egyptians whose wages were much lower.[84]

In early September, Lambros reiterated Averoff's requests in a meeting with the economy minister, Hassan Abbas Zaki, who not only repeated Nasser's assurances but added that he himself had given instructions, even before the Greek minister's visit, that no one was to be dismissed, especially foreigners, from the nationalized companies.[85] Some days later, Lambros also visited the vice president, Zakaria Mohieddin.[86] Referring to the increasing numbers of departures of Egyptiots, Mohieddin declared that this was not his government's intention and that the difficulties that arose could be overcome with goodwill. However, he also emphasized that his government could not modify the laws just for the sake of prominent Greek businessmen. On every occasion, Nasser himself and other Egyptian government officials reaffirmed their intention not to take any measures against Greek employees and workers.

In November, almost four months after the passing of the July laws, the GKA board discussed the issue facing Greek employees.[87] Participants told the meeting that there had been few dismissals of Greek employees. However, they noted that in a number of cases Greek employees were indirectly forced to resign in a number of ways. They were asked to work unfavorable shifts or threatened with criminal proceedings in the event of financial problems. In other cases, the new directors refused to accept important documents from Egyptiots and other foreign clerks that were not written in Arabic. The predominant feeling among those in attendance was that in the following months, almost all of the Greek personnel—employees and workers—would be forced in one way or another to resign. The assurances provided by the Egyptian officials were viewed as meaningless, despite the fact that there was no evidence that Greek personnel were being forced out en masse.

The letters to a *Tachydromos* column published every Friday entitled "Workplace Issues" offer a more differentiated picture of the problems faced by employees and how they dealt with them. Most of those who wrote to the column were men of Greek origin aged between forty and sixty who already had considerable working experience. Zaki Badawi, an Egyptian lawyer based in Alexandria who had been a legal consultant to the GCCA on labor issues in the early 1950s, handled their queries. Almost all the letters published after the introduction of the July laws concerned resignations, not dismissals. While there were some cases that could be considered "forced" resignations, these constituted only a fraction of the described cases, and moreover, it was not always clear what could be considered "forced." The published letters did not always mention the nature of the company, so they could have been Greek, Egyptian, or another foreign company that may have been nationalized. A central, recurring theme was that of severance pay in cases of resignation, especially after a September 1961 law provided that those who resigned before the end of the year had the right to receive full severance, whereas those who resigned after 1 January 1962 would receive a monthly pension, which could not be sent abroad. For those leaving Egypt for good, severance pay could represent a considerable capital sum on which they could rely once they had settled in the destination country. If they were considering the possibility of leaving, the employees' tactic was then to receive the highest possible compensation before they left Egypt for good. Another interesting element of these "dialogues" is that employees often picked the date of departure to coincide with the expiry date of the five- or ten-year residence permit, which the authorities introduced after the 1952 coup. The rationale behind this careful timing by those intent on leaving was to avoid the costly step of renewing these documents.

One of the letters to *Tachydromos* was from KM, a 57-year-old Greek citizen who wanted to retire in late 1961 and whose residence permit was due to expire in March 1964.[88] He envisaged two options: either to resign immediately in order to receive compensation and settle in Greece the following year or to resign immediately and then, after being compensated, to be rehired by the same company and to remain in Egypt until his residence permit expired without having to pay for a new one to be issued. In another letter, dated October 1961, an employee of an Egyptian joint-stock company enquired as to how much compensation he would be entitled to were he to resign before the year's end and then move to Greece in June 1962, namely after the end of the school year.[89]

Another Greek citizen, a radio technician who had a diploma from an Egyptian technical school, described how his company coerced him into resigning.[90] "The only European" employee in the Egyptian company he worked for, the director compelled him to resign before the end of 1961. According to Badawi, the Egyptian director had no legal right to do so. Another person, a sixty-year-old employee in an Egyptian joint-stock company, in which the state had taken a 50 percent share under Law 118, planned to retire and depart for Greece in order to spend his retirement close to his children.[91] His main concern after receiving his compensation was to transfer it immediately to Greece.

Other interesting examples concerned Egyptian citizens of Greek origin whose plans to leave Egypt were considered not repatriation but migration of an Egyptian citizen. As has been mentioned, in most cases Egyptiots deemed the acquisition of Egyptian citizenship more as a flag of convenience in order to remain in Egypt than a decision to integrate oneself into Egyptian society and culture. In one case, a doctor who had obtained Egyptian citizenship sought to retrieve his Greek citizenship. Like other Greeks who had taken this option, he was obliged to leave Egypt and thus lost the right of permanent residence in the country. As a consequence, the Egyptian government was unable to send remittances or even furniture to Greece through the system of Egyptian-Greek clearing.[92] His experience confirmed Egyptiot reservations that changing citizenship would result in difficulties in transferring assets in the event of repatriation.

Another indicative case, which surfaces in the GMFA archives, is that of Georgios Klimis.[93] For as long as he was in Egypt, Klimis worked for the Alexandria Water Company. After he left Egypt to settle in Thessaloniki, he wrote to Averoff in March 1962. The company he had worked for was British, but its chairmen were mainly Greek, Mikès Salvagos being an example. When Law 117 nationalized Alexandria Water, its workforce consisted of four hundred Egyptian and fourteen Greek employees. In a confidential conversation, the Egyptian general manager, with whom Klimis had, as he mentioned, "excellent relations," recommended that he and the other Greek employees resign immediately. He was also willing to help them receive their due compensation as soon as possible before they left. Thus, in late July, all the Greek employees of Alexandria Water submitted their resignations. At the end of September, two months after his resignation and after having settled all his affairs, Klimis departed for Greece permanently. In his letter to Averoff, he explicitly stated that the Greeks were "forced" to leave Egypt. In his case, however, there was no forced resignation and certainly no dismissal. It was a willing resignation based on "reliable" information that the situation might worsen for them.

The above cases and the many others that *Tachydromos* published around this time are indicative of the precise issues employees had to deal with and of how conditions could "force" someone to leave the country. There were no massive dismissals, as the community leadership and diplomatic authorities had feared; neither were there expulsions. The letters dealt with by Badawi confirm that employees, even if the July laws did not affect them, decided to leave on their own accord. Those who had no financial affairs to deal with were able to depart Egypt more easily and more quickly than those who had to transfer a part of their property through clearing, a process that could take up to eight months to complete.[94]

At another level, despite the critical situation, the Greek state did not ease its policy toward the Egyptiot Communists. The consulates had maintained updated lists of Communists since World War II, using them to prevent the definitive departure of those named on them by denying them certificates of social beliefs. Many of those considered Communists who wanted to depart asked that they be declassified. The consulates usually agreed to issue certificates to those not considered active Communists, although in such cases, as Theodoropoulos admitted in a secret letter, "migration is preferable to repatriation."[95]

CRISIS AND DIVERSIONS

On 28 September 1961, Syrian army officers rebelled in Damascus and declared the secession of Syria from the UAR. They said they were reacting to the "incompetency" of the Egyptian authorities and the submission of Syria to Egypt, accusing Nasser of wanting to destroy the Syrian bourgeoisie as he had done with the Egyptian one.[96] Nasser, on the other hand, attributed the Syrian coup d'état to the conspiracies of reactionary circles, imperialist colonizers, Israel, and other forces hostile to Egypt. In reply to what Nasser publicly referred to as a "reactionary secessionist movement,"[97] the government later sequestered the properties of wealthy businessmen in Egypt to "safeguard the people's interests," as an official statement claimed.[98]

In an attempt to find scapegoats, the vice president and interior minister, Zakaria Mohieddin, announced the arrest of thirty-seven "reactionary capitalists" on charges of using their assets "against the interests of the Egyptian people."[99] At the same time, the state sequestered the properties of 167 persons for security reasons. These were mainly Egyptians and members of the traditional *mutamassirun* upper class, mainly Jews, Syrians, Lebanese, and Armenians, whom the authorities accused of collaborating with the enemy and illegal capital exports. The names of eight Greeks were among the 167.[100] As Mohieddin stated, "Those arrested and their supporters are accused of exploiting the people, betraying the revolutionary ideals, cooperating with the colonialists when they ruled Egypt, the smuggling of capital, and tax evasion."[101] For the government, the enemy of the Egyptian people was not only the colonial powers but also Israel, which it accused of collaborating with the members of the traditional Egyptian upper class in order to destabilize the regime.[102] The Israeli press tried to exploit the situation for anti-Nasserite propaganda. In an editorial, the right-wing Tel Aviv newspaper *Ha-Boker* "forecasted" that "when the exodus of the Greeks from Egypt will be completed, Nasser may proclaim in a special speech that the name of Alexandria has been changed to 'Nasseria.'"[103]

Lambros downgraded the importance of these measures, claiming that the decision was taken without much consideration. He cited the example of Theodoros Kotsikas, a Greek industrialist and former Cairo resident, who had already moved to Switzerland, where he regularly received interest payments from his Egyptian bank accounts.[104] Michail Pesmazoglou, the caretaker foreign minister, also raised Kotsikas's case when he met with the Egyptian ambassador in Athens.[105] Adopting a strict tone, Pesmazoglou requested that the Egyptian authorities stop stigmatizing "wealthy and honorable" members of the community and accusing them of being "reactionary capitalists" and participants in the "colonial exploitation of the country" without evidence. The ambassador replied that the sequestration was a temporary measure for the protection of the people's interests and that, in the event of any errors, these would be rectified by a committee that had been established to deal with the issue. Besides, the measure did not concern Greek citizens as a whole, but only a few individuals. It was mainly targeted at Egyptian citizens, and for this reason, no exemption could be made for the benefit of Greeks.

At the same time, the UAR media, which had come under state control in May 1960, agreed with the minister. Populist articles targeted large foreign entrepreneurs, accusing them of exploiting the Egyptians and using their capital against the interests of the Egyptian people. The media presented Nasser, on the other hand, as the guarantor and defender of these interests. The magazine *Images* depicted the Greek and Jewish shareholders of a company under sequestration as exploiters who sucked the blood of the peasants.[106] In addition, Theodoropoulos, the consul general in Alexandria, claimed that the street vendors had advertised the Arabic version of the journal by shouting, "Get your copy and read about the Jews and Greeks."[107] These references, of course, did not concern all Egyptiots but only the large entrepreneurs. However, publications as the one mentioned above, which associated the Greeks with the perceived enemies of the regime, intensified the anxiety in community circles and elicited a vigorous reaction from diplomats. "It is of no interest to us whether they suffer the consequences as wealthy men or as Greeks. It is enough for us that they fraternized with all those accused of being oppressors of the Egyptian people," Theodoropoulos wrote in a secret report to Lambros.[108]

Apart from the article in *Images*, other media pronouncements caused deep concern among the diplomatic authorities. A radio broadcast on *Voice of the Arabs* said that the Greeks enriched themselves so much in Egypt that they could send enough money to Greece to build prisons.[109] Moreover, the consul general of Alexandria reported that on 21 November 1961 the newly established state television showed pictures of the Panathinaiko Stadium in Athens (colloquially, the Kallimarmaro, or "the beautifully marbled"), which had been reconstructed from the ruins of the ancient Greek stadium for the first modern Olympic Games in 1896.[110] The broadcast pointed out that the stadium had been reconstructed with a donation from Georgios Averoff, a prominent community figure. The following commentary accompanied the images: "The Greeks in Egypt not only became rich by exploiting the labor of the people of Egypt, but they also invested their fortunes abroad and made their country of origin rich with beautifully marbled buildings."[111] Similarly, an *Al-Ahram* report from around the same time presented the Egyptiots as having significant financial funds for "beautification projects" in Greece.[112] The press attaché of the Greek embassy in Cairo complained to Osman el-Assal, head of the Press Office of the Foreign Ministry, about these anti-Greek publications. El-Assal qualified the Greek reactions as "excessive," since the above-mentioned cases came from journalists who had no prestige or influence on public opinion. However, he claimed that he would try to prevent similar publications in the future.[113]

In a possible attempt to secure more favorable reporting, on 2 January 1962, the editor-in-chief of *Al-Ahbar* newspaper, Ahmed el-Sawi Muhammad, praised the sentiments of friendship between the Greek and the Egyptian people in announcing a report from Athens by journalist Sohby Abdel Hamit el-Seikh that would appear the following day.[114] The latter referred to the case of "Mitsos," who was born and raised in the Tanta region and who was then "a maître d'hôtel of one of the biggest hotels in Athens."[115] The report quoted Mitsos thus:

> Here I earn five times what I did when I was in Cairo, but my mood is broken. How can I forget Egypt? Is it possible? Never. I was born in the city of Sayyid el-Badawi and my heart and soul have stayed there. ... Because first I am Egyptian and then Greek. ... Egypt is my homeland and I will not forget it for as long as I live.[116]

After mentioning the position adopted by the Greek pilots during the Suez Crisis, the journalist ended his article in the following way: "So, those of our brothers who are Greek, whose families or other conditions dictate that they return to their homeland, will leave good memories here; they will enable the Egyptian Arabic language to be heard in Greece, and our friendship will remain a grand fortress, like the Acropolis was for the city of Athens."[117]

From the above publication, Nasser's declarations and speeches, and the exemptions given to Greeks from Egyptian laws, it is obvious that a distinction was being made between Egyptiot employees and big businessmen. The picture of the likable Greek from Tanta was contrasted with the image of the Greek benefactor. Even before the nationalizations, the media and theatrical plays made this distinction. They presented Greek workers and employees in more positive ways than bankers, big entrepreneurs, or speculators.[118] Harilaos Zamarias, Lambros's successor as ambassador in March 1962, reflected how these categories were linked during the exodus period. "The character of the new measures is anticapitalist, and the foreign element in Egypt is strictly linked to the capitalist economic system, which constituted, especially for Greeks, the starting point of their settlement in Egypt."[119] The scale of the nationalizations of smaller businesses such as maritime agencies and cinema theaters would affect lower-income groups and contribute to the high degree of departures until the mid-1960s.

PROVENANCE, NUMBERS, DESTINATIONS

The statistics kept by the consular authorities on the number of departees are incomplete, since many of those leaving did not declare that they never intended to return. Even if the numbers do not fully correspond to reality, they provide the most representative picture of the mass departure movement and, given that the data were collected monthly, clearly depict its rate and fluctuations in the first half of the 1960s. When referring to Alexandria, Cairo, and Port Said, the data refers to entire consular districts, not only cities. Tables 17 and 18 illustrate the number of declared definitive depar-

Table 17. Number of declared definitive departures of Greeks from Alexandria, per month, 1960–64

	1960	1961	1962	1963	1964	Total
January	–	74	338	85	113	610
February	–	74	288	107	134	603
March	–	127	210	160	125	622
April	–	211	277	128	134	750
May	–	197	320	164	178	859
June	–	191	293	164	181	829
July	–	207	202	190	145	744
August	–	319	138	153	120	730
September	–	351	134	115	100	700
October	–	200	160	116	105	581
November	–	211	103	111	72	497
December	–	179	77	67	56	379
Total	457	2,341	2,540	1,560	1,463	8,361

Sources: AYE/CS/1962/36/7/3/1; AYE/CS/1962/36/7/3/2; AYE/CS/1965/45/3/1/1.

Table 18. Number of declared definitive departures of Greeks from Cairo, per month, 1960–64

	1960	1961	1962	1963	1964	Total
January	27	54	143	101	–	325
February	4	13	172	85	–	274
March	9	170	243	89	–	511
April	21	141	162	66	–	390
May	24	147	126	62	–	359
June	21	62	144	56	–	283
July	51	82	103	100	–	336
August	77	131	17	156	–	381
September	32	80	139	95	–	346
October	81	94	192	174	–	541
November	37	33	180	182	–	432
December	101	110	186	103	–	500
Total	485	1,117	1,807	1,269	772	5,450

Sources: AYE/CS/1962/65/7/1/1; AYE/CS/1965/45/3/1/1.

tures of Greek citizens per month[120] recorded by the two major consulates, Alexandria and Cairo, from 1960 to 1964.

Even though the exodus started in late 1960, the departures increased impressively in 1961 and reached their peak in 1962. In Alexandria, 457 departures were registered in 1960, 2,341 the following year (+412 percent), and 2,540 in 1962. The Cairo consulate, on the other hand, registered 485 departures in 1960, 1,117 in 1961 (+130.3 percent), and 1,807 in 1962. Tables 17 and 18 suggest that the nationalizations had a greater impact on Alexandria's population than that in Cairo. According to the same data, the Greeks of Cairo proved to be more resilient in retaining their positions in this period. In this respect, after the mass departures in 1961 and 1962, the rate of departures fell much faster in Cairo than in Alexandria. The reaction in Cairo was calmer, mainly because Greek Cairenes were not as affected by the July laws. However, the ambassador, Lambros, an Alexandrian Greek himself, offered another dimension for this behavior:

> There was always the tendency in Alexandria to face the difficulties that come up with less sangfroid. I wonder if this tendency should not be accredited to the special mentality of the Alexandria community, especially its governing class, which has been addicted for generations to easy financial and social development, without any obstacles, and therefore, they have less ability to adjust to the new situation.[121]

Where did the departees go? In the early 1960s—and especially in 1961 and 1962—the main destination was Greece. This is depicted in tables 19 and 20, which show the numbers and percentages of departures from the two main consular districts according to destination.

Table 19. Number of departees from Alexandria and Cairo consular districts and destination, 1960–64

	Alexandria			Cairo		
Year	Greece	Other destination	Total	Greece	Other destination	Total
1960	195	262	457	250	235	485
1961	2,065	276	2,341	977	140	1,117
1962	1,959	581	2,540	1,647	160	1,807
1963	951	609	1,560	1,078	191	1,269
1964	940	523	1,463	403	369	772
Total	6,110	2,251	8,361	4,355	1,095	5,450

Sources: AYE/CS/1963/44/5/2/1/2; AYE/CS/1964/43/9/1/1; AYE/CS/1962/65/7/1/1; AYE/CS/1965/45/3/1/1.

Table 20. Percentage of departees from Alexandria and Cairo consular district and destination, 1960–64

	Alexandria			Cairo		
Year	Greece	Other destination	Total	Greece	Other destination	Total
1960	42.6	57.4	100	51.5	48.5	100
1961	88.2	11.8	100	87.4	12.6	100
1962	77.1	22.9	100	91.1	8.9	100
1963	60.9	39.1	100	84.9	15.1	100
1964	64.2	35.8	100	52.2	47.8	100
Average	66.6	33.4	100	73.4	42.6	100

Sources: AYE/CS/1963/44/5/2/1/2; AYE/CS/1964/43/9/1/1; AYE/CS/1962/65/7/1/1; AYE/CS/1965/45/3/1/1.

In 1961, almost nine in ten departees moved to Greece (88.2 percent of those from Alexandria and 87.4 percent from Cairo). This percentage remained high in both cities in 1962 and 1963, before falling in 1964—at least for Cairo—to 1960 levels. In 1962 the percentage dropped by almost 12.5 percentage points compared to 1961 and stabilized at around 60 percent for the following two years. This drop was also due to the intensive efforts of the Greek state, after the first exodus wave, to control the mass departure and direct it toward other destinations.[122] Thus, exodus basically meant repatriation. The choice to move to Greece reflects, to a certain degree, the extent of the panic in the community; migration to a third country required a more composed spirit and greater foresight and planning. Just a few hundred miles from the Egyptian coast, Greece was nearer and more easily accessible than other destinations like Australia, which had more demanding formalities and required more preparation.

Another interesting observation arising from the data is that the repatriation average was lower from Alexandria (66.6 percent) than from Cairo (73.4 percent). This may be explained by the fact that Alexandria had the know-how as regards overseas migration. The city was the basis of the organizations that sponsored the migration process, which was started in 1947 through the GCCA and was systematized by the Greek consulate general of the city in cooperation with the ICEM and WCC. Besides, the seat of the whole operation from June 1960 was the consulate general of Alexandria, and Papantonopoulos, who had many years of experience in ICEM migration programs, was appointed the head of this operation. More than half of the sponsored Egyptiot migrants during the 1950s came from Alexandria. These constituted important human capital for an existing, established network that was the basis for gathering information, providing aid for the issuing of landing permits (in the case of Australia), and settlement in a destination country. The principal destination for the departees continued to be Australia, which received 55 percent of those who migrated from Alexandria and 48 percent of those from Cairo. South American countries, mainly Brazil, and South Africa, which in the 1960s absorbed an important number of Greek migrants from Egypt, followed.[123]

In other Egyptian cities, the departure pattern was not much different during the exodus of the early 1960s. In the consular district of Port Said, for instance, from 1960 to 1961 (years for which data is available) the departure movement was equally massive and almost entirely directed toward Greece: some 201 people moved to the homeland, while 28 went to other countries, corresponding to 87.7 and 12.3 percent, respectively. The simultaneous mass departure of Egyptiots from all over the country shows that the July laws were the last straw. The mass movement had started months beforehand, but the implementation of the socialist legislation during the summer of 1961 accelerated it. This was even clearer in cities like Port Said, where there were no nationalizations and three-quarters of the Greek workforce depended on the Suez Canal.[124] Despite its different social character, "the Greek communities ... are today full of doubts and reservations about the present and worries and fears for the future ... they consider their departure ... as a matter of time and suitable conditions," as the city's consul noted in November 1961.[125]

For most Egyptiots, going to Greece did not amount to repatriation or return migration but was rather the first contact with an "imaginary homeland." Indeed, for many Egyptiots, definitive departure must have felt more as expatriation than repatriation. Despite the mobility between the two countries, the majority of repatriates had never visited Greece before. Nevertheless, the continuous physical contact between the two countries contributed to the maintenance of family and other social bonds with the homeland, which now proved crucial for traversing the Mediterranean. Many of those who left had relatives and friends who had already gone to Greece. For those who were employed in a strictly Greek working environment, they could rely on networks to find a job in Greece linked to the same social and working place. For community organizations, it was easier to provide recommendation letters to employees who wanted to move to Greece than to other countries. In this respect, the GCCA provided letters of reference for employees from Alexandria whom they deemed reliable.[126]

An indicative example of how these networks operated is provided by the French aluminum industry Pechiney, which set up in Greece in 1960. When it began operations in 1966,[127] 11 percent of its personnel were Greeks from Egypt.[128] This was mainly the result of the hiring policy of Dimitrios

Charitatos, who was an executive in a company that was nationalized and was hired by Pechiney in 1962 after he moved to Greece. Charitatos functioned as a pole of attraction for many Greeks, especially from the Suez Canal area,[129] because of his family origins from the island of Kassos, where the majority of Egyptiots in the Suez Canal cities came from. We may assume that similar networks existed for other Egyptiot employees and workers and those in the Suez Canal Authority, which the state nationalized in 1956, who abandoned their positions before their retirement and went to Greece, where they could easily find work in the newly established Hellenic Shipyards in Skaramagas, in western Attica.[130]

But apart from playing the role of real or imaginary homeland, Greece was also an attractive destination for many Egyptiots. Despite strong political cleavages and the marginalization by the postwar Greek governments of a large part of Greek society for ideological reasons, the country showed considerable development potential in the free market system. It gave the possibility for Egyptiot businessmen to continue to live in a free market environment, to which they were accustomed.[131] As Ambassador Zamarias pointed out in March 1962, the upcoming entry of Greece to the European Economic Community (EEC) increased the lure of the former:

> The attraction of Greece is stronger than ever, since the Egyptiots see the homeland not only prospering today more than in any other postwar period, but also laying the foundations for a better future through its connection with the EEC. ... The terms of comparison have been reversed ... and the flow of the Greeks is inevitably turning to where the future seems brighter.[132]

The conditions of near panic, to the degree it existed in Egypt, did not translate into a disorderly departure. Instead, the evidence shows the departures were often well organized. Those who wished to leave took several factors into account: the possibility of transferring assets, the existence of family and other links that could provide assistance in the early stages of their new life, and the possibility to carry on their job in the destination country. Thus, it was also a matter of individual family strategy. The information that circulated through kinship and family networks definitely played a central role in the direction and extent of the departure flow. For instance, diplomats attributed the decrease in the departures during the summer months of 1962 to information coming from Greece claiming that those looking for work faced difficulties. This was the reason for the increase in departures toward third countries during the same period.[133]

The Greek state's policy also contributed to the direction and flow of departures. The assiduity with which it sponsored overseas migration in the 1950s and the 1960s was in blatant contrast to the way it dealt with repatriation. Indicative in this regard is the almost total absence of the Greek state mechanisms during the 1950s and during the exodus in both the organization of the movement and the reception of Egyptiots upon their arrival "home." The inability of the Greek government to balance the clearing arrangement with Egypt resulted in an exchange rate for the Egyptian pound in Greece that was 30 percent below value. While the Greek state compensated the Egyptiot shareholders and company owners for their losses suffered in the nationalizations, it levied customs taxes on furniture and other possessions that had already been taxed in Egypt. This double taxation, along with the LE 10 to 15 per cubic meter cost to ship goods, confronted many Egyptiots with the dilemma of having to leave their furniture and other goods in Egypt and starting from scratch in Greece.[134] The most significant measure adopted by the Greek state for most repatriates was to register all Egyptiots in the social security system and recognize their working years in Egypt.[135]

THOSE WHO LEFT AND THOSE WHO STAYED BEHIND

The exodus began during the final months of 1960 as a result of Law 19/1959 and Decrees 260 and 263/1960 regarding foreign employees and not as an immediate result of the nationalizations of 1961. Despite the fact that the Egyptian state gave favorable treatment to the Greeks, they continued to leave in the first half of 1961. Incidents such as the deportation of Belgian citizens, and of the Greek consuls following the spy affair, served to keep the departure momentum going. The July 1961 laws intensified the exodus wave even more, which was maintained in the following years as a result of the sequestration of properties, more nationalizations, and the 1963 agrarian reform. In all cases, employees, who constituted the backbone of the community, were not directly affected. The legislation was passed in the context of the growth of the country's public sector economy and Egyptian propaganda that deemed the capitalist class, Egyptian and foreign, to be supporters of Israel and the ex-colonial powers. Nonetheless, the laws mainly targeted Egyptian, not foreign or Greek, capital.

Nasser did not expel Greeks from Egypt, as happened with the French, British, wealthy Jews, and Belgians. Consequently, the common belief among the community leadership and the diplomatic authorities since World War II that a wave of persecution awaited the Egyptiot Greeks was not realized. Even those who were directly affected by the nationalization measures were not expelled; they were compensated.[136] The nationalization, though, of the companies and the socialist measures had as an indirect consequence the massive departure of the employees of these companies because the Egyptian government, in the context of the new socialist economy, tried to employ as many Egyptian secondary school graduates as possible and committed itself to offering a job to all university graduates.[137] Companies under state control were to absorb the new labor force, and the mass entry of Egyptians into them contributed to the steep decline in the number of unemployed Egyptians from 325,000 in 1959 to 288,000 a year later, to 211,000 in 1961 and 118,000 in 1962.[138] Such recruitment on a mass scale undoubtedly created pressures on those already working, but it seems that the rights of Greek employees were generally respected. Although there were cases of employees who were dismissed or were compelled to resign and then left Egypt, this pressure, however, was not the direct result of Nasser's or his minister's orders, but came from lower- and medium-ranking public officials, the new Egyptian directors of the nationalized companies, and low-ranking employees. These seem to have acted independently of the hierarchy to serve personal interests and clientelistic networks while Nasser and his ministers sought to reassure Greeks and offer them favorable treatment, as had happened with Decrees 260 and 263 of 1960.

In a speech on 22 July 1961, on the occasion of Revolution Day, just twenty-four hours after the enactment of the nationalizations law, Nasser condemned the "carelessness" and breaches of duty in state-run companies, which he said would be legally prosecuted. "The public enterprise sector," he said, "belongs to every one of you. Anybody who neglects his responsibilities in this respect should be punished. If any person entrusted with responsibility in an enterprise appoints his relatives or makes exceptions, we must punish him and consider this as treason. ... Nobody should be appointed without passing a competitive examination," he continued, condemning a case where a manager "planned a competitive examination in such a way that only a particular man and his wife could pass it." In a paternalistic way, he urged employees to write to him directly should they observe someone who wanted to "appoint his relatives and make exceptions."[139] Nasser's references to breaches of duty in state-controlled companies and his stated intention to prosecute those responsible is also revealing of the extent that nepotism and clientelism had developed in part of the public administration and how this affected Egyptians. Against this background and in the context of the nationalizations, Greek employees were bound to be negatively affected as well.

One incident in particular highlights the gap between official policy and everyday practice in the public administration in relation to issues concerning the community. In November 1961, Labor Ministry inspectors sent signed letters to Greek employers calling for the dismissal of Greek employees under Decrees 260 and 263.[140] After the employers protested to the general director of the ministry and reminded him of the promise the government had made to exempt Greeks, he assured them that the letters had been sent in error and that they would not be bothered about this again.[141] Incidents like this, where lower- and medium-ranking public officials put direct or indirect pressure on employers were not infrequent. Thus, the fear that more disturbances might follow in the future gained momentum, especially given "the existing important unemployment problem, which the dignitaries are trying to resolve with all possible means."[142] The contradictory messages received by Egyptiots from public officials, combined with the fact these messages were issued in a language that many of them had avoided learning, reinforced the fatigue brought about by a long period of uncertainty and contributed to the decision of many to leave Egypt for good.

The fact that promises to exempt Greeks were often verbal, without any written guarantees, did nothing to dilute the feeling of insecurity about the future. It's worth recalling Nasser's words in Athens in June 1960: "An agreement can be reached without changing the law, because when we take any measure we cannot turn back."[143] Laws could not be made or amended to extend favorable treatment or grant exemptions to Greeks, as this would undermine national sovereignty and lead other foreigners to seek similar exceptions. Egypt's capitulatory and colonial past, coupled with the nationalism of the period, left little or no room for more concessions. The vagueness generated by verbal commitments created gray areas where it was difficult for a foreigner to build a future. Not only Egyptian officials and employees but also Greeks exploited such gray areas. Greek employers claimed that such written and verbal guarantees and pressures from public officials left them with no choice but to dismiss Greek employees. These pressures gave "the opportunity to adjust the number of employees to the company's needs" or "to reduce their expenses through the replacement of the better-paid Greeks with Egyptian employees."[144]

Greeks abandoned Egypt en masse because of the general atmosphere of uncertainty about the future, which had built up over the years, and because of rumors that additional and harsher measures lay ahead. The fact that most Egyptiots were employed in clerical positions and had no knowledge of Arabic increased this uncertainty. Adding to the confusion were the contradictory messages coming from the public administration and the general atmosphere of suspicion resulting from the spying revelations involving foreigners and, especially, Greeks. Articles in the press against wealthy Greeks, arrests for smuggling, and the lack of solidarity as demonstrated in the cases of Greeks who blackmailed and denounced compatriots also fueled the panic. The July laws and subsequent sequestrations increased anxiety about the future and pushed more Greeks into leaving. In parallel, the nationalizations that affected large capital holders and prominent community figures in Alexandria and Cairo shook all social levels of the community, which was bound together by social and professional networks and was controlled by the economic elite affected by the measures.[145] It was just a matter of time before these shock waves would hit other cities and undermine the shaky edifice of the community.

For many Egyptiot Greeks, the pressure and uncertainty were just too much to bear, as the consul general in Alexandria, Theodoropoulos, noted in late October 1961. He observed a dangerous swing in the psychology of the Alexandrian Greek, which can be summarized thus: "Let's leave and abandon all our property behind to rid us of the stress of tomorrow." Given the different composition of the community in Cairo, the situation was better than in Alexandria.[146] However, by 1962, uncertainty was also pushing Greeks into leaving the capital, as the city's consul general, Yiannakakis, found: "The Greeks do not leave the country that they feel is their real country and which they loved and still love strictly just for economic reasons. They abandon Egypt for psychological and family reasons and mostly because of the lack of feeling of security about the present and the future."[147]

People often leave one place for a better future in another, and those Egyptiot Greeks who left did so because they were convinced that socialist Egypt offered no future for them or because they had better prospects elsewhere. This may or may not have had an economic meaning, however, and where it had, this may have meant many different things. Despite the latent collective readiness of many Egyptiot Greeks to leave as a result of the uncertainty about the present and future, the specific decision to pack one's bags was affected by the character of each departee as well as his or her personal and family situation. In a snowball effect, each departure served to encourage others to leave. "Many people say that they left only because everybody else was leaving," writes historian Floresca Karanasou.[148]

The majority of those who left Egypt during the exodus must have been white-collar workers and general employees in the nationalized companies, who either resigned of their own volition or were pushed into doing so.[149] Employees of this category, along with the shop assistants, constituted the bulk of the Egyptiot workforce. Trained to perform in a free-market economic environment, they were reluctant to identify themselves with Nasser's vision of Arab socialism and to continue working in state-run companies. Making the use of Arabic compulsory for all clerks created another obstacle. In an effort to combat clientelism, the Egyptian Labor Ministry in 1962 decided that employees in public-sector enterprises with a salary above LE 15 could be recruited only after an exam, which became an insurmountable obstacle to those who wished to enter the labor market and did not know the language.[150] Shop assistants, on the other hand, even if they were not affected directly by any state measures, must have left because of the general pessimistic mood about the future and, additionally, because Greek employers dismissed many of them.[151]

Professionals who worked in the retail trade sector also left. As we have seen, the sector faced severe economic difficulties during the 1950s because of the fall in consumer purchasing power and strict price controls, which diminished profit margins, as well as the departure of well-to-do foreign customers. Besides, diplomats sensed that the decision of the Egyptian government in 1962 to establish cooperative stores, which the state, as their main supplier, controlled, would place additional pressure on Greek retailers. The cooperative stores were able to sell products at much lower prices than the Greeks could. Thus, many of them sought to sell their stores to Egyptian buyers and then leave. The import-export trade, which Law 107/1961 nationalized, directly or indirectly affected a considerable number of foreign professionals. Even though they could continue to work as wholesalers supplied by state organizations, the profit margins were limited. As for the commercial representations, which were to be Egyptianized under Law 24/1957, another law (47/1961) ordered their merger with state organizations. Companies affected by Law 24/1957 had already oriented their business activities toward representing local firms, even though this was less profitable and they faced more competition from Egyptians.[152]

In the early 1960s, the wages offered to Greeks tended to reflect the average wage for Egyptians, except in cases where Egyptians could not replace foreigners. Diplomats considered low wages combined with high taxation of large incomes as one of the main obstacles to Greeks entering the labor market and remaining in Egypt.[153] Higher wages in Greece and in other countries attracted qualified technicians, even if the laws did not affect them. Self-employed architects, civil engineers, and contractors were now barred from receiving public-sector contracts worth more than LE 30,000 per year, unless they cooperated with the State Construction Organization with 50 percent of their capital. The decrease in construction activity by foreign-owned companies reduced their revenue and margin of profit. Moreover, they came under increasing competition from Egyptian companies, which could submit more attractive tenders. In addition, growing state intervention in the economy, where the continuous measures exacerbated the sense of panic, added to the economic difficulties of small- and medium-sized businessmen and professionals. Increasing numbers of liberal professions were restricted to Egyptian citizens, although older professionals could continue practicing.[154] After many years of high departure rates, the Greek population in

Egypt by 1967 was estimated to number 17,000, regardless of citizenship, down from the 47,673 recorded in the official census in 1960.[155]

With the decolonization process under way in many countries, the international context in the early 1960s undoubtedly prompted people to leave Egypt. As colonial empires collapsed, waves of Europeans returned to their respective metropolis from the colonies. The decade from 1956 to 1967 saw massive numbers of repatriates moving from the North African countries of Algeria, Tunisia, and Morocco to France. In 1962 alone—the year that the exodus of Egyptiots reached its peak—651,000 Europeans, mainly French citizens, moved to France after Algerian independence. Of course, Egypt was never a colony in the strict sense, nor were Greeks subjects of a colonial power. The British colonial presence and the privileged environment of the Capitulations, though, had determined its modern history, whereas the anticolonial struggle was behind the expulsion of the British, French, and Belgians from Egypt.

Who stayed behind? First of all, some of those who had been directly affected by Laws 117, 118, and 119 and the agrarian reform of 1963 remained in the country in order to receive compensation. The negotiations between the Egyptian and Greek governments concerning the compensation entitlements of Greek citizens whose properties had been nationalized began in April 1962. After a long process, both sides reached an accord in 1966. The Greek side estimated the value of the nationalized properties at LE 29.4 million and claimed that 1,352 individuals had been affected.[156] The Egyptian side, however, said it would pay only LE 15.5 million in compensation, in annual disbursements of up to LE 800,000 in total over many years.[157] Some of those who were affected by the July laws left immediately, such as Dimitrios Charitatos. Others, such as Dimitrios Zerbinis and Konstantinos Salvagos, remained and passed away a short time later. Not all businessmen affected by the laws left Egypt. Anastassios Theodorakis, GKA president since 1954, and Nikolaos Pierrakos, GKC president, remained and started new businesses in sectors not affected by the state monopoly.[158] The Greek industries that were not fully or partially nationalized not only continued operating in Egypt, but they had considerable profits. The Zottos and Volonakis alcoholic drinks company, which continued operating even though profits fell because of the departure of many foreigners (and main consumers of alcohol) and the reduction in purchasing power in general, was one example. Other industries unaffected by the nationalizations, such as pasta, pastries, tanning, and soft drinks companies, continued to operate without restrictions.[159]

People who had real estate portfolios in Egypt remained in the county or prolonged their stay until they sold out. However, they found it difficult to secure good prices for their properties.¹⁶⁰ Property sales drew the attention of the exchange control authorities, even if many vendors considered the sale price extremely low.¹⁶¹ Others who remained were some senior executives in the nationalized companies whose resignation had not been accepted; some self-employed professionals (doctors, pharmacists, dentists, chemists, civil engineers, and architects); the owners of bars, restaurants, cinemas, and printing houses; shopkeepers; a small number of employees and technicians; old-age pensioners who were not physically mobile; some destitute and unskilled persons whose repatriation was blocked by the Greek authorities; and, finally, a small number of clergymen, educators, and personnel at the *koinotites* who remained active as well as officials of other organizations such as the Alexandria and Cairo chambers of commerce. In 1970, ten years after the exodus began, an official in the consulate general of Alexandria wrote:

> The Greek inhabitants of Egypt form a minority that is chiefly confined to the towns of Alexandria and Cairo. The present Greek population ... either on account of their occupation or on account of their underage children, remains in Egypt, [believing their children] should complete their preuniversity education in Egypt. ... This depletion ... is the logical sequence of the outward stream that has been running for so many years but which is now slowing down; the community comprises people who have close relatives, parents, or children who left Egypt long ago.... The future of "Egyptian Hellenism" is uncertain.¹⁶²

In observing the migration behavior of all these departees, two interrelated questions arise: were all the reasons mentioned in this book enough for them to leave a place that they almost unanimously still considered their "second homeland"? And if Egypt was their "second homeland," where was their first? An easy answer to the latter question is Greece. However, the low appeal of Greece, located some hundred miles away, raises some questions. Even though Greece had seen a decade of relative political stability after the civil war, a significant percentage of Egyptiots still preferred to move to third-country destinations. A number of them, after settling for a while in Greece or other countries, sometimes reemigrated. The relative unattractiveness of Greece can be attributed to some extent to the preventive policy of the Greek state against repatriation. But a more important factor was that after a presence over generations in Egypt, many Egyptiot Greeks did not necessarily identify the homeland with the territory of Greece, a feeling compounded by the diverse origins of their ancestors. For them, the homeland existed more as an imaginary cultural space, and such a space could exist beyond Greece, in the various settings with familiar characteristics where they settled. The choice of these places depended on the networks used, on their specific socioeconomic profile, and on the increasing possibilities for integration. This imaginary cultural space could very well continue to exist in Egypt. In this respect, those who remained did so because none of the reasons mentioned in this book were powerful enough to make them leave, given their professional, social, or personal links with the country. Moreover, some of them had nowhere else to go. For them, Egypt was their ultimate and only home.

NOTES

1. AYE/CS/1961/21/15/2/1, 725, Alexandria, 18 July 1961, Theodoropoulos to Cairo embassy.
2. AYE/CS/1961/16/1/3/1, 171, Alexandria, 9 February 1961, Baizos to Cairo embassy.
3. Ibid.
4. Ibid.
5. AICEM/1959–65, Note, Emigration of Europeans from Egypt, Alexandra Ioannides, Athens, 13 March 1961.
6. AYE/CS/1961/16/1/3/1, 171, Alexandria, 9 February 1961, Baizos to Cairo embassy.
7. "Laws 260 and 263/1960 on Conditions of Employment of Foreigners in the UAR," *Bulletin of the GCCA,* November 1960.
8. Sokratis Kalliarekos et al., *To paroikiako provlima* [The problem of the community] (Alexandria, 1961), 3.
9. Ibid., 4.
10. Themistoklis Matsakis, *To dilimma tou aigyptiotou ellinismou* [The dilemma of Egyptiot Hellenism] (Cairo, 1961), 8.
11. Ibid., 11.
12. CADN/Ambassade de France à Athènes/211, 861/AL, Athens, 10 November 1960, De Charbonnieres to FMFA.
13. AYE/CS/1963/42/8/1/1, 6861, Cairo, 22 May 1961, Katapodis to Khartoum embassy.
14. Pierre Salmon, "Les retours en Belgique induits par la décolonisation," in *L'Europe retrouvée. Les migrations de la décolonisation,* ed. Jean-Louis Miège and Colette Dubois (Paris: L'Harmattan, 1994), 194–95.
15. Jean Ducruet, *Les Capitaux Européens au Proche-Orient* (Paris: Presses Universitaires de France, 1964), 323–24.
16. *Tachydromos,* 28 February 1961, 1.
17. AYE/CS/1961/21/4/1/1, Memorandum (n.p.), 19 September 1961.
18. MAE/Levant 1944–65/République Arabe Unie 1960–65/1001, 765/AL, Athens, 6 October 1960, de Charbonnieres to FMFA.
19. AYE/CS/1961/21/4/1/1, 6005, Cairo, 9 January 1961, Lambros to GMFA.
20. Nikos Katapodis, *Skorpia fylla tis diplomatikis mou zois* [Aspects of my diplomatic career] (Athens: Potamos, 2004), 30.
21. Ibid.

22. AYE/CS/1961/21/4/1/1, Note, Top Secret, 16 February 1961.
23. Ibid.
24. AYE/CS/1961/21/4/1/1, 6259, Cairo, 15 February 1961, Lambros to GMFA.
25. Ibid.
26. Katapodis, *Skorpia fylla*, 30.
27. AYE/CS/1961/16/1/3/2, 224, Alexandria, 9 March 1961, Kontoumas to Lambros.
28. Luise White, *Speaking with Vampires: Rumor and History in Colonial Africa* (Berkeley, CA: University of California Press, 2008), 81.
29. AYE/CS/1962/65/7/1/1, 6072, Cairo, 16 January 1961, Lambros to GMFA.
30. AYE/1961/16/1/3/2, 224, Alexandria, 9 March 1961, Kontoumas to Cairo embassy.
31. AYE/CS/1961/21/4/1/1, 6259, Cairo, 15 February 1961, Lampros to GMFA.
32. Ibid.
33. AYE/CS/1961/16/11/2/2, Note, Athens, 10 June 1961. That is what Lambros claimed to the chief of the Greek General Headquarters Staff, Athanassios Frontistis, when he visited Egypt in June 1961.
34. AYE/CS/1961/21/9/1/1, 6648, Cairo, 9 April 1961, Katapodis to GMFA.
35. AYE/CS/1961/16/1/3/2, 224, Alexandria, 9 March 1961, Kontoumas to Cairo embassy; AYE/CS/1961/21/15/1/1, 650, Alexandria, 3 July 1961, Theodoropoulos to Cairo embassy; AYE/CS/1961/16/1/3/2, 485, Cairo, 14 March 1961, Yiannakakis to Cairo embassy.
36. AYE/CS/1961/16/1/3/2, 485, Cairo, 14 March 1961, Yiannakakis to Cairo embassy; AYE/CS/1961/16/1/3/2, 224, Alexandria, 9 March 1961, Kontoumas to Cairo embassy; AYE/CS/1961/21/15/1/1, 650, Alexandria, 3 July 1961, Theodoropoulos to Cairo embassy.
37. AYE/CS/1961/16/1/3/2, 485, Cairo, 14 March 1961, Yiannakakis to Cairo embassy.
38. AYE/CS/1961/21/15/2/1, 725, Alexandria, 18 July 1961, Theodoropoulos to Cairo embassy.
39. Kalliarekos, *To paroikiako*, 6.
40. Matsakis, *To dilimma*, 10.
41. Ibid., 12–13.
42. Patrick O'Brien, *The Revolution in Egypt's Economic System*, from Private to Socialism, 1952–1965 (London: Oxford University Press, 1966), 130.
43. Ibid.
44. AYE/CS1961/16/3/2/2, 671, Alexandria, 7 April 1961, Theodoropoulos to Cairo embassy.
45. AYE/CS/1961/21/15/2/1, 725, Alexandria, 18 July 1961, Theodoropoulos to Cairo embassy.
46. *Tachydromos*, 20 July 1961.
47. Tewfik Aclimandos, "Les Officiers activistes de l'armée égyptienne, 1936–1954" (Ph.D. diss., Sciences Po, Paris, 2004), 1324.
48. AYE/CS/1961/16/3/2/2, 732, Alexandria, 20 July 1961, Theodoropoulos to Cairo embassy.
49. *Tachydromos*, 21 July 1961, 1.

50. AGCCA/8/General Statistics, Note, 1.
51. Aclimandos, "Les officiers activistes," 1321.
52. AYE/CS/1962/36/4/2/1, 6139, Cairo, 29 January 1962, Theodoropoulos to GMFA.
53. Ibid.
54. AYE/CS1961/16/3/2/2, 745, Secret, Alexandria, 26 July 1961, Theodoropoulos to Cairo embassy.
55. AYE/CS1961/16/3/2/2, 7669, Cairo, 5 September 1961, Lambros to GMFA.
56. Alexander Kazamias, "The 'Purge of the Greeks' from Nasserite Egypt: Myths and Realities," *Journal of the Hellenic Diaspora* 35, no. 2 (2009): 18.
57. AYE/CS/1961/16/3/2/2, 733, Alexandria, 21 July 1961, Theodoropoulos to Cairo embassy; AYE/CS/1961/16/3/2/2, 745, Secret, Alexandria, 26 July 1961, Theodoropoulos to Cairo embassy.
58. AYE/CS/1961/16/3/2/2, 745, Alexandria, 26 July 1961, Secret, Theodoropoulos to Cairo embassy.
59. AYE/CS/1961/21/17/2/1/2, 8124, Cairo, 7 November 1961, Lambros to GMFA. This is a rough calculation based on data published in *Al-Ahram* and mostly concerning former Egyptian-owned companies.
60. AYE/CS/1965/46/9/1/1, 7123, Cairo, 13 July 1965, Mitsialis to Zamarias.
61. AYE/CS/1961/16/3/2/2, 745, Secret, Alexandria, 26 July 1961, Theodoropoulos to Cairo embassy.
62. Elliniki en Alexandria Koinotis, *Logodosia etous 1961* [Greek Koinotita of Alexandria, Annual report of 1961] (Alexandria: T. Kassimatis, 1961), 70.
63. Ibid., 3.
64. Euthymios Souloyannis, *I Elliniki Koinotita Alexandrias, 1843–1993* [The Greek Koinotita of Alexandria, 1843–93] (Athens: ELIA, 2005), 230–34.
65. AYE/CS/1961/16/3/2/2, 745, Secret, Alexandria, 26 July 1961, Theodoropoulos to Cairo embassy.
66. Ibid.
67. AYE/CS/1961/16/1/3/2, 485, Cairo, 14 March 1961, Yiannakakis to Cairo embassy.
68. AYE/CS/1961/16/3/2/2, 7304, Cairo, 21 July 1961, Lambros to Averoff.
69. AYE/CS/1961/21/15/2/2, 735, Alexandria, 11 August 1961, Theodoropoulos to GMFA.
70. AYE/CS/1961/21/15/2/2, 838, Alexandria, 19 August 1961, Theodoropoulos to GMFA.
71. AYE/CS/1961/21/17/2/1/2, 7969, Cairo, 23 October 1961, Lambros to Theodoropoulos.
72. AYE/CS/1961/16/3/2/2, 768, Alexandria, 2 August 1961, Theodoropoulos to Cairo embassy.
73. Ibid.
74. MAE/Levant 1944–65/République Arabe Unie 1960–65/1001/279–80, Athens, 8 August 1961, Laurens-Castelet to FMFA.
75. AYE/CS/1961/16/3/2/2, 7669, Cairo, 5 September 1961, Lambros to GMFA.
76. *Tachydromos,* 10 August 1961, 1.

77. Kazamias, "The 'Purge,'" 20.
78. AYE/CS/1961/16/3/2/2, 880, Alexandria, 29 August 1961, Theodoropoulos to Cairo embassy.
79. AYE/CS/1961/16/3/2/2, 768, Alexandria, 2 August 1961, Theodoropoulos to Cairo embassy.
80. AYE/CS/1961/16/3/2/2, 880, Alexandria, 29 August 1961, Theodropoulos to Cairo embassy.
81. AGCCA/Correspondence, 1960–63: Confidential note of the GCCA, 1962.
82. AYE/CS/1961/21/15/2/2, 838, Alexandria, 19 August 1961, Theodoropoulos to Cairo embassy.
83. AYE/CS/1961/16/3/2/2, 880, Alexandria, 29 August 1961, Theodoropoulos to Cairo embassy.
84. AYE/CS/1961/16/3/2/1, Cairo, 21 November 1961, Yiannakakis to Cairo embassy.
85. AYE/CS/1961/16/3/2/2, 7669, Cairo, 5 September 1961, Lambros to GMFA.
86. Ibid.
87. AYE/CS/1961/21/17/2/1/2, 1103, Alexandria, 13 November 1961, Theodoropoulos to Lambros. The participants of the meeting were A Theodorakis, K Salvagos, K Nanopoulos, S Pialopoulos, L Koutarellis, G Dimitriou, D Zerbinis, and Y Chryssovergis.
88. *Tachydromos,* 27 October 1961, 3.
89. Ibid.
90. *Tachydromos,* 10 November 1961, 3.
91. Ibid.
92. AYE/CS/1965/46/7/2/1, 6189, Cairo, 18 October 1965, Horafas to Cairo embassy.
93. AYE/CS/1962/43/3/2/1, Thessaloniki, 19 February 1962, Klimis to Averoff.
94. AYE/CS/1962/65/7/1/1, 622, Cairo, 4 August 1962, Yiannakakis to Cairo embassy.
95. AYE/CS/1964/44/3/1/1, Secret, 660, Alexandria, 2 November 1963, Theodoropoulos to GMFA.
96. Robert Tignor, *Capitalism and Nationalism at the End of Empire: State and Business in Decolonizing Egypt, Nigeria and Kenya, 1945–1963* (Princeton, NJ: Princeton University Press, 1999), 164.
97. *President Gamal Abdel-Nasser's Speeches and Press-Interviews,* January–December 1961, 281.
98. *Tachydromos,* 23 October 1961, 1.
99. Ibid.
100. Ibid.
101. AYE/CS/1961/21/17/2/1/2, 7976, Cairo, 24 October 1961, Lambros to GMFA.
102. AYE/CS/1963/42/9/1/1, 811, London, 15 February 1961, Seferiadis to GMFA.
103. *Ha-Boker* (n.d.), text translated in AYE/1962/36/7/3/2, Jerusalem, 1 October 1962.
104. AYE/CS/1961/21/17/2/1/2, 7969, Cairo, 23 October 1961, Lambros to Theodoropoulos.

105. AYE/CS/1961/21/17/2/1/2, Note on discussions of the Greek minister of foreign affairs Michail Pesmazoglou with the Egyptian ambassador in Athens, Athens, 26 October 1961.
106. *Images* 1677, 28 October 1961.
107. AYE/CS/1961/21/17/2/1/2, 1066, Secret, Alexandria, 28 October 1961, Theodoropoulos to Cairo embassy.
108. AYE/CS/1961/21/17/2/1/2, 1066, Secret, Alexandria, 28 October 1961, Theodoropoulos to Cairo embassy.
109. Ibid. It refers to Averoff Prison, which was built in Athens in the 1890s with funds provided by Georgios Averoff.
110. AYE/CS/1962/43/6/1/1, 1122, Alexandria, 24 November 1961, Theodoropoulos to Cairo embassy.
111. Ibid.
112. Ibid.
113. AYE/CS/1962/43/6/1/1, 50, Cairo, 16 January 1962, Komninos to Cairo embassy.
114. AYE/CS/1962/43/6/1/1, translation of article from *Al-Ahbar*, 2 January 1962.
115. Ibid.
116. Ibid.
117. Ibid.
118. Ziad Fahmy, *Ordinary Egyptians: Creating the Modern Nation through Popular Culture* (Stanford, CA: Stanford University Press, 2011), 29.
119. AYE/CS/1962/36/5/3/3, 6391, Cairo, 19 March 1962, Zamaris to GMFA.
120. Except for the years 1960 for Alexandria and 1964 for Cairo.
121. AYE/CS/1962/65/7/1/1, 2793, Cairo, 10 October 1961, Lambros to GMFA.
122. AYE/CS/1963/44/5/2/1/2, 553, Cairo, 18 December 1961, Yiannakakis to Cairo embassy.
123. AYE/CS/1963/44/5/2/1/2; AYE/CS/1964/43/9/1/1; AYE/CS/1962/65/7/1/1; AYE/CS/1965/45/3/1/1.
124. AYE/CS/1963/44/5/2/1/2, 3429/EMP/E.F., Port Said, 20 November 1961, Daratzikis to Cairo embassy.
125. Ibid.
126. AGCCA/Correspondence, 1960–63.
127. Ivan Grinberg and Philippe Mioche, *Aluminium de Grèce: l'usine aux trois rivages* (Grenoble: Presses universitaires de Grenoble, 1996), 79.
128. Ibid., 79.
129. Ibid., 80–82.
130. AYE/CS/1963/44/5/2/1/2, 3429/EMP/E.F., Port Said, 20 November 1961, Daratzikis to Cairo embassy.
131. On 9 July 1961, Greece and the EEC signed an association agreement that provided for the possibility of future accession.
132. AYE/CS/1962/36/5/3/3, 6391, Confidential, Cairo, 19 March 1962, Zamarias to Averoff.
133. AYE/CS/1962/65/7/1/1, 622, Cairo, 4 August 1962, Yiannakakis to Cairo embassy.

134. Matsakis, *To dilimma*, 23.
135. This was achieved through decrees in 1963–64. Vassilis Panayotopoulos, "Les Grecs d'Égypte à Athènes," in *L'Europe retrouvée. Les Migrations de la décolonisation*, ed. Jean-Louis Miège and Colette Dubois (Paris: L'Harmattan, 1994), 254.
136. Kazamias, "The 'Purge,'" 20–21.
137. Robert Mabro and Samir Radwan, *The Industrialization of Egypt, 1939–1973: Policy and Performance* (Oxford: Clarendon Press, 1976), 40.
138. International Labour Office, *Yearbook of Labour Statistics, 1965* (Geneva: International Labour Office, 1966), 354.
139. *President Gamal Abdel-Nasser's Speeches and Press-Interviews*, January–December 1961, 152–54.
140. AYE/CS/1963/42/8/1/1, 19760, Cairo, 22 October 1961, Ismail Nahhas to Electrohouse.
141. AYE/CS/1961/16/3/2/1, Cairo, 21 November 1961, Yiannakakis to Cairo embassy.
142. AYE/CS/1963/42/8/1/1, 534, Cairo, 4 November 1961, Yiannakakis to Cairo embassy.
143. *President Gamal Abdel-Nasser's Speeches and Press-Interviews*, April–June 1960, 135.
144. Ibid.
145. See also Kazamias, "The 'Purge,'" 24.
146. AYE/CS/1961/21/17/2/1/2, 1066, Alexandria, 28 October 1961, Theodoropoulos to Cairo embassy.
147. AYE/CS/1962/65/7/1/1, 622, Cairo, 4 August 1962, Yiannakakis to Cairo embassy.
148. Floresca Karanasou, "The Greeks in Egypt: From Mohammed Ali to Nasser, 1805–1961," in *The Greek Diaspora in the Twentieth Century*, ed. Richard Clogg (London: Macmillan, 1999), 43.
149. AYE/CS/1963/44/5/2/2/2, 986, Alexandria, 3 December 1962, Theodoropoulos to GMFA.
150. AGCCA/Correspondence, 1960–63, Confidential note on labor issues of the Greeks in Egypt, May 1962.
151. AYE/CS/1963/44/5/2/1/2, 544, Cairo, 4 December 1961, Yiannakakis to Cairo embassy.
152. AYE/CS/1963/44/5/2/1/2, 553, Cairo, 18 December 1961, Yiannakakis to Cairo embassy.
153. AYE/CS/1963/44/5/2/1/2, 544, Cairo, 4 December 1961, Yiannakakis to Cairo embassy.
154. AGCCA/Correspondence, 1960–63, Confidential note on labor issues of the Greeks in Egypt, May 1962.
155. Dinos Koutsoumis, *Pos kai giati dielythi i paroikia tis Aigyptou;* [Why and how was the Greek community of Egypt dismantled?] (Athens, 1992), 15.
156. AYE/CS/1965/46/9/1/1, 7123, Cairo, 13 July 1965, Mitsialis to Cairo embassy.
157. Manolis Yalourakis, *I Aigyptos ton Ellinon* [Egypt of the Greeks] (Athens: Mitropolis, 1967), 224; Kazamias, "The 'Purge,'" 34.
158. Kazamias, "The 'Purge,'" 20.

159. AYE/CS/1963/44/5/2/1/2, 553, Cairo, 18 December 1961, Yiannakakis to Cairo embassy.
160. Abd Al-Wahhab Bakr, "The Greek Exodus: An Egyptian Perspective," *Journal of the Hellenic Diaspora* 35, no. 2 (2009): 99.
161. AYE/CS/1963/44/5/2/1/2, 553, Cairo, 18 December 1961, Yiannakakis to Cairo embassy.
162. AICEM/1966–73, Alexandria, 4 June 1970.

Conclusion

On 6 June 2008, an international one-day workshop took place in Athens under the title "The Flight of Greeks from Egypt."[1] Most of the attendees were Greeks from Egypt settled in Athens, the majority of whom had hardly any connection with academia. During the workshop, some of them intervened to comment on some of the presentations, some enthusiastically, others critically. They all wanted to present the proper version, as they saw it, of the "flight" because they had personal experience of it, because they had fled. At the center of debate was whether Greeks had been expelled from Egypt or not. The vivid discussion underlined that my research topic was still very much "alive" and that the varying opinions about the departure of the Greeks from Egypt were not due to different interpretations of the historical evidence or to different methodological approaches but to the difference between information and rumors or between the written historical sources and lived experience. To put it in other words, they were due to the difference between history and memory.

The divergent views expressed during the workshop constituted alternative answers to a simple question: why did the Greeks leave Egypt? Contrary to the well-established view to people outside academic circles, as the above Egyptiots were, personal and collective memories do not faithfully represent the past; instead, they are a retrospective integration of collective experiences to socially constructed and ideologically defined perceptions of the past. Behind an apparently simple question, the historical reality is complicated, since it is the product of a dialectic between asymmetric elements, which interact and evolve—not in a linear way—over time. Consequently, it is, or it should be, inconsistent with one-dimensional and simplistic answers. The case of the departure of Greeks from Egypt is just one example.

The Egyptiots' departure was part of wider population movements related to three different historical developments: the dissolution of the Ottoman Empire, the collapse of colonial empires, and the Cold War. Therefore, it has similarities, analogies, but also differences with apparently dissimilar cases of the migration of Greeks and other populations around the globe. When considering Greek populations, the case of Asia Minor offers the closest analogy: not in terms of the refugee drama but because the departure from both areas was linked to the creation of the Turkish and Egyptian nation-states. In contrast, though, to what happened in Turkey or the Balkans, where nation-states replaced Ottoman administrative structures, in Egypt a long period of time elapsed during which the country was autonomous under the Sublime Porte before coming under British control.

British dominion over Egypt and the rest of the colonized world weakened after World War II. Similarly, in other parts of the globe, the other colonial powers, such as France, Italy, the Netherlands, and Belgium, also saw their power greatly reduced. While postcolonial states emerged from the ruins of colonization, certain ethnic or national population groups moved to countries from where they originated or with which they shared a cultural identification, or they just went elsewhere. In most cases, these populations were colonists, such as the French of Indochina, Algeria, Morocco, and Tunisia; the Italians of Libya; the Dutch of Indonesia; or the Belgians of Congo. In other cases, though, they were not subjects or citizens of a colonial force but they had just benefited from colonialism, such as the Asians in Uganda and the Greeks in Belgian Congo, who left these countries after they became independent.

The end of colonization coincided with the emergence of the Cold War. In an effort to protect social peace in postwar Western Europe, the West created international organizations such as the ICEM to reduce social tensions through the promotion of the migration of millions of Europeans to various destinations all over the world. Destitute and unemployed Greeks were also part of this European reality in Egypt and migrated under the auspices of the ICEM and WCC to Australia and other countries—as did mainland Greeks—to protect the social order within the Egyptiot population but most of all in post–civil war Greece.

This book argues that the principal structural component for the Greeks' departure was the abolition of the privileges related to the Capitulations in 1937. Along with the British presence, the Capitulations ensured the economic prosperity of the Egyptiot economic elite and their control over the *koinotites* and the chambers of commerce. This control gave the Egyptiot leadership considerable economic and political influence over the Greek population of Egypt, through the services it provided and through networks based on clientelism and patronage. The prosperity of the community allowed it to cater to new migrants from Greece until the late 1930s and to replace, up to a certain point, those who left.

The domination of foreigners as a consequence of the Capitulations and British presence had not only economic and political but also cultural aspects. It generated a superiority complex toward the Egyptian population, apparent in the reluctance of the majority of Egyptiots to acquire fluency in Arabic. In other words, they refused to integrate themselves in a substantial way into Egyptian society and to "converse" with the Egyptian state after Arabic became one of the basic tools of Egyptian nationalism and its use had extended to all aspects of public life through the 1940s and the 1950s.

Despite the twelve-year transitional period that the Montreux Convention granted for the Greeks and nationals of other ex-capitulatory countries to wean themselves off the Capitulations and adjust to the requirements of the new era, few initiatives were undertaken in this direction. On the contrary, the community leadership, along with Greek state officials, expected that a treaty of establishment would be enough to offer the community a new regime of protection. However, Egypt and Greece never agreed on such a treaty.

The results of the abolition of the Capitulations in real life were not always imminent. Measures that were linked to the process of transforming Egypt from an autonomous Ottoman province under European control to a fully independent nation-state were taken before and after the 1952 coup, and contributed to the decision of Greeks to leave Egypt. According to Themistoklis Matsakis, a prominent figure of the Egyptiot Left in Cairo, these measures concerned among other things the increasing control over imports and exports; the obligation to keep accounting records; the organization and the control of tax issues; the increasing control over foreign exchange; the laws regarding joint-stock companies, schools, associations, etc.; the Egyptianization of banks, insurance companies, foreign commercial representations; and the prohibition on exercising some professions.[2]

However, the Free Officers military coup in July 1952 brought about new political and economic conditions. The bonds of the foreign economic elite with the old regime were now meaningless, and the new status quo required the rapprochement with a new military elite, which officially came under the leadership of Gamal Abdel Nasser in 1954. The new regime promoted foreign investment but Nasser also became a leading figure in the anticolonial struggle. In the new environment, and since the plan for treaties of establishment had been abandoned, confusion and strong contradictions characterized the Greek position toward Egypt at all levels. Prisoners of the capitulatory past and the traditionally close relationship with the Western countries, which the Cold War context reaffirmed, the community leadership and the Greek state tried, without much success, to perform a balancing act between what they considered the national and the community's interest. The Egyptiot Greek Left had some ideas but not the power to implement them. The consular authorities and the traditional conservative leadership resisted all efforts for a substantial democratization of the GKA in the 1950s and intervened in the electoral process to prevent the Egyptiot Left taking control.

In this context, the community, instead of emancipating itself and consolidating its position through a long-term readjustment plan, tried to continue in the most familiar way: under the protection of an external element, which was now the Greek state. There was, however, a discrepancy between the economic power of the Egyptiot elite, the dynamic of Egypt, and the specific weight of the postwar Greek state, devastated after a long period of foreign occupation and civil war. To secure Egyptiot interests, Athens pursued a pro-Arab policy, which was reinforced by the common anti-British struggle with the emergence of the Cypriot question. Based on this policy and on rhetoric of eternal friendship between Greece and Egypt, the postwar Greek governments tried to have Egyptiots exempted from the legislation of a sovereign state, Egypt. The postwar Egyptian governments, on the other hand, not only responded to the expression of goodwill from Athens in kind but also moved some steps forward, by exempting Greek nationals from laws that concerned employees and workers and the running of schools. Thus, the exemptions covered the vast majority of the community.

World War II bequeathed the community with a considerable number of unemployed war veterans. In an attempt to tackle unemployment, the leadership resorted to the clientelistic networks that had been consolidated within the self-sufficient universe of privately owned Greek enterprises during the Capitulations. As the Egyptian population increased and better education and training opportunities made Egyptians capable of performing the professions in which foreigners were once dominant, postwar Egyptian governments started to implement laws that positively discriminated in favor of their nationals. This policy made it more difficult for Egyptiots to access the labor market, but this was not the only reason for the low employment opportunities. Despite the capital accumulated during World War II, Egyptiot businessmen were reluctant to invest in postwar Egypt, and thus, few jobs were created. Changing one's citizenship did not work, and other options, such as joining the auxiliary services of the British Army in the Suez Canal zone or registering at the employment offices of the community, reaffirmed the existence of an introverted labor market that was largely dependent on Western powers and suffered from the lack of a realistic, long-term plan for the employment of the Greek workforce. Even though the departure of other foreigners from Egypt relieved some of the pressure in the labor market, the only realistic solution would have been the rapprochement with Egyptian society and the integration of the Greeks into wider formal and informal mechanisms for securing employment.

Education constituted the principal mechanism that could gradually create the necessary contact points in cultural and economic terms between the community and the new, fluid Egyptian environment. The Greek education system in Egypt, however, remained tied to a classical spirit that may have served the interests of the economic elite, the needs of community's members for upward social mobility, or the interwar and postwar Greek political elite, but certainly not the needs of an ethnic/national community whose members desired to remain in post-Capitulations Egypt. The few efforts the *koinotites* undertook to change the educational orientation were generally unfruitful. The main obstacles in this regard were their economic difficulties, the reluctance of wealthy community members to make substantial donations to education in the postwar period, the anticommunist policy of the Greek state, and the Egyptiot leadership that required the reinforcement of Greek nationalist beliefs. Thus, the majority of community members found themselves unprepared to face the challenges of the labor market and the new Egyptian reality. This situation, in combination with the economic stagnation of the middle and lower strata, gradually encouraged Greeks to make the decision to leave Egypt for a better future.

In the aftermath of World War II, unemployed and destitute Greeks, along with other members of the community who saw reduced profit opportunities in postwar Egypt, were leaving the country. Greek state policy as regards Egyptiots, especially the lower-class elements, was clear: they should either remain in Egypt or move to distant destinations, but not Greece. The postwar unemployment in Greece and the fear that an influx of destitute people might threaten social peace lay behind this decision. Athens's fear increased in line with the flow of Greeks from Istanbul to Greece after the September 1955 pogrom.[3]

The Egyptiot Greek leadership sought to "decongest" the community of the destitute for the same reasons, that is, in order not to disrupt the social peace among Egyptiots and in Egypt in general. In this respect, emigration functioned as a valve for the social pressures within the community. To direct the departure toward third countries, the GCCA, ICEM, WCC, and the Greek government cooperated to come up with a mechanism. Thus, a paradox emerged in which Greek schools galvanized nationalist feeling while community members were sent away from the national center. The movement of destitute and unemployed Egyptiots within the Greek diasporic space was promoted not only out of fear of the communist threat but also on the basis of their usefulness. In moving abroad, these new immigrants could contribute more to Greece's postwar reconstruction through remittances while, at the same time, they could transfer information to putative emigrants and also to the Egyptiot holders of capital, which was stagnating in postwar Egypt, on investment opportunities elsewhere.

The departure of Greeks from Egypt had the character of economic migration, but not only. The employment opportunities that remained unexploited in the early 1950s in Upper Egypt are indicative in this regard. It is difficult to form a typology of the Greek departure, but apart from economic reasons, political, cultural, social, and personal factors also contributed to the decision of Greeks to leave Egypt. The common denominator of the departees was that they were more or less convinced that there was no future for them and their children in the new Egypt. The Suez Crisis proved to be a turning point for some in arriving at the decision to leave Egypt. Its direct impact, however, did not concern the totality of the community, but essentially the people who had worked for the Suez Canal Company, the auxiliary services of the British Army or associated businesses in the canal zone, and Greek Jews. After the dust from the crisis settled and the situation normalized, the rhythm of departure decreased to their pre-1957 levels in 1958 and 1959.

The exodus started in the last months of 1960 and accelerated even more when the Nasserite regime heralded its socialist principles with the July 1961 laws. This mass departure can be explained in the impact of consecutive socialistic legislation, incidents such as the uncovering of the 1960 spy affair involving Greek state officials, the fact that the nationalization laws directly affected the community leadership and in the increasing uncertainty and pessimism about the future, which had been traced at least a decade earlier. Indeed, in the early 1950s Greek diplomatic reports were generally pessimistic regarding the long-term prospects. Ambassador Triantafyllidis thought that this "pessimism" and "uncertainty" was mainly due to the leadership's incapacity to adjust to the new Egyptian reality after the abolition of the Capitulations, noting, "Lack of competition on behalf of the natives, exemption from any kind of taxes, easy profit with relatively little work: this is what the Greeks in Egypt were used to."[4]

The majority of the decisions of Egyptiots to leave en masse in the early 1960s were informed by the overall general situation and by motives stemming from the personal circumstances and character of each individual. However, there is a collective stimulus, which derived from the increasing anxiety about upcoming measures, which in the event never materialized to the anticipated extent. The rumors about what could happen in the future and the lack of solidarity among Egyptiots contributed to this state of almost near panic. Such rumors found fertile ground within the introverted community, where most of the members had the same sources of information, shared the same points of reference, and frequented the same places. Thus, when the exodus started, the world of the community drastically changed, and hence more and more Egyptiots departed in the following years.

Despite the complexity of the phenomenon, the departure of the Greeks from Egypt is often reduced still today by the Egyptiot Greeks to the poet Constantinos P Cavafy's famous farewell to Alexandria, as is clearly evident in historical studies, publications, and their gatherings, which are characterized by intense nostalgia. "In the Western imagination Alexandria has always been associated with loss," says Khaled Fahmy.[5] And in the Greek imagination Alexandria has always been considered a Greek city. This farewell to the lost Alexandria, though, does not reflect the lived experience of Egyptiots. The motion in the Cavafy poem "The God Abandons Antony" is inverted. In the poem Alexandria abandons Antony, but in the case of the Egyptiots they abandoned Alexandria. Of course, the use of the poem by Egyptiots to represent their departure can be explained by the fact that its author also came from Egypt as well as by the poem's theme of abandonment and sorrow. However, this interpretational irregularity of Cavafy's poem and its nostalgic use in the historical representation of the Greek departure have contributed to its misrepresentation. This perspective is dominated by the lyricism and melancholy for lost greatness and a general and abstract notion concerning Alexandria's idealized cosmopolitanism. This vision, apart from the sentimental tension that it emanates, overemphasizes Alexandria's position within the Egyptiot universe to such extent that the city is identified with the entire Greek presence in Egypt. Consequently, it downgrades the Greek presence in other cities, along with the multiple and diverse forms that historically constituted the Greek community. Focusing on Alexandria by using Cavafy's poems is problematic for two more reasons: first, because it implies that the city was Greek from Alexander the Great's time to the twentieth century and, second, because this belief implies that Greeks ended up leaving a city that was "theirs." In other words, if they were not expelled or forced to leave, they had no reason to abandon the city. Thus, two popular national narratives—the uninterrupted continuity of Hellenism from ancient times to the present and that of the "lost homeland," which is traditionally attributed to Asia Minor—are combined to create another paradigm in Egypt.

These considerations are not intended to cast doubt on the use of poetry and literature in understanding an era. Literature is invariably linked to the social context but is not enough for the historical study of a society. The use of literature as a source for historical research is a matter of long academic discussion, which is not the subject of this study. The example of the use of Cavafy's words by Egyptiots, though, suggests that literature and poetry in particular may serve ideological uses in the eyes of the reader. This is not a Greek particularity, of course. The transfer of words, ideas, and concepts from literature to critics, to public history, and from there to academic historiography has contributed to the representation of a rosy, elitist, European cosmopolitanism of Alexandria, which includes Greeks and is implicitly superior to the Egyptian reality.[6]

Historical research in Europe in the 1980s and 1990s, which relied on sources produced by the French-speaking elites of the city, reinforced this image. Since the majority of Egyptians were not visible in such sources, they remained for years on the margins of historical research. As for the Egyptiots, the fragmentary and almost exclusive use of GKA records in some previous studies led to the prevailing view that identifies them with well-off, cosmopolitan Alexandria and links their departure to Nasserite policies. Another problem is that the views of several contemporary Egyptian government protagonists remain unexplored, as the relevant state archives are not accessible to all scholars.

The confusion regarding the social and economic characteristics of the Greeks in Egypt and their departure following Nasser's policies has not only been generated by the literature and archival material. Egyptiots themselves wrote the first studies on their history. Most of them had resided in Alexandria and had moved to Greece in the early 1960s. Their departure was de facto linked directly to Nasserite policies, a conclusion that did not necessarily reflect a criticism of him. However, these authors considered Egyptianization and nationalization of companies in 1957 and 1961, respectively, to have been the main reason for the Greek departure from Egypt. Mainland Greeks made the same direct link; the Greek press saw "extermination" and "persecution" in the policies that Nasserite Egypt claimed were designed to achieve independence from local and foreign capital. Many older Greeks, who in their lifetime had seen refugees from Asia Minor in the 1920s, from Istanbul after 1955, and from Congo and other colonies in the late 1950s, now saw Greeks come in mass numbers from Egypt. With the distance of time and in the studies of a younger generation of scholars who are not Greeks from Egypt or did not experience the exodus, the automatic linking of the Greek departure and Nasserite policy has been challenged.

This book is part of this series of well-documented studies that are sentimentally detached. Instead of focusing on Nasserite legislation, it follows the path to the exodus, using as a starting point the abolition of the capitulatory privileges and relying on unpublished archival material. My aim is not—and could not have been—to present all aspects of the collective and individual experience represented by the departure of the Egyptiots. The book reflects the entangled structures and agency over time, taking into account factors such as the transition from empires to nation-states, the Cold War context, decolonization, and the way these factors were expressed in the Egyptian context. It also analyzes the various responses of the Egyptiot community and Greek state to the multiple transformations that took place in Egypt. The entanglement of these elements shows that the exodus was not a one-way solution. Greeks had always left Egypt, and indeed many remained in the country after the exodus. The exodus period though and the decades preceding it were extremely complex; the agents in this history—the Egyptiots here—interacted with a wide range of structural elements and changes while various push and pull factors influenced them in taking the decision to leave. On the basis of this interaction, they sought logical and profitable solutions to personal, family, and community issues. Consequently, this study did not set out to justify the choices of those who departed or those who remained in Egypt, of the Egyptiot leadership or Egyptiot Left, of Nasser's Egypt or the Greek state. The intention was to approach the topic in an interpretative way, using historical methods to understand this long-term historical process.

NOTES

1. *Journal of the Hellenic Diaspora,* special issue, 35, no. 2 (2009).
2. Themistoklis Matsakis, *To dilimma tou aigyptiotou ellinismou* [The dilemma of Egyptiot Hellenism] (Cairo, 1961), 5.
3. Meropi Anastassiadou and Paul Dumont, *Oi Romioi tis Polis. Travmata kai prosdokies* [The Greeks of Istanbul: traumas and expectations] (Athens: Estia, 2007), 26–27.
4. AYE/CS/1951/10/2/1/1, 507, Cairo, 8 February 1951, Triantafyllidis to GMFA.
5. Khaled Fahmy, "The Essence of Alexandria," *Manifesta Journal* 14 (2012): 64.
6. Will Hanley, "Grieving Cosmopolitanism in Middle East Studies," *History Compass* 6, no. 5 (2008): 1352.

Bibliography

MANUSCRIPT SOURCES

Egypt

Archives of the Averofeio boys' high school of Alexandria, Alexandria
Archives of the Greek Chamber of Commerce of Alexandria, Alexandria
Archives of the Greek Koinotita of Alexandria, Alexandria
Archives of the Greek Koinotita of Cairo, Cairo
Archives of the Greek Koinotita of Suez, Suez
Archives of the Greek Koinotita of Tanta, Cairo

France

Archives of the French Ministry of Foreign Affairs, Paris
    Europe 1956–60/Grèce 1956–60
    Levant 1944–65/Généralités 1953–59—Proche–Orient
Nantes Diplomatic Archives Centre
    Ambassade de France à Athènes, 267
    Consulat de France à Alexandrie, 224/324
    Consulat de France à Port Saïd, 78

Greece

Archives of the Greek Koinotita of Alexandria, Athens
Archives of the Intergovernmental Committee for Migration from Europe, Athens
    Egypt until 1958
    Egypt, 1959–65
    Egypt, 1966–73
Diplomatic and Historical Archives of the Greek Foreign Ministry, Athens
    Central service/Embassies' Correspondence/Egypt/Greeks in Egypt/1936–39, 1941, 1943–54, 1956–58, 1960–64
Konstantinos Karamanlis Archive, Athens
Panagiotis Xenos Archive, Athens

Switzerland

Archives of the International Committee of the Red Cross, Geneva
  B AG 232 065–Égypte–1956–73
Archives of the World Council of Churches, Geneva
  425.3.375/Orthodox-29/I/Near East–Service to Refugees/1950–54

United Kingdom

National Archives, Public Record Office, London
Foreign Office and Foreign and Commonwealth Office (FO)/141: Embassy and Consulates, Egypt
Foreign Office (FO)/371: Political Departments: General Correspondence, 1906–66

PUBLISHED PRIMARY SOURCES

Les Accords de Montreux pour la suppression des capitulations et des tribunaux mixtes en Égypte. Gazette des Tribunaux Mixtes d'Égypte and Journal des Tribunaux Mixtes. Alexandria, 1937.
Annuaire statistique, 1910. Cairo: Imprimerie nationale, 1910.
Annuaire statistique, 1927–1928. Cairo: Imprimerie nationale, 1929.
Annuaire statistique, 1937–1938. Cairo: Imprimerie nationale, 1939.
Annuaire statistique, 1947–1948. Cairo: Imprimerie nationale, 1951.
Australian Immigration. Canberra: Department of Immigration, 1969.
Elliniki en Alexandria Koinotis, *Synoptiki logodosia epi ti etisia geniki synelefsi ton melon* [Greek Koinotita of Alexandria, Short annual report of the members' general assembly]. Alexandria: T. Kassimatis, 1938.
Elliniki en Alexandria Koinotis, *Logodosia etous 1951* [Greek Koinotita of Alexandria, Annual report of 1951]. Alexandria: T. Kassimatis, 1951.
Elliniki en Alexandria Koinotis, *Logodosia etous 1952* [Greek Koinotita of Alexandria, Annual report of 1952]. Alexandria: T. Kassimatis, 1952.
Elliniki en Alexandria Koinotis, *Logodosia etous 1956* [Greek Koinotita of Alexandria, Annual report of 1956]. Alexandria: Th. Kassimatis & Co Printing house, 1956.
Elliniki en Alexandria Koinotis, *Logodosia etous 1958* [Greek Koinotita of Alexandria, Annual report of 1958]. Alexandria: T. Kassimatis, 1958.
Elliniki en Alexandria Koinotis, *Logodosia etous 1961* [Greek Koinotita of Alexandria, Annual report of 1961]. Alexandria: T. Kassimatis, 1961.
Elliniko Emporiko Epimelitirio Alexandrias, *Logodosia dioikitikou symvouliou dia tin chrisin 1958* [Greek Chamber of Commerce of Alexandria, Annual report of the administrative board for the year 1959]. Alexandria: T. Kassimatis, 1959.
International Labour Office. *Yearbook of Labour Statistics, 1960.* 20th issue. Geneva: International Labour Office, 1960.
International Labour Office. *Yearbook of Labour Statistics, 1965.* 25th issue. Geneva: International Labour Office, 1966.

Lefkoma panigyrismou pentikotaetiridas tou Ellinikou Emporikou Epimelitiriou tis Alexandrias [Album for the celebration of the fiftieth anniversary of the Greek Chamber of Commerce of Alexandria]. Alexandria, 1951.
President Gamal Abdel-Nasser's Speeches and Press-Interviews. April–June 1960.
President Gamal Abdel-Nasser's Speeches and Press-Interviews. January–December 1961.
Parliament of Greeks, *Episima praktika ton synderiaseon tis Voulis* [Official proceedings of the Greek parliamentary debates]. Athens, National Printing House, February 1957.
Statitistika apotelesmata tis apografis tis Elladas tou 1928 [Statistic results of Greece's 1928 census], vol. 2. Athens: National Printing House, 1935.
Ta pepragmena tou A en Aigypto ellinikou didaskalikou synedriou [Proceeding of the first Greek teachers' conference in Egypt]. Alexandria, 1931.
Statistique scolaire, 1948–1949. Cairo: Imprimerie nationale, 1951.
Svolopoulos, Konstantinos, ed. *Konstantinos Karamanlis, Archio. Gegonota kai Keimena* [*Archive: Facts and Documents*]. Athens: Ekdotiki Athinon, 1993.
Tableaux analytiques du mouvement migratoire et touristique de la Grèce avec l'étranger pendant les années 1931–1940. Athens: National Statistical Service of Greece, 1946.

NEWSPAPERS AND MAGAZINES

Bulletin of the GCCA (1945–60)
Ellin, Cairo
Images, Cairo
Panaigyptia, Alexandria and Athens
O Paroikos, Cairo
Le Progrès égyptien, Alexandria
Progrès Dimanche, Alexandria
Tachydromos, Alexandria

SECONDARY LITERATURE

Abdel-Malek, Anouar. *Egypt: Military Society; The Army Regime, the Left, and Social Change under Nasser.* New York: Random House, 1968.
——. *Idéologie et renaissance nationale.* Paris: Éditions Anthropos, 1969.
Abdulhaq, Najat. *Jewish and Greek Communities in Egypt: Entrepreneurship and Business before Nasser.* London: I.B. Tauris, 2016.
Abécassis, Frédéric. "École étrangère, école intercommunautaire." In *Entre réforme sociale et mouvement national: Identité nationale et modernisation en Égypte, 1882–1962,* edited by Alain Roussillon, 215–34. Cairo: CEDEJ, 1995.
——. "L'enseignement étranger en Égypte et les élites locales (1920–1960). Francophonie et identités nationales." Ph.D. diss., Aix-Marseille I, 2000.
Abécassis, Frédéric, and Anne Kazanian-Le Gall. "L'identité au miroir du droit. Le statut des personnes en Égypte (fin XIXe–millieu XXe siècle)." *Égypte/Monde Arabe* 11 (1992): 11–38.

Aclimandos, Tewfik. "Regard rétrospectif sur la révolution égyptienne, ou le 23 juillet 1952." *Égypte/Monde arabe,* 2nd ser., 4–5 (2001): 15–39.
———. "Les Officiers activistes de l'armée égyptienne, 1936–1954." Ph.D. diss., Sciences Po Paris, 2004.
Aktar, Ayhan. "Turkification Policies in the Early Republican Era." In *Turkish Literature and Cultural Memory: "Multiculturalism" as a Literary Theme after 1980,* edited by Catharina Dufft, 29–62. Wiesbaden: Harrassowitz, 2009.
Aldrich, Howard E., and Roger Waldinger. "Ethnicity and Entrepreneurship." *Annual Review of Sociology* 16 (1990): 111–35.
Alexandris, Alexis. *The Greek Minority of Istanbul and Greek–Turkish Relations, 1814–1974.* Athens: Centre for Asia Minor Studies, 1992.
Alleaume, Ghislaine. "La production d'une économie 'nationale': remarques sur l'histoire des societies anonymes par actions en Égypte de 1856 à 1956." *Annales Islamologiques* 31 (1997): 1–16.
Althusser, Louis. *Positions (1964–1975).* Paris: Editions Sociales, 1976.
Amary, Al El-. "La crise du chômage en Égypte et ailleurs, ses causes et ses remèdes." *L'Égypte contemporaine* 164 (1936): 465–83.
Amin, Samir. *La nation arabe: nationalisme et luttes de classe.* Paris: Editions de Minuit, 1976.
Anastassiadis, Yiannis. *Mnimes apo tin drasi tou aristerou kinimatos tou aigyptioti ellinismou* [Memoirs from the action of the left movement of Egyptiot Hellenism]. Athens, 1993.
Anastassiadis, Tassos ed., *Voisinages fragiles. Les relations interconfessionnelles dans le Sud-Est européen et la Méditerranée orientale (1854-1923): Contraintes locales et enjeux internationaux.* Athens: École française d'Athènes, 2013.
Anastassiadou, Meropi, and Paul Dumont. *Oi Romioi tis Polis. Travmata kai prosdokies* [The Greeks of Istanbul: traumas and expectations]. Athens: Estia, 2007.
Anderson, Benedict. *Imagined Communities: Reflections on the Origins and Spread of Nationalism.* London: Verso, 1983.
Anscombe, Frederick. *State, Faith, and Nation in Ottoman and Post-Ottoman Lands.* New York: Cambridge University Press, 2014.
Antebi-Yemini, Lisa, and William Berthomière. "Di[a]spositif: Décrire et comprendre les diasporas." In *Les diasporas: 2000 ans d'histoire,* edited by Lisa Antebi-Yemini, William Berthomière, and Gabriel Sheffer, 9–19. Rennes: Presses Universitaires de Rennes, 2005.
Armstrong, John. "Mobilized and Proletarian Diasporas." *American Political Science Review* 70 (1976): 393–408.
'Ashmawi, Sayyid. "Perceptions of the Greek Money-Lender in Egyptian Collective Memory at the Turn of the Twentieth Century." In *Money, Land and Trade: An Economic History of the Muslim Mediterranean,* edited by Nelly Hanna, 244–78. London: IB Tauris.
Assabghy Bey, Iskandar. *La nationalité égyptienne. Etude historique et critique.* Cairo: SOP Press, 1950.
Athanassiadis, Giorgis. *I proti praxi tis ellinkis tragodias. Mesi Anatoli: 1941–1944* [The first act of the Greek tragedy: Middle East, 1941–44]. Athens, 1975.

———. *O paroikiakos ellinismos kai i paideia tou* [The Hellenism of the community and its education]. Cairo, 1948.

Babaoglu, Resul. "From the 'Millet System' to a Hostage Minority: Greek Community of Turkey or a Trump Card in Cyprus Issue, 1954–1955." *International Journal of Social Science and Humanity* 5, no. 6 (2015): 537–45.

Bakr, Abd Al-Wahhab. "The Greek Exodus: An Egyptian Perspective." *Journal of the Hellenic Diaspora* 35, no. 2 (2009): 93–100.

Balta, Paul. "1956." In *Alexandrie 1860–1960. Un modèle éphémère de convivialité: communautés et identité cosmopolite*, edited by Robert Ilbert and Ilios Yiannakakis, 112–24. Paris: Autrement, 1992.

Baring, Evelyn, Earl of Cromer. *Modern Egypt*, 2 vols. London: Routledge, 2001. First published 1908 by Macmillan.

Beattie, Kirk J. *Egypt during the Nasser Years: Ideology, Politics and Civil Society*. Oxford: Westview Press, 1994.

Beinin, Joel. "The Communist Movement and Nationalist Political Discourse in Nasserist Egypt." *Middle East Journal* 41 (1987): 568–84.

———. "Labour, Capital and the State in Nasserist Egypt, 1952–1961." *International Journal of Middle East Studies* 21 (1989): 71–90.

———. "Egypt: Society and Economy, 1923–1952." In *The Cambridge History of Egypt*. Vol. 2, *Modern Egypt from 1517 to the End of the Twentieth Century*, edited by MW Daly, 309–333. Cambridge: Cambridge University Press, 1998.

———. *The Dispersion of Egyptian Jewry*. Cairo: American University in Cairo Press, 2005.

Beinin, Joel, and Zachary Lockman. *Workers on the Nile: Nationalism, Communism, Islam, and the Egyptian Working Class, 1882–1954*. Cairo: American University Press, 1998.

Bertocchi, Graziella, and Chiara Strozzi. "International Migration and the Role of Institutions." *Public Choice* 137 (2008): 81–102.

Botman, Selma. *The Rise of Egyptian Communism*. Syracuse, NY: Syracuse University Press, 1988.

———. *Egypt from Independence to Revolution, 1919–1952*. Syracuse, NY: Syracuse University Press, 1991.

———. "The Liberal Age, 1923–1952." In *The Cambridge History of Egypt*. Vol. 2, *Modern Egypt from 1517 to the End of the Twentieth Century*, edited by MW Daly, 285–308. Cambridge: Cambridge University Press, 1998.

———. *Engendering Citizenship in Egypt: The History and Society of the Modern Middle East*. New York: Columbia University Press, 1999.

Braude, Benjamin. "Foundation Myths of the Millet System." In *Christians and Jews in the Ottoman Empire: The Functioning of a Plural Society*. Vol. 1, *The Central Lands*, edited by Benjamin Braude and Bernard Lewis, 69–88. New York: Holmes & Meier, 1982.

Braudel, Fernand. *La Méditerranée et le monde méditerranéen à l'époque de Philippe II*. Paris: Librairie Armand Colin, 1949.

Brinton Jasper. "Egypt: The Transition Period." *American Journal of International Law* 34, no. 2 (1940): 208–19.

Bromley, Ray. "Towards Global Human Settlements: Constantinos Doxiadis as Entrepreneur, Coalition Builder and Visionary." In *Urbanism: Imported or Exported?*, edited by Joe Nasr and Mercedes Volait, 316–40. Chichester: Wiley-Academy, 2003.

Brubaker, Rogers. "Myths and Misconceptions in the Study of Nationalism." In *The State of the Nation,* edited by John A Hall, 271–306. Cambridge: Cambridge University Press, 1998.

——. "The 'Diaspora' Diaspora." *Ethnic and Racial Studies* 28, no. 1 (2005): 1–19.

Castles, Stephen, and Mark J. Miller, eds. *The Age of Migration: International Population Movements in the Modern World.* London: Macmillan, 1993.

Chiti, Elena. "Ecrire à Alexandrie (1879–1940): Capital social, appartenances, mémoire." Ph.D. diss., Aix-Marseille Université/Università Ca' Foscari Venezia, 2015.

Choate, Mark. *Emigrant Nation: The Making of Italy Abroad.* Cambridge: Harvard University Press, 2008.

Christodoulou, Georgios. *El Alamein, Mesi Anatoli, Bardia: I istoria enos Aigyptioti Ellina stratioti (1915–1966)* [El Alamein, Middle East, Bardia: The story of an Egyptiot Greek soldier, 1915–66]. Athens: Estia, 2002.

Chryssostmidis, Sofianos. "Elliniki paroikia Aigyptou: i exodos" [The Greek community of Egypt: The exodus]. *Archiotaxio* 4 (2002): 117–32.

——. "The Left, Nasser, and the Exodus of the Greeks from Egypt." *Journal of the Hellenic Diaspora* 35, no. 2 (2009): 155–59.

Cochran, Judith. *Education in Egypt.* London: Croom Helm, 1986.

Cohen, Robin. "Repatriates and Colonial Auxiliaries." In *The Cambridge Survey of World Migration,* edited by Robin Cohen, 321–22. Cambridge: Cambridge University Press, 1995.

——. *Global Diasporas: An Introduction.* 2nd ed. New York: Routledge, 2008.

Colonas, Vassilis. "Présence grecque et héritage architectural à Alexandrie." In *Le Caire–Alexandrie: Architectures européennes, 1850–1950,* edited by Mercedes Volait, 77–88. Cairo: IFAO-CEDEJ, 2004.

Connor, Walker. "The Impact of Homelands upon Diasporas." In *Modern Diasporas in International Politics,* edited by Gabriel Sheffer, 16–46. London: Croom Helm, 1986.

Corm, Georges. "Géopolitique des minorités au Proche Orient." *Hommes et Migrations* 1172–73 (1994): 7–17.

——. *Le Proche-Orient éclaté, 1956–2000.* Paris: Gallimard, 1999.

Cottenet-Djoufelkit, Hélène. "L'industrialisation de l'Égypte au 20ème siècle. Des volontés politiques aux réalisations économiques." *Égypte/Monde arabe,* 2nd ser., 4–5 (2001): 135–72.

Cummings, Sally, and Raymond Hinnebusch. "Empire and After: Toward a Framework for Comparing Empires and Their Consequences in the Post-imperial Middle East and Central Asia." *Journal of Historical Sociology* 27, no. 1 (2014): 103–31.

Dahan, Constant. "La question de la nationalité en Egypte et les différents problèmes qu'elle soulève." *L'Egypte contemporaine* 27 (1916): 355–66.

———. "Recherches sur la nationalité des sujets ottomans établis en Egypte." *L'Egypte contemporaine* 37 (1919): 81–94.
Dakhli, Leyla. *Histoire du Proche-Orient contemporaine*. Paris: La Decouverte, 2015.
Dakhli, Leyla, and Vincent Lemire, eds. *Etudier en liberté les mondes méditerranéens. Mélanges offerts à Robert Ilbert*. Paris: Publications de la Sorbonne, 2016.
Dalachanis, Angelos. "Internationalism vs. nationalism? The Suez Canal Company strike of 1919 and the formation of the International Workers' Union of the Isthmus of Suez," in *Social Transformation and Mass Mobilization in the Balkan and Eastern Mediterranean Cities 1900–1923,* edited by Andreas Lyberatos, 343–55. Irakleio: Crete University Press, 2013.)
Damilakou, Maria. *Ellines metanastes stin Argentini* [Greek immigrants in Argentina]. Athens: Istoriko Archeio tis Emporikis Trapezas, 2004.
Deeb, Marius. "The Socioeconomic Role of the Local Foreign Minorities in Modern Egypt, 1805–1961." *International Journal of Middle East Studies* 9 (1978): 11–22.
Dekmejian, R Hrair. *Egypt Under Nasir: A Study in Political Dynamics*. Albany: State University of New York Press, 1971.
Delanoue, Gilbert. "Le nationalisme égyptien." In *L'Égypte d'aujourd'hui: permanence et changements, 1805–1976,* edited by Marie-Christine Aulas; Robert Mantran, et al., 129–56. Paris: CNRS, 1977.
Dertilis, George B. "Dall'emigrazione all'immigrazione: Grecia, 1989–2000." In *Conflitti, migrazioni e diritti dell'uomo,* edited by Maurice Aymard and Fabrizio Barca, 157–82. Soveria Maneli: Rubbettino, 2002.
———. *Istoria tou Ellinikou Kratous, 1830–1920* [History of the Greek state, 1830–1920]. 3rd ed. Athens: Estia, 2005.
Dessouki, Ali E Hillal. "The Shift in Egypt's Migration Policy: 1952–1978." *Middle Eastern Studies* 18, no. 1 (1982): 53–68.
Drettas, Georges. "Des Grecs invisibles. Propos sur l'objet et les méthodes des études consacrées aux phénomènes diasporéiques: l'exemple des Grecs en France." In *La Diaspora Hellénique en France,* edited by Gilles Grivaud, 15–27. Athens: École française d'Athènes, 2000.
Driessen, Henk. "Mediterranean Port Cities: Cosmopolitanism Reconsidered." *History and Anthropology* 16, no. 1 (2005): 129–41.
Droz-Vincent, Philippe. "Le nationalisme de l'État égyptien: Quête identitaire et légitimation du régime politique." In *Nationalismes en Mutation en Méditerranée orientale,* edited by Alain Dieckhoff and Riva Kastoryano, 61–90. Paris: CNRS, 2002.
Dubois, Colette. "Avant-première: Suez, un cas de migration forcée (1956–1957)." *Civilization* 40, no. 2 (1992): 128–53.
———. "La nation et les Français d'Outre-Mer: Rapatriés ou sinistrés de la décolonisation?" In *L'Europe retrouvée. Les migrations de la decolonization,* edited by Jean-Louis Miège and Colette Dubois, 75–115. Paris: L'Harmattan, 1994.
Ducruet, Jean. *Les capitaux européens au Proche-Orient*. Paris: Presses Universitaires de France, 1964.
———. *Statistiques et Perspectives démographiques en République Arabe Unie*. Beirut: Faculté de droit et des Sciences Economiques, 1967.

Dufoix, Stéphane. *Les Diasporas.* Paris: Presses Universitaires de France, 2003.

———. "Un pont par-dessus la porte: extraterritorialisation et transétatisation des identifications nationales." In *Loin des yeux, près du cœur. Les États et leurs expatriés,* edited by Stéphane Dufoix, Carine Guerassimoff, and Anne de Tinguy, 15–57. Paris: Presses de Sciences Po, 2010.

Economides, Jean. "L'action du nouveau régime égyptien dans les domaines économiques et sociaux." *L'Égypte contemporaine* 286 (1956): 5–44.

Emke-Poulopoulou, Ira. *Provlimata metanastefsis-palinnostisis* [Problems of migration-repatriation]. Athens: IMEO-EDIM, 1986.

Esclangon-Morin, Valérie. *Les rapatriés d'Afrique du Nord, de 1956 à nos jours.* Paris: L'Harmattan, 2007.

Etemad, Bouda. "Europe and Migation after Decolonization." *Journal of European Economic History* 27, no. 3 (1998): 457–70.

Fahmy, Khaled. *All the Pasha's Men: Mehmed Ali, His Army and the Making of Modern Egypt.* Cambridge: Cambridge University Press, 1998.

———. "Towards a Social History of Modern Alexandria." In *Alexandria, Real and Imagined,* edited by Anthony Hirst and Michael Silk, 281–306. Cairo: American University in Cairo Press, 2004.

———. "The Essence of Alexandria." *Manifesta Journal* 14 (2012): 63–72.

Fahmy, Ziad. *Ordinary Egyptians: Creating the Modern Nation through Popular Culture.* Stanford, CA: Stanford University Press, 2011.

Fanon, Frantz. *Les damnés de la terre.* Paris: Maspero, 1961.

Fathi, Al-Dib. *Abdel Nasser et la révolution algérienne.* Paris: L'Harmattan, 1985.

Ferro, Marc. *Suez: naissance d'un tiers monde.* Brussels: Complexe, 1982.

———. *Histoire des colonisations.* Paris: Seuil, 1994.

———, ed. *Le livre noir du colonialisme, XVIe–XXIe siècle: de l'extermination à la repentance.* Paris: Robert Lafont, 2003.

Fleming, Katherine. *Greece: A Jewish History.* Princeton, NJ: Princeton University Press, 2008.

Freitag, Ulrike. "'Cosmopolitanism' and 'conviviality'? Some conceptual considerations concerning the late Ottoman Empire." *European Journal of Cultural Studies* 17, no. 4 (2014): 375–91.

Freitag, Ulrike, Nelida Fuccaro, Nora Lafi, and Claudia Ghrawi, eds. *Urban Violence in the Middle East: Changing Cityscapes in the Transformation from Empire to Nation State.* New York: Berghahn Books, 2015.

Gabaccia, Donna R. *Italy's Many Diasporas.* London: Routledge, 2000.

Gal, Allon, Athena S. Leoussi, and Anthony D. Smith, eds. *The Call of the Homeland: Diaspora Nationalisms, Past and Present.* Leiden: Brill, 2010.

Gellner, Ernest. *Nations and Nationalisms.* Oxford: Basil Blackwell, 1983.

Georgelin, Hervé. *La fin de Smyrne.* Paris: CNRS, 2005.

Ginat, Rami. *The Soviet Union and Egypt, 1945–1955.* London: Routledge, 1994.

Glavanis, Pandelis Michalis. "Aspects of the Economic and Social History of the Greek Community in Alexandria during the Nineteenth Century." Ph.D. diss., University of Hull, 1989.

Goadby, FM. "The Present Situation with Regard to the Privileges of Foreigners in the Near East." *Journal of Comparative Legislation and International Law* 6, no. 4 (1924): 258–71.

Goldschmidt, Arthur. *Historical Dictionary of Egypt*. Metuchen: Scarecrow Press, 1994.

Gordon, Joel. *Nasser's Blessed Movement: Egypt's Free Officers and the July Revolution*. Oxford: Oxford University Press, 1992.

Gorman, Anthony. "Aigyptiotis Ellin" [Egyptiot Greek]. *Ta Nea tou ELIA* 58 (2001): 13–18.

———. "Egypt's Forgotten Communists: The Postwar Greek Left." *Journal of Modern Greek Studies* 20 (2002): 1–20.

———. *Historians, State and Politics in Twentieth Century Egypt: Contesting the Nation*. London: RoutledgeCurzon, 2003.

———. "The Failures of Readjustment (Αναπροσαρμογή): The Postwar Egyptian Greek Experience." *Journal of the Hellenic Diaspora* 35, no. 2 (2009): 45–60.

———. "Repatriation, Migration or Readjustment: Egyptian Greek Dilemmas of the 1950s." In *Greek Diaspora and Migration since 1700*, edited by Dimitris Tziovas, 61–72. Farnham: Ashgate, 2009.

Gorman, Anthony, and Sossie Kasbarian, eds. *Diasporas of the Modern Middle East: Contextualising Community*. Edinburgh: Edinburgh University Press, 2015.

Green, Nancy. *Repenser les migrations*. Paris: Presses Universitaires de France, 2002.

———. "The Politics of Exit: Reversing the Immigration Paradigm." *Journal of Modern History* 77, no. 2 (2005): 263–89.

Green, Nancy, and François Weil, eds. *Citizenship and Those Who Leave: The Politics of Emigration and Expatriation*. Urbana: University of Illinois Press, 2007.

Grinberg, Ivan, and Philippe Mioche. *Aluminium de Grèce: l'usine aux trois rivages*. Grenoble: Presses Universitaires de Grenoble, 1996.

Guitard, Odette. *Bandoung et le réveil des peuples colonisés*. Paris: Presses Universitaires de France, 1969.

Güven, Dilek. *Ethnikismos, koinonikes metavoles kai meionotites: ta epeisodia enantion ton mi mousoulmanon tis Tourkias (6/7 Septemvriou 1955)* [Nationalism, social transformations and minorities: The riots against the non-Muslims of Turkey (6–7 September 1955)]. Translated by Sofia Avgerinou. Athens: Estia, 2006.

Hadziiossif, Christos. "La colonie grecque en Égypte, 1833–1856." Ph.D. diss., EPHE-Paris IV, 1980.

———. "Emporikes paroikies kai anexartiti Ellada: ermineies kai provlimata" [Merchant communities and independent Greece: Interpretations and problems]. *Politis* 62 (1983): 28–34.

———. "Apopseis gyro apo ti viosimotita tis Elladas kai to rolo tis viomixanias" [Views concerning the viability of Greece and the role of industry]. In *Afieroma sto Niko Svoromo* [Tribute to Nikos Svoronos], edited by Vasilis Kremmydas, Chrysa Maltezou, and Nikolaos M. Panagiotakis, 330–68. Rethymno: Crete University Press, 1986.

———. "Centre et périphérie: Les activités economiques des Grecs dans les Balkans et le Proche-Orient au début du 20ème siècle." In *The Seas as Europe's External Bor-*

ders: Role in Shaping a European Identity, edited by Marta Petricioli and Antonio Varsori, 49–66. London: Lothian Foundation Press, 1999.
Hanley, Will. "Foreignness and Localness in Alexandria, 1880–1914." Ph.D. diss., Princeton University, 2007.
———. "Grieving Cosmopolitanism in Middle East Studies." *History Compass* 6, no. 5 (2008): 1346–67.
———. "Cosmopolitan Cursing in Late Nineteenth-Century Alexandria." In *Cosmopolitanisms in Muslim Contexts: Perspectives from the Past*, edited by Derryl MacLean and Sikeena Karmali Ahmed, 92–104. Edinburgh: Edinburgh University Press, 2012.
———. "When did Egyptians stop being Ottomans? An Imperial Citizenship Case Study." In *Multilevel Citizenship*, edited by Willem Maas, 89–109. Philadelphia: University of Pensylvania Press, 2013.
Hartog, François. *Régimes d'historicité. Présentisme et expériences du temps*. Paris: Seuil, 2003.
Hasiotis, Ioannis, Olga Katsiardi-Hering, and Evrydiki Ampatzi, eds. *Oi Ellines stin Diaspora 15os–21os ai.* [The Greeks in the diaspora, 15th–20th centuries]. Athens: Greek Parliament, 2006.
Hatzivassiliou, Evanthis. "The Suez Crisis, Cyprus and Greek Foreign Policy, 1956: A View from the British Archives." *Balkan Studies* 30 (1989): 107–29.
———. "Greece and the Arabs." *Byzantine and Modern Greek Studies* 16 (1992): 49–82.
———. *Evangelos Averoff-Tositsas. Politiki Viografia* [Evangelos Averoff-Tositsas: a political biography]. Athens: I Sideris/Konstantinos Karamanlis Institute for Democracy, 2004.
Heikal, Mohammed Hassanein. *Nasser: Les documents du Caire*. Paris: Flammarion, 1972.
———. *L'affaire de Suez, un regard égyptien*. Paris: Ramsay, 1987.
Herlihy, Patricia. "The Greek Community in Odessa, 1861–1917." *Journal of Modern Greek Studies* 7 (1989): 235–252.
Heyworth-Dunne, James. *An Introduction to the History of Education in Modern Egypt*. London: Frank Cass, 1968.
Hoerder, Dirk. *Cultures in Contact: World Migrations in the Second Millennium*. Durham: Duke University Press, 2002.
Hofstede, BP. "An Enquiry into the Reasons for the Decision to Emigrate." In *Characteristics of Overseas Migrants*, edited by G Beijer, NH Frijda, BP Hofstede, and R Wentholt, 3–51. The Hague: Government Printing and Publishing Office, 1961.
Holland, Robert F. *Britain and the Revolt in Cyprus, 1954–1959*. Oxford: Clarendon Press, 1998.
Hopkins, Nicholas S. "La reforme agraire en Égypte." In *Entre réforme sociale et mouvement national: identité nationale et modernisation en Égypte: 1882–1962*, edited by Alain Roussillon, 459–77. Cairo: CEDEJ, 1995.
Hopwood, Derek. *Egypt: Politics and Society, 1945–1990*. London: HarperCollins Academic, 1991.
Hourani, Albert. *Minorities in the Arab World*. London: Oxford University Press, 1947.

———. "Conclusion." In *Suez 1956: The Crisis and Its Consequences,* edited by William Roger Louis and Roger Owen, 393–410. Oxford: Clarendon Press, 1989.
———. *Histoire des peuples arabes.* Paris: Seuil, 1993.
Hussein, Mahmoud. *L'Égypte. Lutte de classes et libération nationale, 1945–1967,* vol. 1. Paris: François Maspero, 1975.
Hyde, Georgie DM. *Education in Modern Egypt: Ideals and Realities.* London: Routledge & Kegan, 1978.
Iakovidis, Ioannis. "I entaxi stin elladiki koinonia ton Ellinon tis Konstantinoupolis (B miso 20ou). Sygrisi me tous Aigyptiotes, Mikrasiates, Pontious" [The integration of the Greeks of Istanbul in Greece (2nd half of 20th century) and comparison with the Greeks of Egypt, Asia Minor and Pontus]. Ph.D. diss., Panteion University, 2005.
Ilbert, Robert. "Qui est Grec? La nationalité comme enjeu en Égypte (1830–1930)." *Relations Internationales* 54 (1988): 139–60.
———. "Une certaine citadinité." In *Alexandrie 1860–1960. Un modèle éphémère de convivialité: communautés et identité cosmopolite,* edited by Robert Ilbert and Ilios Yiannakakis, 20–37. Paris: Autrement, 1992.
———. *Alexandrie, 1830–1930, Histoire d'une communauté citadine.* 2 vols. Cairo: IFAO, 1996.
Iliadis, Manos. *To aporrito imerologio tis K.Y.P. gia tin Kypro* [*The classified journal of KYP concerning Cyprus*]. Athens: I. Sideris, 2007.
Ippolito, Rosa. "L'Impossibile sopravvivenza di una realtà cosmopolita: Cultura, etnia e religione nel declino della comunità Greca di Alessandria D'Egitto." B.A. diss., Università degli Studi di Firenze, 1999.
Issa, M Hossam, *Capitalisme et sociétés anonymes en Égypte. Essai sur le rapport entre structure sociale et droit.* Paris: Librairie générale de droit et de jurisprudence, 1970.
Issawi, Charles. *Egypt at Mid-Century: An Economic Survey.* London: Oxford University Press, 1954.
———. *Egypt in Revolution: An Economic Analysis.* London: Oxford University Press, 1963.
———, ed. *The Economic History of the Middle East, 1800–1914: A Book of Readings.* Chicago: University of Chicago Press, 1966.
———. *An Economic History of the Middle East and North Africa.* New York: Columbia University Press, 1982.
Jankowski, James. *Egypt's Young Rebels, "Young Egypt," 1933–1952.* Stanford, CA: Hoover Institution Press, 1975.
———. "Arab Nationalism in 'Nasserism' and Egyptian State Policy, 1952–1958." In *Rethinking Nationalism in Arab Middle East,* edited by James Jankowski and Israel Gershoni, 150–67. New York: Columbia University Press, 1997.
———. *Nasser's Egypt, Arab Nationalism and the United Arab Republic.* Boulder: Lynne Rienner, 2002.
Jordi, Jean-Jacques. *De l'exode à l'exil. Rapatriés et Pieds-Noirs en France.* Paris: L'Harmattan, 1993.
Judt, Tony. *Postwar: A History of Europe since 1945.* London: Pimlico, 2007.
Kader, Yehia Abdel. *Les passeports et la résidence des étrangers en Égypte.* Alexandria: Journal du commerce et de la marine, 1953.

Kalliarekos, Sokratis, Persis Kitrillakis, and Kostas Stamelos. *Programma anaprosarmogis* [Program of Readjustment]. Alexandria, 1954.

Karanasou, Floresca. "Egyptianisation: The 1947 Company Law and the Foreign Communities in Egypt." Ph.D. diss., Oxford University, 1992.

———. "The Greeks in Egypt: from Mohammed Ali to Nasser, 1805–1961." In *The Greek Diaspora in the Twentieth Century*, edited by Richard Clogg, 24–57. London: Macmillan, 1999.

Katapodis, Nikos. *Skorpia fylla tis diplomatikis mou zois* [Aspects of my diplomatic career]. Athens: Potamos, 2004.

Katsakioris, Constantin. "The Soviet-South Encounter: Tensions in the Friendship with Afro-Asian partners, 1945-1965." In *Cold War Crossings. International Travel and Exchange across the Soviet Bloc, 1940s-1960s*, edited by Patryk Babiracki and Kenyon Zimmer, 134–65. Arlington, TX: A&M University Press, 2014.

Kazamias, Alexander. "The British Occupation of Egypt and Alexandria's Greek Bourgeoisie, 1882–1919." Paper presented at the conference "Bourgeois Seas. Revisiting the History of the Middle Classes in the Eastern Mediterranean Port Cities." European University Institute, Florence, 19–20 September 2008.

———. "Between Language, Land and Empire: Humanist and Orientalist Perspectives on Egyptian-Greek identity." In *Greek Diaspora and Migration since 1700*, edited by Dimitris Tziovas, 177–92. Farnham: Ashgate, 2009.

———. "The 'Purge of the Greeks' from Nasserite Egypt: Myths and Realities." *Journal of the Hellenic Diaspora* 35, no. 2 (2009): 13–34.

Keeley, Edmund. *Cavafy's Alexandria*. Princeton, NJ: Princeton University Press, 1995.

Kerboeuf, Anne-Claire. "The Cairo Fire of 26 January 1952 and the Interpretations of History." In *Re-Envisioning Egypt, 1919–1956*, edited by Arthur Goldschmidt, Amy J. Johnson, and Barak I. Salmoni, 194–216. Cairo: American University in Cairo Press, 2005.

———. "L'incendie du Caire, 26 Janvier 1952. D'un régime à l'autre." Ph.D. diss., Aix-Marseille I, 2007.

Kitroeff, Alexander. "The Alexandria We Have Lost." *Journal of Hellenic Diaspora* 10, nos. 1–2 (1983): 11–21.

———. "The Greeks in Egypt: Ethnicity and Class." *Journal of the Hellenic Diaspora* 10, no. 3 (1983): 5–16.

———. "The Greeks in Egypt, 1919–1937: A Communal Response to Change." Ph.D. diss., University of Oxford, 1983.

———. "I Elliniki paroikia stin Aigypto kai o defteros pagkosmios polemos" [The Greek community of Egypt and World War II]. *Mnimon* 9 (1983): 1–32.

———. *The Greeks in Egypt, Ethnicity and Class, 1917–1937*. Oxford: Ithaca Press, 1989.

———. "The Transformation of Homeland–Diaspora Relations: The Greek Case in the 19th–20th Centuries." In *Proceedings of the First International Congress on the Hellenic Diaspora*. Vol. 2, *From 1453 to Modern Times*, edited by John M Fossey, 233–50. Amsterdam: Gieben, 1991.

———. "Émigration transatlantique et stratégie familiale en Grèce." In *Espaces et familles dans l'Europe du Sud à l'âge modern*, edited by Stuart Wool, 241–70. Paris: Editions de la Maison des Sciences de l'Homme, 1993.

———. "Emporikes Paroikies kai Metanastes" [Merchant communities and immigrants]. In *Istoria tis Elladas tou 20u Aiona* [History of Greece in the 20th century]. Vol. 2, *1922–1940,* edited by Christos Hadziiossif, 361–91. Athens: Vivliorama, 2002.

———. "I Metapolemiki Metanastefsi" [Postwar emigration]. In *Oi Ellines stin Diaspora 15os–21os ai* [The Greeks in the diaspora, 15th–20th centuries], edited by Ioannis Hasiotis, Olga Katsiardi-Hering, and Evrydiki Ampatzi, 75–91. Athens: Hellenic Parliament, 2006.

———. "The Greeks of Egypt in the United States." *Journal of the Hellenic Diaspora* 35, no. 2 (2009): 117–32.

Konstantinidis, A. *I ekatontaetiris tou aigyptiotou ellinismou kai to mellon tou* [The centenary of Egyptiot Hellenism and its future]. Alexandria, 1930.

Kourvetaris, Yorgos A. "The Greeks of Asia Minor and Egypt as Middleman Economic Minorities during the late 19th and 20th Centuries." *Ethnic Groups* 7 (1988): 85–111.

Koutsoumis, Dinos. *Pos kai giati dielythi i paroikia tis Aigyptou;* [Why and how was the Greek community dismantled?]. Athens, 1992.

Kraemer, Gilles. *La presse francophone en Méditerranée.* Paris: Maisonneuve et Larose, 2001.

Kramer, Gudrun. *The Jews in Modern Egypt, 1914–1952.* London: IB Tauris, 1989.

Lacouture, Jean. *Nasser.* Paris: Seuil, 1971.

Lacouture, Jean, and Simone Lacouture. *L'Égypte en mouvement.* Paris: Seuil, 1962.

Landes, David S. *Bankers and Pashas: International Finance and Economic Imperialism in Egypt.* London: Heinemann, 1958.

Laskier, Michael. *The Jews of Egypt, 1920–1970.* New York: New York University Press, 1992.

———. "Egyptian Jewry under the Nasser Regime, 1956–1970." *Middle Eastern Studies* 31 (1995): 573–619.

Laurens, Henry. *Le grand jeu: Orient arabe et rivalités internationales.* Paris: Armand Colin, 1991.

———. *L'orient Arabe: Arabisme et islamisme de 1798 à 1945.* Paris: Armand Colin, 1993.

League of Demobilized Greeks of Alexandria. *Memorandum on the Greek–Egyptian Treaty of Establishment.* Alexandria, 1950.

Lefebvre, Denis. *L'affaire de Suez.* Paris: Bruno Leprince, 1996.

Lefebvre, Jeffrey A. "The United States and Egypt: Confrontation and Accommodation in Northern Africa, 1956–1960." *Middle Eastern Studies* 29, no. 2 (1993): 321–38.

Le Gall-Kazazian, Anne. "Etre Arménien." In *Alexandrie 1860–1960. Un modèle éphémère de convivialité: communautés et identité cosmopolite,* edited by Robert Ilbert and Ilios Yannakakis, 68–80. Paris: Autrement, 1992.

———. "Les Arméniens d'Egypte (XIXe–XXe): La reforme à l'échelle communautaire." In *Entre reforme sociale et mouvement national. Identité et modernisation en Egypte, 1882–1962,* edited by A Roussillon, 501–17. Cairo: CEDEJ, 1995.

Lekkou, Pandelis K. "To Averofeio Gymnasio Alexandrias apo tis idryseos tou eos to 1960" [The Averofeio high school of Alexandria from its foundation to 1960]. Ph.D. diss., Aristotle University of Thessaloniki, 2001.

Lemercier, Claude. "Analyse de réseaux et histoire." *Revue d'histoire moderne et contemporaine* 52, no. 2 (2005): 88–112.
Lewis, Bernard. *Les Arabes dans l'histoire*. Paris: Flammarion, 1993.
———. *La formation du Moyen-Orient moderne*. Paris: Aubier, 1995.
———. *The Multiple Identities of the Middle East*. New York: Schocken Books, 1999.
Lucassen, Jan, and Leo Lucassen, eds. *Migration, Migration History, History*. Berne: Peter Lang, 1997.
Mabro, Robert. *The Egyptian Economy, 1952–1972*. Oxford: Clarendon Press, 1974.
Makrides, Kyriacos. *The Rise and Fall of the Cyprus Republic*. New Haven, CT: Yale University Press, 1977.
Malanos, Timos. *Anamniseis enos Alexandrinou* [Recollections of an Alexandrian]. Athens: Boukoumanis, 1971.
Maragkoulis, Manolis. *"Kairos na syngronisthomen": I Aigyptos kai i aigyptiotiki dianoisi, 1919–1939* [It's time to modernize ourselves: Egypt and the Egyptiot intelligentsia, 1919–39]. Athens: Gutenberg/Panepistiakes Ekdoseis Kyprou, 2011.
Markantonatos, Leonidas G. *Ta en Aigypto ellinika ekpaideftiria* [The Greek schools in Egypt]. Thessaloniki: Society for Macedonian Studies, 1957.
Marsot, Afaf Lutfi Al-Sayyid. *A History of Egypt: From the Arab Conquest to the Present*. 2nd ed. Cambridge: Cambridge University Press, 2007.
Martin, Kevin W. "Baghdad Pact." In *Encyclopedia of the Cold War*, edited by Ruud van Dijk, 55–57. New York: Routledge, 2008.
Massey, Douglas S, Joaquin Arango, Graeme Hugo, Ali Kouaouci, Adela Pellegrino, and J Edward Taylor. "Theories of International Migration: A Review and Appraisal." *Population and Development Review* 19, no. 3 (1993): 431–66.
Matsakis, Themistoklis. *To dilimma tou aigyptiotou ellinismou* [The dilemma of Egyptiot Hellenism]. Cairo, 1961.
Mavris, Georgios. *Ypomnima peri ton en Aigypto Ellinikon Koinotiton* [Memorandum concerning the Greek *koinotites* of Egypt]. Zagazig, 1911.
Mazis, John Athanasios. *The Greeks in Odessa: Diaspora Leadership in Late Imperial Russia*. New York: Columbia University Press, 2004.
Meijer, Roel. *The Quest for Modernity: Secular Liberal and Left-Wing Political Thought in Egypt: 1945–1958*. London: RoutledgeCurzon, 2002.
Melas, Michail. *Anamniseis enos presveos* [Memoirs of an ambassador]. Athens, 1965.
Meletiadis, Haris. "I politismiki diastasi tis ekpaideftikis politikis stin Ellada kata tin proti metapolmiki periodo (1945–1967)" [The cultural dimension of educational policy in Greece during the first postwar period, 1945–67]. In *I elliniki koinonia kata tin proti metapolemiki periodo (1945–1967)* [Greek society during the first postwar period, 1945–67], 442–56. Athens: Sakis Karagiorgas Foundation, 1994.
Memmi, Albert. *Portrait du colonisé. Précédé de portrait du colonisateur*. Paris: Gallimard, 1985. First published in 1957 by Buchet-Chastel.
Miccoli, Dario. *Histories of the Jews of Egypt: An Imagined Bourgeoisie, 1880s–1950s*. London: Routledge, 2015.
Michailidis, Evgenios. *O aigyptiotis ellinismos kai to mellon tou* [Egyptiot Hellenism and its future]. Alexandria: Grammata, 1927.

———. *Bibliographia ton Aigyptioton Ellinon (1853–1966)* [Bibliography of the Egyptiot Greeks, 1853–66]. Alexandria: Emporio, 1966.
Miège, Jean-Louis, and Colette Dubois. *L'Europe retrouvée. Les migrations de la décolonisation.* Paris: L'Harmattan, 1994.
Monte, Palmer. "The United Arab Republic: An Assessment of Its Failure." *Middle East Journal* 20 (1966): 50–67.
Müller, Anita. *Schweizer in Alexandrien: 1914–1963.* Stuttgart: Steiner, 1992.
Mylona, Eftychia. "An Examination of the Massive Greek Departure from Egypt as Depicted in the Greek National Press." M.A. diss., Universiteit Leiden, 2012.
Naguib, Saphinaz-Amal. "Legal Pluralism in the Mediterranean." In *The Intangible Heritage of the Mediterranean: Transmission, Adaptation and Innovation,* 169–80. Oslo: University of Oslo, 2002.
Nasser, Gamal Abdal. *The Philosophy of the Revolution.* Cairo: Dar Al-Maaref, 1954.
Nefeloudis, Vassilis. *I ethniki antistasi sti Mesi Anatoli* [The national resistance in the Middle East]. 2 vols. Athens: Themelio, 1981.
Nikolaou, G. *O aigyptiotis ellinismos kai i mellontiki autou katefthynsis* [Egyptiot Hellenism and its future direction]. Alexandria: Patriarcal Printing House, 1915.
Noiriel, Gerard. *État, nation et immigration. Vers une histoire du pouvoir.* Paris: Belin, 2001.
Noutsos, Haralampos. *Programmata mesis ekpaidevsis kai koinonikos elenchos (1931–1973)* [Secondary educational curriculum and social control, 1931–73]. Athens: Themelio, 1999.
Obdeijn, Herman. "Vers les bords de la Mer du Nord. Les retours aux Pays-Bas induits par la décolonisation." In *L'Europe retrouvée. Les migrations de la décolonisation,* edited by Jean-Louis Miège and Colette Dubois, 49–74. Paris: L'Harmattan, 1994.
O'Brien, Patrick. *The Revolution in Egypt's Economic System: From Private to Socialism, 1952–1965.* London: Oxford University Press, 1966.
Osterhammel, Jürgen. *Colonialism: A Theoretical Overview,* 2nd ed. Princeton, NJ: Markus Wiener, 2005.
Owen, Roger. *Cotton and the Egyptian Economy, 1820–1914: A Study in Trade and Development.* Oxford: Clarendon Press, 1969.
———. "The Economic Consequences of the Suez Crisis for Egypt." In *Suez 1956: The Crisis and Its Consequences,* edited by William Roger Louis and Roger Owen, 363–75. Oxford: Clarendon Press, 1989.
Owen, Roger, and Pamuk Şevket. *A History of Middle Eastern Economies in the 20th Century.* London: Tauris, 1998.
Palaiologos, Tasos. *I elliniki en Aigypto viomichania* [The Greek industry in Egypt]. Alexandria, 1953.
Panayotopoulos, Vassilis. "Les Grecs d'Égypte à Athènes." In *L'Europe retrouvée. Les Migrations de la decolonization,* edited by Jean-Louis Miège and Colette Dubois, 247–54. Paris: L'Harmattan, 1994.
Papakyriakou, Marios. "Setting the Limits of the Nation: Greek Migrants and Religious Faith in Egypt at the Turn of the 20th Century." *Ethnologia Balkanica* 13 (2009): 59–73.

———. "Formulation and Definitions of the Greek National Ideology in Colonial Egypt (1856–1919)." Ph.D. diss., Freie Universität Berlin, 2014.
Parfond, Paul. *Pilotes de Suez.* Paris: France Empire, 1957.
Perruchoud, Richard, ed. *Glossary on Migration.* Geneva: International Organization for Migration, 2004.
Petricioli, Marta. "Italian Schools in Egypt." *British Journal of Middle Eastern Studies* 24, no. 2 (1997): 179–91.
———. "The Italians in Egypt (1936–1940)." In *The Seas as Europe's External Borders: Role in Shaping a European Identity,* edited by Marta Petricioli and Antonio Varsori, 123–34. London: Lothian Foundation Press, 1999.
———. *Oltre il mito. L'Egitto degli Italiani (1917–1947).* Milan: Bruno Mondadori, 2007.
Philipp, Thomas. *The Syrians in Egypt, 1725–1975.* Stuttgart: Steiner, 1985.
Piaton, Claudine, ed. *Ismailia, Architectures, XIXe–XXe siècles.* Cairo: IFAO, 2008.
Pieridis, Giorgos P. "I ellinikes paroikies stin Aigypto" [The Greek communities in Egypt]. *Nea Epochi* 18 (1993): 11–16.
Piquet, Caroline. *La Compagnie du Canal de Suez: Une concession française en Egypte (1888–1956).* Paris: Presses de l'Université de Paris-Sorbonne, 2008.
Podeh, Elie. *The Decline of Arab Unity: The Rise and Fall of the United Arab Republic.* Brighton: Sussex Academic Press, 1999.
Politis, Athanassios. *O Ellinismos kai i Neotera Aigyptos* [Hellenism and modern Egypt]. 2 vols. Alexandria: Grammata, 1928–30.
Politi, Elie. *L'Égypte de 1914 à Suez.* Paris: Presses de la Cité, 1965.
Protopsaltis, Dimitris. *Ta tessera spitia* [The four houses]. Athens: Stafyllidis, 2004.
Psiroukis, Nikos. *To neoelliniko paroikiako fainomeno* [The modern Greek phenomenon of community]. Athens: Epikairotita, 1983. First published 1974.
———. *Aravikos kosmos kai ellinismos* [Arab world and Hellenism]. Nicosia: Aigaion, 1992.
Rappas, Alexis. "Greeks under European Colonial Rule: National Allegiance and Imperial Loyalty." *Byzantine and Modern Greek Studies* 34, no. 2 (2010): 201–18.
———. *Cyprus in the 1930s: British Colonial Rule and the Roots of the Cyprus Conflict.* London: IB Tauris, 2014.
Revel, Jacques. *Jeux d'échelles. La micro-analyse à l'expérience.* Paris: Gallimard, Seuil, 1996.
———. *Un parcours critique. Douze exercices d'histoire sociale.* Paris: Galaade, 2006.
Reynolds, Nancy Y. *A City Consumed: Urban Commerce, the Cairo Fire, and the Politics of Decolonization in Egypt.* Stanford, CA: Stanford University Press, 2012.
———. "Entangled Communities: Interethnic Relationships among Urban Salesclerks and Domestic Workers in Egypt, 1927–61." *European Review of History* 19, no. 1 (2012): 113–39.
Ricoeur, Paul. *La mémoire, l'histoire, l'oubli.* Paris: Seuil, 2000.
Rizas, Sotirios. *I Elliniki politiki meta ton Emfylio Polemo* [Greek politics after the civil war]. Athens: Kastaniotis, 2008.
Rodinson, Maxime. *Les Arabes.* Paris: Presses Universitaires de France, 1979.
———. *L'Islam: politique et croyance.* Paris: Fayard, 1993.
Rodriguez, Marc, and Anthony Grafton. *Migration in History: Human Migration in Comparative Perspective.* Rochester: University of Rochester Press, 2007.

Roussillon, Alain. "Reforme sociale et politique en Égypte au tournant des années 1940." *Égypte, Monde Arabe: droit société, économie* 18–19 (1994): 197–236.

———. *Reforme sociale et identité: essai sur l'émergence de l'intellectuel et du champ politique modernes en Égypte.* Casablanca: Le Fennec, 1996.

———. "Republican Egypt Interpreted: Revolution and Beyond." In *The Cambridge History of Egypt.* Vol. 2, *Modern Egypt from 1517 to the End of the Twentieth Century,* edited by MW Daly, 334–59. Cambridge: Cambridge University Press, 1998.

Roussos, Sotiris. "Greece and the Arab Middle East: The Greek Orthodox Communities in Egypt, Palestine and Syria, 1919–1940." Ph.D. diss., SOAS/University of London, 1994.

Ryzova, Lucie. "Egyptianizing Modernity through the 'New Effendiya': Social and Cultural Construction of the Middle Class in Egypt under the Monarchy," in *Re-Envisioning Egypt, 1919–1952,* edited by Arthur Goldschmidt et al., 124–63. Cairo: American University in Cairo Press, 2005.

Safran, William. "Diasporas in Modern Societies: Myths of Homeland and Return." *Diaspora* (1991): 83–99.

———. "Diasporas in Modern Societies: Myths of Homeland and Return." In *Migration, Diasporas and Transnationalism,* edited by Steven Vertovec and Robin Cohen, 364–80. Cheltenham: Edward Elgar, 1999.

Said, Edward W. *Orientalism: Western Conceptions of the Orient.* London: Penguin, 2003. First published 1978 by Routledge & Kegan Paul.

Sakkas, John. "Greece and the Mass Exodus of the Egyptian Greeks, 1956–1966." *Journal of the Hellenic Diaspora* 35, no. 2 (2009): 101–15.

Salmon, Pierre. "Les retours en Belgique induits par la décolonisation." In *L'Europe retrouvée. Les migrations de la décolonisation,* edited by Jean-Louis Miège and Colette Dubois, 191–212. Paris: L'Harmattan, 1994.

Sayad, Abdelmalek. *La double absence. Des illusions de l'émigré aux souffrances de l'immigré.* Paris: Seuil, 1999.

———. *L'immigration ou les paradoxes de l'altérité.* Paris: Raisons d'agir, 2006.

Schatz, Jean. "La Grèce et ses relations commerciales avec l'Egypte." *L'Egypte contemporaine* 166 (1936): 609–49.

Shafik, Viola. *Popular Egyptian Cinema: Gender, Class and Nation.* Cairo: American University in Cairo Press, 2007.

Shamir, Shimon, ed. *The Jews of Egypt: A Mediterranean Society in Modern Times.* London: Westview Press, 1987.

———, ed. *Egypt from Monarchy to Republic: A Reassessment of Revolution and Change.* Boulder: Westview Press, 1995.

Sifneos, Evridiki. "'Cosmopolitanism' as a Feature of the Greek Commercial Diaspora." *History and Anthropology* 16, no. 1 (2005): 97–111.

Smith, Andrea L, ed. *Europe's Invisible Migrants.* Amsterdam: Amsterdam University Press, 2003.

Souloyannis, Euthymios T. "Comment l'abolition des capitulations s'est preparée en Egypte et comment les Grecs y ont réagi pendant 1927." *Deltion Istorikis kai Ethnologikis Etaireias tis Ellados* [Bulletin of the Historical and Ethnological Society of Greece] 24 (1982): 573–84.

———. *I thesi ton Ellinon stin Aigypto. Apo tin akmi stin parakmi kai tin syrriknosi* [The position of Greeks in Egypt: from prosperity to decline and decrease]. Athens: Politismikos Organismos Dimou Athinaion, 1999.

———. *I Elliniki Koinotita Alexandrias, 1843–1993* [The Greek Koinotita of Alexandria, 1843–93]. 2nd ed. Athens: ELIA, 2005.

Sousi-Tassadit, Hadji. "L'Égypte sous domination britannique (1922–1956)." Ph.D. diss., Montpellier 3, 1986.

Spiliotis, Konstantinos. "The Greek Presence in Egypt: 1914–1962." M.A. diss., University of Manchester, 1999.

Starr, Deborah. *Remembering Cosmopolitan Alexandria. Literature, culture and empire*. London: Routledge, 2009.

Stoler, Ann Laura. "Rethinking Colonial Categories: European Communities and the Boundaries of Rule." *Comparative Studies in Society and History* 31, no. 1 (1989): 134–61.

Syngros, Andreas: *Apomnimoneumata* [Memoirs]. Athens: Estia Bookstore, 1908.

Svoronos, Nicolas. *Histoire de la Grèce moderne*. Paris: Presses Universitaires de France, 1972.

Tamis, Anastasios. *The Greeks in Australia*. Melbourne: Cambridge University Press, 2005.

Tamis, Anastasios, and Efrosyni Gavaki. *From Migrants to Citizens: Greek Migration in Australia and Canada*. Melbourne: National Center for Hellenic Studies and Research, La Trobe University, 2002.

Tignor, Robert. "The Economic Activities of Foreigners in Egypt, 1920–1950, from Millet to Haute Bourgeoisie." *Comparative Studies in Society and History* 22 (1980): 416–49.

———. *State, Private Enterprise and Economic Change in Egypt, 1918–1952*. Princeton, NJ: Princeton University Press, 1984.

———. *Egyptian Textiles and British Capital, 1930–1956*. Cairo: American University in Cairo Press, 1989.

———. "In the Grip of Politics: The Ford Motor Company of Egypt, 1945–1960." *Middle East Journal* 44, no. 3 (1990): 383–98.

———. "Foreign Capital, Foreign Communities, and the Egyptian Revolution of 1952." In *Egypt from Monarchy to Republic: A Reassessment of Revolution and Change*, edited by Shimon Shamir, 103–30. Boulder: Westview Press, 1995.

———. *Capitalism and Nationalism at the End of Empire: State and Business in Decolonising Egypt, Nigeria and Kenya, 1845–1963*. Princeton, NJ: Princeton University Press, 1999.

Tomara-Sideris, Matoula. "Egyptiot Greek Benefaction: Tradition and Modernity." *Journal of the Hellenic Diaspora* 30, no. 2 (2004): 85–96.

———. *Oi Ellines tou Kairou* [The Greeks of Cairo]. Athens: Kerkyra, 2007.

———. "The Demographic Aspect of the Greek Flight from Egypt." *Journal of the Hellenic Diaspora* 35, no. 2 (2009): 61–72.

Torpey, John. *The Invention of the Passport: Surveillance, Citizenship and the State*. Cambridge: Cambridge University Press, 2000.

Traverso, Enzo. *Le passé, modes d'emploi. Histoire, mémoire, politique*. Paris: La Fabrique, 2005.

Trimi-Kyrou, Katerina. "'Kinotis' Grecque d'Alexandrie. Sa politique éducative (1843–1932)." Ph.D. diss., Université des Sciences Humaines de Strasbourg (Strasbourg II), 1996.

———. "Être internationaliste dans une société coloniale: le cas des Grecs de gauche en Égypte (1914–1960)." *Cahiers d'Histoire, Les Gauches en Egypte, XIXe–XXe siècles* 105–6 (2008): 85–117.

———. "The Big Decision: Literary Narrative as a Historical Source." *Journal of the Hellenic Diaspora* 35, no. 2 (2009): 73–92.

Trimi-Kyrou, Katerina, and Ilios Yiannakakis. "Les Grecs: la 'parikia' d'Alexandrie." In *Alexandrie 1860–1960. Un modèle de convivialité: communautés et identité cosmopolite,* edited by Robert Ilbert and Ilios Yiannakakis, 81–87. Paris: Autrement, 1992.

Tsagkaradas, Kostas. *Ta provlimata tis xeniteias* [The troubles of living abroad]. Alexandria: S Grivas, 1946.

Tsaravopoulos, Nikolaos. *I Egkatastasi ton Ellinon stin Aigypto* [The settlement of Greeks in Egypt]. Cairo: K. Tsouma, 1948.

Tsoukalas, Konstantinos. *Eksartisi kai anaparagogi. O koinonikos rolos ton ekpaideftikon michanismon stin Ellada, 1830–1922* [Dependence and reproduction: The social role of the educational mechanisms in Greece, 1830–22]. Translated by Ioanna Petropoulou and Konstantinos Tsoukalas. Athens: Themelio, 2006. First published 1975.

———. *I Elliniki tragodia. Apo tin apeleftherosi os tous syntagmatarches* [The Greek tragedy: From the liberation to the colonels]. Athens: A Livanis, 1981.

Tsourapas, Gerasimos. "Nasser's Educators and Agitators across al-Watan al-'Arabi: Tracing the Foreign Policy Importance of Egyptian Regional Migration, 1952-1967." *British Journal of Middle Eastern Studies,* 43, no. 3 (2016): 324–41.

Tsourkas, Cléobule. *Les Hellènes dans l'intérieur de l'Égypte; leur apport au relèvement économique et social du pays.* Thessaloniki: Institute for Balkan Studies, 1957.

Turiano, Annalaura. "De la pastorale migratoire à la coopération technique. Missionnaires italiens en Égypte: Les salésiens et l'enseignement professionnel (1890–1970)." Ph.D. diss., Aix-Marseille Université, 2016.

Tziovas, Dimitris, ed. *Greek Diaspora and Migration since 1700.* Farnham: Ashgate, 2009.

Valenci, Lucette. "Les relations ethniques au Moyen-Orient et en Afrique du Nord." *Annales (Economies–Sociétés–Civilisations)* 41, no. 4 (1986): 817–38.

Vatikiotis, Panayiotis Jerasimof. *Nasser and His Generation.* New York: St Martin's Press, 1978.

———. *The History of Modern Egypt: From Muhammad Ali to Mubarak.* London: Weidenfeld and Nicolson, 1991.

Vatibellas, Nikolaos. *To kathikon tou aigyptiotou ellinismou kai ta scholia mas* [The duty of Egyptiot Hellenism and our schools]. Alexandria: Typografeio tou Emporiou, 1945.

Venturas, Lina, *Ellines metanastes sto Velgio* [Greek immigrants in Belgium]. Athens: Nefeli, 1999.

———. "Greek Governments, Political Parties and Emigrants in Western Europe: Struggles for Control (1950–1974)." *Revue Européenne des Migrations Internationales* 17, no. 3 (2001): 43–65.

———. "'Deterritorialising' the Nation: The Greek State and 'Ecumenical Hellenism.'" In *Greek Diaspora and Migration since 1700: Society, Politics and Culture*, edited by Dimitris Tziovas, 125–40. Farnham: Ashgate, 2009.

———. "État grec et diaspora. Des 'émigrés' à l'"Hellénisme œcuménique.'" In *Loin des yeux, près du cœur. Les États et leurs expatriés*, edited by Stéphane Dufoix, Carine Guerassimoff, and Anne de Tinguy, 239–59. Paris: Presses de Sciences Po, 2010.

Vgenopoulos, Constantinos G. *La migration de l'après-guerre en Grèce*. Athens: Papazisis, 2003.

Viscomi, Joseph. "Out of Time: History, Presence and the Departure of the Italians of Egypt, 1933-present." Ph.D. diss., University of Michigan, 2016.

Vitalis, Robert. *When Capitalists Collide: Business Conflict and the End of Empire in Egypt*. Berkeley: University of California Press, 1995.

Volait, Mercedes. "Réforme sociale et habitat populaire: acteurs et formes, 1848–1964." In *Entre réforme sociale et mouvement national: identité nationale et modernisation en Égypte: 1882–1962*, edited by Alain Roussillon, 379–409. Cairo: CEDEJ, 1995.

Wahba, Mourad. *The Role of the State in the Egyptian Economy, 1945–1981*. Reading: Ithaca Press, 1994.

Wansbrough, John E, Halil İnalcık, Ann KS Lambton, and Gabriel Baer. "Imtiyazat." In *The Encyclopedia of Islam*, edited by HAR Gibb, 1178–95. Leiden: Brill, 1986.

White, Luise. *Speaking with Vampires: Rumor and History in Colonial Africa*. Berkeley: University of California Press, 2008.

Willets, Peter. *The Non-aligned Movement: The Origins of a Third World Alliance*. New York: Nichols, 1978.

Wright, Richard. *The Color Curtain: A Report on the Bandung Conference*. Jackson: University Press of Mississippi, 1994. First published 1956 by World Publishing.

Yalourakis, Manolis. *I Aigyptos ton Ellinon* [Egypt of the Greeks]. Athens: Mitropolis, 1967.

Yiannakakis, Ilios. "Adieu Alexandrie!" In *Alexandrie 1860–1960. Un modèle de convivialité: communautés et identité cosmopolite*, edited by Robert Ilbert and Ilios Yiannakakis, 125–42. Paris: Autrement, 1992.

Zerbinis, Dimitrios I. *To kathikon ton ithinonton tin paroikian mas* [The duty of the leadership of our community]. Alexandria: I Proodos, 1946.

———. *Histoire d'une entreprise industrielle: The Kafr-el-Zayat Cotton Company SAE, 1894–1956*. Alexandria: Société de publications égyptiennes, 1956.

Index

A

Abu El Matamir, 123
Adjustment and readjustment, 6, 14, 17–9, 21–5, 33–4, 38–9, 41, 49, 63, 66, 78, 85, 120, 122, 124, 136–7, 180, 183–4, 206–7, 221, 227, 241–2, 244
Africa, 30, 39, 40, 51, 68, 141, 154, 161, 164, 165, 180, 182, 183, 185, 194
Agapitidis, Sotirios, 66, 84, 139, 168, 189
Ahbar-Al, 218
Ahram-Al (newspaper), 30, 218
Ahram-Al (studio), 89
Aigyptiotis Ellin (Egyptiot Greek), 20
Alexandria Stock Exchange, 207
Algeria, 50, 67, 230, 240
Anastassiadis, Yannis, 28
Andreadis, Stratis, 65
Anglo-Egyptian Treaty of 1936, 12, 24, 18, 27, 30, 33, 35, 41, 78, 159, 187
Anglo-Greek Association, 20
Antifascist Vanguard (AP), 20–2
Arab-Greek Association, 67, 208
Argentina, 162, 164, 192
Armenian community in Egypt, 3, 4, 88, 90, 91, 152, 155, 217
Asia, 27, 30, 50–1

Asia Minor, 4, 5, 245
  Refugees from, 4, 5, 26, 153, 240, 245–6
Assas-Al, 23
Association of Greek Grocers of Alexandria and suburbs "I Melissa", 89
Association of Greeks from Egypt in Melbourne, 185
Association of Greeks from Egypt in South Africa, 194
Association of Greeks from Egypt and Sudan, 153
Association of Greeks from Egypt in Sydney, 185
Asyut, 123
Aswan (dam), 53, 67
Athanassiadis, Giorgis, 82, 136
Athens, 29, 37, 51, 54, 170, 181, 218–9, 239
Atsaves, Anastassios 128, 133, 140
Australia, 2, 90, 141, 152, 161, 162–9, 180, 182–6, 189, 190–4, 222–3, 240
Austria, 13–4
Averoff, Evangelos, 55, 62, 99, 100, 120, 212–3, 215–6
Averoff, Georgios, 218
Averofeio boys' high school, 16, 127, 131, 144–5

268

B

Badawi, Zaki, 214–6
Baghdad Pact, 50–1
Baizos, Theodoros, 83, 99, 128, 172, 203
Balkans, 4, 240
Balkan Wars, 4, 151
Bandung Conference, 51, 105
Bank of Athens, 69, 171
Belenis, Parisis, 86
Belgian community in Egypt, 5, 27, 30, 111, 204–6, 209, 225, 230
Belgian Congo (see also Congo), 164, 240
Bodossakis-Athanassiadis, Prodromos, 65
Brazil, 13, 163–4, 191–4, 225
Britain (see United Kingdom)
British community in Egypt, 1, 3, 5, 24, 29–30, 55, 60–2, 65, 68, 91, 93–4, 105–6, 110, 132, 152, 155, 204, 209, 225, 230
Buenos Aires, 162, 163

C

Cairo Daily, The, 57
Canada, 164, 191–3
Canberra, 184, 189, 190
Capitulations, 2, 5, 6, 11, 13–8, 21, 24, 26, 28–9, 31–3, 35, 41, 48, 61, 67, 78–9, 85, 92–3, 96, 98–9, 120, 125, 139, 155–6, 169, 204, 230, 240–4
Cavafy, Constantine, 245
Central Intelligence Service (KYP), 170, 205
Charitatos, Dimitrios, 210, 224, 230
Chatzianestis, Errikos, 128
China, 50
Christophoros II, Patriarch of Alexandria, 59
Chryssostomidis, Sofianos, 98, 173
Chryssovergis, Yagkos, 62, 110
Civil War (Greek), 26, 33–4, 35, 48, 127, 138, 166–8, 181, 231, 242

Cold War, 5, 33, 48, 50, 204, 239–41, 247
Cominform, 49
Commercial Bank (N Tepeghiozi & Company), 69
Commercial Bank of Greece, 69
Commercial Bank of the Near East, 69
Communist Party of Egypt, 20–1
Communist Party of Greece (KKE), 20–1
Congo (see also Belgian Congo), 204
Convention of Constantinople (1888), 55
cosmopolitanism, 1, 132, 245–6
Council of Greek-Egyptian Friendship and Cooperation, 36, 59
Cromer, Lord, 13
Cyprus and Cypriots, 48, 51–2, 55–6, 61, 67–8, 87, 193, 242
Czechoslovakia, 51, 53, 105

D

Damanhur, 156
Damascus, 216
Delmouzos, Andreas, 17, 79, 80
Denmark, 13, 14
Dertilis, Leonidas, 206
Dodecanese, 4, 93
Douala, 185
Dragoumis, Filippos, 35, 40, 97, 104, 130, 135, 138
Dulles, John Foster, 51, 55

E

Economic Organization, 62, 111
Eden, Anthony, 54
Efimeris, 151
Egypt, Upper, 4, 83, 123, 155, 158, 160, 244
Egypt, Lower, 158
Egyptian Cotton Committee, 101
Egyptian Cotton Commission, 207
Egyptian Socialist Party, 20

Egyptianization, 60–5, 69–70, 94, 105–6, 110, 241, 246
Egyptiot Left or Left (Egyptiot), 2, 6, 12, 18, 22, 25, 28, 36–8, 48–9, 51, 58–9, 63, 89, 98, 203, 206, 241–2, 247
Ellin, 20, 22–3
Ethnos, 65
European Economic Community, 224

F
Al-Fajr al-Jadid, 22
Farouk, King of Egypt, 18, 35, 47–8
Farouk University, 34–5
Fayid, 159
Fawzi, Mahmoud, 100, 212
Fedayyin, 34, 40, 158
Foni tou Aigyptiotou Ellinismou, I (The Voice of the Egyptiot Hellenism), 39, 49, 51, 59,183
France, 2, 14, 16, 54, 56, 58–61, 64, 67–8, 161, 164
French community in Egypt 1, 3, 5, 24, 27, 29, 30, 55, 60–2, 65, 91, 93–4, 105–6, 110, 132, 135, 152, 155, 204, 209, 225, 230
Free Officers, 6, 6, 12, 28, 33, 47–9, 168, 241–2

G
Gaza, 50, 165
Geneva, 2, 188
George II of Greece, 19
Georgelin, Hervé, 132
Georgiadis, Vassilios, 203
Germanos, Michalis, 188
Germany, 13–4, 18–9, 20, 50, 62, 86, 91, 131–2
Ghana, 68
Glymenopoulos, Periklis, 96
Gorman, Anthony, 82
Greek Chamber of Commerce of Alexandria (GCCA), 2, 20, 22, 39, 41, 52, 62, 86, 90, 95, 98, 101–3, 109–10, 133, 139, 140–1, 158, 161–4, 166, 172, 180, 182–94, 203, 210, 214, 222–3, 243
Greek Chamber of Commerce of Cairo (GCCC), 62, 101
Greek-Egyptian Association, 23
Greek-Egyptian Cooperation Committee, 58, 59, 66
Greek-Italian War, 19–20
Greek Jews in Egypt (see also Jews), 4, 61, 164, 168, 244
Greek Ministry of Foreign Affairs (GMFA), 29, 34, 62–7, 91, 98–9, 106, 163–4, 169–72, 186, 190–1, 205, 215
Greek Orthodox Patriarchate of Alexandria, 20–1, 52, 59, 101, 181, 185
Greek Orthodox Patriarchate of Jerusalem, 52, 59
Greek People's Liberation Army (ELAS), 34
Guinea, 68

H
Hatem, Abdel Kader Muhammad, 208
Heathcote-Smith, Clifford, 20
Heliopolis, 42, 160

I
Ikaria, 167
Images, 68, 123, 218
India, 27, 51
Indian Ocean, 164
Indochina, 27, 240
Intergovernmental Committee for European Migration (ICEM), 3, 187–94, 222, 260, 243
International Labor Office, 84
International Organization for Migration, 3
Ioannides, Alexandra, 189, 190, 203
Irakleio, 154
Iran, 29, 50
Iraq, 50, 52

Ismailia, 1, 4, 34, 40, 41, 56, 58, 83, 129, 142, 163, 188, 190–1
Israel/Israelis, 1, 6, 12, 24, 27–8, 50, 52, 57–8, 60, 67, 91, 104, 152, 164–9, 191, 216–7, 225
Istanbul, 27, 51, 79, 185, 204, 243, 246
Italian community in Egypt, 3, 4, 34, 88, 90–1, 93–4, 131–3, 137, 152, 155, 188, 209
Italian-Turkish War, 93
Italy, 13–4, 16, 19, 62–3, 93, 131, 143, 186, 188, 240

J

Jamati, Habib, 68
Jerusalem, 59
Jewish community in Egypt (see also Greek Jews in Egypt), 1, 3, 4, 20, 50, 58, 61–2, 65, 88, 90–1, 106, 110, 152, 156, 204, 217–8, 225

K

Kafr el-Dawwar, 42, 49, 156
Kafr el-Zayat, 42, 96, 102, 125, 156
Kalliarekos, Sokratis, 57, 137, 183, 203
Kanelidis, Vassilis, 181
Kanellopoulos, Panagiotis, 20–1, 86
Kaoustos, Antonis, 96
Kapsabelis, Georgios, 162–3, 183
Karamanlis, Konstantinos, 51, 55, 62–4, 67–70, 100, 133–9, 203
Karanasou, Floresca, 88, 228
Kasfareet, 159
Kassimatis, Grigorios, 52
Kassos, 224
Katapodis, Nikos, 110, 205
Kazamias, Alexander, 142, 210
Kathimerini, I, 55
Kitrilakis, Persis, 25, 57, 137, 203
Klimis, Georgios, 215–6
Kokkinidis, Georgios, 185
Kokkinos, Antonios, 185
Kotsikas, Theodoros, 217
Koutarellis, Achilleas, 37–8, 49, 88, 110, 210

Koutsoumis, Dinos, 166, 181

L

Lagoudakis, Faidon, 210
Lambros, Dimitrios, 60, 63, 65–7, 91, 171, 189–92, 203–9, 212–3, 217–9, 221
Laskaris, Marios, 86
League of Demobilized Greeks of Alexandria, 25, 101
League of Nations, 12
Lebanese community in Egypt, 205, 217
Leriou, Dimitrios, 186
Lesseps, Ferdinand de, 53
Liatis, Alexios, 31, 35–8, 82, 95, 127, 156, 158, 169, 182–3, 186
Lebanon, 52, 62
Libya, 18, 240
Ligue Pacifiste, 20
London, 19, 54, 69, 165
Lumumba, Patrice, 204

M

Makarios, Archbishop, 51
Makris, Konstantinos, 97
Malanos, Timos, 156
Maltese community in Egypt, 3, 4, 87–8, 90–1
Mansoura, 4, 69, 88, 123, 130, 135, 155, 159–60, 173
  Koinotita in, 16, 160
Madikas, Christoforos, 96
Maraghi Pasha, Mortada el-
Markantonatos, Leonidas, 130
Marseille, 16, 61
Maschas, Iraklis, 59
Maschas, Michail, 102
Matsakis, Themistoklis, 142, 203, 206, 241
Mavromatis, Eleftherios, 164
Mediterranean Sea, 4, 30, 47, 53, 66, 102, 164–5, 223
Mehalla Kebir, 160
Melas, Michail, 11, 39, 84, 138, 158, 164
Melbourne, 164, 140, 184–6

Meletios, I, 17
Metaxas, Ioannis, 16–7, 19, 39, 80, 86, 126
Michailidis, Evgenios, 157
Michailidis, M, 89
Migration Committee (Greece), 66, 189
Migration Fund, 180, 182, 187
Miliarakis, Eleftherios, 180, 184–6
Minya, 42, 81, 123, 130, 135, 157
Misrekis, Ioannis, 1, 21, 23, 29–31, 33, 63, 78, 80, 85, 92, 125, 169, 241
Mit Gamr, 42, 160
Mohieddin, Zakaria, 123, 130, 135, 157
Mollet, Guy, 54
Montreux, conference and convention of, 14–9, 21, 23, 29–31, 33, 63, 78, 80, 85, 92, 125, 169, 241
Morocco, 67, 164, 230, 240
Moscow, 59
Moutselou, Lilika, 172
Muhammad Ali of Egypt, 4, 173
Muslim Brotherhood, 18, 27, 33, 172

N
Naguib, Muhammad, 48–50
Nahhas Pasha, Mustapha al-, 16, 18, 41, 125
Nanopoulos, Konstantinos, 210–1
Nasser, Gamal Abdel, 1, 6, 12, 38, 478, 50–7, 60–5, 67–70, 105, 111, 124, 136, 191, 203–8, 212–3, 216–7, 219, 225–8, 241, 244, 246–7
National Bank of Greece, 69, 172
National Liberation Association (EAS), 20–1
National Liberation Front (EAM), 11, 20–1
National Liberation Front of Algeria (FLN), 50, 67
National Organization of Cypriot Fighters (EOKA), 51
Nationalization, 111, 201–2, 204, 206–15, 219, 221, 223–8, 230–1, 242, 246
Nehru, Jawaharlal, 51

Netherlands and the Dutch, 13–4, 240
New Egypt, 18
New Zealand, 193
Nikodimos, Archimandrite, 185
Nikolaos VI, Greek Orthodox patriarch of Alexandria, 194
Nile delta, 4, 96, 155–6
Non-Aligned Movement, 47
North Atlantic Treaty Organization (NATO), 50–1, 54, 63, 69, 204–6
Norway, 14
Nutting, Anthony, 50, 53

O
October Revolution, 14
Onassis, Aristotle, 65
Ottoman Empire, 5, 13–4, 17, 24–7, 32, 51, 79, 92–3, 239–41

P
Paidousis, Pandelis, 137
Pakistan, 50
Palestine, 24, 27, 128
Palestine War, 30, 41, 91
Palestinians in Egypt, 3
Panaigyptia, 17, 130
Pandelidis, Ioannis, 162, 183
Papantonopoulos, Konstantinos, 191, 193, 222
Pappas, Dimitrios, 21, 23, 25–6, 163
Paris, 17, 56
Paroikos, O, 51, 57, 59, 64, 98, 100, 128, 138, 183–4, 187
Paul, King of Greece, 51
Perth, 182
Persia (see Iran)
Pesmazoglou, Michail, 217
Petronda, Alkmini, 141–2
Petrondas, Christos, 88
Pialopoulos, Simon, 210
Pieridis, Theodosis, 20, 22, 28, 36–7
Pierrakos, Nikolaos, 230
Pikos, Ioannis, 127–8
Piraeus, 167
Politis, Nikolaos, 15–6

Portugal, 13–4
Port Said, 4, 20, 34, 42, 2, 55–6, 60, 63, 81, 83, 84, 87, 103, 109, 122, 129–30, 135, 142, 151, 163–4, 182, 186, 188, 190, 192, 204–5, 219, 223
Pravda, 36
Prussia (see Germany)

Q
Qahira, al-, 52
Qantara, 42, 160

R
Radopoulos, Athanassios, 69, 123–4
Readjustment (see adjustment)
Red Cross, 190
Red Sea, 53
Roilos, Georgios, 62, 167
Romania, 26
Rommel, Erwin, 18
Roussos, Georgios, 21, 86
Royal Greek Army of the Middle East, 19
Rule, Mollie, 188
Russia, 26 (see also Soviet Union)
Russian Orthodox Church, 52

S
Saadist party, 18, 23
Sabry, Ali, 208
Shafei, Hussein el-, 203, 212
Sakellarios, Nikolaos, 39–41, 52, 67, 98, 133, 163
Sakellariou, Alexandros, 19
Salvageios Commercial School, 84, 141
Salvagos company, 88, 100, 157, 159, 210
Salvagos, Konstantinos, 38, 54, 163, 230
Salvagos, Mikès, 16–7, 25, 29, 96, 210–1, 215
Sarpakis, Stylianos, 210
Saudi Arabia, 52, 164
Sèvres, 57
Sibin el-Kom, 160
Sinai, 57, 60
Sidi Barrani, 158

Skarpalezos, Epaminondas, 40, 159
Smyrna, 180
Sofoulis, Themistoklis, 26
Soviet Union, 12, 14, 36, 38, 50–1, 57–8, 67, 90, 105, 204
Souloyannis, Euthymios
South Africa, 19, 164, 194, 223
Spain, 14
Stalin, Joseph, 36, 49, 90, 152
Stamelos, Kostas, 57, 137, 203, 259
State Construction Organization, 229
Suez (town), 77, 83, 160
Suez Canal, 4, 12, 27, 33–4, 39–40, 50, 54, 60,65, 77, 79, 87, 103, 155, 163, 165, 169, 180, 182, 184, 187–91, 205, 224, 223–4, 242
Suez Canal Company, 34, 53–5, 79, 87, 110, 135, 151, 244
  Nationalization of, 54–7, 60, 110
Suez Crisis, 1, 22, 40, 54, 56, 58, 60–5, 69, 83, 91, 99, 105–7, 110, 125, 128, 152, 185, 168–9, 171, 187, 190–4, 202, 204, 219, 244
Sultan, Hamid, 32
Sweden, 13, 14
Switzerland, 62, 217
Sydney, 180, 184–5
Syngros, Andreas, 156
Syria, 52, 62, 67, 110, 203, 216
Syrian community in Egypt, 3, 4, 88, 132, 155–6, 205, 217
Syros, 123

T
Tabakopoulos, Agis, 39
Tachydromos, 39, 57, 68, 88, 110, 166, 181, 183, 214, 216
Tanta, 4, 81, 95, 130, 135, 155, 157, 218–9
  Koinotita in, 42, 160
Tel el-Kebir, 40, 159
Thalassinos, Georgios, 185
Theodorakis, Anastassios, 57, 62, 210, 230

Theodoropoulos, Vyron, 84, 171, 201, 206–13, 216, 218, 228
Thessaloniki, 51, 93, 154, 215
Tignor, Robert, 195, 111, 132
Tito, Josip Broz, 51
Establishment, Treaty of, 15, 18, 21, 25–7, 29–31, 36, 41, 68, 85, 94, 98, 104, 125, 214, 241
Lausanne, Treaty of, 14, 93
London-Zurich Agreements, 68
Triantafyllidis, Georgios, 23, 29, 31, 35, 127, 138, 140, 158, 160, 166, 244
Trimi, Katerina, 88
Tsagkaradas, Kostas, 123
Tsaldaris, Athanassios,, 84
Tsaldaris, Konstantinos, 29–30
Tsaravopoulos, Nikolaos, 23
Tsatsos, Konstantinos, 54
Tsirkas, Stratis, 20
Tsouderos, Emmanouil, 20–1, 165
Tsourkas, Kleovoulos, 160
Tunisia 67, 164, 230, 240
Turkey (see also Ottoman Empire), 3, 19, 27, 29, 50–2, 79, 93–4, 240

U
Uganda, 240
United Arab Republic (UAR), 67, 110, 129, 172, 202, 204, 206, 209, 216–7
United Democratic Left (EDA), 38
United Kingdom, 11, 12, 18–9, 27–8, 30, 50–1, 53–5, 57–8, 68–9, 164–5
United Nations (UN), 24, 30, 51–2, 57, 60, 165
United States of America (US), 12–4, 27, 47, 50–1, 53–5, 58, 62–3, 67, 99, 152, 154, 164–5, 193

V
Valatiadis, Georgios, 77, 103
Valsamakis, Dr, 157
Valtis, Konstantinos, 20, 80, 86
Vatibellas, Nikolaos, 29, 127, 140

Vatsakis, Nikolaos, 102
Venezuela, 191
Venizelos, Eleftherios, 21
Venizelos, Sofoklis, 35
Viscovitch, Evmolpos, 102, 180, 184–6, 188
Vlachos, Alekos, 1

W
Wafd party, 18, 31, 33, 41, 94
Wallace, David Ewan, 15
World Bank, 53
World Council of Churches (WCC), 186–9, 191–3, 222, 240, 243
World War I, 4, 14, 19, 151
World War II, 5, 11, 18, 19, 27, 31, 33, 36–7, 41, 52, 60–1, 78, 84–5, 87, 90, 92, 99, 100, 103, 107, 126, 129, 152, 154–6, 181, 192, 211, 216, 225, 240, 243
  In Greece, 20, 26, 48, 242

X
Xenakis, Aristotelis, 167
Xenakis, Panagiotis, 167
Xenos, Panagiotis, 35, 128

Y
Yalourakis, Manolis, 39, 88, 104
Yiannakakis, Ioannis, 173, 206, 213, 228

Z
Zagazig, 4, 15, 40, 42, 81, 97, 130, 135, 155
  Koinotita in, 160
Zaki, Hassan Abbas, 209, 213
Zamarias, Harilaos, 31, 104, 120, 127, 172, 219, 224
Zarifi, Dolly, 171
Zerbinis, Dimitrios, 20, 22, 34, 37–8, 96, 102, 127, 135–7, 140, 208, 210, 230
Zerbinis, Stratis, 20
Zifta, 42, 160

www.ingramcontent.com/pod-product-compliance
Lightning Source LLC
Chambersburg PA
CBHW072147100526
44589CB00015B/2123